1981

12
55 + 83
248
261
368
395
445

FUNDAMENTALS OF LOGIC

FUNDAMENTALS OF

LOGIC

James D. Carney and Richard K. Scheer

Arizona State University/   Kansas State University/

THIRD EDITION

Macmillan Publishing Co., Inc.

NEW YORK

Collier Macmillan Publishers

LONDON

Macmillan Publishing Co., Inc.
866 Third Avenue, New York, New York 10022
Collier Macmillan Canada, Ltd.

Library of Congress Cataloging in Publication Data
Carney, James Donald.
  Fundamentals of logic.

  Includes indexes.
  1. Logic. I. Scheer, Richard K., Joint author.
II. Title.
BC71.C37 1980   160   78-24377
ISBN 0-02-319480-4 (Hardbound)
ISBN 0-02-978700-9 (International Edition)

Printing: 1 2 3 4 5 6 7 8   Year: 0 1 2 3 4 5 6

PREFACE

What is new in this third edition? First, some material from the earlier editions has been removed. The discussion of uses of language has been omitted, and a shortened version of analogy and dilemma is now found at the end of the chapter on informal fallacies.

Second, new material has been added. The recent work of Saul Kripke and others has prompted us to include a discussion of proper names and natural kind terms in the chapter on words and meaning. In this same chapter, a discussion of euphemisms and ambiguous or vague arguments has been added. The fallacy of inconsistency and an expanded account of special pleading are new for Chapter Two.

Third, some key discussions have been simplified or lengthened, and more illustrations and exercises added. The first chapter, the introduction to the subject matter of this text, has been redone along these lines, along with the introductory chapter to formal logic and the sections on the rules for predicate logic.

Fourth, many new examples and exercises have been added. This is especially evident in the chapter on informal fallacies. An attempt has been made to include examples that are timely and that most students will find interesting. Finally, greater emphasis is placed on formal fallacies and on proving invalidity by the method of counterexamples.

The user of previous editions will note many other changes that we need not enumerate here. However, the basic structure of the text remains the same. The study of logic is divided into the familiar three parts. The first part primarily covers informal fallacies and topics dealing with meaning and language. Formal logic is the focus of Part Two, from sentential logic through monadic predicate logic, with syllogistic logic as a helpful transition between sentential and predicate logic. Part Three deals with some topics in philosophy of science and inductive logic.

We feel that one of the strengths of this text is the wide coverage of topics, to allow instructors the opportunity to pick and choose among a variety of topics in order to tailor their courses to their own interests and to the interests of the students.

Many instructors who have used previous editions of this text have sent us corrections and suggestions on how to improve this third edition. We wish to thank them all. In particular we wish to thank Richard W. Behling, University of Wisconsin, Eau Claire; Lee C. Rice, Marquette University; Michael W. Martin, Chapman College; Duane Willard, University of Nebraska at Omaha; and Donald Gieschen, Arizona State University. We wish also to thank Richard Ylvisaker, Luther College, for the suggestion that the terse paragraph found in the second edition to justify RCP be expanded. We have also followed his suggestion that we should give a similar argument for the justification of RAA and not simply introduce RAA as a short way to do what can be done with RCP and some other rules. Finally we wish to thank Kenneth J. Scott, Senior Editor, Macmillan Publishing Company, for encouraging this new edition and for soliciting many of the helpful comments that guided us in the revision.

J.D.C.
R.K.S.

CONTENTS

PART **I**

INFORMAL LOGIC   1

1. Logic   3

 Arguments 4/ Enthymemes 8/ Deductive and Inductive
Arguments 10/ Correct Deductive Arguments 12/ Correct
Inductive Arguments 14/ Soundness 18/ Argument Dia-
grams 18

2. Traditional Informal Fallacies   29

The Material Fallacies of Relevance 31/ The Material
Fallacies of Insufficient Evidence 59/ The Fallacies of
Ambiguity 69/ Two Additional fallacies 94

3. Words and Meaning   111

 Intension and Extension 111/ Paradigm Examples, Semantic
Features, and Criteria 115/ Proper Names 121/ Real and
Nominal Definitions 126/ Ambiguity and Vagueness 129/
 Factual and Verbal Disputes 139/ Emotive Words 151

vii

PART **II**

FORMAL LOGIC   163

4. Deductive Validity and Logical Form   165

Logical Form 167/ Counterexamples 170/ Sentential and
Predicate Logic 173

5. Truth-Functional Connectives   175

Truth-functional Compounds 175/ "~" and English "not"
176/ "·" and English "and" 177/ "v" and English "or"
179/ "⊃" and English "if, then" 180/ "≡" and English "if
and only if" 184/ The Scope of Sentence Connectives 184/
Determining the Truth Value of Compound Sentences 186

6. Truth Tables   189

Truth Tables for the Sentence Connectives 189/ Logical
Equivalence 191/ Testing Argument Patterns 196/ Testing
Arguments 198/ Formal Sentential Fallacies 201/ Truth
Table Short-Cut Method 205/ Symbolizing Arguments 208

7. Elementary Inferences   213

Rules of Inference 214/ Replacement Rules of Inference
220/ Conditional Proof Rule 228/ *Reductio ad Absurdum*
Rule 232/ Consistency of Premises 236

8. Traditional Syllogistic Logic   241

Categorical Sentences 241/ Disguised Categorical Sentences
246/ Syllogisms 248/ Testing Syllogisms 253/ Immediate
Inferences 263/ Syllogistic Chains (Sorites) and Enthymemes
268/ Formal and Informal Fallacies 272/ Boolean Algebra
274

9. Predicate Logic

278

Singular and General Sentences 279/ Categorical and Other General Sentences 282/ Domains 287/ Truth-Functional Expansions 289/ Valid Argument Patterns 291/ Monadic Predicate Test 295/ Rules for Predicate Logic 301

10. Axioms

319

Truths of Logic 320/ Axioms for Sentential Logic 323/ Some Theorems of PM 328/ Consistency of PM 333/ Independence of the Axioms of PM 335/ Completeness of PM 337

PART **III**

THE LOGICAL STRUCTURE OF SCIENCE

343

11. Science and Hypotheses

345

Inductive Logic 345/ Four Episodes from the History of Science 349/ Empirical and Theoretical Hypotheses 358/ Induction and Deduction 361

12. Crucial Experiments and Mill's Methods

373

Crucial Experiments and Empirical Hypotheses 373/ Crucial Experiments and Theoretical Hypotheses 374/ "Death Blows" 376/ Fact of the Cross 378/ Mill's Methods 384

13. Patterns of Scientific Explanation

397

Deductive Explanations 397/ Probabilistic Explanations 402/ Historical Explanations 403/ Functional Explanations 405/ Empathetic Explanations 406/ Genuine and Pseudo-scientific Explanations 417/ Satisfactory and Unsatisfactory Explanations 425

— **14. Probability**   **436**

Four Problems in Probability Theory 436/ The Calculus of
Probability 442

Name Index   **447**

Subject Index   **453**

FUNDAMENTALS OF LOGIC

INFORMAL LOGIC

I

Logic

Our subject is logic. Logic is primarily the study of arguments and of methods to determine whether arguments are correct or incorrect.

What is an argument? Here are some examples of the kinds of arguments in which we will be interested:

(1) All politicians are pragmatists.
Jimmy Dingey is a politician.
Therefore Jimmy Dingey is a pragmatist.
(2) If Godfrey Daniel passes logic, then he won't leave school.
He won't pass logic.
Thus he will leave school.
(3) Professor Threadbare's tests are easy.
Professor Bounderby's tests are easy.
Professor Goodbody's tests are easy.
Hence all university tests are easy.

These are called arguments, because in each example the claim is made that one statement *follows* in some way from other statements. In the first example, "Jimmy Dingey is a pragmatist" is said to follow from "All politicians are pragmatists" and "Jimmy Dingey is a politician." In (2) "Godfrey Daniel will leave school" is said to follow from the first two statements. And in (3) the statement following "hence" is said to follow from the first three statements. We may define an *argument* as a sequence of statements together with a claim. The sequence is made up of two or more statements. The claim is that one of these statements, called the *conclusion*, follows in some way from the other statements, called the *premises*. Sometimes this claim is made explicitly, and sometimes not. In the first example the argument claim is explicitly made by the word "therefore;" "Jimmy

3

Dingey is a pragmatist" is the conclusion, while the other two statements are premises. Similarly, in (2) the third statement is the conclusion and the remaining two statements are premises. The argument claim is made by the word "thus." And in (3) the argument claim is made by the word "hence;" the first three statements are premises and the fourth, "All university tests are easy," is the conclusion.

Our three examples of arguments can be sorted out in terms of correct and incorrect arguments. For the moment let us understand a correct argument as one in which the argument claim is justified. That is, an argument is correct when the claim that the conclusion follows in some way from the premises is justified. After first clarifying the notion of an argument we will discuss the notion of correctness. It turns out, by the way, that argument (1) is a correct argument, while arguments (2) and (3) are incorrect arguments (unless, in (3), the university has very few professors).

Arguments

Since logic is concerned with determining the correctness of arguments, we must first be able to identify arguments before we apply the methods of logic.

Every argument contains one conclusion and at least one premise. An important clue to the identification of premises and conclusions is sometimes provided by the use of *argument indicator words*. Not all arguments contain them, but when they occur they enable one to see the structure of the argument at a glance. The three arguments in the first section contain the argument indicator words "therefore," "thus," and "hence." Each of these words is an argument claim word, and it generally indicates that what follows it is the conclusion and that what comes before are premises. There are many other words that generally indicate arguments. Here are some examples. *Pr* stands for premises and *C* for a conclusion:

Pr so *C*	*C* because *Pr*
Pr therefore *C*	*Pr* thus *C*
C for *Pr*	*Pr* hence *C*
C since *Pr*	*Pr* consequently *C*
Since *Pr*, *C*	Because *Pr*, *C*

As some of these examples suggest, the conclusion of an argument is not always the last statement in the argument. To illustrate, consider:

All city bosses are Democrats. So all city bosses are pragmatists, since all Democrats are pragmatists.

The conclusion of this argument is the first statement in the second sentence, namely: All city bosses are pragmatists. The above chart has "*Pr* so *C*" as an entry. In this example, what comes before "so" is a premise and the conclusion follows "so." The chart also shows "*C* since *Pr*." In this example what precedes "since" is the conclusion, and what follows "since" is the second premise of the argument. This example also illustrates how one or more statements can be contained in a single sentence. The second sentence of the argument contains the conclusion and a premise. An entire argument can in fact be contained in a single sentence. For example:

Socrates, being a man, is mortal, since all men are mortal.

The word "since" indicates an argument. What follows "since" is a premise. What comes immediately before is the conclusion, "Socrates is mortal." What is left is the other premise. Thus the argument contained in this single sentence is:

All men are mortal.
Socrates is a man.
Therefore Socrates is mortal.

The order of the premises is not important (except in syllogistic logic; see Chapter 8).

EXERCISES 1.1

Identify the conclusion and the premises of each of the following arguments.

1. IBM has plants all over the world, so it has a plant in France.
2. If the Dodgers win the pennant, the Reds will not, because if the Reds win the pennant, then the Dodgers will not win the pennant.
3. Since Cadillacs are larger than Matadors, Cadillacs are larger than Volkswagens, since Matadors are larger than Volkswagens.
4. Anyone religious believes in God. Thus Buddhists are not religious, since they do not believe in God.
5. Jerry Brown will carry either New York or Ohio, but since he will not carry Ohio, he will carry New York.
6. No circles have sides, for all circles are ellipses and no ellipses have sides.
7. All that glitters is not gold, so it is false that all glittering things are gold.
8. Raising animals for protein is a luxury that few developing countries can afford. A 10-acre field produces enough beef to feed one person for a year. But the same field, properly watered, can produce enough

rice to feed 25 people for a year. In rich countries like the United States so much grain is produced that it can be fed to livestock. In developing countries, most or all of the grain is needed by people.

9. Organized labor wants to shorten the present 40-hour workweek, thereby reducing the rate of unemployment. Far from creating more jobs, a shorter workweek would lead to even more unemployment. It would result in higher costs and higher prices and thus fuel the fires of inflation. Companies that have to compete with imports from countries where wages are low would be driven into bankruptcy.

10. Many Senators voted against the Panama Canal treaties because they were representing their constituencies and their constituencies were against the treaties. During the debate in the Senate, majority leader Robert C. Byrd often evoked Edmund Burke, who contended that a Senator's constituency deserves not only his representation but his judgment.

11. If we cannot continue current rates of economic growth and thus create jobs for all, then we must consider the only real alternative. We must accept the idea that people should receive their income as a right.

12. The volunteer army is not working. The Defense Department reported a discharge rate of more than 40 percent, double the draft figures. The volunteer Army includes a disproportionate number of blacks. Ominous disparities exist in economic, geographic, and educational areas. The all-volunteer force is a form of class discrimination. It proclaims that a just society may excuse its privileged classes from its defense. This concept alone should make it anathema.

13. Public utilities' goal is to charge high rates to customers who, of course, have no other source of electricity. At the same time, the power companies do not want to stir their customers to anger lest they make trouble with regulatory agencies. The utilities traditionally have resolved the problem by spending tens of millions of dollars a year on institutional, or "goodwill," advertising campaigns, although the rationale is opaque for monopolies promoting services for which no competition exists. Thus, consumers who have paid too much end up paying more for propaganda designed to influence them to pay still more.   (COHEN and MINTZ, *Power, Inc.*)[1]

14. In deciding to operate, the surgeon is faced with a conflict of interest; he is paid if he operates and not paid if he doesn't. A further conflict arises if he has a choice between performing a major operation, for which he will receive a large fee, or a minor one, for which the fee might be only a fifth as much. Finally, if he knows that he is not expert in performing a certain type of operation and that others would be able to perform it better and more safely, his decision as to whether to do it

[1] Jerry Cohen and Morton Mintz, *Power, Inc.* (New York: Viking Press, 1976), pp. 311–312. Copyright 1976 Jerry S. Cohen and Morton Mintz.

himself is again subject to a conflict of interest. In short, there are many surgical decisions in which the best interest of the patient is in sharp conflict with the financial interest of the surgeon.

(DR. GEORGE CRILE, JR., "The Surgeon's Dilemma," in *Harper's*, May 1975)

15. The best-known characteristic of the culture of the White House is to produce yes-men. It is doubtful that Carter will act to encourage dissent. For Carter's experiences in the Navy and running his own small business successfully without a staff are not the sort of thing that teaches a man to value dissent. Neither does his religion.

   The scriptures, while edifying in most respects, are a dismal guide to sound public administration. The leader is always right; the staff is always wrong. As dissenters, the disciples are a bunch of turkeys. Andrew says the five loaves and two fish aren't enough to feed the multitude. Peter doubts that his belief can make him walk on water. The dissenters are "ye of little faith." The boss, Jesus, is never wrong.

   (CHARLES PETERS, "Blind Ambition in the White House," in *The Washington Monthly*, March 1977)

16. If education is to develop basic learning levels in essential subjects— reading, writing, and mathematics—then it must begin trimming back the exotic kaleidoscope of sense exciting curricula offered today to students. There is only one efficient method of learning to read, and that is to read. And learning to write means writing. And developing a skill with numbers requires endless drills in mathematics.

17. We should oppose programs that would provide federal aid to private and state schools through tuition income tax credits. Such a plan violates the First Amendment because it uses public funds to aid private schools which are integral parts of the religious mission of the churches operating them. Also such a plan would invite continued sectarian pressure on Congress to increase the aid to private education.

ANSWERS

5. *Premise*: Jerry Brown will carry either New York or Ohio.
   Premise: Jerry Brown will not carry Ohio.
   Conclusion: Jerry Brown will carry New York.

10. *Premise*: Senators do not merely represent the will of their constituents, but make judgments in the best interests of their constituents.
   Conclusion: Senators should not necessarily vote the will of their constituents.

15. *Premise*: Carter's background in the Navy and small business does not teach a man to value dissent.
   Premise: Carter is influenced by the scriptures which do not encourage dissent on the part of the nonleaders.
   Conclusion: Carter will not encourage dissent in the White House.

Enthymemes

Many arguments may not be fully stated. The conclusion or one or more premises, or both, may not be stated. Such arguments are called *enthymemes*.

Here are some examples of enthymemes. Each is presented twice; the second time, the missing conclusion or premise or premises is supplied.

(1)   Burgers are bigger at King Kong Burgers. And the bigger the burger the better the burger.

(1')   Burgers are bigger at King Kong Burgers. The bigger the burger the better the burger. Therefore King Kong Burgers are better.

(2)   All Congressmen are corrupt because all men are corrupt.

(2')   All men are corrupt.
All Congressmen are men.
Therefore all Congressmen are corrupt.

(3)   Saudi Arabia has no right to control half the world's oil since it has only a small portion of the world's population.

(3')   No country with a small population has the right to control a large portion of an essential natural resource.
Oil is an essential natural resource.
Saudi Arabia has a small population and controls half the world's oil.
Therefore, Saudi Arabia has no right to control half the world's oil.

A premise is often omitted because it is obvious to those to whom the argument is addressed. For example, with (2) we can easily supply the missing premise, since what is assumed is obvious, namely that all Congressmen are men. In (3) what is assumed as a premise is less obvious, so the original enthymeme is likely to work only among those who share the same world view. In (1) the conclusion is so obvious, it is simply not stated.

As another example consider:

This Broadway play is the best of the season, since all the New York critics say it is.

Here one is obviously assuming the following premise:

If New York critics say a play is the best of the season, then it is the best of the season.

This premise makes the argument a correct one.

A rule for supplying missing premises is called the *principle of charity*. This is the rule that one should supply missing premises that put the argument in the best light. In the above example, we followed this principle in supplying the missing premise. The principle would have been violated if we had, for example, supplied the following as the missing premise for the last argument:

If a play is the best of the season, then New York critics say it is best.

The reason we would violate the principle of charity is that the following argument is incorrect:

If a play is the best of the season, then the New York critics say it is the best.
The New York critics say that this Broadway play is the best of the season.
Therefore this Broadway play is the best of the season.

This argument is incorrect since the premises do not rule out the possibility that the critics may say a poor play is the best. If it is the best then the critics will say it is, but if it is not, they may also say it is. So the conclusion may be false although the premises are true.

EXERCISES 1.2

Some enthymemes are give below. Supply the missing statements following the principle of charity.

1. Everything fattening should be avoided, so McDonald's hamburgers should be avoided.
2. No ghosts are observable, for ghosts are not visible.
3. Art is the expression of economic interest so American painting is the expression of economic interest.
4. If I study I make good grades. If I do not study I enjoy myself. Therefore either I make good grades or I enjoy myself.
5. God exists because the Bible says so.
6. It is impossible for our society to meet our ecological needs, for as long as economic growth is vital to create jobs, it is inevitable that our society will pay more attention to economic needs than to ecological needs.
7. What if Jesus Christ had been aborted? (Anti-abortion bumper sticker).
8. We can travel into the future on one of two paths. The one generally favored by U.S. policy has the nation increasing energy production in all possible ways, but mainly through exploitation of fossil fuels and nuclear fission. This is a road with dire social consequences: energy

wars, depression at home, environmental degradations, and several kinds of catastrophes associated with uranium. Or we can take another path by engaging in frugality. Detroit, Con Edison, and the homeowner learn to conserve truly vast amounts of fossil fuels. In this way, time is bought. This time is used to develop renewable sources of power so that in about fifty years we live off our energy income, chiefly sunshine and the winds.

9. If the gases (chlorofluorocarbon) used to propel various substances out of spray cans continue to increase at the present rate of ten percent a year until 1990 and remain constant thereafter, between five and seven percent of the ozone layer will be destroyed by 1995, and between thirty and fifty percent of it would disappear by the year 2050. To underscore the gravity of even a five percent depletion, the resulting increase in ultraviolet radiation after 2050 would cause forty thousand additional cases of skin cancer each year in the United States alone.

(PAUL BRODEUR, "Annals of Chemistry: Inert,"
New Yorker, 7 April 1975)

10. The greatest single curse in medicine is the curse of unnecessary operations, and there would be fewer operations if the doctor got the same salary whether he operated or not.

ANSWERS

2. Missing premise: All observable things are visible.
4. Missing premise: Either I study or I do not study.
6. Missing premise: Economic growth is incompatible with meeting ecological needs.
10. Missing conclusion: Doctors should be paid salaries not based on the number of operations they perform.

Deductive and Inductive Arguments

In an argument the claim is made that the conclusion follows from the premises. We can distinguish two senses of "follow" and use this to distinguish two kinds of arguments, deductive and inductive arguments.

In a *deductive argument* the claim that the conclusion follows from the premises amounts to the claim that it is impossible for the premises to be true and the conclusion false. Here is an example of a deductive argument:

Most people believe that the continued growth of government cannot be stopped. Whatever most people believe is true. So continued growth of government cannot be stopped.

Typically, we would understand the argument claim in this example to be this: It is impossible for it to be true that most people believe that the continued growth of government cannot be stopped and for it to be true that whatever most people believe is true *and* at the same time false that continued growth of government cannot be stopped. And in this argument the argument claim is justified. With the exception of argument (3) in the first section, all of the previous examples are examples of deductive arguments.

We will call any argument that is not deductive, a nondeductive or *inductive argument*. The characteristic feature of an inductive argument is that the claim of the argument is that the conclusion follows from the premises in the sense that it is improbable that the conclusion is false, given the truth of each premise. The degree of this improbability will vary from argument to argument. An example of an inductive argument is:

> None of Professor Threadbare's tests have contained trick questions. Hence his final exam will not contain a trick question.

In this argument the claim is simply that in all probability the conclusion is true if the premise is true. Thus in this argument one does not suppose that the conclusion *must* be true if the premise is true. One is not ruling out the possibility that the premise is true and the conclusion false. The premise merely supplies evidence to support the conclusion, and nothing more. To claim that it is probably true that the final exam will contain no trick questions on the basis that none of the earlier exams contained trick questions is not to claim that it is impossible that the earlier exams contained no trick questions *and* that the final exam will contain trick questions.

Inductive arguments come in all shapes and sizes. In Part Three, we will see some of the kinds of inductive arguments that are an integral part of our dealings with scientific matters. In everyday life, when we come to believe something on the basis of evidence, our thoughts can be formulated as an inductive argument. Whether or not an inductive argument is correct or not, is, to put it very roughly, a matter of how much evidence there is in the premises for the conclusion. We will look at the matter a little more closely later in this chapter.

EXERCISES 1.3

Which of the following arguments are deductive and which are inductive?

1. That Moses was a historical figure can be doubted because we have no written record of Moses' life.
2. Anne dates only boys that play tennis, so, since Daniel doesn't play tennis, he can't get a date with Anne.

3. Every American should serve a hitch in the Peace Corps, for it certainly did a world of good for Mrs. Lillian Carter.
4. Some socialists are Marxists. All socialists are motivated ecologists. Therefore some motivated ecologists are Marxists.
5. Freshmen generally have trouble with logic. So first year student Henry will have trouble with logic.
6. All the world loves a lover.
   Bob loves Alice.
   So Ted loves Bob.
7. I won't win the State lottery since a million tickets were sold.
8. All circles are figures. So all who draw circles draw figures.
9. In this city 20 percent of the teenagers who want jobs can't find them, so the chances that my teenage brother will find a job are 1 in 5.
10. None but the brave deserve the fair. Only logic teachers are brave. So only logic teachers deserve the fair.

ANSWERS

1. Inductive.   5. Inductive.   10. Deductive.

Correct Deductive Arguments

The essential condition for the correctness of a deductive argument is that the deductive claim be justified. Deductive arguments that fulfill this condition are called *valid arguments*. A deductive argument is valid if it is impossible for the premises to be true and the conclusion false.

Consider the following examples of deductive arguments:

(1) Bertrand Russell is a philosopher.
    All philosophers are scoundrels.
    Therefore Bertrand Russell is a scoundrel.
(2) Bertrand Russell is an atheist.
    All communists are atheists.
    Therefore Bertrand Russell is a communist.
(3) If Shakespeare wrote *Hair*, then Shakespeare was a playwright.
    Shakespeare wrote *Hair*.
    Therefore Shakespeare was a playwright.
(4) If Shakespeare wrote *Hamlet*, then Shakespeare was a playwright.
    Shakespeare did not write *Hamlet*.
    Therefore Shakespeare was not a playwright.

Arguments (1) and (3) are valid and (2) and (4) are not valid.

Correctness = justified conclusion

Again, to say an argument is valid is to say that it is impossible for the premises to be true and conclusion false. With (3) it is false that Shakespeare wrote *Hair*. But it is nevertheless impossible for it to be true that he wrote *Hair*, and for it to be true that if he wrote *Hair* then he was a playwright, and yet for it to be false that Shakespeare was a playwright. So (3) is valid, even though a premise is false. If that premise *were* true and the first premise were true, the conclusion would have to be true. So (3) is valid. Argument (4) is invalid, since even if we suppose he did not write *Hamlet*, and that if he wrote *Hamlet* then he was a playwright, the conclusion could still be false because, for example, he wrote *Othello*. It is instructive to take note at this time of the various relationships between true and false statements and valid and invalid arguments. This can be most efficiently done by the following chart where **T** is true and **F** is false:

Pr	**T**	**F**	**F**	**T**⎫	invalid
C	**T**	**F**	**T**	**F**⎭	

valid or
invalid

The chart may be summarized as follows: The only case in which an argument *must* be invalid is that in which the premises could be true and the conclusion could be false.

In Part Two of this book formal methods are introduced to determine the validity or invalidity of deductive arguments. However, at this early stage of the study of logic a method is at hand to demonstrate why invalid deductive arguments are invalid. All that is required is a little ingenuity.

One way to show that a deductive argument is invalid is by constructing what is called a *counterexample*. In constructing a counterexample one keeps the same argument form, but changes the descriptive content in such a way as to produce an argument with clearly true premises and a false conclusion. Thus we can provide the following counterexamples for the above invalid arguments:

(2′) Emory's hounddog is an animal.   **T**
       All cats are animals.   **T**
       Therefore Emory's hounddog is a cat.   **F**

(4′) If Shakespeare wrote *Hair*, then he is a playwright. **T**
       Shakespeare did not write *Hair*.   **T**
       Therefore Shakespeare is not a playwright.   **F**

We will explain the notion of the *form* of an argument in a rigorous way later. The reader will profit from comparing each of the pairs to find the similarities of form.

EXERCISES 1.4

The following arguments are deductive arguments. Although methods will be introduced later that will enable us to determine whether they are valid or not, use your logical intuition and find the valid arguments. For each of the invalid arguments construct a counterexample if the argument is not already one where each premise is true and the conclusion is false.

Invalid

1. Machines are causally determined, so if human beings were causally determined, they would be mere machines.
2. If a whale is a mammal, then it is warm-blooded. A whale is a mammal. Therefore it is warm-blooded.

Valid

3. All matters of taste are subjective, and all moral judgments are matters of taste; therefore all moral judgments are subjective.
4. All matters of taste are subjective, and no moral judgments are matters of taste; therefore no moral judgments are subjective.

Invalid

5. If the nations disarm, there will be peace; so if the nations do not disarm, there will not be peace.
6. If there is to be peace, then the nations will disarm; the nations will not disarm, so there never will be peace.

Valid

7. If a student is fond of learning, he needs no stimulus, and if he dislikes learning, no stimulus will be of any help. But every student is either fond of learning or dislikes it, so why try to educate?

Invalid

8. Babies are illogical. Anyone who can't pass a test in logic is illogical. Therefore anyone who can't pass logic tests is a baby.
9. If determinism is true, then human beings do not have a free will. But human beings are not free, so determinism is true.

Invalid

10. Every woman is an object, sexually speaking. No woman has a satisfactory feminine experience, so no sexual object has a satisfactory feminine experience.

ANSWERS

2. valid.
4. invalid. Counterexample: All cats are animals. No dogs are cats. Therefore no dogs are animals.
6. valid.
9. invalid. Counterexample: If Shakespeare lived in the tenth century, then he did not write *Hair*. Shakespeare did not write *Hair*. Therefore Shakespeare lived in the tenth century.

Correct Inductive Arguments

One common kind of inductive argument is that which makes a generalization on the basis of samples. Consider:

(1) Ten remelads have been observed.
    Each one has been found to be green.
    Therefore all remelads are green.

Contrast this argument with

(2) Well over two million remelads have been observed.
    Each one has been found to be green.
    Therefore all remelads are green.

The second appears to be a stronger inductive argument than the first because the sample is larger. Let us say that a remelad is a gem stone. Then the small size of the sample in the first argument would ordinarily warrant our saying that the inductive claim is not justified since we would expect that there would be many more remelads. The first argument is an example of an incorrect inductive argument, while the second is a correct inductive argument. In the first argument the inductive claim is not justified, since even if the premise is true it does not provide *good* grounds for saying that the conclusion is likely true. But it is true that if all of the over two million remelads observed up to this time are green then, probably, all remelads are green.

Consider this next pair of inductive arguments which generalize on the basis of samples.

(3) Drug x has been administered to persons between the ages of 20 and 25 years of age who are in good health.
    None of these persons have exhibited any harmful side effects.
    Therefore no person who takes drug x will have any harmful side effects.

(4) Drug x has been administered to persons of all ages and varying degrees of health.
    None of these persons have exhibited any harmful side effects.
    Therefore no person who takes drug x will have any harmful side effects.

Our logical intuition would tell us that (3) is a weaker inductive argument than (4). What accounts for this is that in (3) a generalization is drawn from a sample that is not representative. Since it is not representative one would not be justified in claiming that the conclusion is probably true on the basis of the premises. Thus (3) is an incorrect inductive argument. By contrast, argument (4) is a correct inductive argument.

The next argument is also one in which a generalization is made from samples:

(5) All recorded economic depressions have occurred at the same time that hemlines on women's dresses have gone down.
    Therefore economic depressions occur when hemlines go down.

Here the sample is both large and representative—in fact, it could not be any larger or any more representative. What accounts for the incorrectness of (5) is that we know there is no causal relation between the lengthening of hemlines and economic depressions. Although it is true that in the past they have occurred together, we regard this merely as a coincidence.

A second kind of inductive argument is that in which a hypothesis is made on the basis of evidence. For example:

> (6)   Only two people could have strangled Agatha, her brother or her best friend. Her brother is an abject coward and Agatha has immense strength. Her best friend, a big game hunter, wanted her money and had the opportunity to kill her. He also has a pet boa constrictor.
> Therefore her best friend murdered Agatha.

Whether or not this is a correct argument could only be determined by some more information about the circumstances, but given only what is found in the premises, it appears to be a correct argument.

Finally, some inductive arguments are made on the basis of mathematical probabilities. For example:

> (7)   High card wins.
> My opponent draws a queen.
> Therefore I will probably not win.

This argument is correct since the chances that one will draw a higher card than a queen are only 2 in 13.

EXERCISES 1.5

Sort the following inductive arguments in terms of generalizations from samples, hypothesis-forming inductions, or mathematical inductions. Which are correct and which are incorrect?

1. Because all the past recessions since World War II have been moderate, the next one will be moderate too.
2. I have just rolled a normal die, so the probability that I will roll a six is one in six.
3. Under Wilson we entered World War I, during Roosevelt we became embroiled in World War II, with Truman came Korea and with Kennedy and Johnson we had Vietnam. So Democratic administrations cause wars.
4. The United States spends a larger portion of its GNP on health care than does any other country. Yet the health care in America is inferior to that in many countries. Why? Most of the health-care dollars are

spent in hospitals. Blue Cross is the biggest provider of hospitalization insurance. They tend to pay whatever bills the hospitals submit and to pass on the costs to the consumers in the form of higher rates. Hospital representatives dominate Blue Cross boards and one cannot expect hospital representatives to resist high hospital charges. In most cases Blue Cross operates under special legislation giving it a tax exempt, nonprofit, public service organization status. It does not have to answer to either policy holders or to stockholders, as do profitmaking organizations. Finally, attempts at rate regulation by the states have been ineffective.

5. The automobile induces a peculiar state of mind. Why is it that so many drivers make with all kinds of offensive remarks and gestures from the safety of their steel-and-glass cocoon—remarks and gestures they would not think of using in polite society.

   The same gentlemen who with a benign smile holds the door for a woman when both are on foot gives her a blast of the horn when she does not get out of his way quickly enough in the pedestrian crossing. Somehow, the possession of a ton-and-a-half of steel seems to instill the same destructive instinct in modern man that the possession of a club instilled in the cave dwellers of the past.

6. Medical researchers are telling the truth when they repeat on the basis of sustained and intensive experimentation that they can identify no therapeutic powers in Laetrile that can destroy cancer. Certain patients are telling the truth when they report having recovered from cancer after having taken Laetrile. How is this possible? There are many kinds of cancer which are reversible under certain conditions, and the human body possesses a system which, if properly mobilized, is capable of overcoming various forms of cancer. Laetrile is successful because it is a placebo. Some who use it think it is effective and this belief puts their curative forces to work.

7. The traditional argument used in seeking pay raises for members of Congress is: "They must be paid enough so they won't be open for graft."

   Apparently the $57,000 annual salary that members of Congress now get hasn't achieved that goal.

   Former Rep. Richard Hanna, D-Calif., is serving a sentence in a federal prison for having taken $200,000 in kickbacks from a South Korean businessman.

   Rep. Daniel Flood, D-Pa., faces the same bleak prospect. Rabbi Leib Pinter has pleaded guilty to a charge of paying Flood $5,000 to use his influence in getting federal money for a school in Israel.

   Morality, it is evident, does not depend on the size of one's pay check.　　　　(*Arizona Republic*, editorial, May 18, 1978)

2. Mathematical induction. Correct.
6. Hypothesis-forming induction. Correct.
7. Generalization from samples. Incorrect.

Soundness

In everyday life, when one fully evaluates an argument one demands more than logical correctness. Common sense demands of a good argument not only that it be correct but that its premises be true. Arguments that are correct and also have all true premises are called *sound arguments*.

Earlier we noted that correct deductive arguments can have false premises. This is also true of correct inductive arguments. For example the following is a correct inductive argument with a false premise:

All the millions of emeralds observed up to the present time have been found to be yellow.
Therefore all emeralds are yellow.

If an inductive argument is correct and the premise is true, then it must be the case that *in all probability* (or *very likely*, etc.) the conclusion is true. On the other hand, if a deductive argument is valid and its premises are each true than it *must* be the case that the conclusion is true.

What this shows is that "correctness" and "validity" are terms used in appraising the relationship between the premises of an argument and its conclusion. These terms are not used in appraising statements. "True" and "false" are terms used in appraising statements, but they are not used in appraising the relationship between premises and a conclusion of an argument. There is no such thing, in logic, as a "valid" statement or a "true" argument.

Argument Diagrams

Analysis of an argument in logic involves two steps. The first step is to determine which statements are premises and which statement is the conclusion. The second step is to determine whether the argument claim is justified. That is, one must ask: Is it true that if the premises are supposed true, then it is either impossible that the conclusion is false (deductive arguments) or improbable that the conclusion is false (inductive arguments)? A third step, outside formal logic, is to determine whether the premises are true. If the premises are true and the argument is correct, then the argument is sound and we have rational grounds for affirming the conclusion. But to determine the correctness of an argument the first step is to state the argument clearly. The aim of this section is to aid the reader in stating an argument when the argument is complex.

One perspicuous way to state an argument is to use arrows to indicate the relation between a conclusion and a premise. Thus one can replace

Premise

Therefore (conclusion)

with

Premise
↓
Conclusion

In a complex argument some conclusions may serve as premises or reasons for further conclusions. Such statements are intermediate conclusions. They function both as conclusions from prior premises and as premises for further conclusions. The argument diagram of such an argument may be, for example:

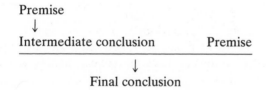

One can usefully use this scheme to diagram complex arguments, as we will illustrate with two examples.

S. I. Hayakawa, Republican Senator from California, was uneasy over the $2.2 million appropriated for an Employment Act in 1977. Those who voted for the act were concerned with the 8 percent unemployment in 1977. Hayakawa opposed the Act, and in an article in *Harper's* indicated why he did. In the following excerpt[2] he gives his reasons for his conclusion, which was: {We need not be alarmed with the 8 percent unemployment in 1977}. In the excerpt and the ensuing diagram, the conclusions are indicated by brackets or curly brackets. The reasons which do not serve as intermediate conclusions are indicated by circled numbers.

The argument I gave was this: [unemployment in 1977 is not the same as unemployment in 1954.]

① In 1954 almost all those registered as unemployed were primary wage-earners for their families. If they were unemployed, then the whole family was in distress. ② Today, with more and more women entering the job market, even if the primary wage-earner (let's say the husband) is employed, the wife, or secondary wage-earner, is likely to *register* as unemployed.

Secondary wage-earners do not have as urgent a need for a job as primary wage-earners. ③ Furthermore, secondary wage-earners do not have the intense job attachment of primary wage-earners. They are more likely to quit if they are unhappy. Also, in the years since 1954 we did something very drastic; we worked out the system of unemployment insurance. So now, if you are bored with your job, you can leave, get the boss to agree that you were laid off, and collect unemployment insurance.

We may now diagram the entire argument as follows:

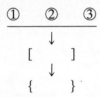

We can further analyze ③. Implicit in ③ is another conclusion, namely: (In 1977 many people are voluntarily unemployed.) The reason for this is: ④ People who are unhappy with their jobs can leave and collect unemployment insurance. So the expanded structure is

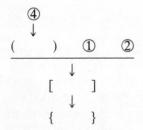

Let us now fill in this structure with summary statements of reasons and conclusion. We obtain something like this:

People who are unhappy with their
jobs can leave and collect unemployment
insurance
↓

(There are many voluntary unemployed in 1977.)	There are many secondary wage-earners unemployed.	Secondary wage-earners do not have urgent needs for work.

↓

[8 percent unemployment in 1977 is
different from 8 percent in 1954.]

↓

{We need not be alarmed with
8 percent unemployment in 1977.}

Is this a correct argument? Is it true, for each argument link in the chain, that if the premise or premises are true then the conclusion must be true? The primary logical weakness of this argument appears to be the reasons for conclusion, enclosed in brackets, that 8 percent unemployment in 1977 is different from 8 percent in 1954. It seems we are to understand by "secondary wage-earners" those who have no urgent need to work. They are those whose unemployment will not result in any family distress since they do not contribute to the wages needed for the basic support of the family. Now it may be true that many secondary wage-earners are unemployed, but also that 8 percent unemployment is a matter for concern. If we assume that 4 percent is an acceptable unemployment figure, then for one to be unconcerned about 8 percent unemployment, the secondary wage-earners and voluntarily unemployed would have to make up 4 percent of the unemployed. So whether the argument is correct or not depends partially on whether the voluntarily unemployed persons and secondary wage-earners constitute 4 percent of the unemployed. One may also remark that the 8 percent figure hides the high unemployment figure for minorities, many of whom are primary wage-earners, and that is a basis for concern.

In the same *Harper's* article Hayakawa presents another interesting argument. It is a somewhat surprising argument with the unlikely conclusion that businessmen in the United States are revolutionaries. Here is the argument, including parentheses and brackets for conclusions and numbers in circles for reasons that are not conclusions.

What kind of people are the most subversive? From whom do we have the most to fear in the way of social change? If you say the people to fear are socialists, communists, anarchists, I think you are wrong. {The most subversive people in the world, I think, are businessmen.}
④ A revolution, to be a revolution in any true sense, must change the relationship of social classes to one another. The United States is a profit-oriented industrial society. Because we are capable of the mass production of consumer goods, we have mass consumption—and advertising to stimulate that consumption. [The unintended revolution created by mass production and mass consumption has come close to producing a classless society in America.]

③ Executives and working-class people alike drive Comets or Cadillacs, drink Coke and Schlitz and Old Grand Dad, eat Nabisco wafers and Hormel ham, and watch the Johnny Carson show. (There is no "ruling class.") ① Anyone can become President, including a graduate of Harvard (John F. Kennedy), of Southwest State Teachers College (Lyndon B. Johnson), of Whittier College (Richard M. Nixon), or of no college at all (Harry S. Truman)—and, after attaining that lofty height, he can still be impeached.

② And the poor of America are not poor by world standards. Our welfare clients live far better than the working people of more than half the world.[3]

We can diagram the argument as follows:

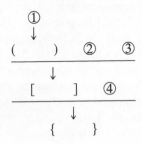

If we fill in the diagram and make a bit more explicit all that is involved in ④ we obtain:

Anyone can become President.
↓

(There is no ruling class.)	There are no poor in the U.S. by world standards.	Americans all drive, eat, and watch the same things.

↓

[The United States is virtually a classless society.]

Mass production and mass consumption have made our society virtually classless.
Any group responsible for changing basic class structure is revolutionary.
U.S. businessmen are responsible for mass production and mass consumption.

↓

{U.S. businessmen are revolutionaries.}

---

[3] Hayakawa, p. 43. Used by permission.

Logically speaking, the primary fault of this argument is the support for [   ]. (   ), ②, and ③ provide weak support for [   ]. The reason for this is that each reason can be true and yet [   ] false. For what does it mean to say that a society has classes? Typically wealth distribution resembles a pyramid in that the wealthy are at the top while the many, the poor, are at the bottom. Also one class, usually the wealthy, runs the state. There may be a wealth pyramid even if everyone watches Johnny Carson and the people at the bottom of the pyramid are better off than people at the bottom of the pyramid in, say, India. And even if the highest executive officers of the state come from different social or economic classes, there may be a ruling class which selects its executives from various classes and which controls the government no matter who the President is.

The two arguments of Hayakawa's are deductive arguments. Their premises are clearly meant as *reasons* for drawing certain conclusions, rather than evidence or data. Such arguments as these are not very rigorous—by no means are all assumptions made explicit. Their persuasiveness rests on how many assumptions one shares with the arguer.

EXERCISES 1.6

Below are some examples of complex arguments. First, use parentheses and brackets to indicate main conclusion and any intermediate conclusion. Second, use circled numbers to indicate reasons that are not conclusions. Third, diagram the argument using arrows, circled numbers, and parentheses and brackets. Finally, fill out the structure with summary statements for reasons and conclusions and break down any reason that may involve implicit conclusions.

1. The idea of a rational democracy is, not that the people themselves govern, but that they have security for good government. This security they cannot have by any other means than by retaining in their own hands their ultimate control. If they renounce this, they give themselves up to tyranny. A governing class not accountable to the people is sure, in the main, to sacrifice the people to the pursuit of separate interests and inclinations of their own.
   (JOHN STUART MILL, *Dissertations: Political, Philosophical, and Historical*)

2. Many among both the intellectual and general publics regard redistribution of income as a deprivation of liberty, in that property is taken away by coercion. I disagree with this. Income and property are certainly the instruments of an individual's freedom. Clearly the domain of choice is enhanced by increases in those dimensions. It is true not merely in the sense of expanded consumer choice but also in broader contexts of career and opportunity to pursue one's own aims

and to develop one's own potential. Unequal distribution of property and of income is inherently an unequal distribution of freedom. Thus a redistribution of income, to the extent that it reduces the freedom of the rich, equally increases that of the poor. Their control of their lives is increased. (KENNETH ARROW, "Taxation and Democratic Values," *New Republic*, November 1974)

3. The idea that the processes that had led half the world to affluence could, with a bit of capitalist investment to prime the pump, lead all the world to the same affluence, was always a mistake. It was based on the age-old centralist conviction in the developed countries that they alone, plus oil, had worked the miracle, and that given the know-how anybody could do it, which was not true. Anyone could do it given the oil, and the know-how, and the raw materials, and an unlimited reserve of people somewhere else willing to work harder under worse conditions on a much lower standard of living than the miracle-worker.

(ELAINE MORGAN, *Falling Apart*:
The Rise and Fall of Urban Civilization)

4. Our forefathers tried to teach us the proper and only real function of a government is the protection of individual and national rights. Remember Thomas Jefferson's statement: "That government which governs least governs best." Our President seems to have the idea that the reverse is true. His philosophy seems to be that little or no protection be afforded to individual and national rights. This is indicated by shelving neutron bomb production, withdrawing U.S. Korean forces, curtailing the cruise missile, cutting back appropriations for an already hopelessly overmatched Navy, methodically wrecking the jurisprudence system and constantly favoring the "rights" of obvious criminals to the detriment of the rights and protection of law-abiding citizens.

Carter and his colleagues seem to think that because a person is a self-reliant, hard-working, law-abiding citizen he should somehow manage to solve all his own problems and then take on all the problems of those loafers and cheaters in the growing community of welfare leechers.

I want our government to protect my national and individual rights with a strong military and police force. I believe every other function that is now being handled by the bumbling bureaucrats could better be handled by private enterprise.

(RONALD L. JOHNSON, letters to the editor,
Arizona Republic, May 30, 1978)

5. A nuclear war has to be started by someone. So the question is, Why should either side want to strike first? Is it true that the Russians, the moment they reach some critical ratio of superiority will have an attack initiated? Some hawks seem to be saying this. But if the Russians

are rational this is the calculation they must make: They must weigh the probable destruction to themselves against their gains through war. And "gains" do not include any pleasure they might take in destroying the United States or in declaring themselves the winner of a nuclear war. So we can dispose of the notion that a nuclear war would start "out of the blue." That's not how it works. At worst a future nuclear war might grow out of an escalating crisis where conflict had already been joined and each side had already developed reasons to be nervous about the other's resort to nuclear weapons.

6. A review of the racial situation in the United States is not encouraging. Whites are fleeing the inner cities and abandoning them to non-whites. Unemployment among blacks has doubled during the last years and now reaches an estimated 40 to 50 percent among urban young male blacks. Welfare aid to non-whites has skyrocketed. What is to be done? There are five alternatives: Ship the minorities out of the country. Simply kill off the offending minority. Slavery. Absorb the minority through intermarriage. Separate-but-equal approach that is now used in South Africa. Slavery and extermination are unthinkable. Expulsion from the country is impractical. Someday we may be emotionally ready for intermarriage, but no one alive now will ever see that day. That leaves the separate-but-equal approach used in the Old South.

7. Why had Congress steadfastly refused to have open TV coverage of its proceedings? The reason is simple. There may be only a handful of congressmen in attendance, and cameras staring at wide open spaces could give a wrong impression of how Congress operates. (Often congressmen not on the floor are working in committee.) However, it is highly unlikely that any of the networks would bother to televise a session of the House or the Senate unless something of vital importance to the nation was happening. To the networks time is money. If what happens on the floor of the House or Senate isn't sufficiently important to capture a sizeable audience, they are throwing money away by televising it. Consequently they won't bother to cover proceedings where only a handful of congressmen would attend. Congress should let TV cover its proceedings.

8. Men and women want to work. Work, private and public, is there to be done. How come, a wandering rationalist might ask, the work and the workers are not happily married? Well, as the radicals of my youth were wont to intone, it is no accident that we tolerate as a nation years of 7, 8, even 9 percent general unemployment and horrifying rates of teenage joblessness which among urban blacks exceed, by some estimates, 50 percent.

    The brutal fact is that unemployment at "moderate" rates confers a good many benefits upon the prosperous and the truly affluent. If everyone could be employed, extraordinarily high wages would have to be paid to toilers in restaurant kitchens, laundries, filling stations, and other humble positions. Whenever decent jobs at living wages are plentiful, it is exceedingly difficult to coax young men and women into our volunteer army. Without a volunteeer army how can the children of the middle and upper classes be spared the rigors of the draft?

Unemployment calms the unions and moderates their wage demands. Business periodicals have been noting with unconcealed gratification that last year's contract settlements between major unions and large corporations were considerably less expensive for employers than those of 1975, even though union members were steadily losing ground to inflation. When people are scared about losing their jobs, they work harder and gripe less. In more dignified language, absenteeism declines and productivity ascends.

(ROBERT LEKACHMAN, "The Specter of Full
Employment," in *Harper's*, February 1977)

9. All presidents, of course, complain about how badly they're treated in the press—and it certainly must be difficult for these nearly imperial figures, surrounded by sycophants and catered to in every way, to find themselves nevertheless so nearly under constant, total, not always friendly scrutiny from people who do not usually know as much as they ought to, let alone as much as they think they know. But however presidents may pity themselves, except in extraordinary circumstances, like those of Vietnam and Watergate, they have overpowering ability to manage the news and shape it to their interests.

Aside from such devices as the backgrounder, the presidency's vast array of powers, its control of foreign affairs, its initiative in domestic legislation, its influence in the national economy and on the atmosphere of American life—all these mean that the presidency is constantly *making* news, causing it to happen. No one else approaches a president's ability of making things happen.

In October 1976, for example, Gerald Ford believed he had come off poorly in his second debate with Jimmy Carter on what the Ford administration had done—actually, had *not* done—to counter the Arab boycott of American companies dealing with Israel. So Ford ordered a quick shipment of sophisticated new weapons to Israel, without customary staff work or clearance. The press had literally no choice but to give headlines to this act taken in Ford's role as commander-in-chief, but in fact designed for domestic political recovery.

Some newspapers and columnists did question editorially whether the arms shipment was justified, at least in the fall of 1976, but immediate headlines always have more impact than later editorials. That is the major advantage any President has in trying to present himself favorably through the press; and before the ink was dry on the headlines about Ford's arms shipment to Israel, he was capitalizing on the publicity by campaigning heavily through Jewish neighborhoods in New York. (TOM WICKER, *On Press*)[4]

10. In 1971 Daniel Ellsberg released to major newspapers the documents known as the Pentagon Papers. These traced the development of American activity in Vietnam in great detail and proved deception of Americans by their government over a period of many years. Though the Nixon administration itself was not covered by the Pentagon Papers, it sought orders to prevent *The New York Times* and *The Washington Post* from printing the papers.

It was not only the government that indicated a failure to understand the Bill of Rights on this occasion. The *Times* and the *Post* retreated in face of government pressure; they stopped printing the papers until the injunctions were overturned by the Supreme Court. They backed off and said in effect, "We hope the Court will save us." They thus weakened their claim to freedom of the press.

They also indicated a serious misunderstanding of that freedom. It is not a private right of newspapers. Essentially it is a matter of the public's right to knowledge and to truth. The newspapers did not have a right to withhold the truth from the people; they had an obligation to publish it. The press is responsible to the people not to the government.

Recognition of this responsibility is essential to democracy. The press must stand as a defender of the people against large concentrations of power, including the power of government. In particular, the press must stand against the notion that the people cannot be trusted with information. If the people of a democracy are to make reasoned judgments, they must have the information on which such judgments can be based.

(EUGENE J. McCARTHY, *The Hard Years, A Look at Contemporary America and American Institutions*

11. No problem in our time is a fraction so important, no source of uncertainty a fraction so valid as the arms competition between the United States and the Soviet Union. . . .

The competition just mentioned rests on two broad currents of thought, both exceptionally ominous in their implications. First, there is the concept of conflict—irreconcilable conflict—between inherently hostile economic, political, and social systems. There can be no reconciliation between Communism and capitalism, authoritarian discipline and personal liberty, atheism and spiritual faith. That is the great fact of life.

---

[4] Tom Wicker, *On Press* (New York: Viking Press, 1978), pp. 128–129. Copyright 1978 by Tom Wicker. Used by permission.

The second and more recent idea is . . . that the arms race is the result of the way we are ruled. It is a manifestation, both in the United States and in the Soviet Union, of the public power of the military establishment and of those who make the arms. It involves a double symbiosis. In the United States the great weapons firms supply the armed services with the weapons they seek. The Air Force, Navy, and Army reciprocate with the orders to the corporations that provide the profits and employment by which they function and flourish. The corporations and the services combine to conduct the research and development which make the current generation of arms obsolete and make necessary the next.

This is the first symbiosis. The second is between the United States and the Soviet Union. The same process in only slightly different form exists there. Each power, by its innovations and acquisitions, then creates the need and incentive for the other power to do the same—or more. Thus each works with the other to ensure that the competition is self-perpetuating. The difference between Communism and capitalism, freedom and authority, progress and reaction, Marx and Jesus, is cited but this is liturgical, not real. No faith sustains the arms competition. All who are knowledgeable agree that neither system would survive the conflict. Both countries are caught in a squirrel wheel, a trap.

(JOHN KENNETH GALBRAITH, *The Age of Uncertainty*)[5]

ANSWERS

9. ① U.S. presidents use backgrounders, they control foreign affairs, initiate domestic legislation, and influence the economy and atmosphere of U.S. life.

② U.S. presidents can make news (e.g., Gerald Ford in 1976 Presidential campaign).

↓

[U.S. Presidents normally have the ability to manage the news.]

↓

{U.S. Presidents ought not to complain about how they are treated by the news media.}

2

Traditional Informal Fallacies

A *fallacy* is an argument that is incorrect, but that may appear to some in some contexts to be a correct argument. Illogical reasoning occurs when people construct arguments that are fallacious without realizing that they are doing so.

Fallacies are divided into formal and informal fallacies. A *formal fallacy* is an invalid deductive argument that so resembles a valid deductive pattern that persons can be misled into thinking it is valid. Consider this example of an invalid deductive argument;

(1)   If Eliza played tennis, then she wore her tennis shoes.
      Eliza did not play tennis.
      Therefore Eliza did not wear her tennis shoes.

But Eliza wears tennis shoes almost all the time, whether she plays tennis or not. So the argument is not valid. We can easily represent the form of this argument by letting *p* and *q* serve as placeholders for the two different statements in the argument. The form of (1) is:

(2)   If *p*, then *q*
      not *p*
      Therefore not *q*

Now consider this valid deductive argument:

(3)   If Eliza played tennis, then she wore her tennis shoes.
      Eliza did not wear her tennis shoes.
      Therefore Eliza did not play tennis.

The form of (3) is:

(4)   If p, then q
not q
Therefore not p

Since forms (2) and (4) appear similar, and (3) is valid, some may be misled into thinking that (1) is a valid deductive argument. Argument (1) is a formal fallacy. Formal fallacies are incorrect arguments because of their logical structure—that is, they are incorrect because they have a form that is logically incorrect. Any argument having the same form is also incorrect. Formal fallacies and the notion of logical form are most conveniently discussed in connection with the study of patterns of valid argumentation, so we will defer consideration of formal fallacies and consider them in later chapters in Part Two of this book. *Informal fallacies*, in contrast, are incorrect arguments but their incorrectness is not a function of having an invalid form but is, for example, a consequence of the ambiguity of language or inattention to the subject matter of the argument.

Informal fallacies have been a topic of study in logic ever since Aristotle wrote *De Sophistici Elenchi*. In accordance with the tradition which goes back to this treatise we will divide informal fallacies into two groups: fallacies of ambiguity and material fallacies. *Fallacies of ambiguity* are generally deductive arguments which appear to be valid but are not, because of a shift in meaning of a word, phrase, or sentence. The *material fallacies* are arguments which are incorrect for reasons other than the ambiguity of language. As Aristotle said, they arise from the subject matter of the argument and cannot be detected and set right by those unacquainted with the subject matter. Material fallacies will be divided into fallacies of insufficient evidence and fallacies of relevance. *Fallacies of insufficient evidence* are incorrect inductive arguments. *Fallacies of relevance* are arguments whose premises are irrelevant to the conclusion. The premises contain information which may appear to be relevant but which in fact is not relevant in establishing the conclusion as true. One might well regard fallacies of relevance as arguments for a conclusion other than the stated conclusion. However the content of the premises of fallacies of relevance can in some circumstances cause some people to accept the stated conclusion as true. An example of such a fallacy is the following which we will later classify as an *ad populum* fallacy:

Most people believe that the continued growth of government cannot be stopped. So continued growth of government cannot be stopped.

The argument is incorrect. Even though most people adopt a certain view it does not follow that it is true. Most people believed at one time that the Earth was flat but it does not follow from that that it was, or is.

This fallacy of relevance can also be construed as having an unstated premise, namely: Whatever most people believe, is true. With this as an added premise, the argument is the following valid deductive argument:

> Whatever most people believe is true.
> Most people believe that continued growth of government cannot be stopped.
> Therefore it is true that continued growth of government cannot be stopped.

But this argument now has a false premise, namely: Whatever most people believe is true. In pointing out that this is false we are not assessing the correctness of this argument. It is valid. But to consider whether this premise is true is in fact to be concerned with whether the argument we started with, the argument without the added premise, is correct. The premise is worthless for the same reason that the original argument is worthless.

As a general rule, fallacies of relevance can be taken as enthymemic deductive arguments. To question the correctness of the original argument is the same thing as questioning the truth of the missing premise. Fallacies of insufficient evidence are meant to be inductive arguments and arguments which are fallacious because of an ambiguity are generally either explicitly deductive or enthymemic deductive arguments.

The Material Fallacies of Relevance

The Ad Hominem *Fallacy*

Instead of presenting relevant reasons against someone's view, a person may try to bring about the rejection of the view by directing his or her remarks at the one holding the view. This is called an *ad hominem* fallacy (argument directed to the person).

There are two main forms of this fallacy. The first is called the abusive *ad hominem*. The second is called the circumstantial *ad hominem*. Abusive *ad hominems* are arguments that have structures like this:

> *A* affirms *p*.
> *A* is defective in such-and-such a way.
> Therefore *p* is false.

The circumstantial *ad hominem* has roughly the following structure:

> *A* affirms *p*.
> *A* is prejudiced because of his special circumstances.
> Therefore *p* is false.

A simple example of an abusive *ad hominem* is: Nietzsche's philosophy of the superman is nonsense since he ended his life in a mental institution. This argument is fallacious because the fact that Nietzsche went insane late in life is irrelevant to the value of his philosophy of the superman. The false assumption operating here is that if a person is defective in some way (for example, psychotic at the end of his life), his philosophical views must also be false.

In 1978 the U.S. Senate voted on the ratification of the Panama Canal Treaties. These treaties had been negotiated with support from the country's last four Presidents. They had been endorsed by the Secretary of Defense and the Joint of Chiefs of Staffs, who were convinced that the treaties would ensure the security of the Canal for the use of the United States. The first treaty provides for Panama to assume territorial jurisdiction over the Canal Zone on December 31, 1999. The second treaty declares that the Canal shall be open to all vessels and that the United States shall be responsible for ensuring the neutrality of the Canal. Many arguments for and against the new Treaties were given, some correct and some fallacious. Here is an example of the latter:

> If the Canal Treaties are approved, then there should be a huge structure at the entrance of the canal higher than the Statue of Liberty. There, on its four sides, etched in big, bold letters for all to see should be the names of each politican and the many others who work so hard on behalf of weakening our country. Then in the years to come after the Statue of Liberty has been taken down our children and their children and others to follow will know who did so much to open the door further for the eventual takeover of our wonderful country by Russia. Only one conclusion follows: Let's keep the Statue of Liberty and forget about the Panama Canal Monument with the names of so many more Benedict Arnolds.

The argument here is essentially that the Treaties should not be ratified because those supporting the Treaties are traitors. (There are appeals to emotion here also. The fallacy involving such appeals is discussed in the next section.) So what we have here is the argument that since the supporters of the Treaties are defective, in this case, are traitors to the United States, their view that the Treaties ought to be ratified by the Senate is mistaken. Needless to say, there were many reasons given for opposing the Treaties which were relevant. For example, opponents claimed that the 1903 Treaty gave sovereignty over the Canal Zone to the United States; that the 1977 Treaties are further evidence of the decline of U.S. power and influence in world affairs; that we are paying the Panamanians to take the Canal; that the new Treaties are a giveaway; and that the rejection of the new Treaties will not impair U.S. world relations. Of course those who supported the 1977 Treaties believed each of these reasons to be false. Nonetheless, whether they are true or false, they are relevant to the question whether the 1977 Treaties should or should not have been ratified.

In the circumstantial *ad hominem* one tries to discredit a person's claim by arguing that because of his special circumstances he or she is prejudiced, biased, or insincere. To illustrate:

> You cannot believe what Professor Threadbare says about teacher's salaries keeping up with inflation. As a teacher he would naturally be in favor of increasing teachers' pay.

> Congress should not consult the Joint Chiefs of Staff about the B-1 Bomber. As members of the armed forces they will naturally want as much money for military purposes as they think they can get.

In the first argument above one ignores reasons why teachers' salaries should not keep up with inflation. In the second argument one ignores reasons why we should not build the B-1 Bomber. Relevant reasons for not building the B-1 would relate to such things as cost, how effective a weapon it is, the need for the weapon, cheaper and more effective alternatives, the arms race and its consequences, and so on. The assumption, the false assumption, in both of these arguments is that if *A* has a special interest in *x*, then you cannot believe what he says about *x*. But obviously, one may have an interest in *x* and yet say true things about *x*.

Circumstantial *ad hominems* are often presented indirectly. For example, consider this interesting case:

One of the few men who see the car as a broad social benefit and who are able to articulate their views is a man (Frank Wylie, head of press relations of Chrysler in 1977) whose automotive syllogisms are terribly vulnerable. One reason is that he may be saying important things, but they are suspect because he is speaking within the halls of the automobile industry. He speaks of what the car has brought to minority groups; his opponents translate that into the failure of the mass transit system to serve such groups better as a result of having been emasculated by the automobile. He speaks of freedom of movement; his opponents understand that as an expression of individual selfishness subverting the common good. He speaks of the automobile allowing random living patterns; his opponents imply that this defeats any attempt at rational regulation of society. He talks about the gaiety, even the frivolity, the car can introduce into lives largely filled with drudgery; his opponents talk about a lack of seriousness of purpose to accomplish the greatest good for the greatest number. He mentions the car's ubiquity; his opponents condemn the same ubiquity as wasteful, selfish, a rape of finite resources, and suffocating.[1]

---

[1] Leon Mandel, *Driven* (Briarcliff Manor, New York: Stein and Day, 1977), p. 20. Copyright 1977 Leon Mandel.

There is no fallacy in "suspecting" Wylie's case for the social benefits of the car since he is head of press relations for Chrysler. However, the argument that since he is head of press relations, his view that the car is responsible for social benefits cannot be believed, is fallacious.

Another kind of circumstantial *ad hominem* is illustrated in this example:

> My uncle Noodles Romanoff, who is now in prison, used to preach to us kids about self-control.
> But I can't see any value in his ideas if he cannot live up to them himself.

This argument supposes that if one's life conflicts with the ethical views one puts forth, then the views are false. But one may endorse noble ethical views and not be able to live up to them. In other words, the fact that one's behavior does not match one's preaching, does not make the preaching wrong any more than it makes the behavior correct.

Needless to say, we often find *ad hominem* arguments persuasive. This is because so often defects in personality manifest themselves in defective views and because our special circumstances often control what we endorse. But even if this is generally true, the most that an attack on a man should do is make us skeptical. For example, suppose A has religious faith and produces an alleged proof for the existence of God. That he has faith and thus may wish to support by reason what he heretofore accepted by faith, may be grounds to be skeptical about his findings, but it is not evidence that his alleged results are false.

Guilt by association is another form of a circumstantial *ad hominem* fallacy. If A stands in some association with B and B is guilty in some way it does not follow that A is guilty. For example liberals and Communists in the United States may share some goals, such as, detente with Soviet Union and Civi Rights. They are "associated" in this way. But they differ in important ways. The most important difference is that while liberals believe that the capitalist system can be maintained as progressive capitalism, Marxists do not. For Marxists capitalism historically is on its way off the world stage. Many Americans feel that Communism implies positions fundamentally opposed to the national interest. If such people, because of these associations between liberals and Communists, inferred that liberals oppose the national interest, they would commit a fallacious inference. Analogously, in 1978 the opposition in the United States to the Panama Canal treaties was primarily from the right while the opposition to the treaties in Latin America was from the Communist left. If one inferred that the right wing in the United States are Communist radicals because of this association one would make a fallacious inference. Various kinds of associations can lead people to such faulty inferences. Bruce Herschensohn describes this interesting case taken from television news during the time of Watergate,

> Watergate is the complex of buildings in which occurred the break-in to Democratic National Headquarters on June 17, 1972. The same com-

mentators who misguided some audiences through the American military involvement in the Vietnam conflict established the word "Watergate" as the umbrella over any and every accusation made against the administration. No matter if it was the President's taxes or the ITT case or the Vesco case or political contributions, it all became "Watergate."

But there was an immensely deceptive and destructive element in the use of that catch phrase for unrelated subjects. The break-in to the Watergate was a *known crime*. By labeling all other charges under the umbrella of "Watergate," they seemed to be linked to that known crime, and there was an implied guilt by association. This was not only done to unrelated incidents, but to people within the administration who had no relationships to that crime.

The technique for its accomplishment was simple. The television commentator would read a report while the screen behind his desk illustrated the Watergate complex of buildings. The implied result of the narrative simultaneous with the visual was that there was some association between the two. The backdrop of the Watergate complex became an all-pervading lethal tool as innocent names were paraded before it. The commentator was not guilty of *saying* something that was inaccurate by the use of this technique, but a combined visual and audible statement was created, and it was untrue.[2]

It should be pointed out that the news media justified their use of such visuals by arguing that visuals of the Watergate Complex were not just symbols of criminal acts by politicians but generic symbols of the whole set of incidents connected with the Nixon administration that eventually led to his resignation and subsequent pardon.

It should be stressed that not all arguments critical of someone are *ad hominem* fallacies. For example, suppose one argues that Richard Nixon should have been impeached because he used illegal means in trying to damage his political opponents and then obstructed justice in trying to cover this up. This is an argument directed against a man. But this argument is correct, for relevant reasons (whether they are true or not) are given for why Richard Nixon should have been impeached. This is not *ad hominem* since one is not arguing that what someone affirms is false because of the character or circumstances of the one making the affirmation.

The Tu Quoque *Fallacy*

Tu quoque means "you're another." The *tu quoque* fallacy is committed when one tries to reply to a charge made by an opponent by making the same or a similar charge against him. Consider these two examples:

> So these are your grounds for criticizing the way we treat our native population. In answer let me just say, "Who was it that killed most of the American Indians?"

[2] Bruce Herschensohn, *The Gods of the Antenna* (New Rochelle, N.Y.: Arlington House, 1976), p. 23. Copyright 1976 by Bruce Herschensohn. Used by permission.

The charge has been made by my opponent that I illegally acquired the money for this campaign. In reply to this I want it to be known that all the money my opponent has for his campaign is illegally acquired.

These arguments are both instances of the *tu quoque* fallacy. In each case someone answers a charge by making a similar charge. These arguments are fallacious because no relevant reason is given for why the policy toward the native population should be continued or for why we should believe that the campaign money was not illegally acquired.

Stuart Chase, in his *Guides to Straight Thinking*, reports this amusing story which can be organized into a *tu quoque* fallacy:

> The story runs that when the Moscow underground was first opened to visitors in the 1930's, an American tourist was invited to inspect one of the stations. He was shown the self-registering turnstiles and the spotless washrooms. "Fine," he said; then, looking down the tracks, "How about the trains?" They showed him the safety devices and the excellent tile frescos on the tunnel walls. He was again impressed, but continued to look anxiously down the tracks. "How about the trains?" snapped his guide. "How about the trains? How about the sharecroppers in Alabama?"

The *tu quoque* fallacy can be regarded as a particular kind of *ad hominem* argument. For in a *tu quoque* A argues that what B says is false (the charge against A is false) by directing the argument at B (trying to show that the same charges or similar charges can be made against B).

The Ad Populum *Fallacy*

An argument in which one bypasses relevant reasons altogether and appeals to popular sentiment, pity, fear, or other emotions to bring about rejection or acceptance of a conclusion is an *argumentum ad populum* (argument to the people).

There are several ways to appeal to popular sentiment. One way is to use expressions that appeal to the emotions of those to whom the argument is addressed, rather than present relevant reasons. A crude but simple example would be:

Don't support DeConcini for governor, for he is one of those Italians.

Here the appeal is made to prejudices that the audience may have—in this case that all Italian politicians are, perhaps, members of the Mafia. Prejudices are often the result of jumping to a conclusion—one judges all members of a group, say, Italians, on the basis of just a few cases, for example, those portrayed in the film *The Godfather*.

A far more complex example of appeal to popular sentiment is contained in the campaign speeches of Governor of California Jerry Brown. He has the ability to stir emotions through what he calls "buzz words." These are expressions which foster the images that appeal to groups of voters that Brown believes he needs for elections. Brown himself has identified these groups as young people, people who are not part of what is going on, and conservatives. How he appeals to the imagination of each of these groups is illustrated by some samples of the rhetoric used in his campaign of 1976 for the Democratic nomination for President: "We have fiscal limits, we have ecological limits, we have human limits." There has been "too much overpromising, too much overselling." "We're on a very small Spaceship Earth." "You have to have a strong defense, but you may have to make choices." "I would come to Washington with a different perspective." "We need continuity just as much as we need change. Just to stay where we are may take some pretty profound changes." He offers "an open spirit, a new generation of leadership." He offers "creative nonaction." "You can't just choose up sides and run the country, there are too many sides." "This is a very young country. This is a very new and vital country. It's a revolutionary country, and I think that that kind of energy is what we need to bring to Washington—honest, open, that's ready to try a few things. There's no one easy answer." As part of a thoughtful presentation of his views these remarks could be illuminating. But as the *substance* of a presentation they led one observer to comment that Brown's campaign speeches are "a jungle of thoughts, themes, moods. They don't seem to be ideas thought through as much as vibrations he has absorbed."[3] This is a use of words intended to appeal to the emotions of the audience, or cause vibrations in their psyches, rather than language used to communicate, for example, one's position on national issues such as unemployment, inflation, energy conservation, wealth redistribution through taxation, the arms race, and so on. Brown's campaign speeches are, therefore, good examples of *ad populum* appeals. It is only fair to say that political speeches are generally appeals to sentiment rather than rational argument.

The function of many television commercials is not to inform but to persuade us to buy a product. And this often is facilitated by an emotional appeal. One is persuaded to accept a claim by an emotional rather than a rational appeal. For example, a commercial for McDonald's hamburgers shows a uniformed servant in a Rolls Royce bringing a covered silver tray to his employer who sits in a mansion before an ornate dinner table. The servant takes the cover off the tray and we see some McDonald's hamburgers, fries, and a shake. What is the point of this commercial? It seems to be this: Anyone can afford a McDonald's hamburger. But here is a rich man who could drink champagne and eat caviar salivating over a McDonald's. So at least some of the good things in life are available to all.

[3] Elizabeth Drew, *American Journal: The Events of 1976* (New York: Random House, 1976).

Commercials seldom present a rational argument. They often exploit our anxieties and weaknesses. Sometimes they suggest life is enhanced by the consumption of the product. Coca Cola reminds us that life is not over yet. Pepsi wishes to allow us to vicariously participate in the "now generation." Advertisements of sugared products such as Count Chocula and Frankenberry are directed at children who are easily convinced. But why direct these commercials at children when it is the parents that have the money? The aim is to convince children of the desirability of the product and then leave it to them to persuade their parents to buy it.

Another kind of appeal to popular sentiment is sometimes called the bandwagon argument. Here is an illustration:

> It is clear from the polls that Senator Snort is going to be reelected by an overwhelming majority, so join the party of victory! Vote for Snort!

This argument is an appeal to popular sentiment because we all want to be part of the group, or some group, so if most people accept something we are also inclined to accept it.

An irrelevant appeal to pity to support a conclusion, or to persuade someone to accept a conclusion, is called an *argumentum ad misericordiam* (appeal to pity argument). This fallacy consists in presenting an appeal to pity as though pity or sympathy were logical or relevant grounds from which to infer a conclusion. The stock example is the defense attorney who argues that his client is innocent of a crime because his client comes from a downtrodden people.

Socrates in 399 B.C. was accused of not worshipping the gods whom the state worshipped and of introducing new and unfamiliar religious practices; he was further accused of corrupting the youth of Athens. Socrates gave a rational and what seems a conclusive defense against these charges. Nevertheless he was found guilty. Socrates in the following passage, indicates the kind of defense which would have led the jury to find him innocent and thus render a just decision. As we can see, it is an appeal to pity:

> Well, Athenians, this and the like of this is all the defence which I have to offer. Yet a word more. Perhaps there may be some one who is offended at me, when he calls to mind how he himself on a similar, or even a less serious occasion, prayed and entreated the judges with many tears, and how he produced his children in court, which was a moving spectacle, together with a host of relations and friends; whereas I, who am probably in danger of my life, will do none of these things. The contrast may occur to his mind, and he may be set against me, and vote in anger because he is displeased at me on this account. Now if there be such a person among you—mind, I do not say that there is—to him I may fairly reply: My friend, I am a man, and like other men, a creature of flesh and blood, and not "of wood and stone," as Homer says; and I have a family, yes, and sons, O Athenians, three in number, one almost a man, and two others who are still young; and yet I will not bring any of them hither in

order to petition you for an acquittal. And why not? Not from any self-assertion or want of respect for you. Whether I am or am not afraid of death is another question, of which I will not speak. But, having regard to public opinion, I feel that such conduct would be discreditable to myself, and to you, and to the whole state.   (PLATO, *Apology*)

The means of defense which Socrates did not choose to use was clearly an argument which appeals to pity. From the context of the *Apology* it can be seen that Socrates is neither directly nor indirectly using an appeal to pity. Most of the jury reacted to this as an insult and Socrates knew that this would be its effect.

The last form of *ad populum* is the argument *ad baculum*—the fallacy of appeal to force. This fallacy is defined as the appeal to the fear of force to cause acceptance of a conclusion. Consider this simple example:

> You ought to vote for a union shop, Utah Jenkins, because it will spare you the surprise of finding shotgun holes in the windows of your home.

If this is construed not as simply an appeal to fear, that is, as a simple threat, it may be regarded as appealing to the fear of force to cause acceptance of a conclusion, namely: The union shop is to be preferred. A threat is embodied in the premise and the premise is logically irrelevant to the conclusion. Just because Utah Jenkins may have his house riddled with shotgun holes is irrelevant to whether union shops are or are not to be preferred. Here is another example:

> In 1961 the Western Powers held that they had certain rights in West Berlin, while the Soviet Union denied that they had such rights. Other nations were placed by both powers in the position of having to take sides. At that time the Soviet Union announced and tested a nuclear bomb that was about a hundred times more powerful than any United States bomb.

Suppose the Soviet Union has argued, "We have the largest bomb in the world, consequently our claims about Berlin are true." This would be an *argumentum ad baculum*. If someone were led to conclude from this argument that the Soviet Union's claims were true, he would have fallen victim to an *ad baculum* fallacy. Here it should be noted that not all appeals to force are or involve fallacies. For example, simple threats ("Your money or your life") are appeals to force, but are not or do not involve fallacies.

There is yet another observation to be made concerning the *ad baculum* fallacy. Of the nuclear bomb example we said that if it is correct that the fear of these new bombs led some to conclude that the Soviet Union's claims were true, then they fell victim to an *ad baculum* fallacy. But it seems to be highly unlikely that the fear of new bombs (or of anything else) would lead anyone to *conclude* that the Soviet Union's claims were *true*. Fear might indeed lead some to *say* that those claims were true, but hardly to *believe* (or conclude) that they were. We suppose that in such a case fear of (possible) consequences would not befog the mind, would not cause one to be duped into thinking a certain claim true, though this fear might well lead one to give lip service to the claim. If this observation is correct, then there exists serious doubt that what have traditionally been called fallacies of appeal to force, or *ad baculum* fallacies, are fallacies at all, since one is not taken in by the "argument," but at best only wishes to appear to be taken in—because he is afraid.

The various methods politicians use to obtain votes are often attempts to persuade voters by *ad populum* appeals rather than attempts to deal with issues and thus give the voters some accurate idea of exactly what they believe. This fact has led Russell Baker, the *New York Times* columnist, to argue that we should not vote. Why? Baker suggests that people who are not well informed about the candidates should abstain from voting and leave it to those who are, for what will make democracy work, if anything will, is not a mass electorate but an informed electorate. But how does one get informed? Usually through political campaigns. But these, Baker says,

> ... are deliberately built to make judgments difficult for the voters. Commonly, they attempt to persuade the voters that the candidate is a good television performer and looks trustworthy. They also strive to show that the candidate has good teeth, a happy family, and a nondescript mind. None of this information is very interesting if you are trying to decide whether the candidate believes in a regressive tax structure, subsidies for the failing corporations, expanded health care programs, or any of the other dull nuts-and-bolts stuff he will have to deal with if elected. ... In 1972 George McGovern spent months trying to defend himself on the "issues" of legalizing marijuana, amnesty for draft evaders and abortion. None of these had much to do with whether McGovern was qualified to deal with the foreign policy and economic problems he would have confronted as President in 1973, but the Nixon people had successfully turned them into "issues" which voters judged important.[4]

Unfortunately, the *ad populum* appeals in campaigns are most effective. Joe Napolitan, the Democratic pollster and media consultant, says he rates a politician's effectiveness on television by turning off the sound and just watching the picture. Many feel that television itself is responsible for the effectiveness of *ad populum* appeals. Television is visual. It emphasizes personality. And the politician is lucky if he gets twenty seconds of attention on the evening news. Thus Americans are being conditioned now to judge the worth of a cause less on its merits than on the appearances of its advocates. Television politics is conditioning Americans to make up their

[4] Russell Baker, "The Case for Not Voting," in *The New York Times*, September 7, 1974.

minds on the basis of their first quick, superficial reaction to style and taste, rather than on the basis of rational consideration of facts and ideas.

The Ad Verecundiam *Fallacy*

It is not uncommon for one to attempt to support a conclusion by citing some person(s) who asserts the conclusion. This type of argument has the form (where p represents some statement):

> A asserts p.
> Therefore p.

Just because A asserts p it does not follow that p is true. However, if A is a reliable authority concerning p, that A asserts p is good grounds for concluding that p. In other words:

> A is a reliable authority concerning p.
> A asserts p.
> Therefore p.

is a correct argument pattern. How can we determine that A is a reliable authority in a field? The answer is simple: If a very high percentage of the assertions he makes with respect to the field in question are true, then he is an authority in the field in question. Now the fallacy of appeal to authority, the *ad verecundiam* fallacy, occurs when an argument is of the first form above and A is not an authority in the area to which p pertains. Thus if someone argues that one model car is superior to another by citing the fact that A said this, and A is not an expert with respect to automobiles, then this argument would be an appeal to authority fallacy. If, on the other hand, A is an expert with respect to automobiles, this would be a correct argument.

In 1958, to consider a real-life example, Robert Welch, the founder of the John Birch Society, in a series of talks which were collected in what is called *The Blue Book*, said such things as: (a) Unless we can reverse the seemingly relentless forces now at work, the United States in only a few more years will become four separate provinces in a worldwide, Kremlin-based Communist dominion. (b) The method by which the Communists are trying to take over the United States is to induce the gradual surrender of United States sovereignty to various international organizations, for example, the United Nations, and to change the economic and political structure of the United States so that it can comfortably merge with Soviet Russia. (c) Although our real danger is internal—from Communist influences and treason in our government—the American people are being led to believe that the danger is external—from Russian military superiority. (d) The only thing which the Communists fear is that, in spite of their tremendous influence in our government and their control of mass media, the American people will someday wake up to what is happening.

According to Welch this is all "the facts," but during these talks little evidence is given other than Welch's testimony. Who then is Welch? He has been in the candy manufacturing business all of his adult life. In addition, to quote Welch:

> ... I should like to make clear in my own defense that my credentials for the task are not based simply on my association with other anti-Communists. It's true that I have been to Formosa, and talked with Chiang Kai-shek and to practially every high official in the Chinese Nationalist Government—with some of them at considerable length. I have been to West Germany, and talked with Chancellor Adenauer. I have been in personal association or continuous correspondence with many if not most of the leading anti-Communists in this country and throughout the world. And I have diligently studied the anti-Communist books and objective histories which reveal piece-meal the horrifying truth of the past two decades.
>
> None of that, however, constitutes the best support of my right to express the opinion I am going to give you. The opinion is: The Communists have already gone at least one-fourth of the way in their third and final step—taking over the United States, and with it the world. That right comes primarily from a study of the Communists' own periodicals and literature.

In another place he says that he has been studying the problem of Communism increasingly over the past nine years and almost full time for the last three years. He also points out that his lifetime spent in the candy manufacturing business enables him to see the weakness of the economic theory of Communism "more readily than might some scholar coming into that study from the academic cloister." His lifetime interest in world history, Welch adds, gives him an advantage over many businessmen in seeing this weakness. These credentials do not, as we can see, reveal Welch as an expert in international matters. Thus his testimony alone is not grounds for affirming the preceding statements. If someone were to affirm these statements and give as his only reason the testimony of Welch or people with similar backgrounds, then he would commit the fallacy of appeal to authority.

Even though it is, of course, not a fallacy to consult an expert, one practical problem is to know what to believe when their opinions conflict. Mintz and Cohen in *Power, Inc.* raise this problem and come to the wise but hardly surprising conclusion that in most serious matters we should not uncritically trust experts. In support of this conclusion they remind us of some failures of experts. Government economists have been wrong about dozens of vital economic predictions. Experts in World War II were confident that Germany could be bombed into submission, but instead, the Allied bombing only strengthened the Nazis' will to resist. Sir Robert Thompson, known as "the British expert on guerilla warfare" once declared that the South Vietnamese would win the war against the Viet Cong. Physicians overprescribe drugs and surgeons remove healthy organs. Expert witnesses in courts, psychiatrists, appraisers, handwriting specialists, give contradictory opinions. Nevertheless it seems that most of us are inclined to believe those we *think* are experts. And we can easily be fooled into thinking someone is an expert. This is evidenced by the following story reported by Mintz and Cohen.

> The pitfalls of uncritical reliance on experts were hilariously illustrated in a paper presented in 1972 by Dr. Donald H. Naftulin, John E. Ware, Jr., and Frank A. Donnelly. They hired an actor to pose as a fictitious "Dr. Myron L. Fox," equipped him with a phony but impressive *curriculum vitae* appropriate to his distinguished appearance and authoritative manner, and coached him to deliver a one-hour lecture and answer questions "with an excessive use of double talk, neologisms, *non sequiturs*, and contradictory statements. All this was to be interspersed with parenthetical humor and meaningless references to unrelated topics."
>
> The title of the lecture was "Mathematical Game Theory as Applied to Physician Education." Dr. Fox had three audiences. The first consisted of eleven psychiatrists, psychologists, and social-work educators gathered for a teacher-training conference. A videotape was made and shown to eleven mental health educators—psychiatrists, psychologists, and psychiatric social workers—and finally to thirty-three educators and administrators, including twenty-one with master's degrees. Each person who listened to Dr. Fox's mutterings and ramblings about game theory was at the end given a written questionnaire to fill out anonymously. In all three audiences the favorable responses far outweighed the unfavorable. A person in the second audience actually claimed to have read the lecturer's publications. None detected the lecture for what it was.[5]

The Ad Ignorantiam *Fallacy*

Arguments called *ad ignorantiam* fallacies must have one of these two forms:

1. There is no proof (or you have not proved) that *p* is false. Therefore *p* is true.
2. There is no proof (or you have not proved) that *p* is true. Therefore *p* is false.

At one time there was no proof that the earth revolves around the sun. If someone had argued:

> The earth does not revolve around the sun, since there is no proof that it does.

---

[5] Jerry Cohen and Morton Mintz, *Power, Inc.* (New York: Viking Press, 1976) p. 307. Copyright 1976, Jerry S. Cohen and Morton Mintz.

this would be an instance of an *ad ignorantiam* fallacy. For, as we can see, man's ignorance of reasons for the earth revolving around the sun does not support the conclusion that the earth does not revolve around the sun. This example is an argument with the second form (2) of an *ad ignorantiam* fallacy.

Here is an *ad ignorantiam* that has the first form; Alexander Hall, a nineteenth-century Methodist minister, defended a theory of physics called substantialism. According to Hall, all forces like gravity are composed of particles. In magazines which he edited, he is supposed to have tried for years to prod scientists into debating with him. They all, of course, refused. It is reported that Hall responded by saying, "Since no one comes up with any reasons against my theory, it must be true." This is an *ad ignorantiam* fallacy. From the fact that no one objected to his view, it does not follow either that the view is true or that it is false. In Hall's case, scientists felt the view was too absurd to take the trouble to refute.

The *ad ignorantiam* fallacy is commonly committed in such examples as the following:

The alarmists have not succeeded in proving that thermal discharge is dangerous to lakes, so it must be safe.

No one has proved that smoking causes lung cancer, so we can go on using cigarettes.

Substance *x* is used in bacon and all lunch meats. But it's perfectly safe since no one has proved that it is a carcinogen.

Often in one set of circumstances an argument is fallacious, whereas in others it is not. This is especially true of arguments with the form of 1. and 2. For example, in a law court if it is not proved that *A* is guilty, it follows that *A* is not guilty. Even though this argument has the form of an *ad ignorantiam*, it is not fallacious because of the wise principle employed in our law courts that a person is presumed innocent until proved guilty. In fact such an argument in a law court can be analyzed as having an additional premise presupposed in the circumstances, so that the argument in reality is

Premise: It has not been proved that *A* is guilty.
Premise (presupposed in the circumstances): If a person is not proved guilty, then he is assumed innocent.
Conclusion: *A* is innocent.

Similarly, scientists sometimes conclude that a statement is false on the basis of the failure to turn up the required evidence for the statement. Such an argument is correct with this added premise presupposed in the circumstances: The scientists are sufficiently expert in the area so that if evidence were available, they would turn it up.

The Petitio Principii *Fallacy*

There are two argument patterns which are traditionally called the fallacy of *petitio principii* (begging the question). They are the following:

1. *p* is true. (Sometimes other statements are included with *p*.) Therefore *p* is true.
2. *p* is true because *q* is true. And *q* is true because *r* is true. And *r* is true because *p* is true. (The length of this chain of arguments can vary.)

Arguments having the second form are called *circular arguments*. When an argument has either form it is as a matter of fact deductively valid. Why this is true will be explained in a later chapter in Part II. Logically speaking, *petitio* arguments amount to little more than concluding that *p* is true because *p* is true. But such an argument fails to provide any grounds for affirming *p*; *p* by itself does not give us grounds for saying *p* is true. That is, *p* does not provide a reason for our concluding that *p* is true. However a *petitio* argument may appear to be an argument where relevant reasons are provided for affirming the conclusion if one fails to see the logical structure of the argument.

Each of the following is an instance of the *petitio principii* fallacy of the first form:

1. A physician in one of Molière's plays accounts for the sleep-giving power of opium by saying that the drug possesses a "dormative virtue."
2. To allow every man unbounded freedom of speech must always be, on the whole, advantageous to the state; for it is highly conducive to the interests of the community that each individual should enjoy a liberty perfectly unlimited of expressing his sentiments.
    (RICHARD WHATELY, *Elements of Logic*)
3. He that hath wife and children hath given hostages to fortune; for they are impediments to great enterprises, either of virtue or mischief.
    (BACON)

That the conclusion repeats the reason or premise is quite obvious in (1), not so obvious in (2), and less so in (3). In (1) "dormative virtue" is a synonym for "sleep-giving power." In (2) "advantageous" and "highly conducive to the interests of the community" are synonymous. And in (3) the "reason" is merely an explanation for "hostages to fortune." Sometimes the reason can be a carefully disguised restatement of the conclusion.

Reasoning in a circle is a more complicated instance of an argument which has the basic form "*p* is true, because *p*." There are some more steps, however, between the conclusion p and the basic reason for p, namely p itself. An example of such an argument is found in the following:

> All the statements in the Koran are true because they are the word of God. We know the Koran is the word of God because Mohammed said it was. We can rely on what Mohammed said because he was God's prophet. And we know he was God's prohet because the Koran says so, and whatever it says is true.

It is clear that this argument is circular and has the second form indicated above.

The famous law of effect in learning theory has at times been so formulated that it mirrors a *petitio*. Here is one formulation of the law:

> Of several responses made to the same situation, those which are accompanied or closely followed by satisfaction to the animal will, other things being equal, be more firmly connected with the situation, so that, when it recurs, they will be more likely to recur; those which are accompanied or closely followed by discomfort to the animal will, other things being equal, have their connections with the situation weakened, so that, when it recurs, they will be less likely to occur. The greater the satisfaction or discomfort, the greater the strengthening or weakening of the bond.

How does one tell when an animal is satisfied or dissatisfied with something? If the answer is: one tells by seeing whether the animal seeks or avoids the thing in question, then the above explanation (that is, the law of effect) is a *petitio* argument.

The Fallacy of Inconsistency

Contradictory statements are statements which must have opposite truth values. That is, p contradicts q if when p is true q is false, and when p is false q is true, and vice-versa. Thus the negation of a statement is a contradictory of the statement. For example the contradictory of

> Dirty work in society is done by the poor.

is

> It is false that dirty work in society is done by the poor.

or

> Some dirty work in society is not done by the poor.

When the premises of an argument contain a contradiction, that is, contradictory statements, the argument is as a matter of fact deductively valid. Why this is true will be explained in later chapters in Part II. But such an argument cannot be *sound*, for a sound argument is one that is correct and one where each premise is true. When an argument has contradictory premises we normally do not regard the premises as providing support for the conclusion because it is ruled out as a matter of logic that the argument can be sound. Furthermore if the premises are contradictory we do not take the premises as providing relevant reasons for the conclusion. As in the case of *petitio* arguments, arguments with contradictory premises do not provide any grounds for affirming the conclusion.

So when one speaks of the fallacy of inconsistent premises, he refers to a formally valid argument but one which is faulty because it is necessarily unsound and is necessarily an argument where the premises do not provide relevant reasons for affirming the conclusion. In any case what is called the *fallacy of inconsistency* is an argument with contradictory premises.

In a recent book the generalist Robert Theobald argues that teachers in institutions of higher learning are primarily concerned with disciplinary rigor and recognition by their disciplinary peers rather than with the transmission of information. Teachers in smaller colleges, community colleges, and adult education programs not only are more interested in transmitting information but they help students look at the assumptions that lie behind disciplinary conclusions. They may also be willing

> . . . to show students that all knowledge is based on challengeable assumptions. (A mathematical proof has been developed that shows that it is impossible to develop a structure of knowledge that does not contain at least one unprovable first assumption.) Few students are aware of this harsh reality; most leave college believing that what they have learned in economics, sociology, political science, and psychology rests on some rational theoretical base, rather than on a nineteenth-century set of assumptions that have long ago been shown to be special cases.[6]

The argument here is that teachers in community college-like schools are better than professors at universities for they may be willing and able to show that all knowledge is based on challengeable assumptions. One reason he gives for this latter claim is that a mathematical proof has shown that any system of knowledge must have at least one unprovable first assumption. Ignoring the question of whether there is any such proof in mathematics, what is appealed to is an alleged mathematical proof. But how can there be such an unchallengeable mathematical proof if *all* knowledge including, presumably, mathematics and logic is based on challengeable assumptions? The reasons Theobald gives for his conclusion contain a contradiction, and we should dismiss the argument for that reason.

[6] Robert Theobald, *Beyond Despair* (Washington, D.C.: New Republic Book Co., 1976), pp. 122–123. Copyright © 1976 by Robert Theobald.

Policies can lead to consequences which are expressible in contradictory statements. We ordinarily call such policies inconsistent. For example, some accuse the current U.S. administration of having inconsistent policies. Those in charge of our economic policies are promoting a higher growth rate to meet human needs and to reduce unemployment. Those in charge of our energy policy are demanding limitations on the use of imported oil and restrictions of other energy development for ecological reasons. But to many it seems contradictory to mesh ecological and economic growth goals.

Similar charges can be leveled at individuals. For example, a candidate for political office may argue in the same speech that we should reduce taxes and also that we should increase the military budget to counter the enormous military superiority of the Soviets. Obviously he is trying to attract two groups of voters—those fearing the Soviets and those who feel they pay too much in taxes—without alienating any groups. Since an increase in military spending can only come from an increase in taxes, unless other government spending is significantly decreased, his position appears inconsistent. If he resolved this apparent inconsistency by, say, supporting large reductions in spending on health, education, or welfare, then he would alienate those who benefit from such spending, something he obviously does not want to do. Lacking an explanation why his position is not consistent, we are justified in charging the candidate with an inconsistency. If a politician's views are inconsistent or appear to be inconsistent, and if an appeal is made to his positions on issues as reasons why he should be supported, this would be a fallacy of inconsistency.

If one says one thing at one time and the opposite at another time without either explaining the change or retracting one of the statements, then one is inconsistent. Jerry Brown, as a young seminarian, stood on principle against capital punishment and persuaded his father, Pat Brown, the then governor of California, to grant a stay of execution to Caryl Chessman, a convicted rapist–kidnapper whose case had become a national symbol of the debate over capital punishment. This ended Pat Brown's dream of the presidency. David Broder outlines how Jerry Brown reacted to this issue when he became governor of California.

> Jerry Brown faced the death penalty issue in 1977 and announced at the beginning of the legislative session that if a bill restoring capital punishment in California should reach his desk he would veto it. He carried out his threat. But as the time for an override vote approached, Brown's role became hazy. A few days before the scheduled Assembly vote, Tony Daugherty, Brown's legislative liaison chief, told me, "In all candor, we have not worked it the way we would a normal override." With the backing of strong Democratic majorities and an able, cooperative speaker, Leo McCarthy, Brown had never been overriden; in fact there had been only two successful overrides of a governor's veto in all the years since Earl Warren. But, Daugherty told me, "If we tried to pressure on this one, it would backfire on the governor. We do have an initiative in this state. It's clear to everyone we'll have a death penalty in

California, and the general political view is, it will hurt him if it's not overridden now and it winds up on the ballot next November." When I asked Brown the next day if that was why he was doing so little lobbying on the issue, he said, "Well, it's a very sensitive subject. The polls show more than 70 percent of the people in California want the death penalty, and it's a matter of both principle and survival to the members of the legislature."

A few days later, the Assembly completed the override process on a 54–26 vote, exactly the two thirds required. Had Brown swayed one vote, the outcome would have been different. Brown told reporters, "I'm not surprised. I don't believe in the death penalty, but as long as it is a valid law, I will carry out my responsibility to uphold it."[7]

The apparent contradiction is that the young Brown vigorously opposed the death penalty, while Governor Brown failed to take the easy, minimal action to sustain his veto of the bill restoring capital punishment in California. Broder explains the switch in terms of a cold-eyed pragmatic move of an ambitious governor. In any case, there are three possibilities here: Governor Brown's actions were not consistent with his beliefs, there is no real contradiction (Governor Brown's view), or Governor Brown has changed his mind about things (Broder's hypothesis). There is nothing wrong with changing one's mind, though it may be embarrassing, especially when you are a politician. What is logically unacceptable is to be inconsistent and to ask for, or expect support because of one's inconsistent positions. Broder remarks that a large part of Brown's appeal "lies in being consistent not in his policies but only in his skepticism. He plays out on a public stage the skepticism many citizens feel about their government."[8]

Can one actually hold two contradictory beliefs? George Orwell thinks so and calls this feat "doublethink." Paradigm examples of doublethink in Orwell's novel *1984* are the enormous lettering on the white concrete face of the Ministry of Truth:

> War is Peace
> Freedom is Slavery
> Ignorance is Strength

The government in *1984* promotes such doublethinking in order to get people to accept indefensible government programs. Doublethinking has to be in part unconscious, according to Orwell, or else it will bring a feeling of falsity and hence guilt. If one holds two contradictory beliefs, then one belief must, logically speaking, be false; thus the conjunction of the two beliefs is false.

---

[7] David S. Broder, "The Canniness of the Long Distance Runner," *Atlantic Monthly*, January 1978.

[8] Ibid.

Complex Question

In Sophocles' *King Oedipus,* Tiresias, the blind prophet, tells Oedipus that he is responsible for the curse that is on Thebes since it was he who slew Laius, the King of Thebes before Oedipus. Oedipus in his rage accuses Creon, his brother-in-law, of getting Tiresias to say this so that Creon might become king. When Creon hears of this he goes to Oedipus to deny the charge since it is not true. When he meets Oedipus, the latter says:

> What brought you here: have you a face so brazen that you come to my house—you, the proved assassin of its master—the certain robber of my crown? Come, tell me in the face of the Gods what cowardice, or folly, did you discover in me that you plotted this? Did you think I would not see what you were at till you had crept upon me, or seeing it would not ward it off?
>
> (SOPHOCLES, *King Oedipus*)[9]

Most of these questions are *complex questions,* for they presuppose that Creon plotted to become king. Take, for example, the last: "Did you think that I would not see what you were at?" If Creon answers no, then he would be assenting to the claim that he was guilty, and if he answers yes, he would also be assenting. Or, to put it another way, Oedipus' question is a complex question because two questions are involved in it: First, "Did you plot to become king?" and, second, "Did you think I would not see it?"

Once one understands what a complex question is, he can understand what error might be made in connection with such a question. Consider the complex question: When will Congress begin to act responsibly? And suppose that the person to whom the question is addressed is sufficiently naive to believe that since the question is asked, the assumptions embodied in it must be true. So when he hears the question he concludes that Congress has not been acting responsibly and that it is high time they should. Since he accepts a view for no worthy reason, his reasoning, such as it is, is fallacious. Obviously, the way to deal with a complex question is to consider first whether the assumption embodied in it is true (e.g., *Is* Congress acting irresponsibly?) and then worry about the answer.

Genetic Fallacy

The genetic fallacy is committed when the genesis of a view is attacked, rather than the view itself. That is, the manner in which one acquires a view or his source of the view is criticized. The effect of this criticism is supposed

---

[9] Sophocles, *King Oedipus,* trans. W. B. Yeats, in *Collected Plays of W. B. Yeats* (New York: Macmillan, 1952), p. 489. Used by permission of Macmillan Publishing Co., Inc.

to be to cast doubt on the view itself. In many of its instances the genetic
fallacy is a variation of the *ad hominem* fallacy. Consider this imagined
argument:

> Lafayette Jones, owner of Special Foods, Inc., an Indianapolis firm
> which produces skim milk, brewer's yeast, wheat germ, yoghurt, tiger's
> milk, and blackstrap molasses, realized how someone could profit from
> the sale of these "wonder foods" if people came to believe that the
> regular use of these foods would maintain good health and add years to
> their lives. So he lectured and published articles making these claims.
> Thus we can clearly see that Mr. Jones' views about these "wonder
> foods" are worthless and erroneous.

Would this be grounds for concluding that Lafayette Jones' claim is false? It
would make us skeptical of its truth, but only evidence that the five foods
have no such value would be reasonable grounds for concluding that the
view is false. The arguer has described what led someone to a view and infers
from this that the view is false.

Another example of this fallacy is found in the following:

> John Stuart Mill's views about the equality of men can be dismissed as
> myths. We all know that John's father, James, told his son, in order to
> prevent Johnny from becoming conceited, that if one showed more
> ability than another, it was entirely due to a better education.

(It should be noted that John Stuart Mill was a genius.) Even supposing that
Mill's father did this, and that this is how Mill came to his views about
equality, this does not provide grounds for dismissing his views.

Our last illustration of the genetic fallacy is from real life:

> A study of primitive tribes shows that early man had many fears—his
> principal fears were those of illness, being crushed under a falling tree,
> and being killed by wild animals. Certain men gained influences in
> tribes by offering various charms and incantations to ward off these
> dangers or by asserting that some benevolent spirit more powerful than
> these dangers would protect those who approached him in the right
> way. The ones who preferred the second policy were those who
> introduced religion. Since this is the origin of belief in God, it is little
> more than superstition, as you can see, and, consequently, the thinking
> man should reject religion.

Even supposing this is what led men at first to religious beliefs, it still does
not follow from this that religious claims are to be rejected. Thus the genetic
fallacy is committed.

Straw Man Fallacy

From time to time the claims of others are misinterpreted (either deliberately or accidentally). The *straw man fallacy* is committed when a claim is misinterpreted and the attempt is made to refute the misinterpreted claim. The argument, however, is presented as a refutation of the original claim. Consider this example of a straw man fallacy:

> The man who said, "Miracles don't happen," is as blind as a mole in a tarbarrel. I guess he never heard of computers. TV is unknown to him. "Astronauts" is a new word to him. The news about Tang hasn't reached him yet. I tell you this is an age of miracles. I could name a thousand more.

In the example the arguer, if serious, has taken "Miracles do not happen" to mean that extraordinary inventions cannot take place. And, obviously, he has successfully shown the statement, understood in this way, to be false. But is this how those who say, "Miracles do not happen," are to be understood? This depends on the context in which the denial is made. Sometimes what is meant by the denial is that events which go against natural law or happen while natural law is suspended and are caused by supernatural forces, do not happen. And, of course, the arguer in our example has not shown or even given a reason why this view is false.

Consider this real-life example of this fallacy:

> Does Communism come out of poverty? Is it true that if you feed the people you can stop Communism? A United States Senator at one time answered no to both questions, and here are the reasons he gave:
>
> (a) "I suppose that some of the people of our country have learned that some Indians and some of the poor people of America have not had enough economic opportunity. But these citizens have not been enrolled among the group led by the Communists or the group of Communist supporters."
>
> (b) "But as to Communists being brewed out of poverty and Communists coming up from hunger, I will venture the statement that there is not a single hungry Communist in Russia. There are only a few million members of the Communist Party there. They are the elite; the privileged class. Lots of people are starving there, but they are the poor people who are oppressed by the Communists."

Now it may well be true that hunger does not breed Communism, but the reasons given by the senator are not relevant to the view that hunger breeds Communism. The first reason is a refutation of the view that if someone is poor, then he is a Communist. His second reason is a refutation of the view that if someone is a Communist, then he is poor. Neither view, of course, is involved in the opinion held by some that hunger breeds Communism.

Often not only is the misunderstood statement in a straw man argument accidentally misunderstood, but the misunderstanding can occur in subtle ways. To illustrate, consider this next example:

The upsurge of Communism, we are informed, is, in part at least, due to the failure of the Church. Specifically, we are told, it is the irrelevance of so much of the nineteenth-century Christianity to the urgent problems of modern industrial mass society that has driven large masses to look elsewhere for salvation and meaning of life; Communism has gained its strength from its ability to fill the spiritual vacuum which the failure of Christianity has produced.

Such is the familiar argument; if taken seriously, however, it leads to some rather extraordinary conclusions. The U.S., the Netherlands, the Scandinavian countries, even Britain, seem to be singularly free from Communist infection; are we to conclude, therefore, that Christianity and the Church are particularly relevant in these countries, in contrast, let us say, to Christianity and the Church in Italy or France where Communism is a powerful mass force?

(WILL HERBERG, "Communism, Christianity and the Judgment of God" in *The National Review*, Janaury 16, 1962)

In the first paragraph is found the claim that is allegedly refuted. The claim is, roughly, that if in a society Christianity satisfies the needs for salvation and meaning of life, then Communism does not take hold. In the second paragraph we find the reasons which are apparently directed against this claim. But what happens here is that the author of the argument erroneously supposes that the following two statements are implied by the original claim: If there is no or little Communism in a country, then it has a strong, powerful Christian church; and if there is a strong, powerful Christian church in a country, then there is no or little Communism. He then presents counter-examples to each of these statements—the United States, the Netherlands, and so on, with no Communism but not so strong a Church; and Italy and France, with a strong Church but also Communism. These two statements are refuted, and if they did follow from the claim in question it would possibly have been refuted, but neither statement follows from the original claim.

Edward Bellamy in a book published in 1880, *Looking Backward*, suggests that some form of basic economic security is essential if we are to get at the roots of crime. In other words poverty generates crime. Many have disagreed with this view. Some argue that if it were true, there should have been a decrease in crime already, because of the rise in the level of income that has occurred in the twentieth century. This argument construes Bellamy's view as the view that if everyone's income level provided for the basic needs of life, then there would be no crime. But is this the most charitable or plausible interpretation of Bellamy's view? The charitable interpretation would be that the lack of an income which persons *regard* as sufficient is the cause of crime. Thus in a society where people need to be made to want more in order for its economic system to function, income levels will seem insufficient to many, and thus crime will continue even though the income level is adequate for the basic needs of life.

EXERCISES 2.1

A. Determine the occurrences of any inconsistencies in the following and explain why you think there is an inconsistency.

1. In 1978 the U.S. Senate debated and then ratified the main Panama Canal Treaty that turns the Canal over to Panama in the year 2000. Before ratifying the treaty, however, the Senate adopted several amendments and reservations to it. One amendment says that the United States has the right to take whatever action necessary to keep the canal open but that the United States does not have the right to intervene in the internal affairs of Panama.

2. Government and industry advocates of nuclear power tell us that a catastrophic reactor incident is wildly improbable. Yet manufacturers of nuclear equipment would not build nuclear plants until the Price–Anderson Act of 1957 became law. This Act limits liability in a single nuclear accident to $560 million.

3. In 1977 the chairman of AT&T, the first corporation in history to announce a one billion dollar quarterly profit, opposed efforts to break his company's monopoly. He warned: There is no question in my mind that if we continue down this road to greater competition, the average customer is going to be hurt.

4. Whites were in South Africa long before blacks and have built a society that is both economically sound and politically stable. So to keep what they built they must attempt to silence black opposition through police power.

5. In 1977 a poll showed that 58 percent of Americans disapprove of government-sponsored welfare programs. And yet when those surveyed were asked a series of questions about the substance of welfare programs a different pattern emerged. For example 81 percent approved of the government's providing financial assistance for children raised in low-income homes in which one parent is missing. (Such dependent children comprise the majority of welfare recipients.) Similarly, 81 percent endorsed helping poor people buy food for their families at cheaper prices and using taxes to pay for health care for poor people.

6. The Department of Health, Education and Welfare makes periodic attempts to wean smokers away from the noxious weed.

They have proposed that larger and more vivid surgeon general's warnings be placed on packs of cigarettes, that there be a limit to the amount of tar and nicotine in cigarettes, that the government pay the cost of stop-smoking programs, and that "Don't Smoke Days" be instituted. While this goes on, Congress provides federal support for tobacco growers. Tobacco farmers say that without support they would go bankrupt. If they went bankrupt, no tobacco would be grown. No tobacco, no cigarettes. We have a government that believes smoking is bad but tobacco is good.

7. If Lincoln were alive today, he would roll over in his grave.
   (REP. JERRY FORD, during a House debate)

8. The traditional American devotion to the work ethic, work as a good in itself, has usually been coupled with a fear that universal devotion to work would result in material abundance that would in turn produce moral and social decay.

9. Can a state that has approved the ERA amendment now withdraw its approval? Four state legislatures have, in fact, voted to rescind their approval. But the ERA sponsors insist an affirmative vote can't be changed, while a negative vote can be.

B. In each of the following passages, first decide whether it is an argument. Second, if it is an argument, state the conclusion and the reasons given for the conclusion. Third, decide whether the argument is fallacious. Fourth, if the argument is fallacious, indicate what kind of fallacy it is, selecting from those discussed above. If some of the arguments are fallacious but of a type not discussed above, use the category "none of these." Fifth, give reasons for your opinion. Each argument can be construed in different ways, so it is important to give your reasons for your classifications.

1. Mayor Ralph Perk, campaigning for the Republican nomination for the Senate in Ohio, said: "People ask me how Republicans will explain the eighteen-and-a-half-minute gap in the [Nixon] tapes. I tell them it will take the Democrats a lot longer to explain the twelve-and-a-half-hour gap at Chappaquiddick."

2. Why should I pay attention to Secretary of HEW Califano's attempts to persuade Americans to stop smoking? Isn't he a three-pack-a-day man? [He was.]

3. The entire graduated income tax structure was created by Karl Marx. It has no justification in getting the government needed revenues. (RONALD REAGAN)

4. "Having made the bomb," Truman was to explain in a broadcast why, "we used it." An estimated 70,000 persons had been killed and at least as many more wounded. That same day Samuel

McCrea Cavert, general secretary of the Federal Council of Churches of Christ in America, had telegraphed to him opposing further use of the weapon. Truman replied: "Nobody is more disturbed over the use of the Atomic bomb than I am, but I was greatly disturbed over the unwarranted attack by the Japanese on Pearl Harbor and their murder of our prisoners of war. The only language they seem to understand is the one we have been using to bombard them. When you have to deal with a beast you have to treat him as a beast. It is most regrettable but nevertheless true."

(ROBERT J. DONOVAN, *Conflict and Crisis*)

5. Recently state officials decided to purchase Kawasaki motorcycles for our police rather than the Harley-Davidson, the No. 1 bike in America for police. As I see it, the real issue is this: Are government bureaucrats going to continue to spend American tax dollars to purchase foreign machines of questionable superiority, thereby helping to undermine tax-paying American Businesses, or should they be required to purchase American-made products wherever possible and in so doing help to maintain the high standard of living enjoyed by American factory workers? I feel the choice is clear.

Tu quoque 6. In 1973 Dan Rather of CBS News asked President Nixon why he felt that he was different from Abraham Lincoln, who had said, "No man is above the law." President Nixon responded that during the Civil War President Lincoln had suspended the writ of *habeas corpus.*

7. President Nixon's speechwriter Patrick Buchanan wrote a piece for the Op-Ed page of *The New York Times*, June 12, 1974 asserting that the Washington, D.C. grand jurors who voted to name the President an unindicted co-conspirator in Watergate were from "the most anti-Nixon city in the United States." (Leon Jaworski, the Special Prosecutor, had suggested to the grand jury that since the question of whether a President could be indicted was unsettled, Nixon be named an unindicted co-conspirator in Watergate.) He pointed out that George McGovern received 78 percent of the votes in the District of Columbia, that seventeen of the twenty-three grand jurors were black, and that blacks across the nation had voted "upwards of 10 to 1 against the President."

ad populum (ad baculum) 8. . . . after the flush of the 1972 Nixon landslide, Clay T. Whitehead as Director of Telecommunications Policy for President Nixon said the local broadcasters must be "responsible." But like "law and order," "responsible" was a code word to Whitehead; to him, it meant that the local station should take steps to end "ideological plugola" in the news, correcting a situation where "so-called professionals . . . dispense elitist gossip in the guise of news analysis." Whitehead threatened station managers at license renewal time "who fail to act to correct imbalance or consistent bias from the networks." He also used the Doctrine in a carrot-and-stick approach which in effect promised that the Administration would fight to get the broadcasters a five-year license (instead of the present three-year term) in return for their squelching anti-Administration viewpoints on network news programs. (FRED W. FRIENDLY, *The Good Guys, the Bad Guys and the First Amendment*)

9. It is silly to talk about abolishing poverty. Even if all your proposals went through, there would always be some people who had less than others. So no matter what steps are taken there will always be poverty.

10. Jesus said, "In very truth I tell you, if anyone obeys my teaching he shall never know what it is to die."

   The Jews said, "now we are certain that you are possessed. Abraham is dead; the prophets are dead; and yet you say, 'If anyone obeys my teaching he shall never know what it is to die.' Are you greater than our father Abraham, who is dead? The people are dead too. What do you claim to be?" (John 8:51–53)

11. A: William Faulkner is a better writer than Tennessee Williams.
   B: Why?
   A: Because the best critics say so.
   B: How do you tell which critics are the best critics?
   A: You can tell which are the best by seeing if they prefer Faulkner to Williams.

12. On the Senate floor in 1950, Joe McCarthy announced that he had penetrated "Truman's iron curtain of secrecy." He had eighty-one case histories of persons whom he considered to be Communists in the State Department. Of Case 40, he said, "I do not have much information on this except the general statement of the agency that there is nothing in the files to disprove his communist connections."

   (Taken from RICHARD H. ROVERE's *Senator Joe McCarthy*)

13. You cannot turn on the television set or hear a politician say something without hearing that discrimination against women in employment is unfair and must end. Yet we must discriminate. We discriminate when we say that a woman cannot be a longshoreman. We discriminate when we say that a woman cannot be hired because she lacks the required degree or special training. We discriminate with our football teams and combat infantry, not to mention. . . .

14. You ought to sell more cars this year, Figby, because it will spare your wife the embarrassment of a letter from the main office telling her you're slipping.

15. A columnist visited the Argonne Laboratories, where the A bomb had been pioneered, and found that neither the institution itself nor any of the scientists he interviewed had a shelter. Even the top government officials seemed to have little faith in the idea, for not a single one of the fourteen high officials of the National Security Council had built a shelter for his own family. Neither had Vice-President Lyndon Johnson or Attorney General Robert Kennedy. Assistant Secretary of Defense Stuart Pittman, who is in charge of the national civil defense program, told a reporter that he had not built a shelter for his family because he was studying the "range of choices." Why should we do anything? If these people don't have shelters, then we shouldn't.

16. Former Navy Captain E. D. Mitchell of the 1971 Apollo flight took 55 special stamp covers on his lunar voyage as part of his "personal memorabilia." These stamp covers are now valued at over half a million dollars. It is difficult to draw the conclusion that condemns these profits from space. Remember that being on the federal payroll, as an astronaut or a politician, has built-in rewards on which people capitalize sooner or later. There hasn't been a President or secretary of state or fallen Watergate man who hasn't written a book or become a television personality and made millions in the process.

Tu quoque

17. How did Freud discover that all dreams are wish-fulfillments? Like this: During an interview it suddenly became clear that the patient who had certain strong erotic or ambitious wishes was having dreams in which these wishes were being fulfilled. He saw, then, how any number of dreams which came to mind and which were reported to him could be regarded in this way, and concluded that dreams are simply wish-fulfillments. If the first patient had had strong fears and was having dreams in which these fears were expressed, Freud might have concluded that all dreams are simply expressions of fear after seeing how many dreams could be looked at in this way. As we can see from this, his views amount to nothing.

18. Scientists today assume that it is likely that there exists intelligent life on other planets. If so, what happens to Christian theology? What happens to the idea that God created man in his own image? Or to the idea that God took the extraordinary step of becoming man in order to redeem one species of bipedal beings on earth? The answer is obvious. Christian theology cannot accommodate the prospect of life elsewhere.

Interesting argument!

19. President Jimmy Carter addressed the 100th anniversary of the Los Angeles Bar Association recently and attacked the lawyers in the United States who do nothing for the little man and spend all their time serving the rich and powerful. "Ninety percent of our lawyers," he complained, "serve 10 percent of our people." But this comes from the man who assembled half his Cabinet from the richest law firms in New York, Atlanta, and Washington. We all know what he is doing. He knows that Americans don't like lawyers. So the one who appointed a Cabinet that groans under the weight of corporate attorneys decided it was time to dump on the legal profession. Attack the same special interests that you are otherwise busy cozying up to. Carter's attack on lawyers is unfair and illegitimate. It is populist posturing and a slanderous assault upon a profession of honorable men.

20. This nation is on the same disastrous course as were some of the ancient nations. We are experiencing decay from within. This nation has given up its principles and constitutional philosophies for circuses, inflation, overtaxation, corruption, and widely known sinister operations. Jimmy Carter and his political henchmen are denying the will of the majority. The government tells us what to do and when to do it. We have no control over our destiny. How long will those silent Americans who grit their teeth, pay their taxes, and bear it continue to retreat and be silent? We don't need fools to manage us. We need a strong leader!

ANSWERS

A. It seems that a case can be made that in each example an inconsistency or an apparent inconsistency is found.

B. 1. *tu quoque* 3. genetic 5. complex question 7. *ad hominem* 9. straw man 11. *petitio* 13. straw man 15. *ad hominem* 17. genetic 19. *ad hominem* and *ad populum*.

The Material Fallacies of Insufficient Evidence

The fallacies studied in this section are examples of incorrect inductive arguments. A fallacy in an inductive argument is the error of thinking that true premises that *in fact* lend no or little support to a conclusion lend it significant support.

False-Cause Fallacy

The *false-cause fallacy* occurs when in an argument one mistakes what is not the cause of a given effect for its real cause. Two frequently discussed variations of this fallacy are the *post hoc* fallacy and the fallacy of accidental correlation.

In most circumstances an argument will be incorrect if it has the form:

Event A occurs, then event B occurs.
Therefore A causes B.

The mere fact that B occurs after A occurs, is not good grounds for concluding that A causes B, though the fact that B occurs after A occurs would be relevant in establishing whether or not A causes B. It is necessary that A occur prior to B if A is the cause of B, but it is not sufficient. Incorrect arguments with this pattern are called *post hoc, ergo propter hoc* (after this, therefore because of this) fallacies. Consider this simple example of a *post hoc* fallacy:

> When Roger Babson, whose prediction of the great stock market crash brought him renown, became ill with tuberculosis, he returned to his home in Massachusetts rather than follow his doctor's advice to remain in the West. During the freezing winter he left the windows open, wore a coat with a heating pad in back, and had his secretary wear mittens and hit the typewriter keys with rubber hammers. Babson got well and attributed his cure to fresh air. Air from pine woods, according to Babson, has chemical or electrical qualities (or both) of great medicinal value.[10]

As we can see, in the preceding passage Babson made this inference:

When I returned to the freezing winter of Massachusetts (A), I was cured of tuberculosis (B).
Therefore the properties of a freezing winter in Massachusetts (A) caused the tuberculosis cure (B).

This argument is incorrect. The reason is not good grounds for affirming the conclusion. The fact that when A happened, B happened, does not thereby provide good grounds to conclude that A caused B.

Our next example involves a claim by a Dr. Melvin Page in his book called *Degeneration–Regeneration*. It is his view that milk is good for babies but is dangerous for adults. He claims that taken by adults, milk is the frequent cause of colds, sinus trouble, colitis, and, most important, cancer. One reason he gives for his view is that in Wisconsin more people die of cancer per capita than in any other state, and more milk is drunk in Wisconsin than in any other state. If Dr. Page made this inference:

More milk is drunk and more people die of cancer in Wisconsin than in any other state.
Therefore milk drinking is a cause of cancer.

[10] Cf. Martin Gardner, *Fads and Fallacies in the Name of Science* (New York: Dover, 1952), p. 97.

then this would be a *post hoc* fallacy. Wisconsin people tend to live longer because they drink so much milk, and cancer is a cause of death in older persons.

The *fallacy of accidental correlation* occurs when an argument has this form:

> *A* occurs when *B* occurs.
> Therefore *A* causes *B* (or vice-versa).

In a *post hoc* fallacy the premise is the claim that *B* follows *A*. In a fallacy of accidental correlation, the premise is simply the claim that *A* occurs when *B* occurs. The premise does not imply that one event followed the other event. It has been noted that whenever there has been a bull market on Wall Street the hemline in women's dresses has gone up, and when the hemline goes down the market goes down. If some manager of institutional money tried to persuade a designer of international reputation to lower hemlines so he could make a killing selling short, he would be a victim of the fallacy of accidental correlation. To cite another example, Soviet propaganda in the Third World, as elsewhere, rests largely on the claim that the Soviet model of socialism has demonstrated its capacity to move a large country into the ranks of advanced industrial societies. This alleged fact is then taken as the vindication of socialism and even of Stalinism. Socialism or Stalinism is the necessary price of achievement. This argument that the Soviet Union uses to show that socialism works has been widely accepted even by those not sympathetic with socialism. But doubts can be expressed concerning the main assumption of this argument. It is that the socialist form of economic organization caused the industrial development of the Soviet Union, and without it there would have been no such development. The evidence is just that they occurred together. There is no evidence that one caused the other. The development of the Soviet Union has not been any more remarkable than that of other comparable countries with different forms of economic organization. It seems that Russia might today be in exactly or perhaps an even better economic position under a different system.

The Fallacy of Special Pleading

Those who fail to mention evidence unfavorable to their claim in a situation in which *all* evidence is presumably being mentioned, are guilty of the *fallacy of special pleading*.

There are at least two sides to most important issues. To avoid a fallacious sort of arguing one should consider both sides of the issue and try to show that a stronger case can be made for the side one favors.

After the oil embargo in 1974 Congress passed a national 55 mph speed limit. There are arguments for and against this national speed limit. Consider the following argument against the "double nickel" speed limit:

> We should repeal the 55 mph speed limit because of the distances that need to be traveled in the West, because of money lost by time consumed on the part of long haul truckers and bus companies and because no one is driving 55 mph anyhow. The double nickel law echoes the unworkable prohibition of alcohol in the 30s.

This argument does consider some of the relevant reasons for the repeal of the 55 mph speed limit. What the argument fails to take into account are the reasons for the speed limit. The most prominent reasons are that the speed limit saves lives and saves oil. (It saves about ten thousand lives a year.) Thus the above argument is an instance of the fallacy of special pleading. To avoid this fallacy one would have to consider reasons both for and against repeal of the national speed limit and, if possible, try to show that the stronger case can be made for repeal of the 55 mph national speed limit.

If one fails to mention facts unfavorable to one's position this is also a fallacy of special pleading. In a recent discussion on television one of the participants argued fallaciously in giving his case for removing warning labels on products harmful to health:

> Some people believe that saccharin may be hazardous to one's health since there is evidence that it causes cancer in laboratory animals. Many of these people want to put warning labels on saccharin products such as soda. But putting such labels on soda cans and bottles *is in itself* hazardous to one's health. The reason is that not using saccharin products can easily result in overweight, and overweight is universally recognized as a far more serious cause of health problems than what might result from using saccharin.

What is suppressed in this argument is the obvious truth that the weight-conscious person has more than the two alternatives mentioned here to choose from: he may avoid sweet soda drinks altogether, whether they are saccharin sweetened or sugar sweetened. It is also obvious that though the dangers of overweight are well known, not everyone may realize the hazards involved in imbibing a great deal of saccharin.

During the impeachment hearings of Richard Nixon, Representative Barbara Jordan gave her reason for voting for impeachment. She said:

> My faith in the constitution is whole, it is complete, it is total, and I am not going to sit here and be an idle spectator to the diminution, the subversion, the destruction of the Constitution.

Watergate has been widely viewed as a matter of maintaining the rule of law under the Constitution. And Jordan's argument is that Nixon should be impeached because he tried to subvert the Constitution. What is suppressed in this argument is something that Jordan and others agree is true. It is that the Constitution has, at times, protected social evils such as slavery. In other words, following the Constitution has not always implied adherence to the moral good. If we add to Jordan's argument what she herself accepts, then her argument is incorrect. It can be true that Nixon tried to subvert the Constitution, but this is not a good reason for concluding that Nixon behaved wrongly if one adds that the Constitution is not necessarily a timeless moral law. However, the reaffirmation of faith in the rule of law by Jordan and others is certainly understandable, for it provided an ostensibly apolitical reason to remove from political office someone perceived as a lawbreaker.

In the 1976 presidential campaign, Ronald Reagan made it plain that as president he would take the federal government out of welfare and other social programs by turning these programs over to the states to let them implement them as they saw fit. This would, he claimed, allow a $90 billion tax savings. What Reagan failed to point out is that in order for there to be a tax savings of $90 billion the welfare program must be abandoned by the individual states. If states took over the welfare programs, then Reagan's plan would simply shift tax burdens from federal taxes to state taxes and Reagan was presumably aware of this. (Later in the campaign when Ford people asked Reagan how all the federal programs he planned to hand over to the states would be financed Reagan said "I would like to hear what their proposal is for reducing the size and cost of the federal government." This reply is very close to a *tu quoque*).

The Fallacy of Hasty Generalization

The *fallacy of hasty generalization* is committed when after observing that a small number, or a special sort, of the members of some group have some property, it is concluded that the whole group has the property. To put it in the language of the statistician, the hasty generalization fallacy occurs when either of the following occurs:

1. One infers from an insufficiently large or quantitatively unrepresentative sample to the whole population. We can call this the *fallacy of small sample*.
2. One infers from a peculiarly selected or qualitatively unrepresentative sample to a whole population. We can call this the *fallacy of biased statistics*.

We are all acquainted with both kinds of incorrect argument. For example, each of the following arguments is a fallacy of small sample.

Every American young person should serve a hitch in the Peace Corps, for it certainly did a world of good for Flossie Snail.

When I was young I worked thirty hours on a job while going to college, so no boy should worry about where he will find money for his college education.

I tell you, Irish workers are no good! The two I hired drank and sang bawdy ballads all the time.

In each case something is concluded about an entire population, all American youth or all Irish workers, from a very small sample, namely, one or two members of each population. If the results of a poll of two or three hundred students around the nation were projected onto the entire U.S. college student population, more than one member of the population would be considered, but even this sample would not likely be large enough to generalize with respect to all U.S. college students.

It is important to have large numbers from the population, but it is also important to avoid selecting them so as to bias the outcome. When farmers take their wheat to the elevator the buyer has a problem in determining the quality of the whole truckload of wheat. If the buyer has his testers take a *large* quantity from the top of the pile, he could easily avoid the fallacy of small sample, but he might well be the victim of the fallacy of biased statistics if he concluded from this sample something about all the wheat (the whole population). After all, it is not ruled out that someone might fill a truck with inferior wheat, putting a small layer of high-quality wheat on top. To be sure to get a representative sample, the buyer will likely have his testers take a portion of grain from the front of the load, a portion from the back, one halfway down, and two on each side from the bottom. The tester then might dump all of this into a sack, shake it, and take out a handful. The quality of the wheat is determined on the basis of this handful of wheat. The inference

This handful is of quality x.
Therefore the whole load is of quality x.

is a perfectly correct argument and avoids both forms of the fallacy of hasty generalization. In many areas, it should be noted, handbooks or standards are available with prescribed guidelines to ensure that a sample of milk, or bolts, or beer, and so on, is large enough and that the sample is representative.

The classic example of biased statistics occurred in the presidential campaign of 1936. Franklin Roosevelt defended his New Deal while Alfred Landon, the Republican nominee, ran on the slogan "Save the American

Way of Life." A poll conducted by a popular national magazine, the *Literary Digest*, predicted Landon's election. Then, in one of the greatest landslides in political history, Rossevelt received 60.7 percent of the popular vote, and won 523 presidential electors out of 531. The old bit of political wisdom faithfully followed by many political pundits, "As Maine goes so goes the nation," was changed to "As Maine goes, so goes Vermont" since these were the only states that Landon carried. About 10 million sample ballots were sent out by the *Literary Digest* and over 2.25 million were returned. Thus no fallacy of small sample occurred. However, the ballots were sent to names taken from lists of telephone subscribers and automobile owners. In 1936, there were 9 million unemployed who, it would seem, did not exactly feel that scrapping the New Deal would "Save the American Way of Life" since before the New Deal there were 12.8 million unemployed. In 1936, an unemployed person or one near the bottom of the economic pyramid had neither telephone nor automobile. Later studies showed, for example, that 59 percent of telephone subscribers and 56 percent of automobile owners favored Landon, whereas only 18 percent of those on relief favored him. Here, clearly, the *Literary Digest* was the victim of a fallacy of biased statistics. The poll had cost the magazine about $1 million (a lot of money in 1936!); shortly after the election, the *Literary Digest* folded.

EXERCISES 2.2

Follow the directions given in 2.1B. For step four, however, substitute fallacies of insufficient evidence.

1. Well, I know a woman who had $10,000 under her mattress and wore a mink coat to collect her social security benefits. I tell you we must stop handing out money. We must do away with social security.

2. Under Wilson we entered World War I, during Roosevelt we became embroiled in World War II, with Truman came Korea, and with Kennedy and Johnson we had Vietnam. Need I remind you that during Republican administrations no new wars have occurred. Can you think of a better reason to vote Republican?

3. It is reported that at the 1956 Republican Convention someone from the platform reported that he had recently seen President Eisenhower and he did not look well. Instantly, as the story goes, a delegate jumped up and cried: "Washington drinks fluoridated water, that's the trouble with Ike!"

4. To fail children who do poorly upsets them and distrubs class morale. The only thing to do, therefore, is to promote everyone.

5. There can be no doubt that the white race is superior to any other race. The nonwhite races are deficient in applied sciences and in their command of nature. The standard of living of the white people today is

not only greater than that of the nonwhites but is the greatest the world has ever known.

false cause

6. Years ago physicians used to bleed patients. Some survived and some did not. The physician credited the bleeding for those who survived.

7. After the plague and the Great Fire of London a House of Commons committee inquired into the causes of the misfortunes. The committee decided that what most displeased the Lord, since these misfortunes were due to His displeasure, were the works of the philosopher Thomas Hobbes. It was decreed that all Hobbes' works be burned and that no work of his should be published in England. This measure was thought by the members of Parliament to have proven effective because there has never since been a plague or a Great Fire in London.

false cause

8. People resort to criminal behavior because, in their view, the likelihood of reward for their criminal acts is higher than the probability of strong punishment if they are caught. Thus the only infallible method to decrease crime is to make it probable that criminals will be caught and to have mandatory incarceration which is followed by throwing away the key.

9. Some want economic sanctions against South Africa. But sanctions are always counterproductive. They never force a country to abandon its policies. They achieve nothing except to make a nation unite around its government. History proves this. The first sanctions ever voted by the old League of Nations were against Italy. They were designed to stop the Italian invasion of Ethiopia. Specifically, they were intended to halt the flow of crude oil that enabled Italy to fuel its airplanes and tanks.

   They didn't work because Soviet Russia saw an opportunity to make a buck. It then had a huge surplus of crude, which it did not hesitate to sell to Italy. The Italian invasion went merrily ahead, and the League became a laughing stock.

   In recent memory, the United States persuaded the Organization of American States to vote an embargo against Castro's Cuba. That proved a flop, too. Franco's Spain, although militantly anti-Communist, saw an opportunity to make money in Cuba and to win an ally as well. Britain saw an opportunity to sell cars, buses and trucks. Soviet Russia saw an opportunity to gain a satellite and a military base in the Caribbean.

   The United Nations, with U.S. approval, voted sanctions against Rhodesia. It cost the United States a great deal of money, but it didn't harm Rhodesia a bit. South Africa and Mozambique made a fortune selling crude to Rhodesia in defiance of the United nations. Soviet Russia made a fortune reselling Rhodesian chromium to the United States. ("Sanctions Don't Work," editorial in the *Arizona Republic*.)

10. The Ku Klux Klan has offered to muster several thousand of its hooded members to patrol the Mexican–United States border to stop illegal

aliens from crossing. We should thank the Klan and accept their help. Vigilantism has proven its effectiveness in the lawless West of yore. Speed and certainty of current American criminal justice is frustrating and imperfect. The KKK's method of dealing with problems is direct and effective. The KKK decides guilt on the basis of a person's skin color, his religion, or his national origin, and through intimidation, lynching, and terrorism it gets results. The Klan will end our nation's futile effort to stop illegal aliens.

11. The Tennessee Valley Authority's Tellico Dam project would turn the free-flowing Little Tennessee River, the snail darter's natural habitat, into a stagnant lake. Since the snail darter, a small fish, is an endangered species protected by a federal law, it was argued that construction be halted on the dam to keep the tiny fish from being wiped out. A lower court ordered construction stopped on the 90 percent completed dam.

12. Carter was often ingratiating on this particular night, so soft-spoken that one sometimes had to lean forward to hear him. (He seemed to do exceptionally well in small groups; newspaper editors whom he visited as he traveled around the country were invariably impressed by him.) His modest style and imperturbable confidence suggested that here was a man unrattled by the scope of his undertaking and by the challenges he would have to embrace if he were successful. But behind this self-assurance the assembled reporters also saw a man who seemed seriously out of tune with the rest of the country concerning the role the United States ought to play in the real world of power politics. This dinner was on April 2, 1972, just weeks before the final fall of the government and army of South Vietnam, and the debacle was easily predictable. But he told the dinner group that American military aid should continue to flow to South Vietnam for a year, and he predicted that the Saigon government would stand for at least that long. It seemed clear that Carter continued to be attuned to old Cold War thinking long rejected by his party's left. By the time Carter had to undergo more widespread public and press scrutiny, however, the Vietnam war was behind the country and he tried to finesse the whole matter by saying he had called in 1971 for American withdrawal, avoiding mention of his earlier support of U.S. policy. He failed to point out that American intervention in Vietnam was wrong, but that "since we are not going to do what it takes to win, it is time to come home."

    (JULES WITCOVER, *Marathon, The Pursuit of the Presidency*)[11]

13. Ronald Reagan during the 1976 campaign for the Republican nomination for President called attention to a few flagrant cases of

[11] Jules Witcover, *Marathon, The Puruit of the Presidency* (New York: Viking Press, 1977), pp. 143–144.

welfare cheating, making it appear that this is the rule rather than a minor exception. Among the best were Reagan's stories about the "welfare queen" in Chicago and Taino Towers in New York. "There's a woman in Chicago," he was fond of recounting, "who has eighty names, thirty addresses, and twelve Social Security cards, and is collecting veterans' benefits on four non-existent deceased husbands." The woman, always unidentified, collected so much on her Social Security cards, Medicaid, food stamps, and welfare, Reagan liked to say, that "her tax-free cash income alone is over a hundred and fifty thousand dollars." In his never-ending diatribe against "welfare chiselers," the woman in Cicago was the centerpiece. The trouble was, though, that the woman, eventually was actually convicted with using *two* aliases, not eighty, and with receiving about $8,000 fraudulently, not $150,000. Even after these facts were published—in an excellent article in *The Washington Star* by John Fialka—Reagan continued to tell the original story.

His other favorite was about New York's subsidized housing project, Taino Towers. "If you are a slum dweller you can get an apartment with eleven-foot ceilings, a twenty-foot balcony, a swimming pool and gymnasium, laundry room and play room, and the rent begins at a hundred and thirteen dollars and twenty cents and that includes utilities," he would say. The digs also had, according to Reagan, a doorman and indoor parking with twenty-four-hour security. But Fialka learned from the project's coordinator in East Harlem that only 92 of 656 units had high ceilings, and these were in six-bedroom units for large families that paid from $300 to $450 a month, depending on income. Also, the pool, gym, and other facilities were public, shared with the surrounding community of 200,000 Puerto Ricans and blacks.

(JULES WITCOVER, *Marathon, The Pursuit of the Presidency*)[12]

14. On March 21, 1973, President Nixon said in a statement that he was pleased to report that $424 million in Federal funds would be made available in the summer for 776,000 public service jobs for youth. The statement went on to say that the outlook for youths in the coming summer was encouraging. Overall, it sounded like a very generous act on the part of the government to offset the chronically high unemployment rate among young people during the summer. Most of the dispatches reported it that way.

Nixon was "special pleading"

Only because of my experience in urban affairs reporting did I become suspicious about a portion of the statement which said the bulk of the funds, $300 million, would come out of money appropriated for the Emergency Employment Assistance Act, which was enacted to

[12] Jules Witcover, *Marathon, The Pursuit of the Presidency* (New York: Viking Press, 1977), pp. 388–389.

provide year-round public service jobs, mostly for adults, and it would be up to local officials to decide whether to use the $300 million for adults or youths.

Under the laws then current, summer youth jobs were to be founded under a separate act. Informed of the President's statement, Senator Jacob K. Javits, Republican of New York, exploded: "Cities are left with the Hobson's choice of firing the father in order to hire the son." It was a classic case of the White House acting in a calculated manner, then making it appear otherwise.

(JOHN HERBERS, *No Thank You, Mr. President*)

ANSWERS

1. hasty generalization   **3.** false cause   **5.** false cause   **7.** false cause   **9.** hasty generalization   **11.** special pleading (Why can't the snail darter be given a new home?)   **13.** special pleading

The Fallacies of Ambiguity

When ambiguity is the reason for the incorrectness of an argument, then the argument is classed as a fallacy of ambiguity. In such arguments the reasons are irrelevant to the truth or falsity of the conclusion.

The Fallacy of Equivocation

Many words and expressions are ambiguous; that is, they can have two or more meanings. For example, the word "fallacy" can mean (a) an incorrect argument; (b) the ability to deceive, as in the "fallacy of the senses"; and (c) a widespread, mistaken opinion, as in the "fallacy that the Soviets are stupid." When a word is used (often knowingly) with different meanings in a context it is said to be used equivocally. When a word or expression is used with two different meanings, and the correctness of the argument depends upon the word or expression maintaining a constant meaning throughout the argument, the *fallacy of equivocation* occurs. Below are two trivial occurrences of the fallacy of equivocation:

Only man is rational.
No woman is a man.
Therefore no woman is rational.

The existence of a power above nature is implied by the fact that in science laws of nature are discovered. For whenever there is a law, there is a law giver.

The first argument is correct if the meaning of the three words "man," "woman," and "rational" stay constant. However, if the premise is to be true, then "man" must mean "humans" and not "human males," for it is false that only human males are rational. On the other hand, if the second premise is to be true, "man" must mean "human male," for it is false that no woman is a man in the sense of a human. We would be misunderstanding the meaning of the premises if we understood "man" to have the same meaning in both premises. We have, then, an argument in which the word "man" is used with two different meanings, "human" and "human male," but in order for the argument to be correct, "man" must maintain a constant meaning in the argument. It is a fallacy of equivocation. In the second argument the conclusion is that science presupposes the existence of a power above nature, or science assumes there is a God (a law giver). For the premise to support this conclusion, "law" must have a constant meaning throughout the argument. But again we would be misunderstanding the statements which make up the premises if we took "law" to have a constant meaning. The argument can be re-expressed in these terms:

Science attempts to discover laws.
Laws imply a law giver.
Therefore science assumes there is a God (a law giver).

In order for the first premise to be true, "law" must mean "relationship in nature," whereas in order for the second premise to be true, "law" must mean "rule of conduct set down by some authority." If the first sense of "law" were injected into the second premise, an absurdity would result. But again if the words maintain a constant meaning in the argument it would be a correct argument.

Not all equivocations in arguments are so obvious. Consider this paraphrase of a U.S. Senator's argument:

Our enemy at this time is not exclusively military. He is far more—he is a political enemy, he is an economic enemy, he is a subversive enemy. The military leader, therefore, in order to perform the duties to which he is sworn, has the responsibility of informing, not only his troops, but the American public concerning the total nature of the Communist menace. For in doing so he is carrying out his oath to defend the Constitution of the United States against all enemies, foreign and domestic.

If we make explicit the steps in the argument, we have this:

1. The military is pledged to defend our country against all enemies, foreign and domestic.
2. Our enemy at this time is not exclusively military but political, economic, and so on.

3. Thus the military should defend against the political and economic threats of our enemy.
4. To educate the American public to the political and economic threats is to defend against these threats of our enemy.
5. Thus the military leaders should educate the American people to the political and economic threats of our enemy.

This argument is incorrect because the phrase "defend against all enemies" is used equivocally. The first use of the phrase is found in (1). Traditionally, the phrase "to defend our country against all enemies," as it appears in the pledge, is understood to mean something like: "To do battle against the attacking military forces of every one of our country's enemies." And, of course, this is what the United States military is trained and prepared to do. In (3) and (4) is found the second use of the phrase. There the phrase is used to cover those things, whatever they might be, which will stop all our enemy's activities, political and economic as well as military. If we use the first sense of "defend against all enemies" throughout the argument, then (3) and (4) turn into these absurd statements: (3) "The military should militarily battle the political and economic threats to our country"; and (4) "To educate the American public to the political and economic threats is militarily to battle these threats of our enemy." If we use the second sense of the phrase throughout the argument, then (1) becomes the false statement, "The military is pledged to do those things, whatever they might be, which will stop all our enemy's activities, political and economic as well as military." What makes this argument persuasive is that this double use of the phrase is not apparent.

Not only can words or expressions which can be true of one or more things—words such as "man," "law," and "defend against all enemies"— shift in meaning in the course of an argument, but so can words such as "is." There are two senses of "is" that sometimes are confused, the "is" of predication and the "is" of identity. The two senses are illustrated by the following:

Mark Twain is an author ["is" of predication].
Mark Twain is Samuel Clemens ["is" of identity].

In the first example a property, "being an author," is attributed to Mark Twain. In the second example Mark Twain is asserted to be identical with Samuel Clemens. An example of equivocation of this sort is furnished in the following argument:

Knowledge is power.
Power corrupts.
Therefore knowledge corrupts.

For the argument to be correct "is" must be the "is" of identity. If knowledge is identical with power and power corrupts, then knowledge corrupts. However, for the premise not to be absurd, the "is" must be the "is" of predication. The premise in order to be true must read: Power is one of the things acquired when one gains knowledge.

Straw man fallacies can be viewed as particular kinds of fallacies of equivocation. For the "miracles-do-happen" example considered earlier can be rephrased as

> Those who say that miracles don't happen say something false; because there are computers, TV, and so on, miracles do happen.

And it is clear that the word "miracle" must shift in meaning if the disputants are to be credited with any intelligence. In "Miracles don't happen" the word "miracle" means something like "events caused by supernatural forces," whereas in "Miracles do happen" it means something like an "extraordinary new invention." Closely related are such examples as the following:

> In this country we believe that all men are created equal, so we should not have entrance requirements for admission to colleges and universities.

This argument may be rephrased so that two occurrences of "equal" can be seen to have different meanings. We might, for example, add this clause to the conclusion: "since if men are equal they would score the same." In this expanded argument "equal" clearly means "treated the same before the law" in one place and "equal in abilities" in another place.

We can also say, however, that the principle found in the U.S. Constitution is misunderstood in the last argument. Arguments in which general principles are applied, intentionally or unintentionally, to cases to which they are not meant to apply are called *fallacies of accident.* When one argues to the falsity of a general principle or general statement from a non-applicable case, this is called the *converse fallacy of accident* and is illustrated in the following example:

> Admission to colleges and universities is based on the fact that some candidates have greater abilities than other candidates; thus it is not true that all men are created equal, as we have been led to believe by Jefferson and others.

The Fallacy of Syntactical Ambiguity

A sentence can have different meanings because of its syntactical structure or because it has a word or expressions which can be understood in at least two ways. Consider the sentence, "The shooting of the hunters is terrible." This can mean that the hunters are terrible at shooting, that it is terrible that the hunters are being shot, or that the fact that the hunters are shooting at all is terrible. Needless to say, how it is to be understood, in general, will be made clear in the context in which the sentence occurs. Another example is, "I like her cooking." This can mean, among other things, "I like what she cooks," "I like the way she cooks," "I like the fact that she cooks," or even, "I like the fact that she is being cooked." This sentence is ambiguous in spite of the fact that it contains no ambiguous words as, for example, this sentence does: "I went to the bank." (By the water? To cash a check?) Such sentences are said to be *syntactically ambiguous.* When awkward grammatical construction accounts for such ambiguous sentences, they are said to be *amphibolous sentences.* A clear example of an amphibolous sentence is, "The fire was extinguished before much damage was done by the local fire department."

When a syntactically ambiguous sentence is used with two different meanings in an argument, and the correctness of the argument depends upon the sentence maintaining a constant meaning throughout the argument, the *fallacy of syntactical ambiguity* occurs.

Consider an admittedly far-fetched example: suppose one is watching a movie in which a group of hunters is being attacked without provocation by a rival tribe. As the fight progresses, your companion remarks that the shooting of the hunters is terrible. Let us suppose also that you conclude from this that your companion has strong feelings of sympathy toward the innocent hunters. But if he was simply condemning their marksmanship, you were misled by the syntactical ambiguity of his remark. With a little imagination this argument could be extracted:

My companion said that the shooting of the hunters is terrible.
If he believes the shooting of the hunters is terrible, then he has strong feelings of sympathy toward the hunters.
Therefore my companion has feelings of sympathy toward the hunters.

If the ambiguous sentence is uniformly understood in the way supposed in the second premise, then the argument is correct. But, as the circumstances show, the ambiguous sentence is understood in a different way in the first premise. The sentence thus shifts meaning in the course of the argument, thereby making the argument incorrect, since it is necessary that the meaning of the sentence stay constant if the argument is to be correct.

Not only a sentence but a group of sentences can be awkwardly put together so that two or more senses can be gotten from the collection. For example, this ad for a time was found in some magazines: "A survey shows many doctors take the fast, pain-relieving ingredients in Brand X. In fact, 3 out of 4 doctors recommend this same type relief to their patients." This is ambiguous since it could be understood in two ways: (1) three out of four doctors recommend Brand X and (2) three out of four doctors recommend a number of drugs which also happen to contain ingredients found in Brand X.

If someone concluded from reading this ad (1) that three out of four doctors recommend Brand X, he would be mistaken and this would be an instance of the fallacy of ambiguity, since this ad should be understood in sense (2).

A humorous example of awkwardly constructed paragraphs is the following letter of appreciation:

> I would like very much to thank both our Walhalla police department and Mayor Snuff for resuming police escorts for funeral processions. It is very definitely a worthwhile function of our police department.
>
> Being one of the first to receive this service, I would like you to know it was very much appreciated.
>
> I was escorted to the edge of the city. The officer then got out and stood at attention until the procession had passed, a very thoughtful and impressive gesture.

To conclude that this was a letter from the dead would be to commit a fallacy.

The Division and Composition Fallacies

The *fallacy of division* is committed when someone argues that something which is true only of the whole is also true of its parts taken separately. Consider these examples of this fallacy:

> Ice cream tastes sweet, so all the ingredients must taste sweet.

Ice cream tastes sweet, but, obviously, it does not follow from this that each ingredient taken separately tastes sweet. For example, salt does not taste sweet.

> Walhalla University produces the best Ph.D's in the country. So Archie Van Dyke, who recently got his degree from the school, must be an excellent man.

The graduates of the best universities are generally excellent, but to infer that a particular graduate is excellent merely from the school's excellence would be an incorrect inference.

The *fallacy of composition* consists in reasoning from what is true only of the parts of some whole to what is true of the whole. The following are both composition fallacies:

> Since each of the ingredients of ice cream does not especially taste good, it follows that ice cream doesn't especially taste good.
>
> A, B, C, D, . . . are all star players, so we can easily have the best team and win the pennant by composing our team of them.

Two things should be kept in mind in connection with the fallacies of composition and division. First, the fallacy of composition should not be confused with the hasty generalization fallacy. When one reasons erroneously from what is true about each of the parts of some whole to the whole itself, this is the fallacy of composition. In the last two examples someone reasons from what is true of *each* of the ingredients and what is true of *each* of the players. Second, sometimes, when one reasons from what is true of the whole to what is true of each part and vice versa, no error is committed. Consider, for example, these two inferences:

> The car is brand new, so the parts of the car are new.
> Each citizen wants Lord Privy Seal to be elected Prime Minister, so the nation wants Privy Seal to be elected Prime Minister.

The reason that composition and division fallacies are classified as fallacies of ambiguity is that many can be regarded as involving words or phrases whose meaning shifts. Many of these fallacies can be regarded as using the verb "to be" equivocally. We can distinguish the distributive use of the verb and the collective use. For example, in "Volkswagens are low priced," the verb "to be" is used distributively. We are saying here that each and every VW is low priced. However, in "Volkswagens are plentiful," we are using the verb collectively. We are not saying that each and every VW is plentiful but that VW's as a class or group are plentiful. Often it will be found that in a division fallacy the verb is used collectively in the premises, then distributively in the conclusion, where in a composition fallacy the order is reversed. To illustrate:

> Goldwater was decisively rejected by the voters.
> William E. Miller (Goldwater's running mate) was a voter.
> Therefore William E. Miller decisively rejected Goldwater.

In saying Goldwater was rejected by the voters one means they collectively rejected him. If one now shifts the verb to distributive sense—each and every voter rejected him—the conclusion follows.

The Fallacy of Accent

Sometimes we can change the meaning of a sentence by accenting some word or phrase. Consider this sentence taken from Jevons' *Lessons in Logic*: "The study of logic is not supposed to communicate a knowledge of many useful facts." It is clear how we are to understand it. Logic, among a number of things, will help to determine when an inference is correct and when it is incorrect, but it will not provide information about the world, as chemistry, for example, does. But we can accent certain words or phrases and change the meaning. For example, we can say, "The study of logic is not *supposed* to communicate a knowledge of many useful facts." This gives the impression that, though logic is not supposed to communicate many useful facts, it does. Or consider our saying, "The study of logic is not supposed to communicate a knowledge of *many* useful facts." Here it sounds as if logic will communicate some useful facts but not many.

The *fallacy of accent* is committed whenever a statement is accented in such a way as to change its meaning, and is employed in an argument. Suppose for example, someone said:

> The famous logician Jevons, to take one example, didn't know that logic is a formal discipline and that to know the propositions in logic is to know nothing about the world. For in his logic book he said: "The study of logic is not supposed to communicate a knowledge of *many* useful facts."

This would be a fallacy of accent.

Quoting out of context, which can be regarded in many of its instances as a fallacy of relevance, is often classed as a kind of accent fallacy. For to quote out of context is in a way to accent some sentence or sentences by neglecting the sentences which surround them. We shall describe this fallacy and consider two somewhat different examples of it.

Sometimes when a statement is removed from its spoken or written context, it may be regarded by many as meaning something different or having an import which is different from what it has in the spoken or written context. When such a statement is employed in an argument in such a way that its import or meaning is changed by not supplying the context, and in such a way that its altered import or meaning figures in a reason relevant to the conclusion, the *fallacy of quoting out of context* occurs.

Suppose a movie critic wrote, "The movie is flawless except for bad acting, a bad plot, and bad photography." A dishonest promoter of the film, let us suppose, advertises the film, indicating that the movie critic wrote, "The movie is flawless. . . ." Since the reviewer's opinion is employed as a reason for seeing the film, this argument is implicit:

> The movie critic wrote, "The movie is flawless . . . ," and that is a good reason for seeing the film.

In this example the phrase out of context quite obviously takes on a radically different meaning. Since it is then employed in an argument, the fallacy of quoting out of context is committed.

The second sample of quoting out of context is a bit different from the first. In the early 1960s many newspapers demanded that direct action be taken to remove Castro's Communist government from Cuba. They cited the Monroe Doctrine in support of such actions. The provision of the doctrine cited was: "an interposition" by a European power in the Western Hemisphere would be the "manifestation of an unfriendly disposition toward the United States." What many of these papers did not tell their readers is that there was more to the message to Congress in 1823 which bears the name "The Monroe Doctrine." The doctrine not only warned Europe to keep its hands off this hemisphere, it went on to assure Europe that we would not meddle in its affairs: "Our policy in regard to Europe is not to interfere in the internal concerns of any of its powers; to consider the government *de facto* as the legitimate government for us; to cultivate friendly relations with it. . . . It is our duty to remain the peaceful and silent, though sorrowful, spectators of the European scene." In this example a phrase from the doctrine is employed to support the conclusion that direct United States action should be taken to remove the Communist government in Cuba. If, however, the complete statement of what is called the Monroe Doctrine had been brought to the reader's attention, the doctrine could not have been used to support the conclusion since the United States, in becoming a world leader, has itself violated the doctrine. Thus the phrase by itself seems to be a good reason for the conclusion, whereas in the context it is not. In the first example the phrase out of context took on a different sense, whereas in this example the import of a phrase changes when the phrase is out of context.

Another example is found in the following:

> In a 1977 ad campaign a Volkswagen ad cited a *Road and Track* article naming the VW Rabbit the "Best Car in the World Under $3,500," as a result of a test. VW advertising did not say that *Road and Track* had suffered many problems with the car in its extended test, most of them after judging the Rabbit "best Sedan in the world under $3,500." Included in those problems was a broken camshaft which is about as serious a mechanical failure as you can have.

If the evaluation that the VW Rabbit is the best car in the world under $3,500 were to appear in conjunction with the total result of *Road and Track's* experience with the car, then it would take on a different meaning for the reader. One would see that the "Best Car" test was only one of many tests, in some of which the VW did not fare so well. Also the VW ad does not indicate another larger contextual feature. This is that *Road and Track*, like most magazines, is supported in part by the manufacturers whose products it reviews. What this implies is that one ought to be a bit skeptical about what such magazines say about products.

Television news has evolved in such a way that accent is a constant threat. Television news coexists with entertainment and often plays the rating game. This, together with the nature of the media, results in television news selecting the interesting over the boring, the simple over the complex, the concrete over the abstract. Finally, its time restraints cause it to condense events. All these factors result in TV news often changing ordinary reality into more exciting television reality. As Daniel Schorr, of CBS News, has written:

> ... Television reduces issues to confrontations of celebrities and polarizes controversies into extreme positions. The middle ground, the uncertain people and all the stammerers tend to be left, in the jargon of the trade, on the cuttingroom floor. As professionals strive to capture the world in a few exciting words and pictures, there emerges a new semblance of the truth, a kind of allegory of events. Deep in their problems of editing, synchronizing, finding the clearest sound and the most telling picture, and saving precious seconds at every point, the professionals forget—until an occasional controversy arises over deceptive excerpting, as in the case of truncated interviews in "The Selling of the Pentagon"—how far behind they have left their audience in understanding how their capsule allegory of events differs from the actual event.[13]

What Schorr is in part pointing out is that the presentation of news on television produces an understanding that differs from the understanding one would have if one had the story in context. For instance Schorr writes that when in 1971 he was obliged to sum up "with staccato brevity" a conflict between the fishing industry and the Food and Drug Administration over the extent of pollution resulting from fishery canning practices, the Bumble Bee Seafoods Company canceled its commercials on all CBS affiliated stations. They regarded Schorr's comments as hostile to the fishery side of the argument. Schorr writes that the real problem was time. In other words a controversial subject packed into a small container resulted in the import of the remarks appearing hostile to some, for example, the people at Bumble Bee. If the remarks had been placed in context this would not have happened. Given the constraints of TV news to put all subjects, including the controversial ones, in small containers, and given the most inevitable erroneous inferences on the part of some of the audience due to accent, pressure naturally exists to avoid controversial subjects.

EXERCISES 2.3

A. For these exercises, follow directions given in 2.1B, but now locate any occurrences of fallacies of ambiguity.

   1. Senator Snort can be trusted to do what is right, for he is a member of the majority, and the majority can be trusted to do what is right in the long run.

   division

   2. The senator is one who says the war is a mistake. The enemy is one who says the war is a mistake. So the Senator is the enemy.

   3. Since each atom is completely determined as to its position or motion by the unchanging laws of nature, and since man's body

[13] Daniel Schorr, *Clearing the Air* (Boston: Houghton-Mifflin Co., 1977), p. 294.

consists entirely of atoms, human actions are completely determined and man does not have a free will.

division

4. The composite American housewife, according to the United States census of 1970, has 2.8 children. You look like an average United States housewife, Mrs. Ogmore-Pritchard. Therefore you can expect your marriage to yield two children, and, after a decent interval, eight tenths of another child. May all your troubles be little ones!

5. As creators, women are superior to men since men can only create works of art, science, or philosophy, whereas women can create life.

composition

6. It is unethical for a physician to invest in a drug company. Therefore it is unethical for the AMA in 1973 to invest $40 million from its members' retirement fund in pharmaceutical firms.

7. In 1977 Bess Myerson on NBC's "Today" show encouraged youngsters to try Hereford Cows, a heavily flavored alcoholic drink. This is a violation of laws pertaining to giving booze to minors, and a lot of folks got upset. However, the district attorney refused to prosecute Myerson on the grounds that the alleged crime was committed while she was acting as a journalist. And as such she is protected from prosecution by the First Amendment guaranteeing freedom of the press.

equivocation

8. After long and solemn deliberations around Reston's desk on January 15, 1962, I was entrusted with a question for President Kennedy that perhaps ten [*New York*] *Times* reporters had honed to what we thought was a fine point. Kennedy could not entirely evade it, we were sure. So as soon as he recognized me later that day, I arose—feeling the cameras aim flatteringly at me—and demanded in my sternest voice: "Mr. President, are American troops now in combat in Vietnam?"

   Kennedy looked at me—six feet away and slightly beneath his elevated lectern—as if he thought I might be crazy.

   "No," he said crisply—not another word—and pointed at someone else for the next question.

   He gave me no chance to follow up, and in any case I was too startled by the brevity of his answer and perhaps not well-enough informed on the matter to have challenged it. It was, we learned later, a lie—unless troops are "in combat" only when they fight by companies and battalions and not when they are acting as "advisers" in combat. That was the one kind of response we did not then expect from a president of the United States; later, we would not have been so naïve.   (TOM WICKER, *On Press*)[14]

[14] Tom Wicker, *On Press* (New York: Viking Press, 1978), pp. 92–93. Copyright 1978 by Tom Wicker. Used by permission.

equivocation

9. Our country is a free nation "under God." Perhaps those who object to our setting aside, by law, a day to honor Him would prefer the kind of freedom found in a country "under Marx."

We pass laws to safeguard our possessions from those who would take them from us; one of our most valuable possessions is our Sundays— our family days of rest and worship.

God in His holy wisdom created the Sabbath as a gift for us, a gift of one day a week from the toils and cares of this world. Are we going to let some men in their rush toward all-out commercialism take it away from us?

equivocation

10. Marx and Engels pursued their activities in the prerevolutionary period (we have the proletarian revolution in mind), when developed imperialism did not yet exist, in the period of the proletarians' preparation for a revolution, in the period when the proletarian revolution was not yet a direct, practical inevitability. Lenin, however, the disciple of Marx and Engels, pursued his activities in the period of developed imperialism, in the period of unfolding proletarian revolution, when the proletarian revolution had already triumphed in one country, had smashed the bourgeois democracy, and had ushered in the era of proletarian democracy, the era of the Soviets.

That is why Leninism is the further development of Marxism.
(JOSEF STALIN, *What is Leninism?*)

11. Improbable events happen almost every day, but whatever happens almost every day is probable. Improbable events, therefore, are probable events.

accent

12. Sir, you unfortunately display ignorance of the religious views of Thomas Jefferson when you call him an agnostic or atheist. The following quotation from the Jefferson Memorial should clearly illustrate this ignorance: "I have sworn upon the altar of God, eternal hostility against every form of tyranny over the mind of man."—Strange language for an atheist or agnostic!

The quote from the Jefferson Memorial is fragmented. The complete quote, from Jefferson's letter to Dr. Benjamin Rush, is as follows: "They [the clergy] believe that any portion of power confided to me, will be exerted in opposition to their schemes. And they believe rightly: for I have sworn upon the altar of God, eternal hostility against every form of tyranny over the mind of man."

13. Senator Robert Byrd and most other members of the Senate Rules Committee believed that Gerald Ford had assured the Congress he would not pardon Nixon. Byrd asked in the confirmation hearings if he believed it would be proper for a vice-president to succeed the presidency and then grant a pardon

to the former president. Ford's answer was that he did not think the American people would stand for such action. In the press conference following his pardon of Nixon he was reminded of what he said in the confirmation hearings. Ford's answer was: "I was asked a hypothetical question. In answer to the hypothetical question I responded by saying that I did not think the American people would stand for such action. I think if you will reread what I said in answer to that hypothetical question, I did not say I wouldn't. I simply said that under the way the question was phrased, the American people would object."

14. Laws passed by Congress require that cars achieve 27.5 mpg by 1985. There is only one way this can be achieved and this is by building smaller and lighter cars. But these laws show a callous indifference to highway safety. We all know that in a collision a heavy object is likely to damage a light object more than itself. An AMC Matador smashing into a Volkswagen will survive better than the VW. A Cadillac smashing into a Matador will come out in better shape than the Matador. It seems clear that the only way to avoid a safety crisis is to build the largest and heaviest cars we can. Is energy conservation worth even one human life? Large, heavy cars save lives, so no argument can prevail against them.

equivocation
"heavy"
and
"light"
not re-
cognized
as relative
terms

15. When Ronald Reagan was Governor of California, he originated the mini-memo. The mini-memo worked this way: When a political, legislative, social, or economic issue required a decision by the Governor, his staff prepared a one-page summary of all its aspects, concluding with a suggested decision. It was divided neatly into four succinct paragraphs, one each for "The Issue," "The Facts," "The Discussion," and "The Recommendation." There was enough space at the bottom of the page for Reagan to pen a check mark to indicate either "yes" or "no" on the recommendation. He and his staff boasted about the mini-memo as the ultimate efficiency, a method by which the Governor became informed and through which he decided. They maintained that there was no issue facing the Governor of California that could not be boiled down to a one-page summary for decision-making.   (EDMUND G. BROWN and BILL BROWN, *Reagan, The Political Chameleon*)

16. It has been claimed that the news media do not hold a liberal bias. News organizations argue that they take an adversary role toward every administration. And an adversary role is in the nation's interest. There is a good deal of theoretical logic behind this explanation, but unfortunately the news media are adversaries only on the conservative side of the political spectrum. President Johnson was met by an adversary relationship not for

a version
of fallacy
present

his liberal programs such as the War on Poverty but for his conservative policies such as his invasion of the Dominican Republic and his escalation of the Vietnam War. There was little if any criticism with Nixon's detente with China and the Soviet Union, his appropriations for the arts and humanities and his proposed Family Assistance Plan. It was only his more conservative policies that drew their criticism, his invasion of Cambodia, his bombing of North Vietnam, and his cover up of Watergate.

17. The transcripts of Nixon's White House tapes on the whole did not seem diabolical: to the contrary, they revealed incompetent bumbling and an utter failure to comprehend what was happening in the real world. The level of discourse was appalling. Over and over the President would return to the same subject; often he had to be reminded by his aides of something he had been told minutes before. Occasionally the President would proclaim forcefully that he had reached a decision on some particular point, only to reverse himself a moment later at the prodding of Haldeman or Ehrlichman. Nixon during his debates with John Kennedy in 1960 excoriated Harry S. Truman for his bad language, promising that if he were elected, "whenever any mother or father talks to his child, he can look at the man in the White House, and whatever he may think of his policies, he will say, 'Well, there is a man who maintains the kind of standard personally that I would want my child to follow.' " To maintain his prissy public image Nixon ordered those who transcribed the tapes to remove swear words from transcripts. Most of the deleted expletives were words like "damn," "Christ," "God" and even less offensive phrases. But the hundreds of "expletives deleted" in the newly published transcripts made the President's language seem a lot more than it really had been. This was one instance where Nixon's hypocrisy had come back to haunt him.

(RICHARD BEN-VENISTE and
GEORGE FRAMPTON, JR., *Stonewall*)

18. Most of us are booby-trapped by our own cultural reactions to death. We have been taught to fear death and to see its coming as the end of everything. But if we learn to think of life as the capacity to grow and to help others to grow, then death does not remove our influence from the world, for the people we have influenced carry us with them. We need to perceive immortality in a new way: to think that one continues in the perceptions of one's wife, one's husband, one's children, the children of others, one's friends, one's neighbors—indeed, all those with whom one has come in contact.

B. Follow the directions given earlier and indicate the fallacies, selecting from *all* those discussed.

1. A Massachusetts legislator was talking to a church group, defending capital punishment. He said, "Christianity would not exist if it weren't for capital punishment. Where would we be if Pilate had given Jesus six to eight years with time off for good behavior? I hope you will support me in my crusade for capital punishment."

2. What prompted the Supreme Court in 1954 in desegregating schools to cast aside the accumulated wisdom of earlier courts and to veer off into the tangled underbrush of sociology where even the best legal bloodhounds lose the trail of law? The explanation is obvious. It is that the Court succumbed to pressures which persuaded the Justices that a desegregation decision could perform a highly useful function in the realm of international relations and enhance the position of the United States in its dealings with the nonwhite nations of the world. (W. D. WORKMAN, *The Case for the South*)

3. In *The Merchant of Venice*, the Duke tells Shylock that he should be merciful and not demand by law that he get his bond (a pound of Antonio's flesh). To this he replies:

   You have among you many a purchased slave
   Which, like your asses and your dogs and mules,
   You use in abject and in slavish parts.
   Because you bought them: shall I say to you,
   Let them be free, marry them to your heirs?
   Why sweat them under burthens? let their beds
   Be made as soft as yours and let their palates
   Be season'd with such viands? You will answer
   "The slaves are ours": so do I answer you:
   The pound of flesh, which I demand of him,
   Is dearly bought: 't is mine and I will have it.

4. Marx held that economic change determines the intellectual, cultural, religious, and political forms of any society. The proof which he gives is taken from history. He shows than an economic change occurred at a certain time and then later a change took place in ideas.

5. The alarmists have so far not succeeded in proving that thermal discharge is dangerous to lakes, so why worry about the new billion-watt nuclear plant which is going to provide new jobs for the community?

genetic
ad hominem

6. Aquinas' and Anselm's proofs for the existence of God are fallacious, for they were just trying to justify through reason what they already believed through faith.

7. Jonathan Swift, in his short essay entitled *A Modest Proposal*, argues that since the children of the poor Irish are so numerous and have created such a burden on the economy and society with their extreme poverty, there should be something done to eliminate the problem. He proposes that the English could well profit from taking these children from their parents and shipping them to England to be slaughtered as food for the English table. After all, Swift reasons, both countries would be better off in many ways. England would be relieved of its food shortage, and the aristocracy would be given a new type of table delicacy. The Irish would no longer be burdened with these hungry infants who most often before the age of twelve are well versed in the art of theft.

If this is fallacious, would be "false cause"!

8. These states are among those whose standard of living is the highest: The United States, Canada, Australia, New Zealand, and England. It is to be noted that all these states are democracies. This raises the question whether they are prosperous because they are democratic or democratic because they are prosperous. Is prosperity the economic reward earned by those who organize their government democratically, or is democracy a political luxury which only the richer members of the international family can afford? Since all these states began and developed at a time when they are not democratic, it is therefore true that they are democratic because they are prosperous.

9. After serving in the armed forces in World War II, Joe McCarthy defeated La Follette in the Republican primary in Wisconsin. As part of his campaign McCarthy passed around flyers which read:
    JOE McCARTHY was a TAIL GUNNER in World War II. When the war began, Joe had a soft job as a Judge at EIGHT GRAND a year. He was EXEMPT from military duty. He resigned to enlist as a PRIVATE in the MARINES. He fought on LAND and in the AIR all through the Pacific. He and millions of other guys kept you from talking Japanese. TODAY JOE McCARTHY IS HOME. He wants to SERVE America in the SENATE. Yes, folks, CONGRESS NEEDS A TAIL GUNNER. Now, when Washington is in confusion, when BUREAUCRATS are seeking to perpetuate themselves FOREVER upon the American way of Life, AMERICA NEEDS FIGHTING MEN. Those men who fought upon foreign soil to SAVE AMERICA have earned the right to SERVE AMERICA in times of peace.
    (Taken from RICHARD H. ROVERE, *Senator Joe McCarthy*)

10. When Joe McCarthy appeared before the Watkins Committee, which was considering censure of his conduct as a U.S. Senator, Edward B. Williams was his counsel. Here is a report of Williams' defense: "When McCarthy's offenses were considered one by one, it turned out that there were very few for which no Senatorial precedent could be found. Had he been inexcusably arrogant and bullying in his treatment of General Zwicker? Indeed, he had been—and to many others besides— but he was not the first man to abuse his power in this way. Williams found an instance, only a few days before the censure hearings, in which Prescott Bush, of Connecticut, had been accused of similar discourtesies in the course of a one-man hearing on public housing. Why not censure Bush along with McCarthy? Had McCarthy given out classified information? He had, but he was not alone in this; a member of the Select Committee, Edwin Johnson, had, only a few years back been widely criticized for giving out classified facts on hydrogen weapons on a television program. Had McCarthy called Senator Flanders 'senile'—yes, but Senator Flanders had compared McCarthy with Hitler; which is worse, to be senile or a Hitler? It was true that McCarthy had urged government employees to give information directly to him whether or not some 'bureaucrat had stamped it a secret,' but was this so different from the action of Watkins himself in signing a committee report that urged 'employees in the executive branch . . . to turn over to committees of Congress any information which would help the Committees in their fight against subversion'?"

(RICHARD H. ROVERE, *Senator Joe McCarthy*)

11. There had been about him [Jimmy Carter] from the moment he had announced his candidacy—to the laughter of most, the wonderment of a few—a sense of purposeful, skilful enigma. He preferred it that way. It suited his purposes perfectly. He believed that the candidate who took clear positions on every issue was not long for the political world. There would be only one issue on which a successful candidate would be judged that year, the amorphous, ethereal concept of integrity, honesty, trustworthiness, credibility. There might be a passing interest in others, but that would be the underlying permanent focal point of the voters, even if they could not articulate it. Abortion, capital punishment, right-to-work laws (he said he favored their abolition but would not actively oppose them), welfare, taxes, the economy, foreign policy—all would crop up in the campaign, of course, and all would be pertinent to one degree or another, of course, but the crux of the election of 1976, he believed, would be the legacy of the war and the scandals that had so thoroughly poisoned the

political well and traumatized the electorate. To step outside that small ring would be fatal, he believed. To answer every question on every topic definitively would be suicidal, he believed. To compete by emphasizing one's governmental experience would be counterproductive, he believed—and so he believed that despite the traditional wisdom that labeled him a long shot, his credentials, or really the lack of them, made him the favorite right from the start.

Being unknown was his most valuable asset. He would be precisely the sort of candidate millions of uncertain Americans might be looking for, even if they did not realize it. They could live with their doubts about his views on abortion or capital punishment or right-to-work laws ("I don't give a damn about any of them," he once said), as long as they felt relatively comfortable with his honesty and integrity and trustworthiness and credibility. Whatever else might be important to them, they would not be nearly so interested in or fascinated by what they already believed or knew or understood; millions of them would be ready and perhaps eager for something quite apart from their past experience as American voters—ready, perhaps, for a stranger. That was Carter's thesis as he began his campaign and from its genesis he worked diligently to remain forever new, forever fresh, and always as enigmatic as possible.

(JAMES WOOTEN, *Dasher*)[15]

ad populum

12.   Tonight, [October 25, 1976, a few days before election day] five minutes before the National Football League game begins on ABC, I see scenes of America—Mt. Rushmore, Indians, cowboys, early machinery, Presidents (Wilson, Roosevelt, Truman, Kennedy, Johnson), and then the White House and, again, Mt. Rushmore. Voice—sounding a lot like the other one—says, "If there's one thing that can bind our country together, that can make us have hope again, and faith in the future, it's a President who is in touch with the American people." Then we see Jimmy Carter saying, "We've seen walls built around Washington, and we feel like we can't quite get through." Then, as a song called "See the Dream, America" plays in the background, we see pictures of tall buildings, of citizens walking briskly and purposefully down the street, of children, and then Jimmy Carter says, "There's only one person in this nation who can speak with a clear voice to the American people . . . that can call on the American people to make a sacrifice and explain the purpose of the sacrifice." Then we see the Carter family walking together, and then photographs of flags, bridges, and a setting

---

[15] James Wooten, *Dasher* (New York: Summit Books, 1978), pp. 36–37. © 1978 by James Wooten.

sun, and then photographs of Jimmy Carter, chin on hand. (ELIZABETH DREW, *American Journal: The Events of 1976*)

13. Our first reaction on reading the interview Charles K. Johnson give to the *Washington Star* the other day was to say to ourselves, "This man's a nut."

Then, we started wondering.

We defy you to find a hole in his reasoning. We can't.

Johnson is president of the International Flat Earth Research Society of America and publisher of its newsletter, *Flat Earth News*.

The *Star* reporter asked him: "Why do you believe the earth is flat?"

He replied: "Well, for the simple reason that it *is* flat."

Don't laugh. Can you think of a flaw in that argument?

"What about the pictures from satellites that show the earth is round?" the reporter continued.

"They are simulated."

"Simulated?"

"The space program is a complete and total hoax?"

Can you prove otherwise? Were you up there on the moon when the astronauts landed? How do you know they *didn't* fake the pictures?

The reporter bored in: "When you are up in an airplane, can't you see the curve of the earth?"

"When you are up in an airplane, you have a slight optical illusion. . . ."

Uh, uh. As the French might put it, "C'est possible." And, in these uncertain times, we can't afford to write off any possibility.

As further proof of his theory, Johnson pointed out that his wife is from Australia, and in the years she was growing up there, she never hung upside down. When she sailed to America, her ship didn't do uphill first, and then over a hump, and then downhill. It went straightaway.

Johnson easily disposed of every argument the reporter raised against his theory. He really impressed us, and he might have convinced us completely, except for one thing.

He said: "If you want to get an idea of the true map of the world . . . take a look at the symbol of the United Nations. The United Nations symbol is the Flat Earth Society's map.

"The symbol of the United Nations is, of course, based on the true knowledge that the earth is flat."

Look, Johnson, if the United Nations believes the earth is flat, it's gotta be round. (Editorial, *Arizona Republic*)[16]

---

[16] Arizona Republic, April 23, 1978. Copyright 1978 *Arizona Republic*. Used by permission.

ad hominem

14. Before Senator Henry Jackson (D—Wash.) went down in defeat in the 1972 Democratic primaries for President he launched a series of vitriolic attacks against Senator George McGovern which (in retrospect) provided the groundwork for the Nixon re-election committee's hatchet work that summer and fall.

By the time he got to Ohio, the neat, strategic plan laid out by Wattenberg had bombed. Jackson was no longer a serious candidate, but instead of acknowledging reality, he gave vent to his pent-up frustrations and began slinging mud at McGovern.

On April 25, in Youngstown, Ohio, Jackson called McGovern "the spokesman for some of the dangerous and destructive currents in American politics." Extremism of the left was gaining respectability, he warned, and "the main vehicle of this suicidal drift is the candidacy of Senator McGovern." Then, using that familiar Nixon tactic, guilt by association, he took a nasty swipe at the South Dakotan: "It comes as no surprise to me that Senator McGovern has just been endorsed by Yippie leaders Abbie Hoffman and Jerry Rubin. It would be unfair to conclude that because Hoffman and Rubin have endorsed McGovern, McGovern endorses Hoffman and Rubin. But it is perfectly fair to ask why these two hate-America leftist extremists, who have been in the forefront of violent demonstrations, should find Senator McGovern's candidacy congenial to their own problems. . . . Apparently the people who tried to wreck the Democratic convention from the outside in 1968 want to do it from the inside in 1972."

Three days later, in Cincinnati, Jackson criticized McGovern for supporting Henry A. Wallace for the presidency some 24 years before. "McGovern's 1948 candidate supported the Communist takeover of Czechoslovakia," charged Jackson. "McGovern's 1948 candidate wanted us to give away tens of billions of dollars in foreign aid to Joe Stalin's Russia." Wallace, in his view, was guilty of "appeasement" and, by implication, so were those who supported FDR's former Vice-President and Agriculture secretary.

(PETER J. OGNIBENE, *Scoop, The Life and Politics of Henry M. Jackson*)[17]

15. Students of history know that no government in the history of mankind has ever created any wealth. People who work create wealth. Increasingly, people in our country see "poverty" as a way of life. They look to government for a free lunch. Let's soberly face the facts of life, their numbers are increasing. They

[17] Peter J. Ognibene, *Scoop, The Life and Politics of Henry M. Jackson* (Briarcliff Manor, New York: Stein and Day, 1975), pp. 21–22.

subscribe to the myth that you get something for nothing so long as the government is footing the bill. But everything that the government gives to the people it must first take from the people in taxes. Poverty is abolished by work, not by government distribution of taxes. "The Idler shall not eat the bread of the Worker." To go against this truism is soul-destroying to the idler and incentive-destroying to the worker. All of us red-blooded Americans who place our hands over our heart and pledge allegiance to our flag need to soberly face the economic facts of life as they are fast taking shape in our country.

16. Recombinant DNA is a new technology that enables scientists to create new living molecules, thus new life. Already scientists have fused a cell of a human with plants and animals and "cloned" from a single cell an adult frog. To some the prospect of creating new life is not pleasing. The possibility of modifying nature alarms those who see the result from man's attempt to modify natural processes so far. Four reasons are often given in defense of recombinant DNA research. First, it is in the very nature of man to continue in research, an inner necessity forever driving him forward to discover. Second, there is a self-perpetrating momentum about technology. Third, there is the impossibility of controlling our affairs in any desirable way. Every time we try to do this it ends badly, either in a way not intended or because small groups of people get control of the mechanisms and use them to hurt others. Finally, the principle of freedom of inquiry is a supreme value. Look what has happened when it has been challenged. Look at Galileo and the Church or Scopes and the Monkey Trial. (JUNE GOODFIELD, *Playing God*)

17. Over the next seventy-five minutes, Dole moved from his light vein, in which he repeated his gag description of the vice-presidency as "indoor work with no heavy lifting," to bitter and cutting sarcasm, delivered unsmilingly. Between suggesting that George Meany, president of the AFL-CIO, "was probably Senator Mondale's make-up man" and even denigrating the host League of Women Voters after Mondale had cited the League's high approval rate of his voting record, Dole managed in effect to lay all twentieth-century wars at the feet of the Democratic Party. Asked about his 1974 comment that Ford's pardon of Nixon was "prematurely granted and mistaken," Dole shot back that the issue of Watergate wasn't a very good campaign issue, "any more than the Vietnam War would be, or World War One or World War Two or the Korean War—all Democrat wars, all in this century." (He used, of course, the abbreviated name of the opposition party that has long been an expression of contempt

special pleading

from the mouths of many Republicans.) And then, noting that he himself still carried the wounds of World War II, he added: "I figured up the other day if we added up the killed and wounded in Democrat wars in this century, it would be about 1.6 million Americans, enough to fill the city of Detroit."

Mondale, who had shaken off his early nervousness and was crisp and aggressive, was incredulous but calm. "I think that Senator Dole has richly earned his reputation as a hatchet man tonight. Does he really mean that there was a partisan difference over our involvement in the fight against Nazi Germany?"

(JULES WITCOVER, *Marathon, The Pursuit of the Presidency*)[18]

18. In a 1974 unanimous decision, Chief Justice Burger stated: It has yet to be demonstrated how governmental regulation of the choice of material going into print can be exercised consistent with First Amendment guarantees of a free press. The First Amendment of the Constitution reads in part: "Congress shall make no laws ... abridging the freedom of speech, or of the press." But in an earlier decision (Red Lion, 1969) it was said that ". . . we hold that Congress and the FCC do not violate the First Amendment when they require a radio or television station to give reply time to answer personal attacks and political editorials." The case supported the Fairness Doctrine which directs broadcasters to devote a reasonable amount of time to discuss controversial issues and to afford reasonable opportunity for opposing viewpoints. But the people's right to know in a democracy is the primary motivation of the First Amendment and free press and most Americans today receive the news from broadcast sources.

It may be argued that there is an inconsistency in the pronouncement of the court.

19. Watson: Moriarty will stop at nothing to end civilization as we know it.
    Sherlock Holmes ("Monty Python's" John Cleese): Then the thing to do is nothing.

20. The central assumption of the social science disciplines [economics, sociology, political science, and psychology] is that there is a simple, correct, objective truth in any given situation. When people disagree, therefore, only one answer can be right; the remainder must be wrong because of stupidity or ignorance. As nobody wishes to admit error, discussions rapidly turn into arguments and conflict is generated. As I have stressed in this book, however, there is no single objective reality. The genetic history, age, sex, and experience of each individual determine what will be perceived in any given situation. People are rarely

equivocation
special pleading

wrong; rather, each person focuses on different parts of the truth, which can then be pieced together to produce a larger vision of reality. Once one understands that subjective diversity is inevitable, then one can consider differences of opinion as healthy and productive and a way of learning more rapidly. One can listen to other people's discussions and ideas without being threatened and enjoy discovering what they add to the total picture. One ceases to listen so that one can argue effectively and begins to listen in terms of what the group can learn together.

(ROBERT THEOBALD, *Beyond Despair*)[19]

21. He [Nixon] was born a human being, but the action of others was less than human. The President was treated as though he had committed a mass murder, and his friends were treated as though they were his instruments in the dropping of hydrogen bombs.

It is a tragedy of human nature that too often we judge others by the darkness of their worst predicament while we judge ourselves in the light of our highest accomplishment.

Hypocritical men are quick to condemn, to act horrified, to discard and depose. Hypocritical men comprehend, but do not aid. They do not attempt to lift others to newer heights, but rush to bury them in greater depths.

"But he lied to the American people," they said.

He did.

The decision of nonrevelation most often leads to lying, whether it be to one or millions, as lying is the grotesque detour that waits unseen beyond the bend of nonrevelation when vigilance is maintained by others. When a man is no longer the master of events, he becomes their slave.

Lying is neither an enviable nor an excusable decision, but it is a decision that has been regrettably made by many of the best of men. It can be said that other Presidents have "covered up" for one reason or another that brought them to lie. Although they lied is not a factor for justification, it is a factor for recognition that they, like their predecessors and followers, may well have been good and decent men, but were not good and decent gods.

(BRUCE HERSCHENSOHN, *The Gods of the Antenna*)[20]

22. Many clergyman have hinted that they should endorse Presidential candidates because of their strong feelings that the very survival of the country may be at stake. That, we believe, would be a mistake. We can understand why a militant minority of

---

[19] Robert Theobald, *Beyond Despair* (Washington, D.C.: New Republic Book Co., 1976), p. 99. Copyright © 1976 by Robert Theobald.

[20] Bruce Herschensohn, *The Gods of the Antenna* (New Rochelle, N.Y.: Arlington House, 1976), pp. 98–99. Copyright © 1976 by Bruce Herschensohn. Used by permission.

If this is a fallacy, would be "special pleading" — perhaps some equivocation

clergymen are leading open-housing marches and burning draft cards. But because such clergymen confuse their spiritual mission with political partisanship is really no reason for the others to follow in their footsteps. That is not the job of religion. People come to religion because of an ultimate metaphysical hunger. But it is surely partly as a reaction against politics in the pulpit that the most recent Gallup Poll found that 60 percent of all persons interviewed said churches should keep out of political and social affairs. However, an even more meaningful statistic is that only 40 percent of those questioned a few years back felt this way. The clerical ministers should not involve themselves deeply in temporal affairs but should be more concerned with providing broad spiritual direction, confining themselves to cultivating the political ethos of a nation, and informing the conscience of the statesmen. They should confine themselves to preaching the Word of God and leave politics to others.

23.   There is an incredible amount of empty space in the universe. The distance from the sun to the nearest star is about 4.2 light years, or 25×10^{12} miles. This is in spite of the fact that we live in an exceptionally crowded part of the universe, namely the Milky Way, which is an assemblage of about 300,000 million stars. This assemblage is one of an immense number of similar assemblages; about 30 million are known, but presumably, better telescopes would show more. The average distance from one assemblage to the next is about 2 million light years. But apparently they still feel they haven't elbow room, for they are all hurrying away from each other; some are moving away from us at the the rate of 14,000 miles a second or more. The most distant of them so far observed are believed to be at a distance from us of about 500 million light years, so that what we see is what they were 500 million years ago. And as to mass: the sun weighs about 2×10^{27} tons, the Milky Way about 160,000 million times as much as the sun, and is one of a collection of galaxies of which about 30 million are known. It is not to easy to maintain a belief in one's own cosmic importance in view of such overwhelming statistics.

(BERTRAND RUSSELL, *The Impact of Science on Society*)

24.   ... [the radical] does not have a fixed truth—truth to him is relative and changing; everything to him is relative and changing. He is a political relativist. ... Does this then mean that ... [he] is rudderless? No, I believe that he has a far better sense of direction and compass than the closed-society organizer with his rigid political ideology. First, the free-society organizer is loose, resilient, fluid, and on the move in a society which is itself in a state of constant change. To the extent that he is free from the shackles of

provocation

✓

"*Truth*"

dogma, he can respond to the realities of the widely different situations our society presents. In the end he has one conviction—a belief that if people have the power to act, in the long run they will, most of the time, reach the right decisions. The alternative to this would be rule by the elite—either a dictatorship or some form of a political aristocracy. I am not concerned if this faith in people is regarded as a prime truth and therefore a contradiction of what I have already written, for life is a story of contradictions.

(SAUL ALINSKY, *Rules for Radicals*)

25. British historian Arnold Toynbee believes that the stimulation of personal consumption through advertising is un-Christian ("I cannot think of any circumstance in which advertising would not be an evil"), and last year advanced the ridiculous proposition: "the destiny of our Western civilization turns on the issue of our struggle with all that Madison Avenue stands for more than it turns on the issue of our struggle with Communism."

. . . In the most effective rebuttal any adman has yet made to Arnold Toynbee, William Bernbach wrote: "Mr. Toynbee's real hate is not advertising. It is the economy of abundance. . . . If Mr. Toynbee believes a materialistic society is a bad one (and I am not saying he is wrong in that belief), then he owes it to mankind to speak out against such a society and not merely against one of the tools that is available to any society."

In fact, as Historian Toynbee should know, taste and cultivation have historically reached their heights in prosperous societies. By helping to produce mass prosperity, advertising has at least indirectly helped to raise the general level of taste in the U.S.—a development that, in turn, has been mirrored in advertising itself. Even its critics concede that advertising has come a long way since the days when national magazines were littered with ads for nostrums that purported to cure everything from consumption to lost manhood, and when a U.S. soapmaker could bugle: "If we could teach the Indians to use SAPOLIO, it would quickly civilize them." Today most ads, if not 99 44/100 percent of them, strive for both taste and believability. And, assuming a continued increase in U.S. affluence and cultivation, tomorrow's advertising should be even more sophisticated and tasteful.

Whatever the state of American culture, all signs are that advertising will always be a conspicuously visible part of it. Fascinated as it is with the business of finding ways to live, the U.S. public wastes little time worrying about whether advertising may be damaging to its collective psyche. It is unlikely that the citizenry will ever take the step some admen seem to yearn for and pass a national vote of thanks to advertising for its part in enriching U.S. life. But it is equally unlikely that the public will ever be suborned out of its unemotional recognition of the adman for what he is: a highly effective salesman without whose efforts the world would be a far more primitive and less pleasant place.

(*Time*, October 12, 1962)[21]

ANSWERS

A. **1.** division   **3.** composition   **5.** equivocation   **7.** equivocation   **11.** equivocation   **13.** accent   **15.** accent   **17.** accent

B. **1.** hasty generalization   **3.** *tu quoque*   **5.** *ad ignorantiam*   **7.** Special pleading   **9.** *ad populum*   **11.** inconsistency   **13.** *petitio, ad ignorantiam*, straw man, appeal to authority, and *ad hominem*   **15.** *ad populum*   **17.** false cause and *tu quoque*   **19.** equivocation   **21.** *tu quoque* and *ad populum*   **23.** equivocation   **25.** *ad hominem*, straw man, *post hoc*, special pleading, and *ad populum*.

Two Additional Fallacies

Analogical arguments and dilemmas are two widely used types of arguments. Often such arguments are incorrect. This gives rise to two additional fallacies, the fallacy of weak analogy and the fallacy of false dilemma. These are discussed in this section. The fallacy of weak analogy is a material fallacy of insufficient evidence. Dilemmas are appraised in a way that does not readily fit in the threefold classification of informal fallacies.

Fallacy of Weak Analogy

One common type of inductive argument is generalization from samples. Earlier we examined some examples of incorrect generalizations from samples classified as fallacies of hasty generalization. For example to argue that

Einstein, Heisenberg, and Bounderby loved music.
Therefore all physicists love music.

is to commit the fallacy of hasty generalization. We argue inductively by analogy as often as we generalize from cases. But while it is not too difficult to recognize incorrect inductive generalizations, the evaluation of arguments by analogy is more difficult. Nevertheless common sense does supply guidelines for appraising arguments that rely on analogy. Let us first

---

[21] *Time*, Vol. LXXX, No. 15, October 12, 1962, p. 87. Courtesy *Time*; copyright 1962, Time Inc.

identify analogical arguments and then outline guidelines for appraising them as correct or incorrect.

In an *argument by analogy* one argues that because two things are similar in some respects they are similar in some other respects. Let a and b be the objects regarded as similar. Let $P_1, P_2, \ldots, P_n$ be the purported similar properties. And let P_{n+1} be the alleged similar-in-other-respects property. Then a common form of an analogical argument is:

> Object a has properties $P_1, P_2, \ldots, P_n$.
> Object b has properties $P_1, P_2, \ldots, P_n$.
> Object a has P_{n+1}.
> Therfore object b has P_{n+1}.

For example, a medical researcher performs experiments upon rats to determine the effect of a chemical substance on humans. He finds that rats given the chemical develop cancer. By analogy he concludes that it is likely that humans will develop cancer if they ingest the chemical substances in the same proportions. This argument can be put in explicit analogical form as follows:

> Rats have such-and-such physiological properties.
> Humans have such-and-such physiological properties.
> Rats develop cancer when they are given chemical substance x.
> Therefore it is likely that humans will develop cancer if they ingest chemical substance x.

Variations on the above pattern can occur when more than one object or type of objects are compared. To illustrate consider the following analogical argument:

> ... we may observe a very great similitude between this earth which we inhabit, and the other planets, Saturn, Jupiter, Mars, Venus, and Mercury. They all revolve round the sun, as the earth does, although at different distances and in different periods. They borrow all their light from the sun, as the earth does. Several of them are known to revolve round their axis like the earth, and, by that means, must have a like succession of day and night. Some of them have moons that serve to give them light in the absence of the sun, as our moon does to us. They are all, in their motions, subject to the same law of gravitation, as the earth is. From all this similitude, it is not unreasonable to think that those planets may, like our earth, be the habitation of various orders of living creatures. There is some probability in this conclusion from analogy.[22]

As can be seen, the argument is:

> The earth (a_1) revolves around the sun (P_1), borrows all its light from the sun (P_2), revolves on its axis (P_3), and is subjected to laws of gravitation (P_4). Saturn (b_1), Jupiter (b_2), Mars (b_3), Venus (b_4), and Mercury (b_5) have P_1 and P_2, P_3, and P_4.

[22] *Essays on the Intellectual Powers of Man*, by Thomas Reid, Essay I, Chapter 4.

The earth is inhabited by living creatures (P_5).
Therefore there is some probability that the other planets are inhabited by living creatures.

Another illustration of an analogical argument follows:

If a doctor is justified in deceiving a sick patient, if there is no harm in telling the children about Santa Claus, if a stage manager in case of fire behind the scenes ought to deceive the audience so as to avert a panic, then it is only logical to conclude that there is no wrong in cribbing at an exam.

The argument in explicit analogical form is as follows:

Doctors (a_1) deceive (P_1) sick patients.
Parents (a_2) deceive (P_1) children about Santa Claus.
Theater managers (a_3) deceive (P_1) endangered audiences.
Students (b) deceive (P_1) when cheating on an exam.
It is justifiable (P_2) for a_1, a_2, and a_3 to deceive.
Therefore it is justifiable for students to cheat on exams.

The *fallacy of weak analogy* occurs when at least one of the following holds:

1. The conclusion of the analogical argument is supposed to follow with certainty from the premises.
2. The relevant dissimilarities outweigh the similarities.

In an analogical argument the objects compared must have some dissimilar properties; otherwise it would not be an analogical argument. If the objects compared were exactly alike, this would insure that the argument is correct; but this would also rule it out as an analogical argument. By its very meaning, an analogical argument involves the comparison of dissimilar objects, so one cannot rationally conclude that the conclusion *must* be true. The comparison of the dissimilar objects can at most lead one correctly to conclude that in all likelihood or with some degree of probability the P_{n+1} property obtains for b. In fact the rule is that the stronger the conclusion of an analogical argument, the less likely the argument is correct, whereas the weaker the conclusion, the less likely the argument is not correct. Suppose Mr. A's Volvo delivers 32 miles per gallon, and his friend Mr. B also buys a Volvo. He reasons by analogy that he will get the same mileage. Suppose Mr. A alters his conclusion to any one of the following weaker conclusions: "I will get between 25 and 40 mpg," or "I will get more than 30 mpg," or "I will get approximately 32 mpg." When any of these weaker conclusions replace the original conclusion, the argument is strengthened. What insures the incorrectness of Mr. B's argument is his concluding that it is certain that he will get 32 mpg solely on the basis of the comparison cited in the premises.

The second way a weak analogy can occur is for the relevant dissimilarities to outweigh the similarities. Recall the familiar argument that, given the similarities between government fiscal policies and family budgeting, and given the fact that continued debt by a family can only lead to ruin, it follows that government deficit spending can only lead to economic ruin. This is a fallacy of weak analogy because of the number of highly relevant dissimilarities between the two cases, the government and the family. To mention only two: the government issues and regulates currency, and the government "owes" the money to itself, but it can cancel the debt at any time. These privileges are unfortunately denied to the family.

By contrast, the medical researcher's inference that it is likely humans will, like rats, develop cancer if they ingest the chemical is a correct analogical argument. First, the conclusion is merely that it is likely to happen. Second, the physiological similarities between rats and humans make it likely that humans would contract cancer from the chemical substance. It should be stressed that just as there are many correct generalizations from samples in everyday life and science, so there are many correct analogical arguments in everyday life and science. The earlier Reid analogy is fallacious, for the similarities betweeen earth and the other planets are insufficient to conclude that life is possible on other planets, whereas the dissimilarities—lack of water and oxygen, difference in temperature, and so on—are sufficient to almost rule out the possibility of life on other planets. Similarly the analogical argument which concludes that it is not wrong to crib on exams is incorrect. The relevant dissimilarity that outweighs the similarities is that the deception in the doctor, parent, and theater manager cases is done for moral reasons. One breaks a low-level moral law, that which says we should not deceive, in order to satisfy a higher level moral law, which is that we should look after the welfare of others.

In 1977 former undersecretary of state George Ball wrote that every white in South Africa will not accept the formula of "one man, one vote," which our government now seems to demand in South Africa. He argued that our political leaders fail to face the realities of South Africa because they are making an incorrect inference based on an analogy. For example, Ball says that the UN Ambassador Andrew Young sees an analogy between South Africa and the American South. And since the American South was able to transform itself into a multiracial "one man, one vote" society through the civil rights movement, so can South Africa. Ball says this inference is fallacious since it ignores relevant dissimilarities between South Africa and the American South. The civil rights movement in the United States only sought to make effective rights already accorded to American blacks by the Constitution. And its success resulted because a large element of the white population was ready to correct old injustices. Most importantly, the civil rights movement in the American South did not threaten white southerners with the total transfer of political control to the blacks. In South Africa "one man, one vote" would mean political control by the blacks since blacks outnumber whites at least four to one. The analogy is a poor one.

There is a notion, which Richard Nixon helped propagate, that the government and the press have an adversary relationship. In 1968 Nixon wrote to Spiro Agnew, "When news is concerned, nobody in the press is a friend—they are all enemies." And many members of the press were Nixon's ferocious adversaries during Watergate. Now the adversary relationship is a relationship that comes up in law. Most believe that justice is served and truth is most effectively discovered when in a court one side does its best to attack while the other defends. There are some similar features in the relationship between government and the press and the relationship between contending lawyers in a court. For example government officials (defense lawyers) try to put their best foot forward, while newsmen (prosecuting lawyers) press to discover what they may be concealing. If one infers from this that since an adversary relation in court ought to exist because it serves justice and truth, such a relationship ought to exist between government and the press, he would have a weak analogical argument. There are relevant differences between the two cases that seem to outweigh the similarities. Thomas Griffith writing in *Time* nicely points out one crucial difference:

> The *judge* is missing—that judge who forbids misleading tactics, freely admonishes both sides, determines which evidence is valid and finally instructs the jury on how it should weigh what it has heard. In the news-gathering process, the press is both prosecutor and sole judge of its own activities— answerable in advance of publication to no one (though it can be sued once the story is out), free to select or disregard evidence as it pleases, free to omit counterclaims, to minimize rebuttals. Such absence of prior restraint is essential to a free press, but the press at least should recognize that it enjoys more unchecked advantages than a courtroom adversary, and therefore incurs some obligations.[23]

Griffith goes on to argue that the relationship between government and the press ought to be an independent relationship rather than an adversary one since the latter has been used to justify one of Washington's major blood sports, the grossly unfair treatment of some public officials by the press.

Finally, it should be noted that to make a comparison is not to construct an argument. Often in order to highlight some features of x one might compare it to y without making any inference. For example in Shakespeare's *King Lear*, Lear says:

> What!, art mad? A man may see how this world goes with no eyes. Look with thine ears. See how yond Justice rails upon yond simple thief. Hark, in thine

[23] Newswatch: "Indegoddampendent is Fine," in *Time*, April 17, 1978.

ear. Change places and, handy-handy, which is Justice, which is the thief? Thou hast seen a farmer's dog bark at a beggar? . . . And the creature run from the cur? There thou mightst behold the great image of authority. A dog's obey'd in office. (SHAKESPEARE, *King Lear*)

Here Lear is stating how he sees justice and authority. Authority is compared with the dog that causes the beggar to run away. The feature Lear sees in authority that is similar to the relation between the dog and the beggar is that authority is just a matter of who has the power. Justice is seen as whatever is the will of those in power.

EXERCISES 2.4

Indicate the analogical arguments found in the following items. Are there any fallacies of weak analogy? Be on the lookout for comparisons that are not arguments.

1. Franklin D. Roosevelt in his acceptance speech in 1932 said, "Revenue must cover expenditures by one means or another. Any government, like any family, can for a year spend a little more than it earns. But you and I know that a continuation of that habit means the poorhouse." *analogical argument – weak*

2. It is no more necessary for there to be two political parties than that a man should have two heads. *– analogical argument, weak*

3. According to Sister Rosetta Stone, the Church's traditional stand on birth control is based on the natural law that it is wrong for man to change the bodily functions.

   If this is so then it is equally wrong for us to use deodorants, perform caesarian sections, or employ any other medical or surgical process that tampers with the body's natural functions. *analogical arguments are weak.*

   Unless the Church can reinforce its argument concerning the natural law, such a pronouncement is an insult to the intelligence of any thinking person. It is like asking us to use candles instead of electricity to light the darkness or to treat plagues and epidemics with prayers and ancient herb brews instead of immunizations and antibiotics, which are all human-made, unnatural, synthetic inventions.

   It would seem that God gave us our intellect and powers of reasoning to set us apart from the rest of nature so that we could subdue and conquer it, not be enslaved by it. So we have probed into the mysteries of earth and the skies and used our knowledge to make a better existence for ourselves and our offspring.

4. Dan Rather, CBS News, compared objectivity to "the Ten Commandments, a goal worth reaching for but impossible to live up to."

5. HEW has launched an antismoking campaign. Some say it is dangerous for government to undertake even modest modification of *analogical argument not very strong*

behavior. But society inevitably is concerned with dampening destructive impulses. Thus government uses incentives to encourage people to become charitable, to become home owners, and many other things. Surely it can encourage them to become nonsmokers.

6. Gay foe Anita Bryant spoke to a convention of religious broadcasters and said gays were not a legitimate minority deserving of civil rights because they were not born homosexual. Thus we have the Anita Axiom: To be a legitimate minority, you have to be born that way. This may come as a shock to religious converts, the handicapped, battered wives, and veterans.

7. If you keep a pack of rats in a confined space large enough for all their physical needs, feeding them well and protecting them against infection, their numbers will increase until eventually, though they still have plenty to eat and drink and room enough to move around and build their nests, their society becomes demoralized. The males fight violently. The rules governing the rank order no longer hold. Sexual behavior becomes deviant, and the young may be neglected or attacked and devoured. The parallels with contemporary urban problems are stiking: increase in violence, contempt for the law, breakdown of family life and social cohesion, sexual permissiveness, child beating, nervous breakdowns. They are sufficiently similar so that we can conclude that the distinctive characteristics of urban behavior can be attributed to the fact of being closely confined, especially with large numbers of one's own kind.

8. Of all persons hospitalized a third of them have been injured in car accidents. Does the auto industry have any blame in this? It's not the industry's fault; it is the nut behind the wheel. Being inanimate, no car can by itself cause an accident any more than a sidewalk can. A driver is needed to put the car in motion. The car is not to be blamed for car accidents. Guns don't kill people, people kill people. The same is true of car accidents. Regulation of the manufacture of cars is no more necessary than regulation of guns.

9. The National Safety Council reports that there were about 46,700 motor vehicle fatalities in 1976. Yet, aside from rather sporadic and desultory efforts, our government has made no very strenuous attempt to reduce this figure. The reason is that we find the fatalities per year on American highways an acceptable level. The U.S. Department of Labor has recently taken the position that any known level of exposure to a suspected carcinogen in a job is too high. The sensible approach is to enjoy the benefits of industrial carcinogens and arrive at an acceptable level of cancer risk by industrial workers, because this is what is done in the case of motor vehicle fatalities.

10. One of the arguments often used by those opposing the Equal Rights Amendment is that the amendment is not necessary because the

Constitution already protects the rights of all persons living within the jurisdiction of the United States. I believe this was the case before the thirteenth, fourteenth, fifteenth, and nineteenth were adopted as well.

This pious protestation ranks along with the age old argument of men attempting the seduction of young women with the ploy, "marriage wouldn't make us love one another more. We don't need a ridiculous piece of legal paper and a ceremony to prove our love. Marriage is unnecessary for us."

I should think that American women would be thoroughly fed up with this kind of phoniness. It seems obvious that if the citizens of this nation really believe in equality and love, that the best way to prove it is to make it legal.

11. Reporters are puppets [Lyndon Johnson told Doris Kearns]. They simply respond to the pull of the most powerful strings . . . Every story is always slanted to win the favor of someone who sits somewhere higher up. There is no such thing as an objective news story. There is always a private story behind the public story. And if you don't control the strings to that private story, you'll never get good coverage no matter how many great things you do for the masses of people. There's only one sure way of getting favorable stories from reporters and that is to keep their daily bread—the information, the stories, the plans, and the details they need for their work—in your own hands, so that you can give it out when and to whom you want.

(DORIS KEARNS, *Lyndon Johnson and the American Dream*)

12. . . . unless something other than the continued arms race is undertaken by governments, it only postpones a war. After all, before 1914 there were crises very similar to the crisis that we've had in the policy of brinkmanship, and those crises didn't lead to war until 1914, and people thought, "Oh, well, if we keep the armaments equal on the two sides, there won't be war." But it wasn't so, and I'm afraid that may happen again. . . .

. . . Everybody remembers that Nobel, who invented the Nobel peace prize and was a very keen advocator of peace, was also the inventor of dynamite. He thought dynamite made war so horrible that there never would be another war. Well it didn't work out that way, and I'm afraid it may be the same with the H-bomb.

(*Bertrand Russell Speaks His Mind*)

13. I think there ought to be no rules whatever prohibiting improper publications. . . . I think prohibitions immensely increase people's interest in pornography, as in anything else. I used often to go to America during Prohibition, and there was far more drunkenness than there was before, far more, and I think that prohibition of pornography has much the same effect. Now, I'll give you an illustration of what I

mean about prohibitions. The philosopher Empedocles thought it was very, very wicked to munch laurel leaves, and he laments that he will have to spend ten thousand years in outer darkness because he munched laurel leaves. Now nobody's ever told me not to munch laurel leaves and I've never done it, but Empedocles who was told not to, did it. And I think the same applies to pornography.

(Bertrand Russell Speaks His Mind)

14. Yes, it certainly is possible [for communism and capitalism to learn to live side by side in the world together]. It's only a question of getting used to each other. Now take the .. Christians and the Mohammedans. They fought each other for about six centuries, during which neither side got any advantage over the other, and at the end of that time some men of genius said: "Look, why shouldn't we stop fighting each other and make friends?" And they did, and that's all right, and just the same thing can happen with capitalism and communism as soon as each side realizes that it can't gain the world.

(Bertrand Russell Speaks His Mind)

15. The men who argue in favor of unrestricted national freedom do not realize that the same reasons would justify unrestricted individual freedom. I will not yield to Patrick Henry, or anyone else, in love of freedom, but if there is to be as much freedom in the world as possible, it is necessary that there should be restrictions preventing violent assaults upon the freedom of others. In the internal affairs of states this is recognized: Murder is everywhere made illegal. If the law against murder were repealed, the liberty of all except murderers would be diminished, and even the liberty of murderers would, in most cases, be short-lived, since they would soon be murdered. But although everyone, except a few anarchists, admits this as regards the relations of an individual to his national state, there is immense reluctance to admit it as regards the relations of national states to the world at large.

(Bertrand Russell, Has Man a Future?)

16. Surely it's about time politicians accused of a crime stop raising the defense that "everybody's doing it."

This was the defense we kept hearing during the Watergate uproar, that every administration since Franklin D. Roosevelt had bugged, burgled and otherwise trampled on the law. So why jump on the Nixon administration?

The cry, "everybody's doing it," did not save the Watergate conspirators from going to jail, but now Rep. Charles Diggs, D-Mich., is raising it again.

Diggs is accused of payroll padding. The other day, his lawyers went into court to argue that he should be let off because it's a common practice in Congress.

[handwritten margin note: analogical argument; questionable]

Now, we know that Capitol Hill is not entirely inhabited by angels, but we doubt that many congressmen have their personal accountant on the public payroll.

And their personal attorney.
And employees of a business they conduct on the side.
That's what Diggs is charged with.

And even if payroll padding were a common practice, well, what kind of defense is that? Should a man caught mugging a little old lady on the streets of New York be let free because mugging little old ladies is a common practice in the city?

("It's Not a Defense," *Arizona Republic*, May 12, 1978)

ANSWERS

2. analogical argument, weak   **4.** comparison   **6.** analogical argument, strong   **8.** analogical argument, weak   **10.** analogical argument, strong   **12.** analogical argument, weak   **14.** analogical argument, weak   **16.** analogical argument, strong

Fallacy of False Dilemma

In logic a dilemma is a particular kind of argument. This kind of argument is found in this example:

Marx, in *Das Kapital*, maintains that there are certain irreversible laws operating in history. One of the consequences of these dialectical laws is that Capitalism will shatter and out of it will come Communism. Communism can emerge *only* from Capitalism. Russia was one of the first countries where the ideas of Communism flourished. Yet Russia at that time was a backward country, ruled by the Tsar, and would take many years to catch up to the stage Marx calls "Capitalism." In 1881 a member of the Populists in Russia wrote to Marx and asked for his support in their movement. Marx was in a dilemma. If he encouraged the movement, then this would conflict with his theory. If he did not encourage it, then perhaps the strongest Communist movement would die or be taken over by other ideologies.

The argument found here is:

If Marx encourages the communist movement in Tsarist Russia, then he will be encouraging actions that conflict with his own theory of history.

If Marx does not encourage the communist movement in Tsarist Russia, then the strongest communist movement will disappear.

Either Marx encourages the communist government in Tsarist Russia or he does not.

Therefore either he encourages actions that conflict with his own theory of history or the strongest communist movement will disappear.

We can indicate the form of this argument as follows by letting p, q, r, and s be placeholders that we can replace with sentences:

If p, then q.
If r, then s.
Either p or r.
Therefore either q or s.

Arguments with this form are dilemmas. Premises one and two are the conditional sentences of the dilemma. The third premise is the disjunctive sentence of the dilemma. A dilemma is said to be constructive when it has the above form, and it is destructive when it has this form:

If p, then q.
If r, then s.
Either not q or not s.
Therefore not p or not r.

The conclusion of a dilemma can be either a disjunctive sentence, as in the above two patterns, or a simple statement, as in the following pattern:

If p, then q.
If r, then q.
Either p or r.
Therefore q.

A complex dilemma is one which has a disjunctive conclusion. A simple dilemma has a simple conclusion. A *dilemma* is an argument with one of the above forms.

A dilemma is formally valid, as is an argument with inconsistent premises. So our interest will be in whether a dilemma is correctly formulated. The error we are interested in is that of thinking one is in a dilemma when one is not. One may believe he is in a dilemma on the basis of insufficient evidence.

The *fallacy of false dilemma* occurs when a dilemma is unrealistic—either the disjunctive premise is false or one or both of the conditional premises are false.

To appraise an argument in terms of the truth or falsity of its premises seems to be a departure from logical appraisal. But this is only partly true. First, to determine whether the disjunctive premise is true is often to simply determine whether the premise is or is not an instance of this logical pattern

p or not p

If it is, then it is a matter of logic that it is true. For it is true in virtue of the meaning of the logical terms "not" and "or." If the disjunctive premise is not an instance of "*p* or not *p*" then, typically, it is false, since in a realistic dilemma the disjunctive premise *must* exhaust alternatives. Second, to determine whether the conditional premises of a dilemma are true is to determine whether, given the truth of the antecedent—what appears between "if" and "then"—this provides sufficient deductive or inductive grounds for affirming the consequent—what appears after "then."

To illustrate the fallacy of false dilemma consider the following dilemma:

> If we are to have peace, then we must not encourage the competitive spirit, while if we are to make progress, then we must encourage the competitive spirit. We must either encourage or not encourage the competitive spirit. Therefore we shall either have no peace or make no progress.

Here the disjunctive premise is immune from criticism since it is an instance of "*p* or not *p*," namely, "either we encourage the competitive spirit or we do not encourage the competitive spirit." However a case can be made that both conditional premises are false. For example consider the second conditional premise: if we are to make progress, then we must encourage the competitive spirit. Progress, even in the sense of expanding the wealth of a nation, can occur in a society in which cooperation is stressed rather than competition (e.g., modern China). So that the fact that a society is making progress does not mean that it encourages the competitive spirit.

The *black and white* fallacy, which is a particular case of the false dilemma fallacy, occurs when the disjunctive premise of a dilemma is not exhaustive and is thus false. This fallacy is committed when the number of possible alternatives is erroneously limited. It has the name black and white fallacy because black and white are just two possible colors among many shades of grey. In a dilemma if the disjunctive premise is false, then what is under discussion is erroneously limited to just two cases. The following argument is an example of the black and white fallacy:

> If men are good, laws are not needed to prevent wrongdoing, while if men are bad, laws will not succeed in preventing wrongdoing. Men are either good or bad. Therefore laws are not needed or laws will not succeed.

Though it is a matter of logic that men are either good or not good or bad or not bad, it is not true that men are either good (i.e., saints) so laws are not needed, or bad (i.e., sinners), so laws will do no good. Men lie on a continuum of virtue ranging from saints to sinners.

In 1974 the U.S. Congress faced a serious dilemma, perhaps the most serious dilemma in its history. Congress was confronted with the problem of whether or not to impeach President Nixon. If the House impeached him, then the resulting trial in the Senate would divide the country perhaps to a degree greater than the Vietnam war, with all the resulting tragic consequences. On the other hand if the House did not impeach him, then it was unlikely that any President would ever be impeached and thus the one sanction that keeps the President of the U.S. within the law would become dormant and idle and the Constitution would be subverted. This dilemma was so uncomfortably realistic that it was a relief to most when President Nixon erased the dilemma by resigning before the House was to vote on impeachment.

EXERCISES 2.5

Locate any dilemmas found in the following examples. If the dilemma is not already in an explicit dilemma form, then put it in explicit dilemma form. Are there any fallacies of false dilemma?

1. Either it is right to kill another human being or it is not right. If it is right, murder is not a crime and should not be punished. If it is not right, there is no justification for putting anyone to death—this would only multiply wrongs. Therefore in either case capital punishment cannot be defended.

2. Either I am fated to pass this course or I am not. If I am fated to pass, I shall do so whether I do the work or not. If I am not fated to pass, I shall not pass, not matter what I do. So why study?

3. If God is benevolent, then He desires to prevent the suffering of helpless human beings. If He is omnipotent, then He has the power to prevent such suffering. The fact that helpless human being are suffering all over the world proves either that God does not desire to prevent such suffering or that He is unable to do so.

4. Conservative solutions to violent crime range from protecting the family with a gun of one's own to deterring the criminal with the threat of capital punishment. Liberal solutions tend towards eradicating the social roots of crime and rehabilitating the criminal. The problem is that the gun the conservatives keeps in his or her house kills a lot more wives and children and lovers than it does criminals. And the evidence that capital punishment actually deters crime is slight indeed. As for the liberals they are right in wanting to eradicate the social roots of crime and to rehabilitate the criminal but wrong in thinking we know how to do either in the near future. It seems, then, there is no way to protect society.

5. SOCRATES: I know, Meno, what you mean; but just see what a tiresome dispute you are introducing. You argue that a man cannot inquire either about that which he knows or about that which he does not know; for if he knows, he has no need to inquire; and if not, he

[handwritten marginal note:] It is not necessarily true that we must adopt either the liberal or the conservative solution

cannot; for he does not know the very subject about which he is to inquire. (PLATO, *Meno*)

6. If we limited economic growth, then we will no longer be able to provide jobs for all. If we don't limit economic growth, then we are not likely to survive on the planet. Lack of employment for all will break the central link of our social organization. If we are to survive on this planet, most who have studied the relationships between economics and ecology now realize that energy use per person must stabilize and probably decrease in the rich countries of the world.

7. A country cannot have full liberty and full equality, for if individual liberty is pushed too far, it creates opportunities for the ruthless and the strong and tends to breed inequalities; if, on the other hand, equality is carried to its fullness, it ends in uniformity and stifles freedom.

8. The dilemma of modern armaments is that the will to use nuclear weapons is indispensable as a deterrent to nuclear and perhaps major conventional aggression; yet if the United States were to exercise its will and use anything like its full arsenal of nuclear weapons it would destroy the very things it was fighting to save.

9. In Shakespeare's *Julius Caesar*, Brutus, a good man, is led by Cassius and the circumstances to believe that Caesar might declare himself king, become a tyrant, and destroy democratic Rome. He cannot let a tyrant destroy his beloved Rome. Since it seems to him that there is no way to kill Caesar's potential tyranny without killing Caesar, Caesar must be stopped by death. On the other hand, how can his death be justified since he has not yet committed any act of actual tyranny? In addition, Caesar is Brutus' friend.

10. Construct the dilemma that the secret agents tried to put Jesus in:

The lawyers and chief priests wanted to lay hands on him there and then, for they saw that his parable was aimed at them; but they were afraid of the people. So they watched their opportunity and sent secret agents in the guise of honest men, to seize upon some word of his as a pretext for handing him over to the the authority and jurisdiction of the Governor. They put a question to him: "Master," they said, "we know that what you speak and teach is sound; you pay deference to no one, but teach in all honesty the way of life that God requires. Are we or are we not permitted to pay taxes to the Roman Emperor?" He saw through their trick and said. "Show me a silver piece. Whose head does it bear, and whose inscription?" "Caesar's," they replied. "Very well then," he said "pay Caesar what is due to Caesar, and pay God what is due to God." Thus their attempt to catch him out in public failed, and, astonished by his reply, they fell silent. (Luke 20 : 19–26)

11. Prior to 1978, the Mormon leadership faced a dilemma. To give blacks full privileges in the church, including the priesthood and participation

in sacred ceremonies, meant repudiation of one of Joseph Smith's holy books, the Book of Abraham. (In the Book of Abraham blacks are not entitled to the priesthood since they are said to have sprung from the loins of the cursed tribe of Ham.) But to repudiate one of Smith's books would make all of Smith's books suspect. And Smith's holy books are the foundations for Mormonism. In contrast, to continue to deny blacks full privileges in the church on the basis of a book that is suspect as history seemed an immoral process, alien to the ideas of intellectual honesty, the Declaration of Independence, and to the fundamental injunctions of Christianity concerning brotherhood and loving one's neighbor as oneself.

12. It may be said, for instance, that, if voluntary actions be subjected to the same laws of necessity with the operations of matter, there is a continued chain of necessary causes, preordained and predetermined, reaching from the original cause of all to every single volition of every human creature. No contingency anywhere in the universe; no indifference; no liberty. While we act, we are, at the same time, acted upon. The ultimate Author of all our volitions is the Creator of the world, who first bestowed motion on this immense machine, and placed all goings in that particular position, whence every subsequent event, by an inevitable necessity, must result. Human actions, there-fore, either can have no moral turpitude at all, as proceeding from so good a cause; or if they have any turpitude, they must involve our Creator in the same guilt, while he is acknowledged to be their ultimate cause and author. For as a man, who fired a mine, is answerable for all the consequences whether the train he employed be long or short; so wherever a continued chain of necessary causes is fixed, that Being, either finite or infinite, who produces the first, is likewise the author of all the rest, and must both bear the blame and acquire the praise which belong to them. Our clear and unalterable ideas of morality establish this rule, upon unquestionable reasons, when we examine the consequences of any human action; and these reasons must still have greater force when applied to the volitions and intentions of a Being infinitely wise and powerful. Ignorance or impotence may be pleaded for so limited a creature as man; but those imperfections have no place in our Creator. He foresaw, he ordained, he intended all those actions of men, which we so rashly pronounce criminal. And we must there-fore conclude, either that they are not criminal, or that the Deity, not man, is accountable for them.

(DAVID HUME, *An Enquiry Concerning Human Understanding*)

13. According to the latest polls conducted by Lou Harris, George Gallup, and others, public confidence in government has sunk to another low point.

The only thing surprising about that is that everyone would be surprised.

From coast to coast, Americans are constantly reminded how untrustworthy politicians usually are after they get elected.

When he was campaigning for our votes, Jimmy Carter promised such things as the appointment of U.S. attorneys solely on merit, a balanced budget and a simplified income tax system.

After election, the new president gave us the David Marston case, abandoned the idea of a balanced budget, and as we all found out on April 17, couldn't deliver on a simplified income tax.

In New York City, Mayor Edward Koch endorsed the Westway highway project which he had bitterly opposed during his campaign and pledged would never be built as long as he was mayor.

In California, Governor Jerry Brown dismisses his campaign promises by saying they were "just words". That clearly implies that whatever the candidate says is meaningless after he gets elected.

These are just three examples of a disappointing trait shared by most politicians all over the country at every level of government. Is it any wonder that fewer and fewer people are bothering to vote? They realize that politicians cannot be trusted to do what they promise.

So what is the solution?

How about the people hiring politicians to perform certain tasks, in much the same way we hire other contractors to perform services?

Each candidate would file a public contract stating what he will do if elected. Based on this written contract, the voters can decide which candidate to elect.

If the elected official then fails to perform according to his written promise, a citizen could sue him for breach of contract.

Sound crazy? Well, maybe. But the current setup doesn't make much sense, either.

(GEORGE MAIR, "Make Campaign Pledges Binding?")[24]

14. During his campaign Jimmy Carter repeatedly pledged that he would never lie to the American people. We could depend on that. Now the President is running into the issue of veracity. Carter during his campaign made an unequivocal commitment that all federal judges and prosecutors should be appointed strictly on the basis of merit. Carter caused gas producers to believe that he favored deregulation of natural gas. Carter promised Catholics that he would support some form of tuition grants for schools. He said he would reduce the White House staff by 30 per cent and balance the budget before the end of his four-year term. He told farmers that they would have price supports at least equal to production costs. Now Black spokesmen charge him with

[24] George Mair, "Make Campaign Pledges binding?" in the *Arizona Republic*, May 12, 1978.

"callous neglect" of his pledges. Jews believe he broke his word on arms sales to Arab enemies. Liberal senators have had the rug pulled from under them in the energy debate. Either Carter made promises that he thought he could keep, or it was not duplicity but ignorance that produced these fatuous promises. He either has perfectly good intentions or is merely naive.

ANSWERS

1. Unrealistic dilemma. Second conditional is false if capital punishment can be justified as a way to prevent killing.

2. Unrealistic dilemma. Even if one is fated, he may be fated to do a little work.

3. Valid dilemma with this form: If p, then not q. If r, then not q. q. Therefore not p or not r. Weak or strong depending on the viability of theological efforts to solve the problem of evil.

5. Unrealistic dilemma. Second conditional is false.

7. No dilemma, but a valid deductive argument. In Part Two we would symbolize it as follows:

$$(x)(Lx \supset \sim Ex), \qquad (x)(Ex \supset \sim Lx) \qquad \therefore \quad \sim(\exists x)(Lx \cdot Ex)$$

8. Realistic dilemma if it is formulated as follows: Either we have the will to use nuclear weapons or we do not. If we do not, then there is no deterrent. If we do, then "having the will" implies "being willing to exercise it," and thus we are willing to destroy what we are trying to save by having the deterrent.

9. One can, it seems, question whether the only way to stop Caesar's "potential tyranny" is to murder him.

10. The dilemma is: If Christ says to pay taxes, then he is telling his followers to submit to an unpopular colonial government. If he says not to pay taxes, then he runs the risk of arrest by this government. According to the poet John Milton "Pay Caesar what is due Caesar" is to be understood as implying "My conscience I have from God and I can therefore not give it to Caesar."

11. In 1978 the leader of the Mormon Church received a revelation that blacks can be members of the priesthood. The continuous revelation doctrine found in Mormonism weakens the first conditional. Smith's book is only part of the revelation and is to be interpreted in the light of later revelations.

12. Actions have moral turpitude or they do not. If they do, then God is also guilty. If they do not, then there are no criminals. Again, problem of evil. If it can be solved then first conditional is weak.

3

Words and Meaning

George Orwell wrote that political language has to consist mostly of euphemisms, question-begging, and sheer cloudy vagueness, for political speeches and writings are largely the defense of the indefensible. No doubt some political language is question-begging, and contains contradictions, vagueness, ambiguities, and euphemisms, as do some nonpolitical uses of language. In any case, and for whatever reasons, such language is sometimes used in arguments, and the result is a faulty argument. In Chapter 2 some examples of question-begging and contradictory language in fallacious arguments were studied. In this chapter the practical interest is in the ambiguous, vague, and euphemistic language in faulty arguments.

Considerations of words and meaning are helpful in providing a general framework for the discussion of ambiguity, vagueness, and euphemisms. Such a framework is outlined in the first four sections of this chapter.

In section five arguments which are faulty because of ambiguity and vagueness are considered. A certain kind of vagueness gives rise to disputes that many find troublesome because they are neither about facts nor just about words. Such disputes, when misunderstood, consist of a pair of fallacies due to ambiguity. These disputes are considered in the section on factual and verbal disputes. In the last section the use of euphemisms to deceive people is discussed along with another verbal ruse called persuasive definition.

Intension and Extension

It accords with common sense to distinguish two dimensions or aspects of meaning for a word or expression: The denotation or extension of a word or expression and the connotation or intension of a word or expression. For reasons of brevity let us just use "word" for the longer phrase "word or expression." The things or individuals to which a word can be truly applied are said to constitute the *denotation* or *extension* of the word. Thus some of the individuals found within the extension of the word "logician" would be Aristotle, George Boole, John Venn, Bertrand Russell, Kurt Gödel, and W. V. Quine. There are at least nine things to which the word "planet" can be truly applied and thus nine things are found within the extension of the word "planet"; namely, Mars, Venus, Mercury, Saturn, Pluto, Jupiter, Uranus, Neptune, and Earth. The *connotation* or *intension* of a word, for example, the intension of the word "logician," consists of the features something must have for the word to apply truly to it. In order to qualify as a logician a thing must have the properties or features of being a person and being knowledgeable about logic. The intension of the word "planet" would be this set of properties: any natural body, except a comet or a meteor, that revolves about the sun of a solar system. Put in other terms, the extension of a word is the class of things to which a word truly applies, whereas the intension of a word is the collection of properties which determine whether a thing is a member of the class denoted by the word.

As an aid to understanding these notions it is useful to notice several things. First, words can have intension without extension. If there is nothing which a word or phrase denotes, then it has no extension. There is a type of word that denotes nothing but which nevertheless connotes a set of properties. Such words are called *empty terms*. Illustrations of empty terms would be "furry fish," "unicorn," "square circle," and presumably "perfect husband." Also, a word or phrase may have only one thing that comes within its extension but it may be possible that it could be truly applied to more than one thing. This is true of the phrase "natural satellite of the earth." Some words may have extension without intension. One view of the matter is that many proper names are words with extension but without intension. Interestingly, two words can have the same extension and yet have different intension; consider, for example, "Indian head nickel" and "buffalo nickel," or the classic example, "human beings" and "featherless bipeds" (ignoring plucked chickens). However, if two words have the same intension, then they must have the same extension, for if the intension of a word determines the class of things denoted by the word, then the same intension insures the same denotation. Two different words can have the same intension. For example, "ascend" and "climb" have the same intension, as do "slender" and "slim," along with "man" and "rational animal," or "square" and the phrase "rectangle with equal sides."

Since there are these two aspects of meaning, it follows that when we speak of the meaning of a word we can be talking about the intension of the word, when the word has an intension; the extension of the word, when it has an extension; or both. Typically, a definition for a word is regarded as giving the meaning of the word. We commonly speak of sentences which indicate the intension of a word as giving the definition for the word. For example, the following would be commonly taken as clear examples of definitions:

> "Pentagon" means "plane figure with five sides."
> "Septuagenarian" means "a person who is seventy or more but less
>   than eighty years old."
> "Hammer" means "an instrument having a hard, solid head, usually of
>   metal, set traversely to the handle, and used mostly for pounding."

However, one can also give definitions by enumeration or by ostensive
definition and thus work on the level of extension. If one lists the things
which come within the extension of a word, one gives what is called a
definition by enumeration. For example, "word" is used in this chapter in a
certain way, and one can identify its use by indicating that a word is either a
general term (a term which can be true of one or more things) or a singular
term (a term which can be true of only one thing, e.g., a proper name). In
turn, what is meant by "logical term" can be indicated by enumeration of the
things which are logical terms; one such enumeration would be "not,"
"and," "or," "if, then," "all," "some," and identity. There are limits to
definition by enumeration. Such definitions are theoretically ruled out
where the word denotes an infinite class, e.g., "positive integers," or when
the word denotes an endless number of things, e.g., "atoms" or "dogs."

But a type of extensional definition is possible for even these last kinds of
words. We can give what are called ostensive definitions. In indicating the
meaning of a word, we give what is called an *ostensive definition* when we
somehow present a thing which is found within the extension of the word. To
explain the meaning of the word "sepia" by pointing to the rich brown color
prepared from the inky secretion of the cuttlefish, or "dog" by showing
someone a picture of Fido is to give an ostensive definition. If one explains
the meaning of "equivocation fallacy" by drawing attention to:

> Only man is rational.
> No woman is a man.
> Therefore all women are irrational.

or if one explains the meaning of "positive integer" by drawing on the
blackboard:

> $\{1, 2, 3, \ldots\}$

he would in each case be using an ostensive definition.

An ostensive definition is a *nonverbal* definition for a word. When an
ostensive definition is given for a word, other words need not be used to
explain the meaning of the word in question, as they need to be used in an
intensional definition. One must use a verbal definition to give the intension
of a word, but in an ostensive definition, one directs attention to actual

objects denoted by that word. A moment's reflection should be sufficient to realize that some words must be defined nonverbally for language to be possible. Unless some words had their meaning given nonverbally, there would be no words with meaning which could be used to explain the meaning of other words. Ostensive definitions are necessary, in other words, to link language to reality. Without ostensive definition or definitions by enumeration, all definitions would be circular; or else explaining the meaning of any word would lead to a vicious regress. In most natural languages the meanings of words such as "red," "sweet," "pain," "between" are learned in an ostensive way through exposure to things they denote.

It is helpful to note that, in general, definitions are designed to show how the various words are used. To exhibit the extension of a word, by enumeration or an ostensive definition, is to call attention to those things we use the word to refer to. To give an intensional definition is simply to list those properties or characteristics a thing must have in order for one to use the word to refer to it. And, with simple words and some other words, one often learns how to use them by observing how others use them. Thus, there is a close connection between the meaning of a word and how it is used.

EXERCISES 3.1

A. For each of the following words indicate part of their extension and their intension.

1. university (She goes to the university.)
2. uncle (He plans to visit his uncle.)
3. river (He is looking for the source of the Nile River.)
4. history (Arnold Toynbee writes history.)
5. senator (Joe McCarthy was a senator.)
6. men (All men are created equal.)
7. mobilization (Meet the enemy's bluff with mobilization.)
8. argument (Arguments ought to be sound.)

B. Sort out the pairs below in terms of potential intensional definition or extensional definition.

1. mother/a parent of the female sex
2. courage/Samson's killing the young lion with his bare hands
3. sulky/sullen
4. love/never having to say you're sorry
5. a is soluble/if a is placed in water a will dissolve
6. politician/Richard Nixon and Hubert Humphrey and men like them
7. a is *harder* than b/a can scratch b, but b cannot scratch a
8. a basketball team/a center, two guards, and two forwards

ANSWERS

A. 1. Partial extension: Harvard University, University of California, Arizona State University.

Intension: "university" means "an institution of higher learning providing facilities for teaching and research and authorized to grant advanced academic degrees."

B. 1. Intensional.   **3.** Intensional.   **5.** Intensional.   **7.** Intensional.

Paradigm Examples, Semantic Features, and Criteria

Let us understand by a *paradigm example* for a word, a clear example of a thing which comes under the extension of the word. For most words we have no difficulty indicating paradigm examples. Monopoly is a paradigm example of a game, the Hancock Building in Chicago is a paradigm example of a skyscraper, Alonzo Church is a paradigm example of a logician, and tampering with a computer program so that the computer which tallies the votes in an election favors one candidate is a paradigm example of political fraud.

If one asks what the features are in paradigm examples which justify applying the word in question to the paradigm, one is asking for what will now be called *semantic features*. If one asks what the semantic features of the man who is coming down the driveway are that justify our speaking of him as a "bachelor," then the answer would be "an unmarried adult male." As another illustration, the civil conflict in France in 1789 may be regarded as a paradigm example of a revolution. What justifies our calling this event a revolution? That is, what are the semantic features of this event which is found within the extension of the word "revolution"? They are more or less this: it is an event in which the group wielding power in the country was expelled by force, and a new government was established. Let us call the set of semantic features (such as, an event in which the group wielding power in a country is expelled by force, and a new government is established) a *criterion* for applying the word "revolution." In general a set of features which justify our speaking of a thing as W is a criterion for the word "W."

It is obvious that there is an intimate connection between semantic features, criteria for a word, and the intension of a word. To make clear the nature of these relations it will prove useful to construct three models. For simplicity let us suppose that objects a_1, a_2, a_3, a_4, and a_5 are the complete extension of the word "W," and that each is a paradigm example of a W. Furthermore let us suppose that F is the one and only semantic feature for applying the word "W" to a_1–a_5. This state of affairs can be illustrated as follows:

$$W$$

Model I	a_1	a_2	a_3	a_4	a_5
	F	F	F	F	F

To say that "W" means "F" when the word "W" satisfies model I, is to give the intension of the word "W," and it is also to give the one and only criterion for applying the word "W," since F is the only semantic feature. If we now suppose that a word satisfies model I whether there are n number of a's or an infinite number of a's, and if F is taken as designating either a simple or a compound property, then it is easy to give examples of words in our language that satisfy model I. In ordinary discourse "bachelor," "pentagon," and "septuagenarian," from the previous section, all satisfy model I. The general term "red" can be construed as satisfying model I, since the possession of the property red is the one and only criterion for saying that a thing is red (this is not to suggest that one can give an intensional definition for "red"). Usually words that satisfy model I are so used that a decision has been made that not only is F the criterion or sufficient condition for something being W, it is also a necessary condition. In other words, the term is used such that both of the following are true by convention or practice:

If F, then W. (F is a sufficient condition for W.)
If W, then F. (F is a necessary condition for W.)

If a word satisfies model I in this way, one can give what is called an *exact definition* for the word; thus an exact definition is a definition that has the form:

"W" means "F"

where F is a single property or conjunction of properties and where having F is by convention or practice necessary and sufficient for W. For example,

"triangle" means "a polygon having three sides"

is an exact definition. If anything has the sum of these properties:

is a polygon
has three sides

then this is sufficient for it to be a triangle. And each feature or property is such that if anything is a triangle it must have both features. Both features are necessary for something to be a triangle. It goes without saying that in any context where precision is needed—for example, in any rigorous development of a discipline such as mathematics, logic, or physics—exact definitions for words used are to be prized. Many exact definitions are given for the working words in this text, for example: "fallacy" means "an incorrect argument that can erroneously seem to some to be correct."

Not all words can be given exact definitions if not all words are so used that they satisfy model I. And this state of affairs seems to obtain. For it seems that there are many words for which we cannot provide an exact definition. When we propose exact definitions for words like "building," "pen," "ball," and "game," we can without too much trouble come up with *counterexamples* to the proposed exact definitions. For example, will the following exact definition work for the word "building"?

> "Building" means "a constructed object with walls and roof built for permanent use."

If anything is a building must it have each of these features? Cannot we have buildings not built for permanent use, say temporary prefabs? Must a building have walls? What about wall-less structures in warm climates, or geodesic-dome apartment houses? Cannot there be roofless buildings, say, a tent-shaped building? Does a building have to be constructed? Also, is the sum of these features sufficient for something being a building? Might not a nonbuilding have each of these features? Consider, for example, a mobile home. If an exact definition cannot be given for "building" as it is used in the ordinary context, then the word so used cannot satisfy model I. What kind of model does it satisfy?

Many words, especially words used in nonformal contexts, seem to satisfy other models. Two such models will now be outlined. In the second model each of the paradigm examples will have one semantic feature in common but will have other semantic features as well. Let the common feature be designated by F. As before, F may be either a simple or a compound property. However, we also wish to have different criteria for the paradigms, or at least not have each paradigm with the same criterion. In short, we want "W" in this model to have criteria for its application. To indicate this possibility, G, H, I, and J will be used. These letters may also be simple or compound properties. The second model follows.

			W		
Model II	a_1	a_2	a_3	a_4	a_5
	F, G, I	F, H, I	F, H, J	F, G, J	F, G, H

In the next model we wish to have *no* common semantic feature. Here is the third model:

			W		
Model III	a_1	a_2	a_3	a_4	a_5
	F, G, K, I	F, G, H, J	F, G, I, J	F, H, I, J	G, H, I, J

We again treat the models as allowing for n number of individuals or infinite numbers of them, and we suppose there may be any number of semantic features. Let us consider some examples of words which seem to satisfy these latter two models. The word "ball" as used in "The player hit the ball down the third-base line" satisfies, it seems, the second model. Though the many things denoted by the word "ball" have different semantic features, a pervasive feature of them seems to be: being spherical. The word "pen" as it is used to refer to those familiar objects people write with also seems to satisfy the second model. We call feathers and quills "pens," we call ballpoint pens "pens," we call instruments we fill with ink "pens," we call instruments with felt tips "pens," and so on. In each case there are certain semantic features not found in other cases; however, a common feature is this: being a thing used to write with.

Ludwig Wittgenstein (1889–1951) in *Philosophical Investigations* suggests the following paradigm of a word that satisfies the third model:

> Consider for example the proceedings that we call "games." I mean board games, card games, ball games, Olympic games, and so on. What is common to them all?—Don't say: "There *must* be something common, or they would not be called 'games' "—but *look and see* whether there is anything common to all.—For if you look at them you will not see something that is common to *all*, but similarities, relationships, and a whole series of them at that. To repeat: don't think, but look!—Look for example at board games, with their multifarious relationships. Now pass to card games; here you find many correspondences with the first group, but many common features drop out, and others appear. When we pass next to ball games, much that is common is retained, but much is lost.—Are they all "amusing"? Compare chess with noughts and crosses. Or is there always winning and losing, or competition between players? Think of patience. In ball games there is winning and losing; but when a child throws his ball at the wall and catches it again, this feature has disappeared. Look at the parts played by skill and luck; and at the difference between skill in chess and skill in tennis. Think now of games like ring-a-ring-a-roses: Here is the element of amusement, but how many other characteristic features have disappeared! And we can go through the many, many other groups of games in the same way; can see how similarities crop up and disappear.
>
> And the result of this examination is: we see a complicated network of similarities overlapping and criss-crossing: sometimes overall similarities, sometimes similarities of detail.

The *Oxford English Dictionary* provides this definition for the word "game": "Game" means "a diversion of the nature of a contest, played according to rules, and decided by superior skill, strength or good fortune." As we can see, this is a fairly accurate list of most of the semantic features of the paradigm examples of the things we call games. The use of "or" in the definition shows that some of the semantic features need not be present in each paradigm. But do any of these features need to be present? Is it true that all things that we call games have these features? It seems not; for example, not all games are diversions, in the sense of being played for fun. War games are not played for fun, but are part of training for officers and men. Folk games are not contests, though they involve rules, skill, and so on. Children's games are not always played according to rules, as, for example, the games children play in the bath tub. And so forth.

The mechanism which explains why an *a* in model I comes under the extension of the word "*W*" is the common criterion. The common criterion determines the class of things which come within the extension of the word "*W*." But what explains the extension with respect to words which satisfy models II and III? The answer is, in the main, *resemblance*. The common feature found in model II helps to promote this resemblance. And with models II and III we have what is now called *family resemblance*. As we know, members of the same family may resemble each other in, for example, manner of talking, way of smiling, way of holding the head, expression of pleasure, facial features (high cheekbones, bushy eyebrows, green eyes, aboriginal nose, high forehead, cleft chin, dimpled cheeks, ruddy complexion, and so on), intellect, and so on. Yet in, say, nine members of the family, not all these features need to be present, and possibly, the members of the family will have no single family distinguishing feature in common. But still they could all be unmistakably members of the same family. We should note that members of a family a_1 and a_5, taken *by themselves*, may not resemble each other, would not be taken to be members of the same family, but taken with the other members they can be seen to belong to the same family. Or to put this in another way, a_1 and a_5 may have no family distinguishing features in common yet still may resemble each other *via* the other members of the family.

Many words used in ordinary discourse are learned in connection with paradigm examples. The child notices that a thing is called *W* (usually a paradigm). The child then calls this thing and things like it *W* and is corrected by parents and others if he strays. In this process children learn when and when not to call something *W* because of the paradigms and the similarity of things to these paradigms. People understand each other when they use words learned in this way because if asked what they mean they would cite similar paradigms, or their behavior exhibits that they use words with similar paradigms. Again, what determines whether *a* is similar to a paradigm is what society takes as similar, there being, of course, explanations for why certain properties are selected.

The intension of words that satisfy model II or model III can also be given by using an intensional definition. This is properly done by citing the inclusive disjunction of typical criteria for the paradigms. In other words, intensional definitions for such words take the form:

"W" means "C_1 or C_2 or . . . or C_n"

where the C's are typical criteria for the word "W," the criteria for the paradigms. And where by "or" is meant "either one or the other (or both)," the inclusive use of the word "or." Frequently, however, in response to a requested definition for a word which satisfies model II or model III, only one or two criteria are given, with the intention that the listener will pick up the family resemblance. Also it is not infrequent that a person might use such a word with only one criterion in mind. Thus, for example, if he were asked to paraphrase the word out of his sentence, he would replace it with just one C rather than C_1 and the disjunction of the other C's.

One procedure for determining the intension of words that satisfy model II or model III is first to consider a number of cases in which persons use the word "W" and in which the things referred to are all paradigmatic. Then formulate a hypothesis to account for the fact that the word "W" is used in these cases. The hypothesis can take this form:

H: If x is W, then x has _____

where names for hypothesized semantic features replace _____ and are linked using "and" or "or" or "usually." For example such an H might be "If x is a book, then x is printed words on sheets of paper bound together usually between hard or soft covers." Third, one considers nonparadigmatic uses of the word "W" to see if H holds, and one considers more paradigmatic uses to see if H holds. In this way one sharpens up the H. This procedure in fact is followed by those who write dictionary entries.

If a word "W" satisfies model I, then if the same word "W" is also used in connection with paradigms that lack F, we would say that the word has a second intension. Analogously, if a word, "W," satisfies model II or model III, then a family resemblance exists among the paradigms because of the semantic features. If this same word, "W," is used in connection with a's that lack all these semantic features, then we would say that the word has a second intension, since any family resemblance is ruled out. Or if an a simply lacks a family resemblance to the other a's which fall within the extension of "W" and "W is used to denote the first kind of a's, then it would be said that "W" has more than one intension. Most ordinary words have two or more intensions. For example, the word "table" has at least these six intensions: (1) a piece of furniture, (2) a set of laws (the twelve tables of Rome), (3) an indelible record (the everlasting tables of right reason), (4) a tabular arrangement of data (a truth table in logic), and (5) a parliamentary procedure: to remove from consideration indefinitely. And "connotation" has at least two intensions: (1) intension and (2) subjective association one has with a word.

EXERCISES 3.2

1. Formulate some possible exact definitions for words (select any words) and consider whether counterexamples are possible. *e.g. brother*
2. Try to give some examples of words which satisfy each of the three models. The last exercise may have suggested such words.

   Be sure to justify your answer. *for III – philosophical words*

   Hint: If a dictionary entry for a word uses a word for disjunction, "or," or the word "usually," then this normally indicates a model II or model III word (or at least a nonmodel I word). For example, "table" means "a piece of furniture consisting of a smooth flat slab fixed on legs *or* other supports and *usually* used for eating, writing, working, *or* playing of games."

Proper Names

If every word has an intension and an extension—and this is the claim of one theory of meaning—then so do proper names. Consider, for example, the proper name "Thales." What is its intension? The only possibility would appear to be the description or descriptions we associate with the name. The description we usually associate with this name seems to be this one:

The philosopher who said that everything is water.

If this is the intension of "Thales," then to say

(1) Thales is a philosopher.

is to make a claim logically analogous with

(2) Triangles have sides.

But this view faces difficulties. On this view (2) is necessarily true. It expresses a state of affairs that cannot be otherwise. It is impossible, logically impossible, that triangles do not have sides. But it seems that even though Thales was the philosopher who said that everything is water, he might not have said this. He might not even have been a philospher, just as Plato might not have been a philosopher. So (1) might be false, and thus is not analogous to (2).

This difficulty has suggested to some that the intension of a proper name should be construed as the proper descriptions associated with the name in a *loose* sort of way. To explain this view consider the proper name "Aristotle."

Here is a partial list of the descriptions we associate with this name.

D1   the teacher of Alexander the Great
D2   the author of the *Poetics*
D3   the founder of the Lyceum
D4   the best student of Plato
D5   the Greek philosopher born about 348 B.C.

On the view in question, none of the following is necessarily true:

Aristotle is the teacher of Alexander the Great.
Aristotle is the author of the *Poetics*.
and so on.

The following, however, are necessarily true:

(3)   If x is Aristotle, then some of the D's are true of x.
(4)   If a sufficient number of D's are true of x, then x is Aristotle.

On this view descriptions give the intension of names. But no one description does, nor does a certain set of descriptions. When we say "x is Aristotle" we are not saying:

x has D_1 and . . . and D_n

but rather

A sufficient number of D's are true of x.

But this view also faces difficulties. Neither (3) nor (4) appears necessary. It is possible that Aristotle did none of the things we associate with him. And could not someone else have done all the things we associate with him?

The view that a proper name has intension and that the intension is the descriptions we associate with the name is nevertheless attractive. It explains and gives a simple, easy to understand account of how the reference of a name is determined. If the intension of "Thales" is "the philosopher who said everything is water," then whatever x satisfies this description is the referent of "Thales" when we use the name. Let us call the view that the reference of the names we use is determined by the descriptions we associate with the names, the *description theory of reference*. Now the descriptions we associate with a name can fix reference without these descriptions being the intension of the name. The description "the philosopher who said everything is water" can fix the reference of "Thales" without our meaning by "Thales," "the philospher who said everything is water." This description can fix the reference of "Thales" without (1) being necessarily true. So if proper names have intensions, then the description theory follows. But the description theory can be true even if names have no intension. That is, names may not have intensions; nevertheless, the way that we fix the reference of a name may be through the descriptions we associate with the names we use.

On the description theory of reference someone, say, S, refers to x using a name "a" because S associates with "a" a description or descriptions that x uniquely satisfies. But this theory of how the reference of a name is determined faces its difficulties. People often use names without knowing any description that their referents satisfy uniquely, or they use names with descriptions that satisfy things other than their referent. For example, I may not know anything about Karim Abdul Jabbar other than that he is a great basketball player, yet I can still refer to him. Most likely we associate one or both of the following descriptions with the proper name "Columbus":

> The man who first realized that the earth is round.
> The first European to land in America.

Probably neither of these things is true of Columbus. The man who first realized that the earth is round was most likely a Greek and, no doubt, some Viking "discovered America." So when we use the proper name "Columbus" are we really referring to some Greek or some Norseman? Of course not.

But if the descriptions we associate with the names we use do not determine reference, what does? One theory recently given is that the referent of a name is the object that has a particular causal relation to that name, regardless of whether that object has any of the properties the user of the name believes its referent to have. This is commonly called the *causal theory of reference*. It is to be contrasted with the description theory of reference. Saul Kripke, a contemporary American philosopher, has sketched an outline of the causal theory of reference.[1] Here is his discussion of one case:

> Someone, let's say, a baby, is born; his parents call him by a certain name. They talk about him to their friends. Other people meet him. Through various sorts of talk the name is spread from link to link as if by a chain. A speaker who is on the far end of this chain, who has heard about, say Richard Feynman, in the marketplace or elsewhere, may be referring to Richard Feynman even though he can't remember from whom he ever heard of Feynman. . . . He then is referring to Feynman even though he can't identify him uniquely.[2]

Although Kripke does not put it exactly this way, his words suggest the following procedure for finding the referent of a name that speaker S uses. First, find the point at which S acquired the use of the name from A; if A's

---

[1] Saul Kripke, "Naming and Necessity," Davidson and Harmon (eds.), *Semantics of Natural Language* (Dordrecht: Reidel, 1972), pp. 253–355.
[2] Kripke, pp. 298–299.

use is derived from someone else's, say *B*'s use of the name, trace the origin of *B*'s use, and so on. Eventually, if the name has a referent, the chain will end with an initial act in which an object is given the name, and this object is then the referent of *S*'s use of the name. Such causal chains can be quite short or they may be exceedingly long, reaching back many years. On this view the descriptions we associate with a name do not determine reference for names. Rather, reference for names is determined by tracing a historical chain back to the original dubbing occasion.

Two points can help in understanding this view. First, descriptions can be used to fix the reference of a name when an object is given a name. A name need not be introduced by ostensive dubbing. In the original dubbing one need not actually point to the bearer of the name. For example, we can dub the first man born in 2000, "Newman." This description:

The first man born in 2000.

fixes the reference of the name and only this description fixes the reference of the name, since Newman does not now exist. Yet even in this case it is not necessarily true that

Newman is born in 2000.

For it is possible that the first person born in 2000 might have been delivered a few days earlier. In other words even in cases where a name is introduced not by ostensively dubbing an object but by the use of a description it seems natural to say that the meaning of the name is not the meaning of the description.

Second, the original semantic reference of any proper name can be overridden by another semantic reference. The *semantic reference* of a name is its conventional meaning and it is determined by a causal chain. This is to be contrasted with the *speaker's reference* which is the object which the speaker wishes to talk about on a given occasion. Generally, these coincide, but they need not. One might have watched TV last year and seen Carter's look-alike in a TV commercial. One might have thought that it was Carter and said, "Jimmy Carter is now endorsing Billy's Beer." In this example the speaker's reference would be the man in the TV commercial, while the semantic reference of "Jimmy Carter" is the 39th president of the United States. To illustrate how the original semantic reference of a proper name can be overridden, consider the following case: Scholarly consensus is that the prophet Jonah is an historical person, but that the Old Testament account of him is not history but myth. It may well be that it has become habitual in our speech community to use "Jonah" in such a way that the reference of "Jonah" is exclusively fixed in terms of the fellow who was tossed overboard for displeasing God, who was swallowed up by a big fish, and three days later was cast up upon the shore unharmed. If so, the semantic reference of "Jonah" has shifted from the historical prophet to the person in the myth.

Do proper names have intension? It seems that the descriptions we associate with names do not constitute the intension of names, even if the descriptions are loosely related to a supposed intension. Proper names in the language do not have verbal definitions. But even if descriptions cannot be identified with the meaning of names, do descriptions fix reference in the manner claimed by the description theory of reference? Or is reference fixed in the way claimed by the causal theory of reference? It is our view that these theories need to be worked out in more detail before these questions can be answered.

EXERCISES 3.3

For each of the following italicized names, indicate some descriptions that are associated with the name. Are any of these descriptions, *D*, such that for the name *N* the following sentence

If *x* is *N*, then *x* is *D*.

is necessary?

1. Richard Wagner wrote *Götterdämmerung*.
2. The Greeks once called *Dionysius, Bacchus*. *nec.*
3. *Gottlob Frege* initiated the modern development of deductive logic. *not nec.*
4. *Douglas MacArthur* directed Allied forces in the Pacific during World War II. *not necessary*
5. *Teddy Kennedy* may become President of the United States. *- not nec.*
6. *Hamlet* killed *Ophelia*. *- may be necessary*
7. *Columbus* discovered America. *- not nec.*
8. *Sleeping Beauty* was awakened by a prince. *- may or may not be nec.*

ANSWERS

1. the last opera of the Ring Cycle
   "If *x* is *Götterdämmerung*, then *x* is the last opera of the Ring Cycle" is not necessary. Wagner might have written *Götterdämmerung* and never had any ideas concerning writing any other operas.
5. the brother of Robert and Jack Kennedy
   "It *x* is Teddy Kennedy, then *x* is the brother of Robert and Jack Kennedy" is not necessary.
6. son of Queen Gertrude
   "If *x* is Hamlet, then *x* is the son of Queen Gertrude" may be necessary; thus fictional names may have intensions.

Real and Nominal Definitions

If proper names do not have intension, may not all or some general terms also lack an intension? Recently it has been suggested that words for natural kinds like "gold," "water," "heat," "red," "lightning," and "pain" do not have intensions. For example, consider the word "gold" and this plausible account of how it gets a use in the language: The term "gold" is introduced by dubbing some original samples of gold "gold." Descriptions may be used to pick out samples, say: "the yellow, malleable, shining metal on the table," but the meaning of "gold" is not the meaning of "the yellow, malleable shining metal." The extension of "gold" is determined by the actual nature of the originating samples and other paradigms, not by any description that the user of "gold" may have in mind. When we introduce such a term we do not have to know the nature of the stuff we are naming. We hope that such knowledge will come with empirical scientific investigations. If x has the same internal constitution as the original sample, then x is gold. If the supposition that there is one constitution in the initial samples proves wrong, we drop the term "gold" or declare that there are two kinds of gold. If we are in doubt whether x is gold, we rely on experts, if there are any, to determine if x is gold. The experts rely on scientific theories. Experts tell us that gold is an element with atomic number 79, so whether x is gold is determined by whether x is an element with atomic number 79. Iron pyrite looks and behaves in many ways like gold, but it is not gold because it is not the element with atomic number 79.

Now we typically associate descriptions with natural kind words, for example:

"gold" and "the heavy, yellow, highly malleable, precious metal"
"tiger" and "the large carnivorous quadrupedal feline, tawny yellow in color with blackish transverse stripes and white belly"

It may be thought that such descriptions constitute the intension of these words. Against this, it may be argued that these descriptions just fix reference of words and it is not necessary that gold be yellow, for example, or that tigers have stripes. But what about these descriptions:

"gold" and "the element with atomic number 79"
"water" and "H_2O"

Aren't these intensions? Again, it may be argued that these descriptions simply fix the reference of the words. These descriptions are part of our scientific theories about gold and water, but our theories evolve and are not immune from changes. They do not express necessary truths.

If natural kind terms do not have intensions, how does one explain the role of dictionary definitions for natural kind terms such as "gold" and "tiger"? Some have suggested that dictionary definitions for natural kind words are not presentations of the intensions of these words but are ways to fix the reference of the words. Dictionary definitions for natural kind terms function in a way analogous to descriptions which are used to fix the reference of proper names. A dictionary may define "gold" as "being a heavy, yellow, highly malleable, precious metal." Clearly, we look to these features to determine whether x is gold. But on this view these features are only contingently related to gold. For it is conceivable that gold could turn out not to be yellow, for example. An item may possess all the characteristics we customarily use to pick out gold and yet fail to be gold. A dictionary defines "tiger" as "a large carnivorous quadrupedal feline, tawny yellow in color with blackish transverse stripes and white belly." But is it a contradiction to suppose that tigers never have four legs? If "feline" just means having the appearance of a cat, might x be a cat and yet have none of these features? Also one might find animals in some parts of the world which, though they look just like tigers, on examination were discovered not even to be mammals. They are, let's suppose, very peculiar looking reptiles. (The English sparrow was found to be a finch.) Whether x is a cat is determined by whether x belongs to a particular biological family.

Let us call the view that all words have intensions and that the intension of a word determines its extension, the *traditional theory of meaning*. Let us call the view that words have extensions but not intensions, the *new theory of meaning*.

There seems to be an important difference between terms like "gold," "water," "tiger," and "pain," and terms like "bachelor," "game," and "triangle." In using the latter we do not have some kind of thing before our eyes, name it, and then seek to discover the properties of what it is we have named, as we do in the case of "gold" or "tiger." Rather we have a certain description in mind in speaking of bachelors and games, and every object that satisfies the description constitutes part of the term's extension. In other words, terms like "bachelor" seem to satisfy the traditional theory of meaning, not the new theory. By "bachelor" we mean any unmarried male of marriage age. This definition does not represent an empirical discovery about bachelors. It is a rigid specification of what it is to be a bachelor. Thus some version of the traditional theory of meaning seems correct for non-natural kinds or what are called *nominal kinds*. In the case of *nominal kinds*, the essence of the thing (its essential properties) is expressed by definition. If so, it seems that both theories are needed to achieve an understanding of language. Language does not operate in just one way. So the two theories can be qualified in such a way that rather than exclude each other, they complement each other.

A tradition going back to Plato and Aristotle holds that we define things rather than words. Indeed, Aristotle defined "definition" as "a phrase signifying the essence of a thing." Aristotelian definitions are known as *real definitions*. In contrast, when we define a word or term with the aid of other words we give a *nominal definition*. Words that satisfy the traditional theory of meaning can be given nominal definitions, such as

"bachelor" means "unmarried adult male"

One cannot give a nominal definition for a word that satisfies the new theory of meaning since the word has no descriptive content. Thus there is no intension to fix by giving a nominal definition. If "definition" is restricted to sentences used to fix the intension of a word, then words satisfying the new theory of meaning cannot be given definitions. However, if "definition" is used in such a way as to include giving the essences of things, then sentences such as

Gold is the element with atomic number 79

would be an example of a non-nominal or real definition. Such definitions express our scientific theories. What this suggests is that the new theory of meaning applies to those general terms naming things which are in the scope of scientific theories, whereas the traditional theory of meaning applies to other general terms.

EXERCISES 3.4

Which of the following are real definitions and which are nominal definitions?

1. Human beings are rational animals.
2. An allergy is a hypersensitivity to a specific substance, such as food, pollen, or dust, or a condition, as heat or cold, which in similar amounts is harmless to most people.
3. Psychology is the science that deals with the mind and with mental and emotional processes.
4. Psychology is the science of human and animal behavior.
5. A marathon is a foot race of 26 miles, 385 yards, run over an open course.
6. Intelligence is what is measured by intelligence tests.
7. A public school in the United States is an elementary or secondary school that is part of a system of free schools maintained by public taxes and supervised by local authorities.
8. Petroleum is an oily, flammable, liquid solution of hydrocarbons, yellowish-green to black in color, occurring naturally in the rock strata of certain geological formations.
9. A tide is the alternate rise and fall of the surface of oceans caused by the attraction of the moon and sun.

10. Heat is a form of energy produced by the accelerated vibration of molecules.
11. A relation R is transitive if for all objects a, b, c, if R holds between a and b and between b and c, then it holds between a and c.
12. "Pusillanimous" means "faint-hearted."
13. x is a *prime number* if x is an integer and the only divisors of x are x and 1.
14. Full employment in the United States is a jobless rate of 5 percent or less.

ANSWERS

4. real **5.** nominal **10.** real **11.** nominal **12.** nominal

Ambiguity and Vagueness

Most words admit of what are called *borderline cases*. What this means is that for most words there are things which are such that we are uncertain (not as a result of lack of knowledge) whether to call them W or non-W. In other words, if a word "W" admits of borderline cases, then there are things which clearly come within the extension of "W," and things which do not clearly come within the extension of "W," and things which do neither, the borderline cases. Words that satisfy any of the previously discussed models can have borderline cases, though because of the lack of a sum of semantic features which is both sufficient and necessary for W in models II and III, words that satisfy these latter models are generically more prone to borderline cases than are words that satisfy model I. When a word "W" admits of borderline cases, then the following state of affairs obtains:

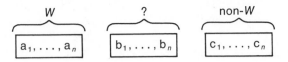

In this diagram $a_1, \ldots, a_n$ are paradigmatic individuals which fall within the extension of the word "W." $c_1, \ldots, c_n$ are all the individuals which do not fall within the extension of the word "W." $b_1, \ldots, b_n$ are the individuals that we are inclined to put in neither the right nor the left box, and this indecision is not a function of lack of knowledge about $b_1, \ldots, b_n$. What creates our uncertainty is that $b_1, \ldots, b_n$ are sufficiently similar to $a_1, \ldots, a_n$ not to be called non-W's, but, on the other hand, they are not sufficiently similar to $a_1, \ldots, a_n$ to be called W's. In the question mark cases, there simply has not been any good reason or motivation to make a decision as to whether these things are *W*'s. It is not that a (more-or-less) arbitrary decision cannot be made, it just has not been made. No convention has been adopted. A good reason to adopt such a convention would be, for example, to avoid constant misunderstandings.

Let us consider some examples of borderline cases. We are surrounded by objects some of which are and some of which are not colored red, but it is not difficult to find an object of a shade that falls just in between, an object of which we might, for example, want to say, "It is red and it is not red." Some people have little money, they are definitely not rich; others have millions; but there are others, who fall between, of whom we cannot say whether they are or are not rich. As "democracy" is often used in certain contexts, Britain, the United States, the Scandinavian countries, and the older countries of the British Commonwealth are all governed democratically. The Soviet Union, China, Greece, and Egypt are not democracies. But what about some South American republics? When one country stimulates and aids the revolutionary forces in another country, is this aggression? Is a U.N. peace force an army? Are we today living in a time of peace or of war? Is an agnostic or atheist who, on moral grounds, opposes killing in war a conscientious objector? Is the Pill medicine? Is a man who sees a crime committed while watching his television set, as millions saw Jack Ruby shoot Lee Harvey Oswald, a witness of the crime and therefore ineligible to sit on the jury that tries the offender? Are nuclear arms defense weapons? Does an unborn baby have any legal rights? Can you murder a creature from another planet? Are taxes collected on gambling winnings income tax? Is a person who lives only in the summer in a house he owns a resident of that community? Examples of borderline cases can be multiplied indefinitely.

Sometimes people find perplexing such questions as, "Are South American republics democracies?" "Does an unborn baby have legal rights?" "Are all athletes on Olympic teams amateurs?" In some ways these questions are perplexing and in some ways they are not. And the way in which they are not perplexing is often what accounts for people's being perplexed about them. Some people tend to think that these questions have answers in the way, say, that such questions as, "Is New York City the largest city in the world?" 'Is there life on Mars?" or "Is the United States a democracy?" have answers. But the former questions do not have such answers. Neither facts about the world not our use of language would provide a yes or a no answer to borderline case questions. All that we can say in response to such questions is that the thing in question is a borderline case, and if the circumstances are appropriate, we can give reasons for why the word in question should or should not be extended to cover the borderline cases. One should not think that such questions are unimportant questions since they are not about brute facts. Sometimes they deal with a vital issue, as will be illustrated in the next section. In any case, in a borderline question a *decision* needs to be made, and to appeal only to facts or usage is not sufficient to answer such questions.

When a word is said to be *vague*, at least three things can be meant, though these are not always distinguished. First the word can be intensionally vague. To say a word is *intensionally vague* is to say that it does not satisfy model I: it does not have a single criterion for its application; there is no sum of features that is both necessary and sufficient for things to come under the extension of the word. Any term for which one cannot provide an exact definition is intensionally vague. Generally speaking, in formal contexts the aim is to reduce intensional vagueness as far as possible. Second, to say that a word is vague can mean that it is extensionally vague. To say a word is *extensionally vague* means that it admits of borderline cases. Finally, to say a word is vague can mean that in some contexts we cannot understand it, not in the sense of finding one or more possible intensions for the word, but in the sense of not being able to recognize at all what its intension may be. Let us call this *contextual vagueness*. An executive committee member of an important society in the United States said at one time: "We of the solid right equate the Democratic Party with the welfare state, and the welfare state with socialism, and socialism with communism." It seems that the word "equate" here suffers from contextual vagueness. A psychologist ended a large volume on dreaming by asking the question, "Is wakefulness the more natural and fundamental state, in which sleep is only a restorative interlude, or is sleep the truly normal condition?" How, for example, are the words "natural and fundamental state" to be understood in this context? Finally, consider what "the people" might mean in the slogan "Return the government to the people."

To say that a word is ambiguous can mean at least two things. It can mean that the word is lexically ambiguous or contextually ambiguous. A word which has two or more definitions is said to be *lexically ambiguous*. Most words are lexically ambiguous. To illustrate, "fallacy" is lexically ambiguous since it has at least the following intensions: (1) an incorrect argument, (2) a widespread erroneous view (as in the "fallacy that the government will go broke if it has deficit budgets"), or (3) the use of "fallacy" in the "fallacy of the senses." "Argument" is lexically ambiguous since it has at least the following intensions: (1) a group of two or more statements, one of which is affirmed on the basis of the other or others, and (2) a dispute among two or more people.

Sometimes, however, a word is so used that even with careful inspection of the context, one can understand the word in two or more ways. Such words are *contextually ambiguous*. For example, if my sister-in-law said at the dinner table that her eight-year-old boy knows the meaning of the word "cybernation," this probably would be an instance of contextual ambiguity. "Knows the meaning" in this context could mean several things, among them: (1) can use the word "cybernation" correctly, or (2) can give the intension of the word. In a context "Hitler is alive" could mean that some are keeping the faith or that the Nazi leader is presently living in Argentina. In the 1940s a U.S. senator from Ohio placed this amendment in the Soldiers'

Voting Laws: "It is unlawful for any officer or executive to deliver to the troops any motion picture film containing political propaganda of any kind which might affect the result of an election for President." When a new biography of Justice Holmes and a film about Woodrow Wilson were withheld from the troops, the senator was indignant and said he had been misunderstood. It seems fair to say that in the senator's amendment the word "propaganda" can be understood in at least two ways, the way the army understood it—"propagation of a particular political view"—and the way the senator understood it—"false or distorted statements usually put out by some special interest group."

A word of caution: Just because one finds that a word can be understood in two or more ways does not mean that it is contextually ambiguous; it might be merely lexically ambiguous. Only if in context it can be understood in at least two ways can one say that the word is contextually ambiguous. During the riot-torn summer of 1967 a U.S. senator and party leader was asked the question, "Will the riots hurt the Democrats more than the Republicans?" He replied by saying that the question could be understood in several ways; for example, "Will Republicans suffer more property or bodily harm than Democrats?" He was guilty of failure to pay attention to the context or some other sin.

Fully analyzing an argument involves three steps. First, determine which statements are premises and which statement is the conclusion. Second, determine whether or not the argument claim is justified. That is, determine whether it is true that if the premises are supposed true then it is either impossible that the conclusion is false (deductive arguments) or improbable that the conclusion is false (inductive arguments). Third, determine whether or not the premises are true. If the premises are true and the argument is correct, then we have rational grounds for affirming the conclusion. But if contextual vagueness or ambiguity is present in the sentences which make up the argument, then we are frustrated in analyzing the argument and thus unable to judge whether the argument provides rational grounds for affirming the conclusion. We are unable to determine exactly what is being stated. So we may not be able to determine the structure of the argument, whether it is correct or not, or whether the premises are true. So a primitive requirement of a sound argument is freedom from contextual ambiguity or vagueness. An argument that does not have clear statements is a faulty argument, since a necessary condition for correctness is not satisfied.

To illustrate with a *simple* example let us consider again one of the dilemmas discussed in the previous chapter:

If we are to have peace, then we must not encourage the competitive spirit, while if we are to make progress, then we must encourage the competitive spirit. We must either encourage or not encourage the competitive spirit. Therefore we shall either have no peace or make no progress.

Here the structure of the argument is quite clear; it is a dilemma. But the argument suffers from contextual ambiguity. "Progress" can be understood in several ways in this context, for example: (1) increasing the wealth of a nation, (2) moving toward a more just society, (3) elimination of poverty and fairly distributing the wealth of a nation, (4) becoming the most powerful nation in the world, and so on. "Progress" means moving forward to some goal, and generally when we speak of progress we have some goal in mind. So different goals give us different criteria for "progress." In the above context the argument is too lean for us to be sure what the goal is, so we are unable to evaluate the conditional premises for correctness. (When we encountered this argument earlier we simply stipulated (1) and argued that the antecedents in the conditional premises do not provide good grounds for affirming the consequences.)

EXERCISES 3.5

A. First, imagine a paradigm case of a thing denoted by each word and a paradigm case of a thing not denoted by each word. Then for each word imagine a thing which is such that we would hesitate in calling it W or non-W; that is, imagine a borderline case for the word.

1. horse (People still ride horses.)
2. offensive weapons (Missiles are offensive weapons.)
3. magazine (*Time* is a weekly magazine.)
4. rain (It is raining.)
5. war (Two nations are at war.)
6. luxuries (Americans enjoy many luxuries.)
7. disturbing the peace (He was arrested for disturbing the peace.)
8. fanatic (He's a fanatic.)
9. religion (There are many religions of the world.)
10. spoon (Put the spoons on the table.)

B. In light of the discussion in this section, criticize the following arguments and statements:

1. Since the term "luxury" is a vague term—that is, since you cannot draw a line between those things which are luxuries and those things which are not luxuries—there is no real distinction between luxuries and things which are necessities. So stop looking that way at my new three-speed electric comb.
2. The only adequate way to explain the meaning of a word is by giving an exact definition. We cannot give exact definitions for most of our ordinary words, so we cannot make adequately clear what we mean.

3. The question is constantly debated in this assembly whether some country is an aggressor in some action. It is evident that we can never come to an agreement as things stand. I propose we appoint an impartial committee made up of members from both the East and the West and from neutral countries to find out what aggression *is*, so we can settle all these disagreements.

4. We cannot define a word without using other words. But we must understand the meaning of the words used in the definition. This can be done only by using still other words which in their turn will have to be defined, and so on. Thus it is theoretically impossible really to define a word.

5. Definitions are neither true nor false.

6. They tell me that we cannot provide exact definitions for most of our words because we don't use them in accordance with strict rules. Well, this is our fault. We should do something about it. Just think how clear our statements would be if our language was set straight. Just think of the misunderstandings which could be avoided.

7. Vagueness can be reduced, but it is impossible to eliminate it.

8. As we all know, there are a number of acts which we speak of as "just." There must be something in common in all these acts since we say they are all just. If we could find out what this is, then we could tell whether any act is just by seeing if it has that which just acts have in common. Philosophers have always wanted principles to tell just acts from unjust acts. Why don't they just work together and find out what this common characteristic (or characteristics) is!

9. Now, I continued, if two things, one large, the other small, are called by the same name, they will be alike in that respect to which the common name applies. Accordingly, insofar as the duality of justice is concerned, there will be no difference between a just man and a just society.   (PLATO, *The Republic*)

10. Words are poor instruments for the communication of thoughts. Although dictionaries give what may be called the official meaning of a word, no two people who use the same word have just the same thought in their minds. Words are ill-fitting garments for the thoughts they clothe.

11. "I don't know what you mean by 'glory,'" Alice said.

   Humpty Dumpty smiled contemptuously. "Of course you don't—till I tell you. I meant 'there's a nice knock-down argument for you!'"

   "But 'glory' doesn't mean 'a nice knock-down argument,'" Alice objected.

"When *I* use a word," Humpty Dumpty said, in rather a scornful tone, "it means just which I choose it to mean—neither more nor less."

"The question is," said Alice, "whether you *can* make words mean so many different things."

"The question is," said Humpty Dumpty, "which is to be master—that's all."

Alice was too much puzzled to say anything; so after a minute Humpty Dumpty began again. "They've a temper, some of them—particularly verbs: they're the proudest—adjectives you can do anything with, but not verbs—however, *I* can manage the whole lot of them! Impenetrability! That's what *I* say!"

"Would you tell me please," said Alice, "what that means?"

"Now you talk like a reasonable child," said Humpty Dumpty, looking very much pleased. "I meant by 'impenetrability' that we've had enough of that subject, and it would be just as well if you'd mention what you mean to do next, as I suppose you don't mean to stop here all the rest of your life."

(LEWIS CARROLL, *Through the Looking-Glass*)

12. SOCRATES: What is piety, and what is impiety?

EUTHYPHRO: Piety is doing as I am doing; that is to say, prosecuting anyone who is guilty of murder, sacrilege, or of any similar crime . . . and not to prosecute them is impiety. . . .

S: But . . . I would rather hear from you a more precise answer, which you have not as yet given, my friend, to the question, What is "piety"? When asked, you only replied, "Doing as you, charging your father with murder."

E: And what I said was true, Socrates.

S: No doubt, Euthyphro; but you would admit that there are many other pious acts?

E: There are.

S: Remember that I did not ask you to give me two or three examples of piety, but to explain the general idea which makes all pious things to be pious. Do you not recollect that there was one idea which made the impious impious, and the pious pious? . . . Tell me what is the nature of this idea, and then I shall have a standard to which I may look. (PLATO, *Euthyphro*)

13. . . . the meaning of the term will be what is common to the various examples pointed out as meant by it.

(C. I. LEWIS, *Mind and the World-Order*)

14. The purpose of Newspeak was not only to provide a medium of expression for the world-view and mental habits proper to the devotees of Ingsoc, but to make all other modes of thought impossible. It was intended that when Newspeak had been

adopted once and for all and Oldspeak forgotten, a heretical thought—that is, a thought diverging from the principles of Ingsoc—should be literally unthinkable, at least so far as thought is dependent on words. Its vocabulary was so constructed as to give exact and often very subtle expression to every meaning that a Party member could properly wish to express, while excluding all other meanings and also the possibility of arriving at them by indirect methods. This was done partly by the invention of new words, but chiefly eliminating undesirable words and by stripping such words as remained of unorthodox meaning, and so far as possible of all secondary meanings whatever. To give a single example. The word *free* still existed in Newspeak, but it could only be used in such statements as "This dog is free from lice" or "This field is free from weeds." It could not be used in its old sense of "politically free" or "intellectually free," since political and intellectual freedom no longer existed even as concepts, and were therefore of necessity nameless. Quite apart from the suppression of definitely heretical words, reduction of vocabulary was regarded as an end in itself, and no word that could be dispensed with was allowed to survive. Newspeak was designed not to extend but to *diminish* the range of thought, and this purpose was indirectly assisted by cutting the choice of words down to a minimum.   (GEORGE ORWELL, *1984*)[3]

Would Newspeak prevent heretical thoughts? Would it make *impossible* the concept of political or intellectual freedom? How would you go about stripping words of unorthodox meaning? In what way are thoughts dependent on language?

C.   Identify any occurrences of contextual ambiguity or vagueness in the following:

   1.   Alex Mair, vice-president of General Motors, has this to say against the 55 mph speed limit: "We have taken a step to modify the forward advancement of the country. . . . I don't think we should continue doing that. The nation needs a return to its feelings of leadership. Part of that is to lead in all things that we do. And, since the transportation system is a key to the nation's system, whichever nation exceeds in transportation is going to be a leader in other ways, and I think we Americans need to be and should want to be leaders. . . . We shouldn't look forward to the year 2000 and decide we're still going to be moving our system

[3] From *Nineteen Eighty-Four* by George Orwell. Copyright 1949. Used by permission of Secker and Warburg Ltd. and Brandt and Brandt (New York).

around at 55 mph. That is not fast enough to retain leadership as a nation." (LEON MANDEL, *Driven*)[4]

2. The Democratic Party has accepted since the New Deal the principle of national socialism. The only principle that represents a viable alternative to national socialism is the principle of rugged individualism. This made America become the wealthiest and the most free country in the world. Obstructing a political renaissance in our country is the fact it takes just plain guts to accept personal responsibility and risks inherent in the kind of freedom essential if everybody is to enjoy the maximum real peace and prosperity they want and need. The political party that provides leaders who inspire rugged individualism will win elections and can turn this country around. Then, and only then, can we reject national socialism and get back on the road to prosperity, freedom, and greatness.

3. A panel investigating the 1976 collapse of Idaho's Teton Dam, which caused the deaths of 14 persons and millions of dollars of damage, concluded that the collapse was caused by an unfortunate choice of design carried out with less than conventional precautions.

4. International terrorism is to be deplored. It is brought about by thrill seeking youth who have rationalized their activities by Marxist ideologies to end imperialism. The only way to fight these deluded "freedom fighters" is for nations to disarm. For you cannot end terrorism of the weak by terrorism of the strong.
    (Taken from SHANA ALEXANDER, *60 Minutes*, April 9, 1978)

5. On April 17, 1973 Ron Ziegler, President Nixon's press secretary, announced that all previous White House statements on Watergate were "inoperative."

6. It is argued that when government acts to discourage use of cigarettes it is dangerously tampering with the citizen's free will. But eighty percent of smokers acknowledge that smoking is harmful, and most smokers have tried to quit, but failed. And in what sense do smokers freely will the accumulation of tar in their chests?

7. Although the motives of the supporters of Equal Rights Amendment may be praiseworthy, the ERA, as a blanket attempt to help women, may bring even more restraints and repressions. I fear that the ERA may stifle many God-given feminine instincts. Men and women are equally important before the Lord, yet they have differences biologically, emotionally and in other ways. Unfortunately, ERA fails to recognize these differences. I am convinced there are better means than the ERA for giving women the rights they deserve.

---

[4] Leon Mandel, *Driven* (Briarcliff Manor, New York: Stein and Day, 1977), p. 102.

8. As a concerned citizen, I am interested in the fight against obscenity. The most repulsive form of obscenity is being allowed to manifest itself today wholly unchecked. I speak of the Nazi Storm Troopers who intend to parade again in Skokie, Ill., commemorating Hitler's birthday on April 29 [1978].

A learned judge has ruled that as Americans they have that privilege under the right of freedom of speech, even though this group of Nazis' shouting "Heil, Hitler!" can incite a riot just as surely as a man in a crowded theatre shouting "fire!" when there is no fire. Freedom of speech does not mean freedom to incite riot.

You question why their activities should be called obscene? Webster defines obscenities as "the immoral or offensive quality of thought, speech or representation."

Hitler, alone, has been affirmed as the "No. 1 war criminal" for his immoral and degrading acts against all mankind. His name and the Swastika, the symbol of his despotism, represent the most vicious forms of torture, murder and genocide. Were these not immoral and indecent—were they not obscene acts against mankind?   (THEODORE D. STEVENS, letter to the editor, *Arizona Republic,* April 13, 1978)

D. Locate any occurrences of contextual ambiguity or vagueness in the arguments given in Chapter 2.

ANSWERS

A. 9. The traditional religious faiths are religions and paradigm cases of things denoted by "religion." The body of beliefs that make up a scientific theory is not a religion (nor are telephones, for that matter). Some argue that the bodies of beliefs which conjoin members to modern political parties in industrial democratic countries are such that we would hesitate to speak of them as religions or as nonreligions.

B. 1. Vagueness, either intensional or extensional, does not imply that there is not a sharp distinction between clear-cut cases of things which are W and those which are not W.

2. If "adequate" means "successful," then there are many adequate ways. If "adequate" means "the only way open so as to prevent misunderstandings," then even exact definitions, in some circumstances, could be "inadequate." If "adequate" means "giving a description of the necessary and sufficient conditions," then the first sentence is a logical truth and it becomes impossible to give an adequate definition for any word which does not satisfy model I.

3. If "aggression" does not satisfy model I, there is no exact definition to be found.

4. Children pick up words without being given verbal definitions. We also give ostensive definitions. There is no infinite regress.

5. When someone reports the fact that a certain word means a certain thing to some particular group of people, then it seems appropriate to appraise such definitions as true or false insofar as they are factual reports.

6. If such rules were set down it would be difficult to enforce them, so such activity would be idle and silly. If such rules were followed, certain undesirable consequences would follow. For example, new metaphors would be ruled out. There would also still be the possibility of misunderstanding since ostensive definitions can be misunderstood and since borderline cases occur for model I words.

7. If this means that things imagined or otherwise can be borderline cases for any word, then this statement seems true.

8. Seems to presuppose that "just" is a model I word, and that conventional use of the word "just acts" determines whether an act is just or not.

10. For most ordinary words we have more or less the same paradigm examples in mind when we use them. We can always explain what we mean when we run into trouble.

11. There are certain contexts where stipulative definitions (in which we assign a word a meaning) are appropriate. Humpty Dumpty's use of them, as is clear, creates misunderstanding and confusion and hence negates the value they have in appropriate circumstances. Also one would hope that stipulative definitions would not be used to intimidate persons.

C. 2. "rugged individualism" 4. "disarm" and "terrorism of the strong" 6. "free will" 8. "obscenity"

Factual and Verbal Disputes

People sometimes find themselves in disagreement about facts. Sometimes their disputes can be resolved and sometimes they cannot. Disputes about what causes a particular disease or what Christ did when he was nineteen may not be resolvable at a given time. But sometimes what look like factual disputes turn out to be disputes arising because of some purely verbal difficulty, and it is to these disputes that we will turn presently.

But first, one should notice that there may be disputes generated by an error as to what a word, in fact, means. This is still a factual dispute, since the dispute will be settled once the facts about the meaning of the word or phrase generating the dispute are known. For example:

UTAH JENKINS: President Andrew Johnson was not impeached because to impeach a president is to find him guilty of a crime while in office and, as we know from reading our American history books, he was found not guilty.

UTAH WATKINS: President Johnson was impeached, though you are of course correct in saying that he was not found guilty of any crime, for to impeach a president is not to find him guilty of something, but merely to charge him with a crime or misbehavior in office.

The disagreement here is over what it means to impeach a president. Utah J. says it means one thing and Utah W. says it means another. There is a clear meaning for the word in this context, which can be found in a dictionary. Utah W. is correct.

It may also be the case that two disputants are using the same word or phrase in different senses, without realizing that they are doing so. This is no doubt common, but it is uninteresting and we need not spend too much time on this sort of pseudodispute. Here is an example:

FATHER: I wish you would turn off that radio. There is too much noise to read.

SON: That's not noise. That's a new group—the Bronx Cheer.

FATHER: It is noise. Turn it off.

The father is using "noise" as acoustical engineers do: "noise" is "unwanted sound." But his son, we may suppose, is using the word to mean "sound that is strident, loud, and displeasing." And, we may suppose, they would agree as to whether it is noise to one or the other when they agree or admit that they are using the word differently. We will call these disputes *pseudo-disputes*.

What distinguishes a pseudodispute from another kind of verbal dispute, which we will call the *definitional dispute*, is that in the pseudodispute the parties are not aware of the fact that they are using the key words in different ways and that once this is pointed out, they will cease and desist. They are not really disputing. In the definitional dispute, however, each party not only knows he is using words in a different way from the other party, but is arguing, essentially, that they *should* be used as he is urging. These are curious arguments, generally, since words have meanings resulting from the conventions governing their use, and, except in special circumstances, the meaning of a word cannot be decided upon by someone who has spotted a reason for changing it. Such special circumstances might arise when two people are inventing a technical term.

A subclass of this sort of argument is the argument as to whether a word is applicable to certain borderline cases, things that lack characteristics which would make the words unequivocally applicable, but possess enough of these characteristics to incline some to apply the word. We will speak of this inclination as an inclination to *extend* the use of a word. Sometimes we will have good reasons to extend the use of the word and sometimes we will not. Sometimes we will judge that something in the question mark area so strongly resembles our paradigm cases for a certain word that the word should be extended to cover this instance, and there will be times when the resemblance is so weak that we will decide not to extend the word, and so on.[5]

Such a judgment is made in an amusing way in *Alice in Wonderland.* Alice swallows a morsel of the left-hand side of a mushroom and grows an immense length of neck. Her head goes into a tree, where she encounters the Pigeon. Here is part of their conversation:

> "And just as I'd taken the highest tree in the wood," continued the Pigeon, raising its voice to a shriek, "and just as I was thinking I should be free of them at last, they must needs come wriggling down from the sky! Ugh, Serpent!"
>
> "But I'm not a serpent, I tell you!" said Alice. "I'm a— I'm a—"
>
> "Well! *What* are you?" said the Pigeon. "I can see you're trying to invent something!"
>
> "I—I'm a little girl," said Alice, rather doubtfully, as she remembered the number of changes she had gone through, that day.
>
> "A likely story indeed!" said the Pigeon, in a tone of the deepest contempt. "I've seen a good many little girls in my time, but never *one* with such a neck as that! No, no! You're a serpent; and there's no use denying it. I suppose you'll be telling me next that you never tasted an egg!"
>
> "I *have* tasted eggs, certainly," said Alice, who was a very truthful child; "but little girls eat eggs quite as much as serpents do, you know."
>
> "I don't believe it," said the Pigeon; "but if they do, why, then they're a kind of serpent: that's all I can say."

In this example, the Pigeon considers the fact that Alice has a long, snake-like neck and eats eggs enough to extend the use of the word "serpent" to cover Alice. Alice feels that the differences between a serpent and Alice in her strange state are great enough not to extend the use of "serpent" in this way.

Often we hear political liberals called socialists. What prompts this seems to be the following: Socialists (1) desire federal welfare legislation which would provide inexpensive medical care for everyone, unemployment compensation, old age retirement under Social Security, and the like. Socialists also (2) desire to remove concentrations both of poverty and of

---

[5] Resemblance between x and y is not the only reason we have to call y by the same name as x. The fact that x and y stand in the same relation to z might be a good reason, the fact that x and y are caused by the same z might be a good reason, and so on. See J. L. Austin, "The Meaning of a Word," *Philosophical Papers* (London, Oxford University Press, 1961). But we will ignore these cases in this chapter.

great wealth from among the people. Socialists (3) want government planning in the operation of the economy. Traditionally, political liberals also want (1), (2), and (3). This similarity has led to liberals being called socialists, even though socialists want, for example, (4) government ownership of the means of production. What we see here is an extension of the word "socialist." The similarity in (1), (2), and (3) has led people to extend the word. Some people, of course, feel that with (4) missing, the similarity is not sufficiently strong to extend the use of the word in this way.

It is obvious how these disputes arise, but it would be optimistic to suppose that all such disputes can be easily resolved. For example, in 1933 a United States district court considered the question of whether James Joyce's *Ulysses* was pornographic. In this case a great deal rested on whether the book was to be included in the class of pornographic literature. If the court decided it was pornographic, the book could be neither printed nor admitted into the United States. The presence of "dirty words" in *Ulysses* and the preoccupation with sex in the thoughts of the characters are what led those who instituted the suit to claim that it was pornographic. The decision that the Honorable John M. Woolsey made was that *Ulysses* is not pornographic, for commonly, if a piece of literature is pornographic, there must be the desire by the author to exploit the obscene. In addition, the judge said that *Ulysses* was not obscene within the legal definition of "obscene" ("tending to stir the sexual impulses or to lead to sexually impure and lustful thoughts"). This decision follows the convention that in order for a book to be pornographic there must be the desire on the part of the author to exploit the obscene, and he must have some success in doing this. Woolsey decided that the use of "pornographic" could not be extended so as to apply to *Ulysses*.

Important consequences were to follow from the following example: In March 1927 the case of *Olmstead* v. *United States* came to the Supreme Court. Roy Olmstead was head of a bootlegging ring in Seattle, Washington, which annually sold $2 million worth of liquor smuggled from Canada. Orders for liquor were telephoned. Four federal agents intercepted some of these telephone calls. No tapping of wires had been done on Olmstead's premises. The question before the Court was whether the Fourth Amendment to the Constitution can be extended to include the tapping of telephone wires. The Fourth Amendment reads, "The right of the people to be secure in their persons, houses, papers, and effects, against unreasonable searches and seizures, shall not be violated, and no warrants shall be issued, but upon probable cause, supported by oath or affirmation, and particularly describing the place to be searched and the persons or things to be seized." The defense argued that wiretapping is a case of "unreasonable search" and thus the evidence that Olmstead is a smuggler, since it comes from telephone calls intercepted without a warrant, is illegal. The prosecution argued that wiretapping does not come under the extension of the phrase "unreasonable search" as used in the Fourth Amendment, that the Amendment "cannot be extended and expanded to include telephone wires reaching to the whole world from the defendant's house or office.... Congress may, of course, protect the secrecy of telephone messages ... and thus depart from the common law of evidence. But the courts may not adopt such a policy by attributing an enlarged and unusual meaning to the Fourth Amendment." Justice Brandeis, for the dissenting opinion, wrote, "Whenever a telephone line is tapped, the privacy of the person at both ends of the line is invaded.... As a means of espionage, writs of assistance and general warrants are but puny instruments of tyranny and oppression when compared with wiretapping.... Decency, security and liberty alike demand that government officials shall be subjected to the same rules of conduct that are commands to the citizen.... Our government is the potent, the omnipresent teacher. Crime is contagious. If the government becomes a lawbreaker it ... invites anarchy."[6]

In this case a great deal rested on whether wiretapping of this kind is or is not considered a case of "unreasonable search" as the expression is used in the Fourth Amendment. Not only are Roy Olmstead's millions and his freedom at stake, but since judicial decisions, especially those given by the highest court of a country, serve as rules or norms for similar cases, the property, the privacy, and freedom of us all are affected.

Another dispute, which William James called a typical "metaphysical" problem, is the following:

> Some years ago, being with a camping party in the mountains, I returned from a solitary ramble to find every one engaged in a ferocious metaphysical dispute. The *corpus* of the dispute was a squirrel—a live squirrel supposed to be clinging to one side of a tree-trunk; while over against the tree's opposite side a human being was imagined to stand. This human witness tries to get sight of the squirrel by moving rapidly around the tree, but no matter how fast he goes, the squirrel moves as fast in the opposite direction, and always keeps the tree between himself and the man, so that never a glimpse of him is caught. The resultant metaphysical problem is this: *Does the man go round the squirrel or not?* He goes round the tree, sure enough, and the squirrel is on the tree; but does he go round the squirrel? In the unlimited leisure of the wilderness, discussion had been worn threadbare. Every one had taken sides, and was obstinate; and the numbers on both sides were even. Each side when I appeared therefore appealed to me to make it a majority.

William James thought that this was a verbal dispute which could be resolved in this way:

> Mindful of the scholastic adage that whenever you meet a contradiction you must make a distinction, I immediately sought out and found one, as follows: "Which party is right," I said, "depends on what you *practically* mean by 'going round' the squirrel. If you mean passing from the north of him to the

[6] From 277 U.S. 438.

east, then to the south, then to the west, and then to the north of him again, obviously the man does go round him, for he occupies these successive positions. But if on the contrary you mean being first in front of him, then on the right of him, then behind him, then on his left, and finally in front again, it is quite obvious that the man fails to go round him, for by the compensating movements the squirrel makes, he keeps his belly turned towards the man all the time, and his back turned away. Make the distinction, and there is no occasion for any further dispute. You are both right and both wrong according as you conceive the verb 'go round' in one practical fashion or the other."

Although one or two of the hotter disputants called my speech a shuffling evasion, saying they wanted no quibbling or scholastic hair-splitting, but meant just plain honest English "round" the majority seemed to think that the distinction had assuaged the dispute.[7]

James, as we can see, believes that if two senses of "going round" are distinguished, "there is no occasion for any further dispute." For the one party is using the phrase in one way, thus what they say is true; and the other party is using it in another way, and what they say is also true. The two senses of "going round" are

1.   Passing from the north of something, to the east, then to the south, then to the west, and then to the north again.
2.   Being first in front of something, then to the right, then behind, then to the left, and finally in front again.

Now James' solution is open to question. There is not a simple ambiguity that accounts for the dispute. His solution implies that one party *meant* (2) by "going round." But would anyone mean this by "going round"? If he did, then a man sitting on a couch would go around a man in a spinning swivel chair. A more realistic way to look at this dispute is as a word extension dispute. As we ordinarily use the phrase "going round," both (1) and (2) are true. The squirrel–tree–man situation is an unusual case, for (1) is true in this situation but (2) is not. One party thought the presence of (1) even with (2) missing was enough to extend the use of "going round" and the other did not. It is a case which falls in the question mark area discussed in the previous section.

Finally, let us consider another example that is even more complex and perhaps more typically philosophical, since it cannot be represented as simply a disagreement about extending the use of a word. It is more a matter of changing the use of a word.

When a tree falls in the wilderness with nobody around, will there be a sound?

JOHNNIE CRACK: No, there is no sound because no one is there to hear it.

---

[7] William James, *Pragmatism* (London: Longmans, Green, 1907), pp. 43–44.

FLOSSIE SNAIL: Of course there is a sound, regardless of whether anyone is there to hear it.

Frequently this dispute is represented as involving no disagreement either in fact or over the use of a word. "Sound" is said to have two meanings: (1) the physical phenomenon—the waves in the air—and (2) the auditory sensation—the experience of hearing the sound. Johnnie is thinking of sense (2), Flossie of sense (1). Now in some cases this might be all the dispute comes to, but generally this is not the case. Is the word "sound" ordinarily used in either sense? As we ordinarily use the word, we do not hesitate to speak of the noise that things make when no one is around: "Can you imagine the deafening sound that rocket made when it hit?" However, the fact that we do not hesitate to speak of unheard sounds does not mean Flossie is right, since the word "sound" had uses long before anyone knew about waves in the air. What we have here is not a disagreement as to facts, of course, but neither do we have no disagreement. For some reason (perhaps he has been reading Berkeley), Johnnie thinks that "sound" should be used in sense (2), whereas Flossie disagrees and for some reason (she has been reading elementary physics books) believes that this would be a mistake and that "sound" really should be used in sense (1).

None of these last three examples is a factual dispute. Each is a dispute arising because two people are using words in different ways, and each is of such complexity that it might very well be baffling to those who do not understand what gives rise to the disagreement.

Often the origin of a dispute has to do with a disagreement in attitudes. Such disagreements can occur as an element in a verbal or nonverbal dispute and, of course, there can be disputes which are simply disagreements in attitudes. A paradigm of such a dispute is the debate in which one party says something is good or right while the other party argues that it is bad or wrong. How disagreements in attitude can be found along with verbal disputes can be illustrated in this example:

A: All the leaders of the German "conservative" party are not conservatives. A conservative wants to remove government from economic matters and leave all of this to free enterprise.

B: They are conservatives. They are not like our Republicans or even like many of our Democrats. They conceive the role of government as one of partnership with industry and labor in pursuit of a common national goal, which is an expanding economy in which all can share fruitfully. Government intervention is natural and necessary, and public spending and planning, within reasonable limits, are essential ingredients of that concept. Without them capitalism cannot long survive as a healthy way of life. They believe deeply in the free enterprise system, but they believe, too, that only through prudent use of public spending and planning can the system live and grow.

There are at least two recognized uses for the word "conservative." And it is fair to say that in this example, A is using "conservative" with one distinct criterion and B is using a different criterion. The criterion for A's use of the term "conservative" seems to be more or less this: one who opposes government interference with business, one who endorses the old *laissez-faire* relationship between government and business. On the other hand, B is using the term "conservative" with this criterion: one who maintains as much of the status quo as possible by adjusting free enterprise in capitalistic countries to changing times and problems.

There is another element present in this dispute, however. For A and B "conservative" seems to have prescriptive force. That is, for them to call an individual a conservative is implicitly to commend the man. If this is so, a conflict of attitudes would be implicit in this dispute. A disapproves of the German leaders, and he approves of the old kind of conservatives, whereas B approves of the kind of conservatives found among the German leaders. The conflict of attitudes implicit in this dispute is thus A's disapproval of the German leaders and B's approval. Since terms with prescriptive force can be employed in any kind of dispute, including factual ones, a conflict of attitudes of this kind could be an element in any kind of dispute. If, for example, the revelation that a dispute is a pseudodispute leaves the parties in opposition, this is a good indication that a conflict of attitudes exists.

EXERCISES 3.6

Which of the following items can be regarded as involving a verbal dispute? Indicate the type of verbal dispute found. It may be that some are verbal disputes of a kind different from those distinguished in this section. Are there any disagreements in attitudes?

1. How conservative is America?
   A: Recent polls have shown that those who call themselves conservatives substantially outnumber those who call themselves liberal.
   B: But many who call themselves conservatives don't really mean it. Careful polling reveals that many of those who call themselves conservatives favor liberal objectives.
   C: If all this conservatism exists, why hasn't it manifested itself in a Republican Party revival?
   D: It doesn't matter if Americans are conservative or liberal. The public opinion in this country that counts must be formed by leadership.
2. A: Man hasn't progressed at all in 2,000 years—still the same old sinner, more plagued by guilt than ever.
   B: Of course he has progressed. Look at our blessings: TV, wonder drugs, satellites, space travel, modern art, etc.

A: But progress is movement toward redemption. It does not consist in sinking deeper into the muck of this world.

C: No, progress consists actually in finding ways to enjoy the most agreeable form of misery—physical comfort.

3. I have no doubt that the First Amendment—Congress shall make no law . . . abridging the freedom of speech and the press—intended that there would be no libel or defamation law in the United States, just absolutely none. My view is, without exception, that freedom of speech means that you shall not do something to people either for the views they have or the views they express or the words they speak or write.

   DISPUTER: But surely the Bill of Rights doesn't grant absolute freedom of speech and press. The Bill of Rights doesn't nullify libel and slander laws. In addition, it doesn't or shouldn't cover the peddlers of filth, those advocating the violent overthrow of the government, the one who spills security secrets, etc.

4. Since marriage is forbidden between members of the same sex, what happens if a husband undergoes sexual reassignment and is reclassified as the same sex as his/her spouse? If the marriage is dissolved wouldn't he/she be required to pay alimony to the ex-wife?

   A: The marriage is automatically dissolved, because both are the same sex and the law rules out marriages of the same sex.

   B: The postoperative transsexual has not actually changed sex, so they are still legally married. You can't change anatomical differentiations, only the sense of sexual identity.

   C: The marriage laws suppose the immutability of one's sex. Since this assumption no longer holds, the law does not apply here, so it is left open whether they are or are not married.

5. . . . a man's earnings are his property as much as his land and the house in which he lives. . . . It has been the fashion in recent years to disparage "property rights"—to associate them with greed and materialism. This attack on property rights is actually an attack on freedom. It is another instance of the modern failure to take into account the whole man. How can a man be truly free if he is denied the means to exercise freedom? How can he be free if the fruits of his labor are not his to dispose of, but are treated, instead, as part of a common pool of public wealth? Property and freedom are inseparable: to the extent government takes the one in the form of taxes, it intrudes on the other.   (BARRY GOLDWATER, *The Conscience of a Conservative*)

   DISPUTER: When we speak of "freedom" in a democratic context we have in mind the freedom of the general public. If a few are allowed to accumulate great wealth while a great many are left with very little, then freedom is granted to a few but denied to the many. Since without some "property" the many cannot exercise their freedom, if we are interested in freedom, then the government should tax so as to distribute the wealth.

6. In 1964 former Republican Governor of Illinois William G. Stratton was indicted on charges of failing to report $94,000 in income for the period 1957–60, while he was governor. The prosecution suggested that most of the money came from cash political contributions which were diverted to personal use. The defense did not deny that Stratton spent more than he reported, but they argued that it came from gifts or campaign funds that were spent on political expenses, both of which are not taxable. The prosecution then reviewed some of these expenses which included: $63,000 lodge overlooking the Sargamon River; $5,000 for remodelling his family home; $4,750 for a houseboat; a payment once made for $1,400 for four suits and a tuxedo; cash purchase in the thousands for dresses for Mrs. Stratton and their two grown daughters; portraits; organs; a manure spreader for Stratton's farm; and a European trip for one of his daughters. The defense countered by maintaining that both the lodge and the family house were used for official entertainment. Meetings were constantly going on aboard the boat, in fact once a State Supreme Court Justice fell overboard. Mrs. Stratton was the First Lady of Illinois and needed to be properly dressed. The Governor had to think of his image. In short, all of these items were related to the former governor's political career. The defense attorney frankly said: "It is hard to say that even his toothpaste was not a deductible expense." The prosecution argued that these things were not tax-deductible. The federal court, after a nine and a half week trial, acquitted Stratton of income tax evasion.

(Adapted from *Time*, March 19, 1965)

7. A lumberman is asked by a passerby, "How long have you had *that* axe?"

"For about ten years now. Had the handle changed three times and the blade twice."

"But then you haven't had *that* axe for ten years."

8. A: It takes about eight minutes for the sun's light to reach us, and it takes much longer in the case of the other stars. It is quite possible, for example, that that star which we are looking at ceased to exist eight minutes ago. This only brings to light the not often recognized fact that what we are seeing is not the star but what it looked like about eight minutes ago.

   B: Nonsense! Let's face it, it sounds paradoxical, but if that star ceased to exist eight minutes ago what we are seeing is an object which doesn't exist. Let's be tough-minded.

   C: Enough of those virile adjectives. It is all quite simple. Science has found out that we are really seeing sensations in the mind which are caused by the star which no longer exists.

9. A: Dr. Jekyll and Mr. Hyde were the same person who merely changed his physical appearance.

B: No, they were two persons who inhabited the same body—the body of course changed its appearance.

10. A: The proper yardstick to be used in measuring the value of education is that it directly contributes to making life useful for students, that it helps prepare them for a better life. Now much has been written about some perfectly ridiculous courses which certain universities have offered from time to time. One that comes immediately to mind was given by a midwestern state university on "The Origins of the Ancient Greek Language." This course was offered for four years, until a newspaper exposed the absurdity of the course. Such courses which have no objective for making students more useful citizens should not be included in the curriculum of a university supported by public tax money.

B: My point is that the conclusion you want to draw rests on a false premise, namely, that a course contributes to making a useful citizen if and only if it helps the student to become useful in contributing to the material wealth of the country. How else can you go from your claim that courses in tax-supported schools should help prepare for a better life and make more useful citizens to concluding that specialized courses should be dropped from the curriculum. At bottom the issue is whether public institutions should broaden individual choice or serve the corporate needs of industry, government, and the military.

11. In 1954 Harry A. Jones, sixty-six, of Long Beach, California, was found by his wife, slumped over his desk. She called a doctor. The doctor could find no pulse, no heartbeat, nor any sign of breath. Jones was pronounced dead and an ambulance was called to take him to the mortuary. On the road the blankets began to move, causing the driver a very bad moment. Mr. Jones "came back to life" and made a full recovery. Was he dead?

A: Of course he wasn't dead. He didn't "come back to life" for he never left life. He is alive and was alive; the doctor must have made a mistake.

B: But he was dead. The doctor found no pulse, no heartbeat, and no breath. If this is true of someone, then we say he is dead. No, he was dead. This was a true resurrection.

12. A: The government in 1962 seized 5,400 Giant Economy Size jars of Grandma's instant coffee. Their reason: It was discovered that the *Economy* jar costs the American housewife 1.9 cents per ounce more than the ordinary 6-ounce jar of the same coffee. This is false advertising.

B: No, it isn't. Time is money, don't you know! Just think of the time that's saved by buying the giant jar. It saves the housewife a trip or two to the store. Also it's cheaper at current garbage-disposal rates to throw away three big jars than five little ones.

13. During Prohibition two young men ran through the Elks Convention train at a quick stop selling "cold tea" at $5 a pint. After the train started, the Elks discovered that what they had bought was cold tea. Was this false advertising?

A: No. They announced that they were selling cold tea and it was cold tea. How can this be called false advertising?

B: It was false advertising. In those circumstances anyone saying that he was selling cold tea at $5 a pint would be understood to be selling whisky, so it was false advertising.

14. On August 24, 1962, twenty-three Cuban refugees shelled Havana with 20-mm shells from two 36-foot motorboats. These Cubans were living in and came from Miami. Should they be indicted under the Neutrality Act, which reads that it is a crime for a group to launch "a military expedition or enterprise" from the United States against a country with which the United States is at peace?

A: Yes. They launched a military attack and the United States is not at war with Cuba.

B: No. We are not certain that these boats did not touch down at some Caribbean island en route to Havana, in which case they wouldn't have departed from the United States. Also does shooting up the Havana waterfront with 20-mm cannon constitute a military expedition? No. It is a symbolic act.

C: No. Twenty-three men are not a group, much less a military expedition. Shooting does not make a military expedition. In addition, if the United States is on bad terms with the country to which the nongroup goes, we are not at peace with it, although we may not be at war either.

D: Yes. What would you have said if Canadian refugees had shelled Quebec or Toronto?

ANSWERS

3. If the dispute is over what the authors of the Constitution meant by "freedom of speech and the press," then the dispute is factual.

6. This is a dispute over what is to come under the extension of "tax-deductible expenses," namely, are all those items related to a governor's political career to be considered tax-deductible expenses? It would seem that they are not clearly not deductible, for witness the court's decision; on the other hand, the fact that the prosecution argues that many are not deductible lends support that they are not clearly tax deductible. Thus a word-extension dispute.

7. Pseudodispute. The lumberman and passerby have, in these circumstances, different criteria for their use of the phrase "the same axe." The passerby counts being of the same material among his criteria for saying x is the same axe. The lumberman includes material, possibly changing, having been used in such-and-such a way over a period of time, among his criteria for saying it is the same axe.
9. Word-extension dispute. An extraordinary case. Commonly when we speak of "the same person" such characteristics as same physical appearance, same character, same memories, and so on, are present. In the Jekyll and Hyde case some are present and some are missing. Should we extend "same person" to cover Jekyll and Hyde?
13. A good case can be made for this being a word-extension dispute. The case in question has several of the characteristics of paradigm cases of false advertising. For example, most were deceived by what the salesmen said. The salesmen intended to deceive in exactly this way. They said just those things which in these circumstances would so deceive. The story goes that this case came to court and the judge said that this was not a case of false advertising.

Emotive Words

Today, according to a U.N. survey, to call a government a "democracy" is, anywhere in the world, to commend implicitly the government in question. In turn, to call a government a "dictatorship" is implicitly to condemn it. (We may thus safely predict that the next dictatorship will be called a democracy.) Such words as "democracy" and "dictatorship" are said to have *prescriptive* or *emotive force*. Such prescriptive force may be either commendatory or condemnatory. Thus to say "*a* is *W*," when "*W*" has prescriptive force, may imply either the speaker's approbation of *a* or his censure of *a*. Examples of other words that generally have commendatory force today, at least in the United States, are "freedom," "justice," "art," "realistic," "moderate," "Christian," "constitutional," "education," "patriot," "open-minded," and "American." Words with condemnatory force are "extremist," "radical," "reactionary," "bureaucrat," "atheist," "fascist," "communist," "racist," and "loophole." Words with such condemnatory forces are also called pejorative words. A hundred years ago or so the word "democracy" was generally used pejoratively, but this changed after the world wars. The Nazis in the 1930s attempted to use "democracy" as a term of abuse. In some circles in the United States "welfare state" is commendatory whereas in other circles it is a pejorative word. We may imagine the pejorative force of "Western capitalism" in the U.S.S.R. or China. Thus, as these last examples illustrate, whether a word has prescriptive force depends on the time and place of its use and on those using it. It is interesting to note that sometimes a word can have prescriptive force while its synonym or near equivalent can lack such force.

It is a remarkable fact that people's attitudes toward a thing can be changed merely by replacing an emotive expression with a neutral expression referring to exactly the same thing (and vice-versa). That is, two expressions can have the same extension and intension and yet the emotive force of one of the expressions can determine whether people will approve or disapprove of those things referred to by the emotive word. To illustrate, in 1977 a poll taken by *The New York Times* and *CBS News* questioned 1,447 persons selected to represent the entire American adult population. Fifty-eight percent said they disapproved of government sponsored welfare programs. Yet when those surveyed were asked about welfare programs in terms in which the word "welfare" was omitted, 81 percent approved of welfare. For example, 81 percent approved of the government providing financial assistance for children raised in low-income homes where one parent is missing (Aid to Families with Dependent Children, the main component of welfare), helping poor people buy food for their families at cheaper prices (food-stamp program), and using taxes to pay for health care for poor people (Medicaid program). What was all the more remarkable was that the response was much the same among almost all types of people—rich and poor, liberal and conservative, Democrat and Republican. Another example is the Panama Canal Treaties. In 1978, at one time, polls showed that most Americans disapproved of the Treaties, and yet when questions involving the substance of the Treaties were asked, most approved of them.

When one uses an expression which has less condemnatory prescriptive force than another expression which refers to the same thing, one makes use of what is called a *euphemism.* Some examples of euphemisms are the following where the expression that the euphemism replaces is in parentheses:

> Careless with the truth (liar)
> Economy class (second class)
> Medicare (socialized medicine)
> Defense department (war department)
> Planned economy (regimented state)
> Family assistance (guaranteed income)

Each pair of expressions is typically used to refer to the same thing. Thus each euphemism and the paired expression have the same extension, and in most cases they have the same or close to the same intension. However, the euphemism lacks the condemnatory force associated with the expression in parentheses.

Euphemisms are often found in political language. Typically euphemisms are used to defend government actions that might be otherwise hard or harder to defend without the use of euphemisms. George Orwell provides three illustrations of such uses of euphemisms:

> In our time, political speech and writing are largely the defense of the indefensible. Things like the continuation of British rule in India, the Russian purges and deportations, the dropping of the atom bombs on Japan, can indeed be defended, but only by arguments which are too brutal for most people to face, and which do not square with the professed aims of political parties. Thus political language has to consist largely of euphemism, question-begging and sheer cloudy vagueness. Defenceless villages are bombarded from the air, the inhabitants driven out into the countryside, the huts set on fire with incendiary bullets; this is called *pacification*. Millions of peasants are robbed of their farms and sent trudging along the roads with no more than they can carry: this is called *transfer of population* or *rectification of frontiers*. People are imprisoned for years without trial, and shot in the back of the neck or sent to die of scurvy in Arctic lumber camps: this is called *elimination of unreliable elements.*[8]

Here are the examples of euphemisms that Orwell cites:

> Pacification (bombing away in a village)
> Transfer of population (driving people away from their land)
> Elimination of unreliables (sending political prisoners to Siberia)

The use of euphemisms may have reached the status of an art form during the Vietnam War. Here are some examples:

> Winding down the war (surrendering)
> Surgical strike (precision bombing)
> Pacification center (concentration camp)
> Incontinent ordinance (bombs falling outside a target area)
> Incursion (invasion, as in "Cambodian incursion")
> Advisor (military personnel)

Here are some current examples of euphemisms:

> Mature (fat, as in "mature figure")
> Low-income (poor)
> Correction facility (prison)
> Life insurance (insurance to provide money in case of an early death)
> Convenience food (junk food)
> Arms limitation (not building all the weapons possible)
> Subsidizing business (federal handouts to business)
> Sanitation workers (garbagemen)
> Radiation enhancement weapon (neutron bomb)
> Overdependence on drugs (drug addiction)

[8] *A Collection of Essays on George Orwell* (New York: Doubleday–Anchor, 1954), pp. 172–173.

When would one want to use a euphemism? When one wishes to refer to x, but wishes to eliminate any condemnatory prescriptive force from the usual expressions used to refer to x. One would do this because one wishes to persuade (or better, to con, to avoid a euphemism here) one's audience into thinking that x is not as bad as it is (or as they think it is). This type of persuasion is used in lieu of giving rational reasons why x is not as bad as it is perceived to be. Thus euphemisms are like fallacies in that they are irrational ways to get people to believe things. The fallacious use of euphemisms is illustrated in this example: E. Howard Hunt, one of the Watergate burglars and a former CIA agent and consultant to the Nixon White House, appeared before a federal grand jury in April 1973 and this exchange occurred:

Q: Well, in your terminology, would the entry into Daniel Ellsberg's psychiatrist's office have been clandestine, illegal, neither, or both?

A: I would simply call it an entry operation conducted under the auspices of highest authorities. = *illegal entry*

Here Hunt is referring to a crime, but saying that it is "an entry operation." The hope is that his audience will be persuaded to believe that what he did is not criminal. That is, rather than argue that the breaking in was not criminal, if this is indeed possible, Hunt referred to it with a euphemism, thus disguising the criminal nature of the act. The grand jury was not, in fact, persuaded, since Hunt eventually went to jail for his "entry operation."

Often words can be used for their prescriptive force and without any fixed intension or even any intension at all—for example, when nations disapprove of certain actions of other nations and call them aggressors. In orthodox Marxian context any comrade who does not enthusiastically support one's divining of the dialectic is called a bourgeois. "Anti-American" is applied by some to anyone who disagrees in a fundamental way with their political views. Such a state of affairs makes lexical definitions theoretically impossible, for in order to supply a lexical definition—set down how the selected group uses the word—the word must be used by the group in accordance with a detectable intension. If a definitionlike utterance were constructed that would be acceptable to most people, this, no doubt, would be because the "definition" would be interpreted in as many ways as the word itself. Often lexicographers will report the way some particular group at some time in history used the word when a discernible intension exists. They may report, for example, the way the term "democracy" is used in some first-class political science textbook, or they might give an earlier meaning of such a word, an intension it had before it came into wide and wild use. For example, we may find this dictionary entry for the turn-of-the-century use of "radical": someone who holds the most advanced views of political reform.

Sometimes in order to influence people and get them to act in a desired manner a definitionlike utterance is offered for a prescriptive word. When the prescriptive word lacks the intension set down in the definitionlike utterance, this activity is called giving a *persuasive definition*, the definition-like utterance being the persuasive definition. In other words, when the prescriptive word lacks the intension given in a definitionlike utterance, and when one gives such a "definition" consciously or unconsciously to influence people's behavior, one has given a persuasive definition. All persuasive definitions are illegitimate in the sense that the definition is represented as the standard intension of a word when the word lacks this intension or, perhaps, has no accepted intension at all.

Let us consider a simple example of a persuasive definition. Imagine someone addressing a group of people who, on the whole, approve of those things which come under the extension of the word "education." In the course of his talk he utters this profundity: "Education in the real sense of the word is stirring up students so that they will be driven to think for themselves." He says this, let us suppose, in order to get those in the audience to approve of his teaching methods which consist of little more than efforts to stir up students. In this example, all of the necessary features for a persuasive definition are satisfied. First, an intension is given to "education," which it lacks as it is commonly used. Second, this intension is not a matter of stipulation but is offered as the real meaning of the word in question. Third, the definition is given to a prescriptive word. And, finally, whether the speaker realizes it or not, this activity is done to influence people's behavior, in this case to get his audience to approve of his teaching methods.

In context a persuasive definition is an argument. In effect when a persuasive definition occurs there is an implicit argument which takes this form:

You approve (or disapprove) of things that come within the extension of the word "W."

"W" has such-and-such an intension ("W" really means "...").

Therefore you should approve (or disapprove) of a since it comes within the extension of "W," supposing "W" means "...."

An argument of this sort is a fallacy of ambiguity. The class of things denoted by "things which come within the extension of 'W'" in the premise is a different class than that denoted by the word in the conclusion. Here, then, is a fallacy of ambiguity in which the extensional dimension of meaning of a word shifts.

It is convenient to extend the definition of a persuasive definition so as to include another closely related pseudodefinition. Sometimes a word with or without prescriptive force may be given an intension it does not have and the words used in the definition may be highly prescriptive. When this is done to influence people's behavior we may also speak of this activity as giving a persuasive definition. Thus when an exuberant communist leader on May Day declared:

> Communism means the abundance of the best products for the population. Communism means that a man should have good clothing and a good place to live so that people can learn to work in self-denial for the good of society and make use of the achievements of science, culture and art.

he was taking the word "communism," which presumably is still a term of approbation in the U.S.S.R., and affixing to it an intension which heavily reinforced its prescriptive force because of the prescriptive nature of the defining words. The purpose of this exercise is as self-evident as the purpose of the House Un-American Activities Committee member who wrote in a government publication:

> Is is possible to translate communism into plain English?
> Yes. In brief, communism is the dogmatic worship of a self-righteous idol derived from logical absurdity and deceit, and sustained on fanaticism, power, and blood.

and thus provided for us a second example of this second kind of persuasive definition.

EXERCISES 3.7

A. Do you find any euphemisms in the following? Why are they used?

1. Dr. A. Dale Console resigned in 1957 as medical director of Squibb and Sons. One of the reasons he gave up his job is that he was required to word warning labels on drugs so that they would appear to be an inducement to use the drug rather than a warning of the danger inherent in its use.

2. The government speaks of full employment when 4 percent of the workforce is unemployed.

3. The United States gave military aid to Pakistan. But Pakistan used that aid to put down an independence movement in Bangladesh. Of this Senator William Proxmire (D-Wisc.) in *Uncle Sam: The Last of the Bigtime Spenders* said: "Through the force of arms, much of it supplied by the United States, they killed, burned, raped, tortured, and devastated an entire countryside. They drove ten million people from their homes. They murdered and slaughtered others. Some were driven into the sea. Others escaped· to refugee camps in India, where thousands remained uncared for. India retaliated and drove the West Pakis-

tan Army from Bangladesh. Weapons for both sides had been supplied by the United States. In the budget we call that international security assistance."

4. The Vietnam War was just the flow of history.

5. Politicians do not deprive children of school funds or minority persons of jobs. They trade off highways for schools and missiles for jobs.

6. The CIA at one time conducted experiments in sensory deprivation and human behavior control through an organization called "Society for the Investigation of Human Ecology."

7. Recently the U.S. Senate began calling its recess a "nonlegislative period" and the House began calling its recess a "district work period."

8. In a Virginia Slims ad campaign aimed at an aggressive exploitation of young women by means of words and images, smoking is presented as a decision for freedom and independence.

9. In legal circles a rainmaker is a law-firm partner who brings business because he has held high government office. Among the most famous was Richard Nixon, who managed to attract Pepsi-Cola for the New York firm of Nixon, Mudge, Rose partly because as Vice-President in 1959 he steered Nikita Khrushchev to the Pepsi Kiosk in Moscow as photographers clicked away.

10. We speak of the "free world" and mean by it, in addition to the United States and Britain, Chile, South Korea, and South Africa.

11. The Committee on Public Doublespeak, established by the National Council of Teachers of English to honor those who make significant contributions to semantic distortion, gave one of its first annual "Doublespeak Awards" to Air Force Colonel David Opfer, air attache at the U.S. Embassy in Phnom Penh in 1973. He complained to reporters "You always write it's bombing, bombing, bombing. It's not bombing. It's air support."

12. In 1973 Nixon's man for telecommunication policy, Clay T. Whitehead, was traveling about the country to publicize a Congressional bill that would place a local station's license in jeopardy if the station could not demonstrate "meaningful service to the community." One way to demonstrate such service, Whitehead was suggesting, was to eliminate reporting and analysis of the administration.

13. Six months ago, in presenting the military budget for fiscal 1973, Nixon and Laird were asking for certain escalations as a hedge in case the SALT talks failed. Now they are asking for the same escalations on the grounds that the SALT talks succeeded. An exasperated Fulbright in the Senate Foreign Relations Committee hearings on the SALT accords told Laird he had "a genius

for semantic confusion." There could be no better illustration than the use of "strategic arms limitation agreements" as an excuse for—literally—billions of dollars worth of new weapons. The total bill cannot yet be added up but the specific projects and policies could easily cost a hundred billion in this decade.

(I. F. STONE, "The New Shape of Nixon's World," in *The New York Review of Books,* June 29, 1972)

14. Assistant FBI Director J. Wallace LaPrade, who has been under recent pressure by [Attorney General] Bell for his alleged activities in illegal acts committed in investigating the Weatherman Underground, said Thursday that investigations conducted without warrants such as those that resulted in the indictments of former acting FBI Director Gray and his own proposed discipline are still being conducted by the FBI, with presidential authority.

"At the present time, there are warrantless investigations that the attorney general, with the president's executive authority, is having the FBI conduct," he said at a news conference. He did not say whether President Carter had specific knowledge of them.

Asked what he meant by "warrantless" he replied: "I would describe it this way: The activities that are alleged in connection with the Weatherman investigation (in the early 1970s) would categorize as warrantless activities."

LaPrade would not elaborate on what those were, but said "the executive power of the president permits the types of things that we're discussing of a warrantless nature."

(Associated Press, April 14, 1978)

15. In 1978 Alabama Governor George C. Wallace was a candidate for the Democratic nomination for a seat in the U.S. Senate. Wallace and his political aides, who blamed his wheelchair for his poor showing in the 1976 presidential primaries, counted on voter sympathy—they called it appreciation—to carry him through what would be one of his toughest political struggles.

16. The Transsexual movement speaks of "sexual reassignment" rather than sex-change operations. Transsexual patients claim that they are members of one sex trapped within the bodies of the other sex.

B. Do you find any occurrences of persuasive definitions in the following?

all

1. A liberal is a man who cultivates the skills that make freedom operational. He is always a man on special assignment.

(MAX ASCOLI, editor and publisher of *The Reporter* magazine)

2. The root difference between the Conservatives and the Liberals of today is that Conservatives take account of the *whole* man,

while the Liberals tend to look only at the material side of man's nature. The Conservatives believe that man is, in part, an economic and animal creature; but that he is also a spiritual creature with spiritual needs and spiritual desires. What is more, these needs and desires reflect the *superior* side of man's nature, and thus take precedence over his economic wants. Conservatism therefore looks upon the enhancement of man's spiritual nature as the primary concern of political philosophy. Liberals, on the other hand—in the name of a concern for "human beings"— regard the satisfaction of economic wants as the dominant mission of society. They are, moreover, in a hurry. So that their characteristic approach is to harness the society's political and economic forces into a collective effort to *compel* "progress." In this approach, I believe they fight against Nature.

(BARRY GOLDWATER, *The Conscience of a Conservative*)

3. "Fabian Socialists," the general explained to the senators, could be more or less defined as "some of those to the left who seem to appear at various times, usually anonymously, and who are not in the records of Mr. Hoover as are the card-carrying communists, who sometimes raise questions as to where we are going or where they would like us to go."

4. Every truly civilized and enlightened man is conservative and liberal and progressive.

   A civilized man is conservative in that his deepest loyalty is to the Western heritage of ideas which originated on the shores of the Mediterranean.

   Because of that loyalty he is the indefatigable defender of our own constitutional doctrine, which is that all power, that all government, that all officials, that all parties, and all majorities are under the law—and that none of them is sovereign and omnipotent.

   The civilized man is a liberal because the writing and the administration of the laws should be done with enlightenment and compassion, with tolerance and charity, and with affection.

   And the civilized man is progressive because the times change and the social order evolves and new things are invented and changes occur. (WALTER LIPPMAN in a speech to the Women's National Press Club in Washington)

5. Philosophy is a battle against the bewitchment of our intelligence by means of language.

   (WITTGENSTEIN, *Philosophical Investigations*)

William James was once asked to define philosophy and he replied, "Just words, words, words!"

Russell said philosophy consists of speculation about matters where exact knowledge is not yet possible.

Philosophy is the body of highest truth, the organized sum of science; the science of which all others are branches.

(The Century Dictionary)

6. You said just now that the government in 1933 gave a lot of work to the unemployed. It is a great mistake to believe this. It is false. Oh yes, the men built roads and planted forests and things like that. But I don't call that *work*. *Real work*, *real* employment, doesn't have to be invented. It doesn't need any government to create it. It springs naturally from the economy.

7. A leading member of several nationalist groups has defined American nationalism as "an awareness that the United States is at least potentially a great, powerful, and superior nation." Bertrand Russell defines nationalism in this way: ". . . nationalism is not a single world-wide system, but is a different system in each nation. It consists essentially in collective self-glorification and in a conviction that it is right to pursue the interests of one's own nation however they may conflict with those of others." And here is another definition: "The Nationalist opposes the belief that the world is one, that all human beings are 'brothers' in the broadest sense, and that all men everywhere in the world must cooperate with each other and live together in peace under world law."

8. His [George Wallace] basic technique had always been to discover what most of the voters were thinking and tell them that was what he thought too. He had never been a genuine ideologue, even in his younger days, although he had shown certain liberal tendencies during his tenure in the state legislature in Montgomery and had run a relatively liberal-to-moderate gubernatorial campaign in 1958, losing the election but winning the endorsement of the Alabama chapter of the National Association for the Advancement of Colored People. But Wallace reasoned that his opponent had won precisely because he had spoken the words voters wanted to hear and he never forgot that lesson. "Leadership," he would pompously intone years later, "derives from the people to the politician, not the other way around."   (JAMES WOOTEN, *Dasher*)[9]

[9] James Wooten, *Dasher* (New York: Summit Books, 1978), p. 282. Copyright © 1978 by James Wooten.

ANSWERS

A.   **2.** full employment
      4. flow of history
      5. tradeoff
      9. rainmaker
   11. air support
   13. arms limitation
   15. voter appreciation

B.   **8.** Persuasive definition for "leadership." Wallace sets the definition so that his responding to whatever the voters (most of the voters) want comes under the extension of "leadership."

PART

II

FORMAL LOGIC

4

Deductive Validity and Logical Form

The principal task of logic is to provide methods for determining the validity of deductive arguments. Let us briefly review what an argument is and what a deductive argument is. An *argument* is a sequence of two or more statements together with the claim, sometimes implicit, that one of these statements, the conclusion, follows from the other statements, the premises. An argument is *deductive* if the claim is that it is impossible for the conclusion to be false if the premises are all true. Consider the following arguments:

(1) All emeralds which have been found are green.
    Therefore all emeralds are green.
(2) If Shakespeare wrote *Hamlet*, then Shakespeare is a playwright.
    Shakespeare wrote *Hamlet*.
    Therefore Shakespeare is a playwright.
(3) If Shakespeare wrote *Hair*, then Shakespeare is a playwright.
    Shakespeare did not write *Hair*.
    Therefore Shakespeare is not a playwright.

These are all arguments, but only (2) and (3) are deductive arguments. Clearly the argument claim in (1) is not that it is impossible for the premise to be true and conclusion false but only that it is improbable that the conclusion is false if the premise is true. The claim is that if the premise is true, then in all probability the conclusion is true. Thus (1) is not a deductive argument. However in (2) and (3) the claim is that it is impossible for the premises to be true and conclusion false.

A deductive argument is *valid* if the deductive claim is warranted. Argument (2) is a valid deductive argument. Argument (2) is valid because it is impossible for the premises to be true and the conclusion false. Argument

165

(3) is an invalid deductive argument. It is not impossible for the premises to be true and the conclusion false. In fact each premise of (3) is true and the conclusion is false.

To say that an argument is valid is not to comment on the truth or falsity of its component statements, although if an argument is valid it is impossible for the premises to be true and the conclusion false. Validity is a relation that may or may not exist between premises and conclusion, while truth is a property of statements. In this regard it is instructive to note that invalid arguments may have all true component statements and that valid arguments may contain false premises or a false conclusion or both. To illustrate, let us consider the following arguments:

If Shakespeare wrote *Hamlet*, then Shakespeare is a playwright.
Shakespeare is a playwright.
Therefore Shakespeare wrote *Hamlet*.

Invalid argument. Both premises true, conclusion true.

Hamlet is a comedy and is badly written.
Therefore *Hamlet* is a comedy.

Valid argument, premise false, conclusion false.

All Shakespeare's plays are musicals.
Hair is a play by Shakespeare.
Therefore *Hair* is a musical.

Valid argument. Both premises false, conclusion true.

If Shakespeare wrote *Hamlet*, then Shakespeare knew English.
Shakespeare wrote *Hamlet*.
Therefore Shakespeare knew English.

Valid argument. The first premise is true, the second true, and the conclusion is true.

EXERCISES 4.1

The following are deductive arguments. Though methods will be introduced later to determine whether such arguments are valid, at this point, use your logical intuition to find the valid ones.

1. All bankers are Republicans. All Republicans favor tax reduction. So all bankers favor tax reduction.

2. Either there will be nuclear war or the nations will disarm. The nations will not disarm. So there will be nuclear war.
3. If we are to conserve our natural resources, then we must no longer encourage the competitive spirit. We will conserve our natural resources, so we will give up promoting competition.
4. All capitalists are born-again Christians. Jimmy Carter is a born-again Christian. So he is a capitalist.
5. Jimmy Carter is the President of the United States, so the President of the United States is Jimmy Carter.
6. If we reduce unemployment, there will be inflation. We will never reduce unemployment, so there will be inflation.
7. Either we reduce unemployment or there will be inflation. We will never reduce unemployment. So there will be inflation.
8. All Arabs are rich, so Sheik Amani is rich.
9. Jack and Jill went up the hill, so Jill went up the hill and so did Jack.
10. Jack and Jill were married, and Jill became pregnant. Hence Jill became pregnant and then Jack and Jill were married.

ANSWERS

Only **4**, **6**, and **10** are invalid, the rest are valid.

Logical Form

What determines validity of an argument is the *logical form* of the sentences that make up the argument. What is logical form? This can be explained most easily by using some examples. Consider the following two arguments:

(1) Plato is a mathematician or Plato is a philosopher.
Plato is not a mathematician.
Therefore Plato is a philosopher.
(2) Shakespeare is an actor or Shakespeare is a playwright.
Shakespeare is not an actor.
Therefore Shakespeare is a playwright.

They have something in common. What this is can be exhibited by letting "p" and "q" be placeholders or variables for sentences and by writing down the following argument pattern:

(3) p or q
Not p
Therefore q

Both arguments (1) and (2) can be obtained from (3). By replacing "*p*" with "Plato is a mathematician" and "*q*" with "Plato is a philosopher" one obtains argument (1). By replacing "*p*" with "Shakespeare is an actor" and "*q*" with "Shakespeare is a playwright" one obtains argument (2). Since (1) and (2) can be obtained from argument pattern (3), they have the same logical form. They are instances of the same argument pattern and this pattern is a logical pattern. It is a *pattern* for it contains variables for sentences. It is an *argument* pattern because it contains an argument claim indicated by "therefore." It is a *logical pattern*, for the only non-variables, excluding the argument claim, are syntactical or logical terms. Both "or" and "not" will count as logical terms. Others will be introduced subsequently.

The notion of logical form can also be illustrated by these next two arguments.

(4)   All wealthy persons are dishonest.
All successful politicians are wealthy persons.
Therefore all successful politicians are dishonest.

(5)   All men are infallible.
All logicians are men.
Therefore all logicians are infallible.

Notice that these arguments contain terms which stand for classes of things. Expressions such as "men," "dishonest persons," "dog," "gold" are general terms. Proper names would be one kind of example of nongeneral terms. Let the letters "*S*," "*M*," and "*P*" be placeholders or variables for general terms. Now consider the following argument pattern:

(6)   All *M* are *P*.
All *S* are *M*.
Therefore all *S* are *P*.

Both arguments (4) and (5) are instances of this logical argument pattern. "All" is another example of a logical term. Since both (4) and (5) are instances of (6), they have the same logical form.

The validity of an argument depends on its logical form. This is shown by the fact that any argument that is an instance of argument pattern (3) is valid, and any argument that is an instance of argument pattern (6) is valid. An *instance* of an argument pattern is obtained when one *uniformly* replaces the placeholders or variables of the pattern with appropriate expressions. Thus (4) and (5) are instances of (6), and (1) and (2) are instances of (3). Uniform replacement occurs when the same replacement is put in for all occurrences of the variable in question. The arguments below are *not* instances of (3) and (6), respectively, since the replacement is not uniform:

Plato is a mathematician or Plato is a philosopher.
Plato is not a scientist.
Therefore Plato is a Philosopher.

All cats are animals.
All tigers are cats.
Therefore all cats are tigers.

However, the next examples are instances of (3) and (6), since the replacement is uniform even though the same replacement is made for different placeholders (resulting in rather absurd sounding examples):

(7)   Plato is a philosopher or Plato is a philosopher.
       Plato is not a philosopher.
       Therefore Plato is a philosopher.
(8)   All cats are animals.
       All animals are cats.
       Therefore all animals are animals.

To construct an instance of an argument pattern is to provide an *interpretation* for the pattern. That the validity of an argument depends on logical form is shown by the fact that any interpretation of pattern (3) or (6) results in a valid argument. [Note that (7) is a valid argument for it is impossible for the premises to be true and the conclusion false. This is ruled out since the premises cannot possibly be true.]

Argument patterns (3) and (6) are both examples of valid patterns. A *valid argument pattern* is a pattern that results only in valid arguments on interpretation. Here are some other examples of valid argument patterns using *p*, *q*, and *r* as placeholders for sentences. All these are familiar enough so that they now have the indicated names.

p ∴ Not not p	Double negation	Not not p ∴ p	Double negation
p q ∴ p and q	Conjunction	p and q ∴ p	Simplification
p or q Not p ∴ q	Disjunctive syllogism	If p, then q p ∴ q	*Modus ponens*
If p, then q Not q ∴ Not p	*Modus tollens*	If p, then q If q, then r ∴ If p then r	Hypothetical syllogism

EXERCISES 4.2

Each of the following arguments is an interpretation of one of the eight valid patterns above. Identify by name the pattern exemplified in each argument.

1. If we reduce pollution, then our standard of living will go down. Our standard of living will not go down. So we will not reduce pollution.

modus ponent

2. If we conserve energy, then the economy will not grow. We will conserve energy, so the economy will not grow.
3. Either we will conserve energy or we will have low unemployment. We will not conserve energy. So we will have low unemployment.

hypothetical syllogism

4. If we protect our environment, then we will have a no growth economy. If we have a no growth economy, then we must have incentives other than profit. So if we are to protect our environment we must have incentives other than profit.
5. We will have high unemployment and inflation. Thus we will have high unemployment.

conjunction

6. We will reduce pollution. We will solve the unemployment problem. So we will both reduce pollution and solve the unemployment problem.
7. It is not the case that we will not end pollution. So we will end pollution.
8. Inflation and unemployment are facts of the energy crisis. Thus inflation

simplification

is a fact of the energy crisis.

ANSWERS

1. *modus tollens*   3. disjunctive syllogism   5. simplification
7. double negation

Counterexamples

There is an invalid pattern corresponding to each of the valid patterns discussed in the previous section. For example, corresponding to *modus ponens* we have:

If *p*, then *q*
q
Therefore *p*

Corresponding to *modus tollens* there is:

If *p*, then *q*
Not *p*
Therefore not *q*

And corresponding to the hypothetical syllogism there is:

(1) If p, then q
     If r, then q
     Therefore if p, then r

One can demonstrate the invalidity of each of these invalid patterns by providing interpretations that result in arguments where each premise is true and the conclusion false. Such interpretations are *counterexamples* to the patterns. For example, if we make these replacements for the last pattern (1)

p: It rains
q: The streets are wet
r: It floods

we have this interpretation:

If it rains, then the streets are wet.
If it floods, then the streets are wet.
Therefore if it rains, then it floods.

Here, in most circumstances, each premise is true and the conclusion is false.

One can thus demonstrate the invalidity of an invalid pattern by constructing a counterexample, that is, by providing an interpretation for the pattern that results in an argument in which each premise is true and the conclusion is false. How can one demonstrate the validity of valid patterns? Logic has provided methods for doing this. These will be introduced in the next chapters.

If an argument is valid, then it has a valid logical form. And this means that it is an interpretation of a valid logical argument pattern. Validity of an argument is exclusively a function of the logical form of the argument. It is necessary to point out, however, that although valid arguments must be interpretations of valid argument patterns, there may be valid arguments that are interpretations of invalid argument patterns. For example, the following can easily be demonstrated to be an invalid pattern by the method of counterexamples:

(2) p
     Therefore q

and yet the valid argument below is an interpretation of this pattern:

(3) Some lazy persons are students.
     Therefore some students are lazy persons.

where p: Some lazy persons are students; q: Some students are lazy persons. Similarly the next argument below is valid and also is an interpretation of argument pattern (2):

> (4)   Today is Monday and today is sunny.
>   Therefore today is Monday.

where p: Today is Monday and today is sunny; q: Today is Monday.

Arguments (3) and (4) are valid, and they are valid because of their logical form. But the form which accounts for their validity is not (2). In the case of (3) it is:

> Some S are P.
> Therefore some P are S.

and in the case of (4) the form that accounts for its validity is:

> p and q
> Therefore p

Arguments thus can have more than one logical form. But if an argument is valid, it is because it has a valid logical form. When we speak of "the form" of an argument this is to be taken as reference to the form of the argument upon which rests its validity or invalidity.

EXERCISES 4.3

Each pattern below is invalid. Prove that each pattern is invalid by the method of counterexample.

1. p or q
   p
   $\therefore q$
2. If p, then q
   q
   $\therefore p$
3. If p, then q
   Not p
   $\therefore$ Not q
4. If p, then q
   If r, then q
   $\therefore$ If p, then r
5. If q, then p
   If q, then r
   $\therefore$ If p, then r

6. Not both p and q
   $\therefore$ Not p and not q
7. p
   $\therefore p$ and q
8. If p, then q
   $\therefore$ If q, then p
9. If p, then q
   If r, then s
   Either q or s
   $\therefore$ Either p or r
10. p only if q
    q
    $\therefore p$

ANSWERS

1. *p*: Democrats are the majority party in Congress.
   q: Republicans are the majority party in Congress.
3. *p*: Shirley Chisolm is President of the United States.
   q: A Democrat is President of the United States.
5. *q*: Felix is a cat.
   p: Felix is an animal.
   r: Felix has whiskers.
7. *p*: Jimmy Carter is the 39th President of the United States.
   q: Jerry Ford is the 39th President of the United States.
9. *p*: Dr. Perkins is a Republican.
   q: Dr. Perkins can register to vote.
   r: Dr. Perkins is a Democrat.
   s: Dr. Perkins can register to vote.
   (Dr. Perkins is an Independent)

Sentential and Predicate Logic

We have encountered two kinds of argument patterns. First, there are patterns that use variables or placeholders for sentences and logical words, such as "or," "not," "and," and "if, then." These logical words are called *sentence connectives*. Second, there are patterns that use variables or place-holders for general terms and logical words like "all" and "some." These logical words are called *quantifiers*. Argument patterns of the first kind are examples of what are called *sentential* argument patterns. Argument patterns of the second kind are examples of what are called *predicate* argument patterns. *Sentential logic* is the study of methods for determining the validity or invalidity of sentential argument patterns. *Predicate logic* is the study of methods for determining the validity of predicate argument patterns.

In this introduction to formal logic we begin with the study of sentential logic and end with predicate logic. The methods of logic introduced are ways to determine the validity of sentential and predicate argument patterns. Sentential logic will be applied to what we will call *sentential arguments*. These are arguments whose validity or invalidity is a function of how sentences are related by sentence connectives. Predicate logic will be applied to what we will call *predicate arguments*. These are arguments whose validity is also a function of how general terms are related by quantifiers and sentence connectives. The examples of sentential and predicate arguments to which these methods will be applied will be arguments that occur in everyday contexts.

The first task before us is to set down methods for determining the validity of sentence argument patterns. To do this we first need a precise account of sentence connectives. This is the topic of the next chapter.

EXERCISES 4.4

Which of the following arguments are sentential arguments?

1. If determinism holds, then man does not have free will. Man has free will. Therefore determinism does not hold.
2. Machines are causally determined, so humans are machines since they are causally determined.
3. If I study I am likely to make good grades. If I do not study I can enjoy myself. Therefore I will either have good grades or enjoy myself.
4. All departures from law should be punished. Whatever happens by chance is a departure from law. Hence whatever happens by chance should be punished.
5. All athletes are muscular. Georgia is muscular, so she is an athlete.
6. A fool can win your heart only if you are a bigger fool. A fool can win your heart. Thus you are a bigger fool.
7. Christ died for our sins. Any life on other planets is not part of us. So life on other planets cannot be saved.
8. Either we will end pollution or not. If we do, then we will have a no growth economy. If we do not, then man will not survive. Man will survive, so we will eventually end pollution.
9. Nixon loves San Clemente, so San Clemente loves Nixon.
10. All the world loves a lover. Bob does not love Alice. Therefore Alice does not love herself.

ANSWERS

Only **1**, **3**, **6**, and **8** are sentential arguments.

5

Truth-Functional Connectives

Natural languages have devices that connect simple sentences to form compound sentences. In this chapter we will introduce symbols which correspond to these devices. We need these symbols in order to formulate efficient methods of determining the validity of sentential argument patterns and thus sentential arguments. A noteworthy feature of the sentence connectives to be introduced in this chapter is that they form truth-functional compound sentences. We begin by explaining the notion of a compound sentence, and then we will take up the notion of truth-functional compound sentences.

Truth-Functional Compounds

Any sentence that contains another sentence as a part is a *compound sentence*. Thus the following are all compound sentences:

(1) If the book is blue, then the book is colored.
(2) Agatha believes that Mars is inhabited.
(3) It is false that Mars is inhabited.

Since "the book is blue" and "the book is colored" are sentences that are parts of (1), (1) is a compound sentence. Since "Mars is inhabited" is part of (2) and is part of (3), both (2) and (3) are compound sentences. A sentence that is not compound will be said to be simple.

The devices for forming compound sentences in sentential logic are patterned after the ordinary language expressions

and; or; if, then; if and only if

175

and the adverb

not

These words are used to form compound sentences. They are sometimes called compound sentence formers, but we will follow the usual practice and call them sentence connectives.

The sentence connectives in sentential logic have the property of being truth-functional. To say that a sentence connective is *truth-functional* is to say that the compound sentence it forms is a truth-functional compound. A truth-functional compound sentence is one whose truth or falsity depends entirely on the truth or falsity of its component sentences. To find out whether a truth-functional compound is true or false *all* one needs to know is the truth value of its component sentences.

To illustrate, consider

(4)   It is not the case that Mars is inhabited.

There are two possibilities with respect to the truth or falsity of the simple sentence in (4) "Mars is inhabited". These can be indicated as follows, letting "**T**" be "true" and "**F**" be "false":

Mars is inhabited
T
F

Now we say of (4) that it is **F** in the first case and **T** in the second. In other words, if "Mars is inhabited" is true, then (4) is false, and if "Mars is inhabited" is false, then (4) is true. Schematically,

Mars is inhabited	(4)
T	**F**
F	**T**

(4) is thus a truth-functional compound, since its truth or falsity is exclusively determined by the truth or falsity of its component sentence.

"~" and English "not"

We will now introduce the symbol "~". The name of this symbol is "*tilde*." It forms compounds called negations. The rule for its use is that the compound it forms is **T** if and only if the component is **F**; and the compound it forms is **F** if and only if the component is **T**. Clearly, (4) is the negation of "Mars is inhabited," and is a truth-functional compound.

There are various ways in English to form a negation of a sentence. For example, here are some ways we can form the negation of "He is patriotic":

He is not patriotic.
He is unpatriotic.
It is false that he is patriotic.
It is not the case that he is patriotic.
That he is patriotic is untrue.
He is a traitor.

If one represents "He is patriotic" by the "p," then each of these negations can be expressed as "$\sim p$." We often deny that a sentence is true in more elaborate ways than by using "not" or "it is false that." We deny a sentence, for example, when we say "That's absurd," "Whatever possessed you to say that" or "You've got to be kidding." However, it is not always obvious what the negation of a sentence is. The denial of

Some students are lazy.

is not

Some students are not lazy.

for *both* sentences are true. If p is the negation of q, then they must have opposite truth values. If p is the negation of q, then if p is **T**, then q is **F** and if p is **F**, then q is **T** and vice-versa. The negation of "Some students are lazy" is in fact

No students are lazy.

"·" and English "and"

Next consider a compound sentence formed by using "and":

(1)   Eliza is playing tennis and Mini is playing tennis.

There are four possibilities with respect to the truth or falsity of its two component sentences and here they are:

Eliza is playing tennis	Mini is playing tennis
T	**T**
T	**F**
F	**T**
F	**F**

Looking at the rows, both can be **T**, one **T** and the other **F**, and so on. We say of (1) that it is true if both component sentences are true, otherwise we say (1) is false. In other words, we have this situation:

Eliza is playing tennis	Mini is playing tennis	(1)
T	**T**	**T**
T	**F**	**F**
F	**T**	**F**
F	**F**	**F**

For example, the third row indicates that when the first sentence is false and the second true, (1) is false. (1) is a truth-functional compound. The truth or falsity of (1) is exclusively determined by the truth or falsity of its component sentences.

In sentential logic "·" the dot, is used as "and" is used in (1). The dot is used to form conjunctions. The compound formed by "·" is true if and only if both components are true; otherwise it is false.

"And" in English is not always used to connect sentences. Consider:

Eliza and Mini are at school.

But this sentence can naturally be rephrased as one in which two sentences are connected, namely:

Eliza is at school and Mini is at school.

In other cases such a rephrasing becomes less promising. Consider the following:

(2)   Grant and Lincoln were contemporaries.
(3)   Eliza and Mini are sisters.
(4)   Two and two make four.

One could, with some effort, manipulate the first into

Grant lived from 1882 to 1885 and Lincoln lived from 1809 to 1865.

But there might very well be some question whether this states what (2) states. In any case, in neither (3) nor (4) is "and" used to connect two sentences.

One feature of "·" is that it is commutative. That is "$p \cdot q$" means the same as "$q \cdot p$." "And" is used commutatively in (1). But "and" is not always used commutatively when it is used to connect sentences. For example:

(5)   Dick and Jane were married and Jane became pregnant.

Here the second "and" is not used commutatively. For (5) does not mean the same as

Jane became pregnant and Dick and Jane were married.

The reason is that the second "and" in (5) is used to express temporal succession and is synonymous with "and then."

"∨" and English "or"

The word "or" in English is ambiguous. It has two uses. These correspond to:

either but not both

which is called the *exclusive* "or," and the *inclusive* "or," which is

either or both

An illustration of the exclusive use of "or" would be:

(1)   Either today is Tuesday or today is my birthday.

We are saying that one of these things is true, but not both. An illustration of the nonexclusive use of "or:" suppose one thinks that Kripke is a philosopher or Frege is, and perhaps *both* are. He may express this by saying:

(2)   Kripke is a philosopher or Frege is a philosopher.

Here one would be saying that either one or the other or both are philosophers. One might replace "or" here with "and/or." Assuming that (2) is the nonexclusive use of "or" we obtain the following truth analysis for (2):

Kripke is a philosopher	Frege is a philosopher	(2)
T	T	T
T	F	T
F	T	T
F	F	F

(2) is false only in the event that both of its component sentences are false. If they are both true, or if one or the other is, then (2) is true. (2) is a truth-functional compound. If (1) is analyzed in the same way, the following results:

Today is Tuesday	Today is my birthday	(1)
T	**T**	**F**
T	**F**	**T**
F	**T**	**T**
F	**F**	**F**

(1) is also a truth-functional compound. Notice (1) is false when both components are true. If one says "This is so, *or* that is so (but not both)," then if both are true, what he says is false.

The symbol "∨," the wedge, will now be introduced and patterned after nonexclusive use of "or." It is used to form disjunctions. And compounds it forms are **F** if and only if both components are **F**; otherwise they are **T**.

"⊃" and English "If, then"

"If, then" performs various duties in English. For example, consider these uses:

(1)   If John can recite the first stanza of "The Raven," then he has studied it.
(2)   If the pipe is not fixed, then the plaster will be ruined.
(3)   If either you or he has broken the window, and you did not, then he did.
(4)   If we have a cold spell, then the tomatoes will die.

The sentence which is between "if" and "then" in an "if, then" sentence is called the *antecedent*. The sentence that follows "then" is the *consequent*. All these uses of "if, then" have a parallel feature of special interest. For example in (2), if the pipe is not fixed and if the plaster is not ruined, (2) is said to be false. If we have a cold spell but the tomatoes do not die (because, for example, they are a hardy variety), then (4) is false. The same considerations apply to (1). What all of these "if, then" sentences have in common is that if the antecedent is true and the consequent is false then the "if, then" sentence is false. "If, then" sentences in logic are called *conditionals*. If a conditional is true, then it is not the case that the antecedent is true and the consequent is false. Using some of the symbols just introduced, we can put the point this way: If a conditional, "if p, then q," is true, then $\sim(p \cdot \sim q)$.

We are now ready to introduce the symbol "⊃" the horseshoe. It will be used to form conditionals. Thus $p \supset q$ will be read "if p, then q." $p \supset q$ will mean the same as $\sim(p \cdot \sim q)$. This connective will form truth-functional compounds, and its behavior can be indicated as follows:

p	q	$p \supset q$
T	T	T
T	F	F
F	T	T
F	F	T

The compound formed by $p \supset q$ is false if and only if the antecedent is **T** and the consequent is **F**.

It is important to notice, however, that the significance of the conditionals in sentences (1)–(4) is not maintained by replacing "if, then" with "$\supset$." As we can see in the above table, $p \supset q$ is true if p is false. But of (1) through (4) we would not say that they are true if their antecedents are false. For example, if the pipe is fixed we would not say that (2) is true on *that* account. (2) is true if the pipe is not fixed *and* if the plaster is ruined because of the pipe's not being fixed. Similarly, if we did not have a cold spell we would not suppose that (4) is true because of *this*. (4) is shown to be true by observation of tomato plants in a cold spell and by knowledge about the relation of cold to the life of plants and, in particular, of tomato plants. (1) would not be true if the person cannot recite the first stanza of "The Raven"; rather, (1) is true because the "ability to recite" requires "study." Also if the consequent is true in $p \supset q$, the conditional is true whether the antecedent is true or false. This too does not accord with our uses of "if, then." Often if the antecedent is false, we do not judge the statement as being true or false.

If we take the above conditionals as representative samples of conditionals in English, that is, as sentences of the form "If . . . , then . . . ," then conditionals in English are not truth-functional. We might say they are truth-functional only with respect to falsity. For each, if the antecedent is true and the consequent is false, the conditional is false. But for each conditional to be true, no combination of **T** or **F** antecedent or consequent is sufficient. For in each case a relation of a certain sort must exist between what is referred to in the antecedent and the consequent for the conditional to be true.

There are, in fact, conditionals in English that are not even negatively truth-functional. For example:

(5) If Sen. Chitterlings is elected President in 1980, then the moon is made of blue cheese.

We would *not* ordinarily say that if (5) is true, then it is false that both Chitterlings will be elected and that the moon is not made of blue cheese, for we would not, in most contexts, speak of (5) as true or false. (5) would commonly be used as an expression of pessimism about Chitterlings' chances, as a joke, and the like. For example, (5) may mean:

(6) It is absolutely impossible for Chitterlings to be elected.

(6) is not, as we can see, an "if, then" statement.

Here is another example of an "if, then" statement which lacks the common feature:

(7) If Nixon had lost the 1972 election, he would not have had to suffer through Watergate.

new idea

This is known as a contrary-to-fact conditional—for obvious reasons. In the case of these conditionals it is understood that the antecedent is, as a matter of fact, false, so that the falsity of (7) could not result from the truth of the antecedent and the falsity of the consequent. The conditions under which such conditionals are true and false is a topic of the philosophy of science.

The last examples to be considered here are known as generalized conditionals. As one could guess, the generalized conditional is a generalized version of the ordinary conditional:

(8) If one can recite the first stanza of "The Raven," then he has studied it.
(9) If a number is divisable by 4, then it is even.

Notice that it makes no sense to speak of the antecedent as being true, since the antecedent is not a statement; that is, one cannot say that

One can recite the first stanza of "The Raven."
A number is divisible by 4.

are true or false because no particular person or number is being referred to. The consequent, as is easily seen, is also neither true nor false. So the truth conditions of the conditional are not applicable to the generalized conditional. Later it will be seen that the generalized conditional must be analyzed into more complex components than whole statements.

The fit between "∼," "·," "∨," and their English counterparts is quite close. Where there are deviations one will be able to handle them by analyzing them into more complex paraphrases than simple negations, conjunctions, and disjunctions. This seems not to be the case with English conditionals and "⊃." "If, then" in English is seldom used to form truth-functional conditionals. How then can sentence logic be applied to English arguments using conditionals if "⊃" is truth-functional and "if, then" is not?

First, the truth-functional conditional is indispensible in mathematics. All essential uses of "if, then" in mathematics are truth-functional. In mathematics theorems are derived from axioms and postulates. Such derivations constitute deductive arguments and, therefore, can be judged valid or not by the methods of logic since the connectives (and other logical terms) are truth-functional. Second, it is widely believed that in a scientific language which is expressively complete (can express what needs to be expressed in the sciences) the conditionals along with the other connectives will be truth-functional.

Finally, when "if, then" is used in sentential arguments to connect sentences, these uses of "if, then" generally share the common feature discussed above. An English conditional used to connect sentences is false if the antecedent is true and the consequent is false. And this allows us to apply sentence logic. To illustrate, consider the following sentential argument:

(10) If Socrates is a man, then Socrates is mortal.
      Socrates is a man.
      Therefore Socrates is mortal.

The "if, then" in (10) is not a truth-functional horseshoe. That is,

If Socrates is a man, then Socrates is mortal.

would not be considered to be true merely because Socrates is not a man. So we need to distinguish (10) from interpretations of the argument pattern

$p \supset q$
p
Therefore q

But still (10) comes within the scope of sentence logic. Argument (10) is close enough to truth-functional structure to apply sentence logic, because only the common feature of conditionals is essential to its logical form. The conditional in (10) expresses, in part:

$\sim$(Socrates is a man $\cdot$ $\sim$ Socrates is mortal)

Now if

Socrates is a man (second premise)

then from what is said it follows that

Socrates is mortal (conclusion)

For

$\sim(p \cdot \sim q)$
p
Therefore q

is a valid pattern. Later this will be formally verified.

"≡" and English "if and only if"

The final connective that we wish to introduce is the symbol "≡." It is called the *biconditional*. $p \equiv q$ is read "p if and only if q." Normally when we say "p if and only if q" we mean that if p then q and if q then p. That is how $p \equiv q$ will be understood, but now the conditionals will be "⊃." That is, $p \equiv q$ will express the same thing as the conjunction of $p \supset q$ and $q \supset p$. The biconditional sentence is true if the sentences connected have the same truth value. That is, $p \equiv q$ is true if either both p and q are true or both p and q are false, otherwise it is false. Note that since $p \supset q$ expresses no more than $\sim(p \cdot \sim q)$, $(p \supset q) \cdot (q \supset p)$ is true if p and q are both true or if p and q are both false, otherwise it is false. This is why $p \equiv q$ expresses the same thing as $(p \supset q) \cdot (q \supset p)$.

Earlier we reviewed some of the uses of "if, then" and noted that these uses do not always exactly parallel $p \supset q$. Thus any such discrepancies accrue to $p \equiv q$, since $p \equiv q$ expresses that conjunction of $p \supset q$ and $q \supset p$, and yet it is nevertheless read "p if and only if q."

Before going on it will prove useful to review some of the nomenclature for these sentence connectives. The symbol "∼" is called the negation sign and any sentence having the form $\sim p$ is called a negation. The symbol "·" is called the conjunction sign. Any sentence having the form $p \cdot q$ is called a conjunction, with the component sentences being called conjuncts. The symbol "∨" is called the disjunction sign. Any sentence having the form $p \vee q$ is called a disjunction. The sentences connected by "∨" are called disjuncts. The symbol "⊃" is called the conditional sign. Any sentence having the form $p \supset q$ is called a conditional. The sentence following "if" is called the antecedent of the conditional and the statement following "then" is called the consequent of the conditional. Finally the symbol "≡" is called the biconditional sign. Any sentence having the form $p \equiv q$ is called a biconditional. In what follows we will freely use this terminology. In addition a simple sentence is one which contains no sentence as a part. All statements formed by using sentence connectives are thus nonsimple, or compound, sentences. Compound sentences formed by simple sentences plus these sentence connectives are said to be truth-functional compounds. A compound is a truth-functional compound if its truth value is determined by the truth values of the component sentences.

The Scope of Sentence Connectives

The *scope* of a sentence connective comprises those parts of a compound sentence governed by the connective. The compound sentence:

John went home or Mary went home and Susan went home.

is ambiguous with respect to the scope of "or" and "and." This sentence could be understood as either:

(1) Both John went home or Mary went home and Susan went home.
(2) Either John went home or Mary went home and Susan went home.

Replacing "or" with "$\vee$" and "and" with "$\cdot$" the ambiguity can be resolved using parentheses as follows:

(1′) (John went home $\vee$ Mary went home) $\cdot$ Susan went home.
(2′) John went home $\vee$ (Mary went home $\cdot$ Susan went home).

In both (1) and (1′) the scope of "or" is "John went home" and "Mary went home," whereas the scope of "and" is "John went home or Mary went home" and "Susan went home." In both (2) and (2′) the scope of "or" is "John went home" and "Mary went home and Susan went home," whereas the scope of "and" is "Mary went home" and "Susan went home." If we wish to negate:

$$p \vee q$$

that is, if we wish to negate the disjunction of p and q, it will not do to write

$$\sim p \vee q$$

for this will be understood as the negation of p, it being disjoined to q. That is, "$\sim$" will be taken to have merely the scope of p, not the disjunction of p and q. To negate the disjunction we use parentheses to indicate that the scope of "$\sim$" is the disjunction as follows:

$$\sim (p \vee q)$$

When more than one set of parentheses are needed to indicate the scope of connectives we will go from parentheses to brackets to curly brackets, and so on. To illustrate, in:

$$\sim \{[(p \supset \sim q) \vee r] \cdot [p \supset (q \cdot r)]\}$$

the first pair of parentheses indicates the scope of "$\supset$," the second pair of parentheses indicates the scope of the second "$\cdot$." The first pair of brackets indicates the scope of "$\vee$," whereas the second pair of brackets indicates the scope of the second "$\supset$." Finally the curly brackets indicate the scope of "$\sim$." The connective with the greatest scope will be called the *main connective* in a compound sentence. In the last example "$\sim$" is the main connective. It goes without saying that in English, various methods other than parentheses are used to indicate the scope of the connectives we use. Commas, semicolons, voice inflection, and gestures are some methods we use to indicate the scope of connectives. For example, (1) and (2) could be written, respectively:

John went home or Mary went home, and Susan went home.
John went home, or Mary went home and Susan went home.

Similarly, this next compound sentence:

If either Mary pops her balloon or George doesn't, and Dierdre lets hers go into the clouds; then we will all go home happy.

could be rendered using symbols and parentheses and brackets as:

[(Mary pops her balloon ∨ ~ George pops his balloon) · Dierdre lets hers go into the clouds] ⊃ we will all go home happy.

Determining the Truth Value of Compound Sentences

In this chapter five sentence connectives have been introduced. They are: "~," "∨," "·," "⊃," and "≡." Generally these will be used to replace "not," "or," "and," "if, then," and "if and only if" in symbolizing statements. The rules for these truth-functional connectives can be summarized as follows:

1. ~p is opposite in truth value to p.
2. $p ∨ q$ is false when and only when both p and q are false.
3. $p · q$ is true when and only when both p and q are true.
4. $p ⊃ q$ is false when and only when p is true and q is false.
5. $p ≡ q$ is true when and only when p and q have the same truth value.

These rules can be used to determine the truth value of sentences composed of sentences and sentence connectives given the truth value of the component sentences. Suppose the variable p is interpreted as a true sentence and q is interpreted as a false sentence. What would be the truth value of the following formula?

~$[p ⊃ (q · ~ ~p)]$

To solve this problem one first replaces the variables with their supposed truth values, letting **T** stand for "true" and **F** stand for "false:"

~$[\mathbf{T} ⊃ (\mathbf{F} · ~ ~\mathbf{T})]$

Next, as the second step, determine the truth value of the smallest compound formed by a connective. The compound with the connective that has the least scope is the smallest compound. In this case ~**T** is the smallest compound, then ~ ~**T**, then **F** · ~ ~**T**, and so on. The truth value of ~**T** is **F** by rule 1 above for negation. So the second step applied gives us:

$$\sim[\mathbf{T} \supset (\mathbf{F} \cdot \sim\mathbf{F})]$$

Finally, repeat the second step until all that is left is a **T** or **F**. Applying this to the example, we obtain (dropping idle parentheses as we go along):

$\sim[\mathbf{T} \supset (\mathbf{F} \cdot \mathbf{T})]$	by rule 1
$\sim[\mathbf{T} \supset \mathbf{F}]$	by rule 3
$\sim[\mathbf{F}]$	by rule 4
T	by rule 1

The final **T** shows us that if p is **T** and q is **F** then the preceding formula is **T**.

Using the five rules for the sentence connectives and the method just described, one can easily determine the truth value of a compound sentence given the truth value of its simple components. What, for example, is the truth value of the following sentence:

> Tom Sawyer is captain if and only if it is not true that either Ben is second captain or Jo is treasurer.

if we suppose:

> "Tom Sawyer is captain" is **T**
> "Ben is second captain" is **F**
> "Jo is treasurer" is **T**

To solve this problem, first replace each English connective with the appropriate symbol and replace the simple sentences with their supposed truth value, obtaining:

$$\mathbf{T} \equiv \sim(\mathbf{F} \vee \mathbf{T})$$

Continually applying the rules to the smallest compounds gives us:

$$\mathbf{T} \equiv \sim\mathbf{T}$$
$$\mathbf{T} \equiv \mathbf{F}$$
$$\mathbf{F}$$

Thus given the assigned truth values, the compound is false.

EXERCISES 5.1

A. Supposing that *p* is true, *q* is false, and *r* is true, determine whether the following compound formulas are true or false:

1. $(p \lor q) \equiv \sim(\sim p \cdot \sim q)$
2. $\sim(p \lor \sim q)$
3. $\sim[\sim q \lor (p \cdot \sim r)] \cdot (\sim p \lor \sim q)$
4. $\sim(p \lor \sim q) \cdot \sim(\sim r \lor \sim p)$
5. $(p \equiv q) \equiv \sim[\sim(\sim p \lor q) \lor \sim(\sim q \lor p)]$
6. $\sim\{\sim[\sim q \lor (p \cdot \sim r)] \cdot (\sim p \lor q)\}$
7. It is not the case that both *p* and *q*.
8. It is not the case that *p* and it is not the case that *q*.
9. It is not the case that either *p* or *q*.
10. It is not the case that *p* or it is not the case that *q*.
11. If *p* and *q* then *r*.
12. Both *p* and if *q* then *r*.

B. Supposing that "Ben Rogers is captain" is true, "Jo Harper is captain" is true, and "Tom Sawyer is captain" is false; determine whether the following compound sentences are true or false:

1. Either Ben Rogers is captain or if Jo Harper is captain then Tom Sawyer is not captain.
2. If either Tom Sawyer is captain or Jo Harper is captain then Ben Rogers is captain.
3. If Jo is not captain, then it is false that both Tom and Ben are captains.
4. Both Ben Rogers is captain and either Jo or Tom is captain.
5. It is not the case that if Ben Rogers is captain then Tom is captain and Harper is not captain.
6. Either Tom and Jo are captain, or Rogers and Tom are captains.
7. Jo is captain, and either Rogers is captain or Jo and Tom are captains.
8. If either Ben or Tom is captain and Tom isn't, then if Ben is captain, then Tom isn't and Ben isn't.

ANSWERS

A. 2, 3, 4, 8, and 9 are false; the rest are true.

B. 2. $(F \lor T) \supset T$, T; 4. $T \cdot (T \lor F)$, T; 6. $(F \cdot T) \lor (T \cdot F)$, F;
8. $[(T \lor F) \cdot \sim F] \supset [T \supset (\sim F \cdot \sim T)]$, F.

Truth Tables

In this chapter the first techniques for establishing the validity of sentential arguments are introduced. These techniques are called truth table analyses. Since sentential arguments are valid if they are interpretations of valid argument patterns made up of sentence connectives and variables for statements (recall Chapter 4), the techniques introduced in this chapter are directed at determining whether a sentential argument pattern is valid or not valid. As was just indicated, sentential argument patterns are argument patterns made up exclusively of sentence connectives ("$\sim$," "$\vee$," "$\cdot$," "$\supset$," and "$\equiv$") and sentence variables (p, q, r, . . .). It should be recalled that p, q, and so on are letters which will function as sentence variables, that is, blanks in which any sentence may be put. It should also be recalled that one obtains an interpretation of such a pattern when one uniformly replaces the variables with sentences, that is, when one replaces each occurrence of a given variable with the same sentence. The valid sentential argument patterns are those argument patterns which always result in valid arguments no matter how they are interpreted.

Truth Tables for the Sentence Connectives

In the last chapter the connectives—"$\sim$," "$\vee$," "$\cdot$," "$\supset$," "$\equiv$"—were introduced. The functions of these connectives are given in the following rules:

1. $\sim p$ is opposite in truth value to p.
2. $p \vee q$ is false when and only when *both* p and q are false.
3. $p \cdot q$ is true when and only when *both* p and q are true.

189

4. $p \supset q$ is false when and only when p is true and q is false.
5. $p \equiv q$ is true when and only when p and q have the same truth value.

Each of these rules can be expressed by use of what are called *truth tables*. Consider "$\sim$" and this table:

Rule 1

	p	$\sim p$
1.	**T**	**F**
2.	**F**	**T**
	(a)	(b)

(1) and (2) are the *rows* of the table. (a) and (b) are the two *columns* of the table. In the first column are listed all possible truth values for p. In row (1), where p is given as **T**, $\sim p$ is **F**, and in row (2) where p is given as **F**, $\sim p$ is **T**. This table sets down how we are understanding the symbol "$\sim$." Using a table we have expressed the rule for "$\sim$." Similarly, the rule for "$\cdot$" is expressed in this table:

Rule 3

p	q	$p \cdot q$
T	**T**	**T**
T	**F**	**F**
F	**T**	**F**
F	**F**	**F**
(a)	(b)	(c)

All possible combinations of truth values for p and q are given in columns (a) and (b). In column (c) is given the truth value of $p \cdot q$, given the truth value of p and q on each row. For example, on row 1, given that p is **T** and q is **T**, $p \cdot q$ is **T**; on row 2, given that p is **T** and q is **F**, $p \cdot q$ is **F**. This last table can also be written in this way:

p	$\cdot$	q
T	**T**	**T**
T	**F**	**F**
F	**F**	**T**
F	**F**	**F**

Truth table representations for the rules of the other three connectives are given as follows:

	Rule 2			Rule 4			Rule 5	
p	$\vee$	q	p	$\supset$	q	p	$\equiv$	q
T	T	T	T	T	T	T	T	T
T	T	F	T	F	F	T	F	F
F	T	T	F	T	T	F	F	T
F	F	F	F	T	F	F	T	F

EXERCISE 6.1

As noted in the last chapter "or" is ambiguous. It can be used to express "either p or q or both" or "either p or q but not both"; $p \vee q$ expresses the first (the inclusive sense of "or"). Let $p \veebar q$ express the second (the exclusive sense of "or"). Provide a rule and a truth table for "$\veebar$."

ANSWER

Rule: $p \veebar q$ is true if and only if p and q have opposite truth values.

Logical Equivalence

The next use to which truth tables can be put is showing whether or not one sentential formula is logically equivalent to another formula. By sentential formula is meant a sentence composed of sentence variables and sentence connectives. One such formula A is said to be *logically equivalent* to another such formula B when they agree in their truth value no matter what truth values are assigned to the component variables in A and B. If two formulas A and B are logically equivalent, then A expresses what B expresses. By one natural account of "meaning" they mean the same. Since a truth table shows the truth value of a formula under the various possible combinations of truth values for the component variables, truth tables can be used to verify whether or not one formula is equivalent to another.

To illustrate, recall that in the previous chapter it is remarked that to say $p \supset q$ amounts to saying $\sim(p \cdot \sim q)$. It can now be said that $p \supset q$ is logically equivalent to $\sim(p \cdot \sim q)$ and truth tables can be used to verify this. The component variables of the formulas are p and q. The possible assignments of truth values to this pair are:

p	q
T	T
T	F
F	T
F	F

For each of these possible combinations of truth values for p and q the truth value of $p \supset q$ is (by rule 4):

$p \supset q$
T
F
T
T

What is the truth value of $\sim(p \cdot \sim q)$ for each of these possible combinations of truth values for p and q? For $\sim q$ we have (by rule 1):

$\sim q$
F
T
F
T

when q is **T**, **F**, **T**, and **F**. And for $p \cdot \sim q$ we have (by rule 3):

$p \cdot \sim q$
F
T
F
F

when we have the preceding assignments of truth values to p and q. According to rule 1, the truth value of $\sim(p \cdot \sim q)$ is the opposite of $(p \cdot \sim q)$. So for each of the possible combinations of truth values for p and q the truth value of $\sim(p \cdot \sim q)$ is the following:

$\sim(p$	$\cdot$	$\sim q)$
T		F
F		T
T		F
T		F

These results can be put together in one table as follows:

·p	q	p ⊃ q	~q	p · ~q	~(p · ~q)	
T	T	T	F	F	T	F
T	F	F	T	T	F	T
F	T	T	F	F	T	F
F	F	T	T	F	T	F
		(a)			(b)	

By observation we can now easily verify that $p \supset q$ is logically equivalent to $\sim (p \cdot \sim q)$. Column (a) and column (b) match. This means that $p \supset q$ and $\sim (p \cdot \sim q)$ agree in their truth value no matter what truth value is assigned to their component variables. Thus $p \supset q$ is logically equivalent to $\sim (p \cdot \sim q)$.

$p \supset q$ is also equivalent to $\sim p \vee q$ (and thus $\sim (p \cdot \sim q)$ is equivalent to $\sim p \vee q$). We can now show that they are equivalent by using a truth table like the preceding one. First we fill in the possible truth values for p and q.

p	⊃	q		~p	∨	q
T	T	T		F		T
T	F	F		F		F
F	T	T		T		T
F	T	F		T		F

We have eliminated the p and q columns to avoid unnecessary notation. One can easily see how to fill in the "∨" column of $p \vee q$, but certain things need to be kept in mind with $\sim p \vee q$. Earlier, the notion of the *scope* of connectives was introduced. In $\sim p \vee q$, the "$\sim$" has the least scope. Since the "∨" has the greatest scope, it is the main connective in $\sim p \vee q$. (In $\sim (p \cdot \sim q)$, the first "$\sim$" is the main connective.) Under the main connective will be found the truth value of the whole formula $\sim p \vee q$. Thus we first fill in the value for the connective with the least scope, the "$\sim$," then for the connective with the next greatest scope, the "∨," which is also the main connective in this case. We obtain:

p	⊃	q		~p	∨	q
T	T	T		F	T	T
T	F	F		F	F	F
F	T	T		T	T	T
F	T	F		T	T	F
	(a)				(b)	

The same truth values are given under the *main* connectives of each, thus the two formulas are equivalent.

The truth values of $p \equiv q$ and $(p \supset q) \cdot (q \supset p)$ are also the same, as shown on this table:

p	≡	q		(p	⊃	q)	·	(q	⊃	p)
T	T	T		T	T	T	T	T	T	T
T	F	F		T	F	F	F	F	T	T
F	F	T		F	T	T	F	T	F	F
F	T	F		F	T	F	T	F	T	F
	(a)						(b)			

In $(p \supset q) \cdot (q \supset p)$ the "⊃" are tied for having the least scope. In these cases it makes no difference which column of truth values is listed first. The "·" is the main connective.

The truth values of $\sim p \cdot \sim q$ are not the same as that of $\sim (p \cdot q)$, and thus the two formulas are not equivalent, though they might appear to be equivalent. That they are not equivalent can be shown in this table:

~p	·	~q		~	(p	·	q)
F	F	F		F	T	T	T
F	F	T		T	T	F	F
T	F	F		T	F	F	T
T	T	T		T	F	F	F
	(a)				(b)		

In $\sim (p \cdot q)$ the "~" is the main connective. Clearly, columns (a) and (b) do *not* match.

Another way to determine whether two formulas or sentences expressed in symbols are equivalent is by using "≡." When two formulas or sentences are equivalent, as, say, $\sim (p \cdot q)$ and $(\sim p \vee \sim q)$ are, then the truth table for $\sim (p \cdot q) \equiv (\sim p \vee \sim q)$ will have all **T**'s under the "≡." For according to rule 5, $p \equiv q$ is true when p and q have the same truth value. Thus we have this table:

~	(p	·	q)	≡	(~p	∨	~q)
F	T	T	T	T	F	F	F
T	T	F	F	T	F	T	T
T	F	F	T	T	T	T	F
T	F	F	F	T	T	T	T
				(a)			

In column (a), the column of the main connective, there are all **T**'s. The equivalence of any two formulas, then, can be tested by joining the formulas with "≡," and seeing what is obtained for the "≡" column in the truth table.

If there are all **T**'s, the formulas are equivalent; if there are one or more **F**'s, the formulas are not equivalent.

To determine the equivalence of two formulas with one component variable, say p, the possible truth values for the component variable, in this case just p, are, of course:

$$p$$

T
F

If there are three different kinds of component variables in the two formulas, say p, q, and r, then the possible truth values for these components are:

p	q	r
T	T	T
T	T	F
T	F	T
T	F	F
F	T	T
F	T	F
F	F	T
F	F	F

In general the number of rows for n number of variables when setting down possible truth values for n number of variables is 2^n. Thus if a pair of formulas A and B had four different kinds of sentence variables, a sixteen-row truth table would be needed to determine the logical equivalence of A and B.

EXERCISE 6.2

A. Use truth tables to determine which pairs of formulas are equivalent:

1. $\sim(p \cdot q)$ and $(\sim p \cdot \sim q)$
2. $\sim(p \vee q)$ and $(\sim p \cdot \sim q)$
3. $\sim(p \supset q)$ and $\sim(\sim p \vee q)$
4. $p \supset q$ and $(\sim q \supset \sim p)$
5. $p \supset q$ and $(\sim p \supset \sim q)$
6. $p \vee q$ and $q \vee p$
7. $p \supset q$ and $p \supset (p \cdot q)$
8. $\sim p \supset q$ and $\sim[p \supset (p \cdot q)]$
9. $(p \supset \sim q) \vee p$ and $p \vee \sim q$
10. $(p \supset q) \cdot (q \supset r)$ and $\sim(r \supset p)$

11. $(p \supset \sim q) \cdot (r \supset q)$ and $(p \supset \sim r)$
12. $p \vee (q \cdot r)$ and $(p \vee q) \cdot (p \vee r)$
13. $p \cdot (q \vee r)$ and $(p \cdot q) \vee (p \cdot r)$
14. $p \supset (q \vee r)$ and $(p \supset q) \cdot (p \supset r)$
15. $(p \cdot q) \cdot r$ and $(p \cdot r) \cdot q$
16. $(p \vee q) \vee r$ and $(p \vee r) \vee q$
17. $(p \vee q) \vee r$ and $r \vee (q \vee p)$

B. Show the equivalence of $p \underline{\vee} q$ and $(p \vee q) \cdot \sim (p \cdot q)$.

C. Construct formulas using only "$\sim$" and "$\cdot$" plus sentence variables equivalent to $p \supset q$, $p \vee q$, and $p \equiv q$.

D. Let $p \mid q$ read "not both p and q." Construct a truth table for $p \mid q$. Show that $p \mid p$ is equivalent to $\sim p$ and that $(p \mid q) \mid (p \mid q)$ is equivalent to $p \cdot q$. If C above shows that any formula can be expressed using the pair "$\sim$" and "$\cdot$," what does D show?

ANSWERS

A. **2**, **3**, **4**, **6**, **7**, **12**, **13**, **15**, **16**, and **17** are equivalent. The rest are not equivalent.

D.

p	q	$p \mid q$	$p \mid p$	$\sim p$	$(p \mid q) \mid (p \mid q)$	$p \cdot q$
T	T	F	F	F	T	T
T	F	T	F	F	F	F
F	T	T	T	T	F	F
F	F	T	T	T	F	F

Testing Argument Patterns

An argument pattern is valid if a valid argument is always the outcome of interpreting the pattern. An argument is valid if it cannot be the case that its premises are true and its conclusion false. From this it follows that if no matter what truth values are supplied for the component variables of an argument pattern, one can never obtain premises that are each true and a conclusion that is false, then the pattern is valid. Truth tables provide a procedure for determining whether or not a sentential argument pattern is valid.

To see how this works, suppose we wish to establish which of the following argument patterns are valid and which are not:

$$p \supset q \qquad p \supset q \qquad p \supset q \qquad p \supset q$$
$$p \qquad\qquad q \qquad\qquad \sim q \qquad\qquad \sim p$$
$$\therefore q \qquad\quad \therefore p \qquad\quad \therefore \sim p \qquad\quad \therefore \sim q$$

It will first be convenient for purposes of truth table analysis to rewrite these patterns so that each can occur on one line as follows:

$$p \supset q, p \therefore q \quad p \supset q, q \therefore p \quad p \supset q, \sim q \therefore \sim p \quad p \supset q, \sim p \therefore \sim q$$

where "$\therefore$" here and above is the familiar sign for "therefore," indicating that what comes before it are premises and what follows is a conclusion. The premises are separated by ordinary commas. The second step is to construct a truth table for the argument pattern that has been re-expressed on one line. A truth table for an argument pattern is a table that indicates the truth value of each premise and the truth value of the conclusion for all possible truth-value assignments to the component variables found in the argument pattern. The truth table for the first of the preceding argument patterns is

p	$\supset$	$q,$	p	$\therefore$	q
T	T	T	T		T
T	F	F	T		F
F	T	T	F		T
F	T	F	F		F

Having now constructed a truth table for the first argument pattern, we can, by observing each row, confirm whether the pattern is valid or not. If for each row there is no case where each premise is **T** and the conclusion **F**, then the pattern is valid. Observe in connection with the first argument pattern that there are no such rows; thus the pattern is valid. The following are tables for each of the other three argument patterns:

p	$\supset$	$q,$	q	$\therefore$	p		p	$\supset$	$q,$	$\sim q$	$\therefore$	$\sim p$		p	$\supset$	$q,$	$\sim p$	$\therefore$	$\sim q$
T	T	T	T		T		T	T	T	F		F		T	T	T	F		F
T	F	F	F		T		T	F	F	T		F		T	F	F	F		T
F	T	T	T		F		F	T	T	F		T		F	T	T	T		F
F	T	F	F		F		F	T	F	T		T		F	T	F	T		T

By examining the first of the preceding tables we find that in the third row each premise is true and the conclusion is false, so the second argument pattern is invalid. On the next table there are no rows where each premise is true and conclusion false, so the third argument pattern is valid. On the last table, row 3 reveals the invalidity of the last argument pattern.

EXERCISES 6.3

A. Determine by using truth tables whether the following sentential argument patterns are valid or invalid.

1. $p \cdot q \therefore p$
2. $p \cdot q \therefore q \cdot p$
3. $\sim\sim p \therefore \sim\sim\sim\sim p$
4. $(\sim p \vee \sim q) \therefore p \cdot q$
5. $(p \vee q) \cdot \sim p \therefore q$
6. $p \supset q \therefore \sim(p \cdot \sim q)$
7. $(p \supset q) \cdot \sim q \therefore \sim p$
8. $(p \supset q) \cdot \sim p \therefore \sim q$
9. $p \vee (q \cdot r) \therefore (p \vee q) \cdot (p \vee r)$
10. $p \vee (q \equiv r) \therefore p \vee q$
11. $(p \cdot q) \cdot r \therefore \sim[(\sim p \vee \sim q) \vee \sim r]$
12. $p \cdot (q \cdot r) \therefore p \vee q$
13. $(p \supset q) \cdot (q \supset r) \therefore r \supset p$
14. $(p \vee q) \cdot \sim(p \vee q) \therefore s$
15. $(p \supset q) \cdot p, r \therefore q \cdot r$
16. $p \equiv q, p \cdot \sim q \therefore p$
17. $(p \supset q) \cdot (r \supset s), (q \vee s) \therefore p \vee r$
18. $(p \equiv q) \cdot p, \sim q \therefore p \cdot \sim q$
19. $(p \supset q) \cdot (r \supset s), (q \cdot s) \therefore p \cdot s$
20. $p \vee q \therefore \sim(\sim p \cdot \sim q)$

B. Do the same for Exercises 4.3.

ANSWERS

A. **1, 2, 3, 5, 6, 7, 9, 11, 12, 14, 15, 16, 18**, and **20** are valid.

Testing Arguments

If an argument is an interpretation of a valid argument pattern, then it is valid. Since the validity of sentential argument patterns can be established by using truth tables, the validity of those arguments whose validity is a function of the way sentences are related by sentence connectives, what are being called sentential arguments, can be established. To see how this works let us apply the procedure to this rather complex sentential argument:

If the warranty is in force, then the motorist was responsible and the company is liable; and if the warranty is not in force, then the motorist is not responsible and the company is not liable. Therefore the company is liable if and only if the warranty is in force and the motorist is responsible.

To handle this complex argument one must first reveal all of its sentential structure. This means that one must display all of its sentence connectives including all the "nots." To do this, replace each simple sentence (if a sentence contains no sentence connective, it is simple; otherwise it is compound) with an appropriate capital letter and replace each English connective, including negation, with its symbolic counterpart. This first step is called *symbolizing the argument*.

Using W for "The warranty has expired," M for "The motorist is responsible," and C for "The company is liable," we symbolize the preceding argument as follows:

$$[W \supset (M \cdot C)] \cdot [\sim W \supset (\sim M \cdot \sim C)]$$
$$\therefore C \equiv (W \cdot M)$$

The second step is to replace uniformly all occurrences of each capital letter with a different statement variable. The pattern we obtain by replacing W with p, M with q, and C with r is:

$$[p \supset (q \cdot r)] \cdot [\sim p \supset (\sim q \cdot \sim r)]$$
$$\therefore r \equiv (p \cdot q)$$

The third and final step is to use a truth table to determine whether or not this argument pattern is valid. After a truth table for this argument pattern is constructed, the results will show that the pattern is valid. Thus the validity of the preceding argument is demonstrated.

To speed up these procedures one can omit replacing each capital letter with sentence variables. In other words, one can treat the capital letters as if they were variables, thus counting the symbolized argument as an argument pattern, and test it using a truth table.

Since the arguments we shall consider in this and the next chapter are all sentential arguments, it follows that if the truth table test shows the pattern to be invalid, the argument is invalid. In other words, if we restrict application of truth tables to sentential arguments, as we are doing, then truth tables can be used to demonstrate either the validity of the argument or the invalidity.

To illustrate these points, suppose the premise and conclusion of the last argument are switched. The resulting argument, treating it as an argument pattern, is tested overleaf.

$$C \equiv (W \cdot M) \quad \therefore \quad [W \supset (M \cdot C)] \cdot [\sim W \supset (\sim M \cdot \sim C)]$$

T	T	T	T	T		T	T	T	F	T	F	F	F
T	F	T	F	F		F	F	F	F	T	T	F	F
T	F	F	F	T		T	T	F	T	F	F	F	F
T	F	F	F	F		T	F	F	T	F	T	F	F
F	F	T	T	T		F	F	F	F	T	F	F	T
F	T	T	F	F		F	F	F	F	T	T	T	T
F	T	F	F	T		T	F	F	T	F	F	F	T
F	T	F	F	F		T	F	T	T	T	T	T	T

Checking down the rows we find that with rows 6 and 7 the premise is true and the conclusion false. Since the argument is a sentential argument, these results confirm that the argument is invalid.

EXERCISES 6.4

Determine whether the following sentential arguments are valid or not, by first symbolizing the argument and then testing the indicated argument pattern using a truth table. Use the suggested capital letters as abbreviations for the simple sentences.

1. If you take the final, then you can pass Professor Black's course. If you pass her course, then you must take her final. So taking the final is both necessary and sufficient for passing her course. (T, P)

2. Logic makes no sense. Therefore either I give it up or logic makes sense if and only if I give it up. (L, G)

3. If either Mitchell or Agnew winds up with the nomination, then Kennedy will be nominated and a Democratic victory will be assured. Therefore either Mitchell will not win the nomination or Kennedy will be nominated. (M, A, K, D)

4. A student passes logic only if he does the exercises. But students never do exercises. Therefore a student never passes logic. (P, E)

5. If inflation ceases, then price controls are initiated. If inflation ceases, I shall be able to make ends meet. Thus if price controls are initiated, I shall be able to make ends meet. (I, P, E)

6. It is not true that both the price of gold is fixed and people speculate on the price. People do speculate on the price of gold, so the price of gold is not fixed. (G, S)

7. Either you can reach the roof with the ladder or we need a new ladder. We do not need a new ladder, so you can reach the roof with the ladder. (R, N)

8. Either it is too late to study or someone has gone to bed early. Since not everyone went to bed early, it must be too late to study. (L, B)

9. If the pool is closed, we can't practice dives; and if we can't practice, we'll lose the meet. So if the pool is closed, we'll lose the meet. (C, P, L)

10. If the pizza is done we will either split it with our roommates or eat it all and get sick. Since we will not share it when it's done, we will eat it all and get sick. (*P, S, E, G*)

11. Either Edgar will get his degree in June or he will drop out of school and take a job with his father. If I know him, he will not drop out of school; consequently, he will get his degree. (*D, S, T*)

12. If the high-pressure system has moved in, the weather back home is clear and the temperatures are mild. But since the system has not yet moved in, the weather must be either cloudy or hot. (*H, W, T*)

13. We either stand up to China or we don't. If we save the free world, then we stand up to China, whereas if we die as a civilization, we don't stand up to China. Therefore we either save the free world or die as a civilization. (*C, S, D*)

14. If the president has the long-range interest of the college in mind, then he would obtain new money for the philosophy department. Since this year the philosophy department has received a great deal of new money, it follows that the president does indeed have the long-range interests of the college in mind. (*P, N*)

15. If Nightly is a city boss then he is a Democrat. If he is a pragmatist then he is a Democrat. So Nightly is a pragmatist, provided that he is a city boss. (*C, D, P*)

ANSWERS

1. $T \supset P, P \supset T \therefore T \equiv P$ valid
3. $(M \lor A) \supset (K \cdot D) \therefore {\sim}M \lor K$ valid
5. $I \supset P, I \supset E \therefore P \supset E$ invalid
7. $R \lor N, {\sim}N \therefore R$ valid
9. $(C \supset {\sim}P) \cdot ({\sim}P \supset L) \therefore C \supset L$ valid
11. $D \lor (S \cdot T), {\sim}S \therefore D$ valid
13. $C \lor {\sim}C, (S \supset C) \cdot (D \supset {\sim}C) \therefore S \lor D$ invalid
15. $C \supset D, P \supset D \therefore C \supset P$ invalid

Formal Sentential Fallacies

A *formal fallacy* is an invalid deductive argument which resembles a valid pattern so closely that persons can be misled into thinking it is valid. Consider the following example of a formal fallacy:

(1) If Godfrey Daniel passed logic, then Godfrey Daniel can do the exercises.

Godfrey Daniel can do the exercises.

Therefore Godfrey Daniel passed logic.

The validity of this sentential argument is a matter of this pattern's being valid:

(2) $p \supset q$
    q
    $\therefore p$

And one can easily verify that it is not valid. Now contrast (1) with

(3) If Godfrey Daniel passed logic, then Godfrey Daniel can do logic exercises.
Godfrey Daniel passed logic.
Therefore Godfrey Daniel can do logic exercises.

This is a valid sentential argument and an interpretation of the following valid pattern (*modus ponens*):

(4) $p \supset q$
    p
    $\therefore q$

Since patterns (2) and (4) are somewhat similar, it can happen that some may be misled into thinking that (1) is a valid argument.

(1) is an example of the fallacy of affirming the consequent. The *fallacy of affirming the consequent* occurs when an argument is an interpretation of pattern (2) and when the validity of the argument is a matter of (2) being a valid pattern. This last clause is needed because invalid argument patterns can have interpretations which result in valid arguments. For example if we make these replacements in (2):

"Godfrey Daniel passed logic" for p
"Godfrey Daniel can do logic exercises and Godfrey Daniel passed logic" for q.

The resulting argument is valid because its validity is a matter of the following pattern being valid:

$p \supset (q \cdot p)$
$q \cdot p$
$\therefore p$

And it is easily seen that this pattern is valid.

Another example of a formal fallacy is the fallacy of denying the antecedent. The *fallacy of denying* the antecedent occurs when the validity of an argument rests on whether the following pattern is valid (which it is not):

$p \supset q$
$\sim p$
$\therefore \sim q$

It is the resemblance of this pattern to the following valid pattern (*modus tollens*):

$p \supset q$
$\sim q$
$\therefore \sim p$

which accounts for some thinking it is valid.

Three other formal fallacies arise out of the following invalid patterns:

$p \supset q, r \supset q \therefore p \supset r$ or $p \supset q, p \supset r \therefore q \supset r$
$p \supset q, r \supset s, q \lor s \therefore p \lor r$
$p \supset q, r \supset s, \sim p \lor \sim r \therefore \sim q \lor \sim s$

The first gives rise to the *fallacy of invalid hypothetical syllogism*. The second and third give rise to the *fallacy of invalid dilemma*. The valid patterns that they closely resemble are, respectively:

$p \supset q, q \supset r \therefore p \supset r$ (hypothetical syllogism)
$p \supset q, r \supset s, p \lor r \therefore q \lor s$ (constructive dilemma)
$p \supset q, r \supset s, \sim q \lor \sim s, \therefore \sim p \lor \sim r$ (destructive dilemma)

We will count an argument an interpretation of one of the above patterns even when the order is changed or when premises are conjoined. Thus exercise 13 in Ex 6.4 will count as an interpretation of the first form of invalid dilemma even though, as written, it would be symbolized as:

$C \lor \sim C, (S \supset C) \cdot (D \supset \sim C) \therefore S \lor D$

Here S goes in for p, C for q, D for r and $\sim C$ for s. The disjunctive premise comes first, and the two conditional premises are conjoined. Ex 12 in Ex 6.4 will also count as a fallacy of denying the antecedent. Symbolizing it as it stands, we obtain

$H \supset (W \cdot T), \sim H \therefore \sim W \lor \sim T$

But since $\sim W \lor \sim T$ is equivalent to $\sim (W \cdot T)$ this argument is a fallacy of denying the antecedent.

EXERCISES 6.5

A. Identify any formal fallacy in the following arguments. Remember that the argument may not be in the same order as the pattern, and it may have conjoined premises and still be an interpretation of the pattern. Also an argument is an interpretation of a pattern if a part is equivalent to the corresponding part of the pattern.

1. If Jimmy Carter tells Andrew Young to shut up, he will shut up. Andrew Young will not continue to express what is on his mind, so Jimmy Carter will tell Andrew Young to shut up.

2. No cloned baby exists. If there is a cloned baby then someone knows more about human cloning than almost anyone in the world. So there is no one who knows more about human cloning than almost anyone in the world.

3. If Jane enjoys a significant improvement in her night vision, then it is Jane's time for ovulation. If Jane has enhanced night vision, then Jane can see dimly lit objects ordinarily undetectable in the dark. So if it is Jane's time for ovulation, then Jane can see dimly lit objects ordinarily undetectable in the dark.

4. If there are price controls, then inflation can be held at a tolerable level. If there is a recession, then inflation can be held at a tolerable level. Runaway inflation will not go away. So there will neither be price controls nor a recession.

5. If men are good, then there is no need for laws. If men are bad, then laws are useless. But men are neither good nor bad; there are no saints nor are there pure sinners. So it is not true that either there is no need for laws or laws are useless.

6. If Jane favors the Equal Rights Amendment, then she is a bitter woman seeking a constitutional cure for her personal problems. Jane is such a woman, so she naturally favors ERA.

7. Either Jane favors ERA or she is a woman who finds her greatest fulfillment at home with her family. Jane, however, favors ERA. Thus she does not find fulfillment at home.

B. Do you find any instances of formal fallacies in exercises 6.4?

ANSWERS

A. 1. affirming the consequent 3. invalid hypothetical syllogism
   5. denying the antecedent (twice) 7. denying the antecedent
B. 5. invalid hypothetical syllogism   13. invalid dilemma
   15. invalid hypothetical syllogism

Truth Table Short-Cut Method

The number of rows that a truth table has for a given argument pattern can be calculated by using the formula 2^n, where n is the number of different variables found in the pattern. Thus if a pattern contains p, q, and r there will be 2^3, or eight rows, and if it also contains s there will be 2^4, or sixteen rows, and so on. Clearly the truth table method so far described becomes unwieldly when one has more than three different sentence variables to consider. What is needed is some way to abbreviate a truth table analysis, a truth table short-cut method.

Such methods are available and one such method is called the truth table *reductio ad absurdum* test. This test is made up of the following three steps. To determine whether a given argument pattern is valid or not valid:

1. Assume that each premise of the pattern can be **T**, and the conclusion **F**. In other words, assume that the pattern is not valid.
2. Follow out the consequences of this assumption and try every possible way to make each premise true and conclusion false.
3. If one fails in step 2 the pattern is valid; the assumption of step 1 is false. If one succeeds in step 2 the pattern is not valid, since one has succeeded in assigning truth values to the variables so that each premise comes out true and the conclusion false.

This method is used on the following pattern:

$$(p \cdot q) \supset (r \cdot \sim r) \therefore p \supset \sim q$$

Following out step 1, one obtains

$$(p \cdot q) \supset (r \cdot \sim r) \therefore p \supset \sim q$$
$$\text{T} \qquad \text{F} \quad \text{F}$$

Step 2 tells us we must follow out the consequences of these assignments and see if we can make truth value assignments to the variables so that each premise is true and the conclusion is false. We note that if this conditional conclusion is true, one is not *forced* to make any truth value assignments; however, if the conclusion is **F**, then since it is a conditional the antecedent must be **T** and the consequent **F**, which means that one *must* make p **T** and q **T** and do this everywhere in the argument, as follows:

$$(p \cdot q) \supset (r \cdot \sim r) \therefore p \supset \sim q$$
$$\text{T} \quad \text{T} \, \text{T} \qquad \qquad \text{TF F T}$$

We are now forced to make additional truth value assignments. In the antecedent of the premise we have a conjunction with two **T**'s as conjuncts; thus the antecedent is **T**, so if the conditional is **T** then the consequent must be **T**. We arrive, then, at

$$(p \cdot q) \supset (r \cdot \sim r) \therefore p \supset \sim q$$
T T T   T   T F F T

Now *r*, the only variable for which we have not made a value assignment, must be both **T** and **F** if the conjunction in the consequent of the premise, $r \cdot \sim r$, is to be true. But clearly if we put in **T** for *r* we have:

$$(p \cdot q) \supset (r \cdot \sim r) \therefore p \supset \sim q$$
T T T T T F   T F F T

and this line indicates an impossible state of affairs, an inconsistent truth value assignment. A conjunction cannot be true if one of its conjuncts is **F**. On the other hand, if we assign **F** to *r* we run into another inconsistency, namely:

$$(p \cdot q) \supset (r \cdot \sim r) \therefore p \supset \sim q$$
T T T T F T   T   T F F T

We have thus failed on trying to make good on the assumption of step 1. We cannot possibly make the premises **T** and the conclusion **F**, so step 3 indicates that the argument pattern is valid. Note that if one reaches a choice point following out these steps, i.e., reaches a place where he is not forced to make a truth value assignment in doing step 2, he should select one of the unassigned variables and try out **T** and then **F** (always selecting the most frequently occurring variable; it makes the solution easier). If in making assignments to the remaining variables, one can make consistent truth value assignments, the argument pattern is not valid. If *both* the **T** route and **F** route end up in inconsistent truth value assignments, then the argument pattern is valid. Note that in some cases one may have more than one choice point. All alternatives must lead to inconsistencies if the pattern is valid.

In the next example the *reductio* test is used on an invalid argument pattern:

$$r \vee (q \cdot p), p \supset \sim r \therefore \sim q \vee \sim p \qquad \text{step 1}$$
T   T   F

At this point the only place one is forced to make a truth value assignment is in the conclusion in following out step 2. Both *q* and *p* must be **T**. Thus,

$$r \vee (q \cdot p), p \supset \sim r \therefore \sim q \vee \sim p \qquad \text{step 2}$$
T T T T   T T   F T F F T

It is now ensured that the first premise is **T**. If the second premise $p \supset \sim r$ is to be **T** with p **T**, r must be **F**. And we can consistently make r **F** in the problem. The following is a consistent assignment of truth values to the variables which makes the premises true and conclusion false: step 2 (completion)

$$r \vee (q \cdot p), \; p \supset \sim r \therefore \sim q \vee \sim q \qquad \qquad \text{step 2 (completion)}$$
$$\textbf{F T \; T \; T \; \; TT TF \; \; FT F FT}$$

In other words, if p is **T**, q is **T**, and r is **F** each premise is true and the conclusion is false. What we have in effect succeeded in doing is to show that if this argument pattern were placed on a truth table, the row where p is **T**, q is **T**, and r is **F** would be the row which verifies the invalidity of the argument pattern. Having been able consistently to follow out the assumption of step 1, we verify that the argument pattern is not valid.

This short-cut truth table method is called the *reductio ad absurdum* test because it is the application of a valid pattern commonly called *reductio ad absurdum* (reduce to absurdity) or indirect proof. Here are the two important variations of the pattern:

$$p \supset (q \cdot \sim q) \qquad \qquad (p \cdot q) \supset (r \cdot \sim r)$$
$$\therefore \sim p \qquad \qquad \qquad \therefore p \supset \sim q$$

It is the first valid pattern that is capitalized on in the short-cut method. In step 1 we assume that the argument pattern in question is not valid. This is our p. From this we try to show that an absurdity follows, namely, an inconsistent truth value assignment must be made to the component variables of the pattern. This is our $q \cdot \sim q$. In other words, we try to show the truth of the premise of the first pattern above. If we succeed, then we can conclude that p is false; in this case, our assumption is false. $\sim p$ is true. The pattern is valid.

EXERCISE 6.5

Use the *reductio ad absurdum* truth table method in determining which of the following argument patterns are valid and which are not valid.

1. $p \supset q$
    $r \supset s$
    $\sim q \vee \sim s$
    $\therefore \sim p \vee \sim r$

2. $p \equiv (q \vee r)$
    $\sim q \supset \sim r$
    $\therefore q \vee \sim p$

3. $q \supset \sim p$
    $\sim r \vee q$
    $\therefore p \supset \sim r$

4. $(p \cdot q) \vee (\sim p \cdot \sim q)$
    $\therefore p \equiv q$

5. $(p \cdot q) \supset r$
   $(p \cdot \sim q) \supset \sim r$
   $\therefore p \supset (r \equiv q)$

6. $(p \cdot q) \supset r$
   $\therefore (p \supset r) \vee (q \supset r)$

7. $p \equiv q$
   $q \equiv r$
   $\therefore \sim p \equiv \sim r$

8. $(p \supset q) \vee (p \supset r)$
   $\therefore p \supset (q \cdot r)$

ANSWERS

Only **8** is invalid. These assignments establish the invalidity of **8**: p, **T**; q, **F**; and r, **T**.

Symbolizing Arguments

To apply truth table analysis to sentential arguments one must first symbolize the argument. This involves replacing each simple sentence with an appropriate capital letter and replacing the connectives with symbolic connectives. In ordinary language, however, conditionals, conjunctions, or disjunctions can often be expressed in a variety of ways. For example, conditionals are often expressed in ways other than with the expression "if, then." Here are some familiar variants of "if, then," each of which can be rephrased as "if p, then q":

p only if q	p is sufficient for q
q if p	q is necessary for p
q provided that p	q when p
q in case p	

Some especially troublesome variants of disjunctions are

p unless q	p or else q
p except q	

That each of these can be rendered $p \vee q$ may at first seem odd, but often this is a legitimate paraphrase of the English. For example, "You won't pass logic unless you do the exercises," can be expressed as, "You won't pass logic or you do the exercises." And since $\sim p \vee q$ is equivalent to $p \supset q$, this sentence can also be paraphrased as, "If you pass logic, then you do the exercises." Doing the exercises is a necessary condition that must be met if one is to pass logic. Sometimes, though not often, one says something stronger than $p \vee q$ in saying "p unless q". Namely, one says $\sim p \equiv q$. For example, consider certain contexts in which mother says to the child: "You cannot go out and play (G) unless you first clean up your room (C)." Not only is mother saying that the room must be cleaned up before the child goes out:

$G \supset C$

but they both understand her to be saying, in addition,

$C \supset G$

when the child goes out with mother's approval after cleaning up the room.
Among the variants for conjunction there are, for example,

p but *q*	*p* despite *q*
p although *q*	*p* yet *q*
both *p* and *q*	*p* while *q*
p however *q*	*p* albeit *q*
not only *p* but *q*	

Finally it should be noted that "neither *p* nor *q*" can go into $\sim (p \vee q)$ or $\sim p \cdot \sim q$, these being equivalent to each other.

A recommended procedure in symbolizing complex statements is first to symbolize the outermost structure and then symbolize inwardly step by step. For example, consider the sentence.

If Herman and Morris don't show up, then neither will the ETT deal be concluded nor will the directors meet and confer with the members from the Justice Department unless Sam comes to his senses and takes matters into his own hands.

First we make a decision as to the main connective in the sentence. Taking "if, then" as the main connective we expose just this connective, obtaining:

Herman and Morris don't show up $\supset$ neither will the ETT deal be concluded nor will the directors meet and confer with the members from the Justice Department unless Sam comes to his senses and takes matters into his own hands

Next we can consider the consequent and establish its main connective. Selecting the "unless" we turn the last into:

Herman and Morris don't show up $\supset$ (neither will the ETT deal be concluded nor will the directors meet and confer with the members for the Justice Department $\vee$ Sam comes to his senses and takes matters into his own hands)

Taking next the "neither, nor" idiom we have:

Herman and Morris don't show up $\supset$ [~(the ETT deal be concluded $\vee$ the directors meet and confer with the members from the Justice Department) $\vee$ Sam comes to his senses and takes matters into his own hands]

Finally if we replace the simple sentences with the appropriate capital letters and put in the three conjunctions we obtain:

$$(\sim H \cdot \sim M) \supset \{\sim [E \vee (D \cdot C)] \vee (S \cdot T)\}$$

EXERCISES 6.6

Symbolize the following arguments and test each one for validity using the *reductio ad absurdum* truth table method. Use the suggested capital letters for abbreviations of simple sentences. Indicate any occurrences of formal fallacies.

1. Only actors are good politicians unless only clever people are actors. But not all good politicians are good actors, so not all actors are clever people. (A, C)

2. Blue is at the top of the batting order only if our team has a chance of winning. But since his slump, he has been batting seventh. Therefore our team doesn't have a chance. (B, T)

3. Canby did not put up the campaign signs because it is not the case that both Canby and Lee put up the signs and Lee always puts up campaign signs. (C, L)

4. Either the hypothesis will be tested or it will be ignored (by not testing it). And so if it is tested it will not be ignored. (T, I) (Hint: use exclusive "or.")

5. Church will start early only if Elder Older is home from the convention and he will be home from the convention only if he has a lot of will power. Since church is already late, Elder Older has no will power. (C, H, W)

6. The president will either obtain money for the psychology laboratory or persuade Dr. Freund to stay another year and raise Dr. Freund's salary, provided that he has the long-range interests of the college in mind. But he won't do any of these things, so, obviously, he is taking a short-range view. (M, P, R, L)

7. Either the Dirty Sox or the Greenskins will wind up in the cellar unless Ned Witt keeps hitting. But Ned won't keep up his hitting and the Dirty Sox will win more than the Greenskins, so the Greenkins will wind up in the cellar. (D, G, N)

8. Dr. Freund will not speak to Dr. Fiendish in case that Dr. Fiendish will not cut down the tree that is about to fall on Freund's garage, but Fiendish will never speak to Freund. Therefore, if either Freund speaks to Fiendish or Fiendish speaks to Freund, Fiendish will cut the tree. (*FR, FI, S*)

9. Unless you fish early in the morning or in the evening, you do not catch bass in August. So if you do not fish in the evening, but you catch bass in August, you fish early in the morning. (*M, E, C*)

10. If there is no test, then the students will be happy only if the professor stays in bed. The professor is in class every day. If the students are happy, then there is no test. Therefore the students will not be happy. (*T, H, P*)

11. Either the students will be happy and there will be no exam or the students will be happy and class will be dismissed. The students are happy. They were not dismissed. Therefore there was no exam. (*H, E, C*)

12. If either the students are happy or classes are dismissed, then Roger loses his bet. If Roger loses his bet, then Stan gains. Classes are to be dismissed and Stan will not gain anything. So the students are not going to be happy. (*H, C, R, S*)

13. If you are interested in history or in scenery, then you will leave the main road. If you are not interested in history, then you won't leave the main road. Therefore you are interested in history provided that you are interested in scenery. (*H, S, L*)

14. If Canby puts up campaign signs then if Lee puts them up, all of them will go up. So if Lee puts them up then if Canby puts them up, they all go up. But neither Lee nor Canby put any of them up, so not all of them are up. (*C, L, A*)

15. The instructor will be pleased if Anderson takes the test and passes. But if Anderson takes the test and writes illegibly, the instructor will not be particularly pleased. In fact, Anderson will pass the test only if he writes illegibly. (Then the instructor won't be able to see how bad his exam is.) So Anderson won't both take the test and pass. (*I, T, P, W*)

16. If JB has his way and KF is defeated, then the Fitzwig dynasty will come to an end if KF is defeated. Therefore if KF is defeated and the Fitzwig dynasty does not continue, JB will not have his way. (*J, K, F*)

17. If you love her and give her gifts, then she will love you. Hence if you love her, she will love you if and only if you bring her gifts. (*L, G, S*)

18. Although knowledge is virtue only if the will is not predetermined, decision making is morally relevant nonetheless. There is no responsibility except when the will is free. Decision making is morally irrelevant if and only if there is no responsibility. Therefore, whatever else it might be, knowledge is surely not virtue. (*K, P, D, R*)

19. Butkus runs, passes, blocks, and even blows up the football. He runs if and only if he is neither blocking nor passing. He blocks provided that he does not blow up the football. Therefore if Butkus blows up the football, then he passes but does not run. (R, P, B, F)

20. It is not the case that a woman succeeds if and only if she has ability. A woman has ability provided that she displays it once in a while. If a woman displays her ability once in a while but does not succeed, then either she is unlucky or someone is against her. In case a woman is unlucky, she cannot display her ability. Thus it is sufficient for a woman's succeeding that she not have someone who is against her. (S, A, D, U, G)

ANSWERS

1. $A \vee C, \sim A \therefore \sim C$ invalid
3. $\sim (C \cdot L), L \therefore \sim C$ valid
5. $(C \supset H) \cdot (H \supset W), \sim C \therefore \sim W$ invalid
7. $(D \vee G) \vee N, \sim N \cdot \sim D \therefore G$ valid
9. $(M \vee E) \vee \sim C \therefore (\sim E \cdot C) \supset M$ valid
11. $(H \cdot \sim E) \vee (H \cdot C), H, \sim C \therefore \sim E$ valid
13. $[(H \vee S) \supset L], \sim H \supset \sim L \therefore S \supset H$ valid
15. $(T \cdot P) \supset I, (T \cdot W) \supset \sim I, P \supset W \therefore \sim (T \cdot P)$ valid
17. $(L \cdot G) \supset S \therefore L \supset (S \equiv G)$ invalid
19. $R \cdot P \cdot B \cdot F \cdot R \equiv \sim (B \vee P), \sim F \supset B \therefore F \supset (P \cdot \sim R)$ valid

7

Elementary Inferences

If the reader of this book were asked to determine the validity of the following argument:

Either Godfrey Daniel will get his degree in June or he will drop out of school and live off his parents. He will not get his degree, so he will live off his parents. (G, D, L)

following the procedures introduced in the last chapter, he would first symbolize the argument as follows:

$G \vee (D \cdot L), \sim G \therefore L$

He would then use a truth table method to verify that the symbolized argument is valid. However, if one were unacquainted with truth table methods one would most likely use a different method to establish the validity of the argument. One might reason in this way: If $G \vee (D \cdot L)$ and if $\sim G$, then $D \cdot L$ follows. And if $D \cdot L$, then L, the conclusion, follows. So the argument is valid. It is not without justification that this way of determining that the argument is valid is said to be a more natural method than a truth table analysis.

This method of establishing that an argument is valid is discussed in this chapter. Whether or not one fully realizes it, in using this method one assumes rules of inference. For example, in going from $D \cdot L$ to L one assumes the following rule:

From $p \cdot q$ one can infer q.

We now turn to some of these rules and the form by which one can set up "natural" proofs for sentential arguments. Such systems are called *natural deduction* systems for sentential logic.

Rules of Inference

When a sentential argument is valid the premises truth-functionally imply the conclusion. Premises *truth-functionally* imply the conclusion if and only if "premises ∴ conclusion" is an interpretation of a valid sentential argument pattern. The rules of inference studied in this chapter are truth-functionally valid rules, in that when one of them is applied to a given sentence or given sentences, the inferred sentence is truth-functionally implied by the given sentences. To ensure that the rules have this feature each rule will be determined by a valid pattern. That

$$p \lor q, \; \sim p \therefore q$$

is a valid pattern is easily established. This pattern suggests a rule of inference which can be stated as follows:

Rule 1:   From $p \lor q$ and $\sim p$ one can infer q.

This rule is applied in the following two inferences. (Regard these as arguments already symbolized.)

1.	$A \lor B$	
2.	$\sim A$	
3.	B	from 1 and 2 by rule 1

1.	$(A \cdot B) \lor C$	
2.	$\sim (A \cdot B)$	
3.	C	from 1 and 2 by rule 1

In each example above a third line is entered because it can be inferred from the previous two lines by rule 1. Note that in rule 1 and in the rest of the rules, statement variables p, q, r, and s are used. These function, as always, as places for simple or compound sentences. Thus, we can apply a rule of inference such as rule 1 when p or q are replaced with simple sentences, as both are in the first example above, or when p and q are replaced with compound sentences, as with p in the second example above.

The valid patterns:

$$p \cdot q \therefore p \qquad\qquad p \cdot q \therefore q$$

suggest the rule discussed at the beginning, namely:

Rule 2: From $p \cdot q$ one can infer p.
From $p \cdot q$ one can infer q.

This rule plus the first rule are applied in the next sequence of sentences:

1. $A \vee (B \cdot C)$
2. $\sim A$
3. $B \cdot C$ from 1 and 2 by rule 1
4. B from 3 by rule 2

In this numbered sequence of lines two inferences occur. The nature of each is made explicit by indicating on the right of the inferred sentence the lines from which it comes and by what rules. Indicating origin and rule in this way makes clear the *justification* for each inferred line.

These two rules plus others to be introduced will be used to construct proofs for sentential arguments. A proof for a sentential argument will be a sequence of sentences in which the premises occur first, the conclusion last, and in which each sentence is either a premise or is inferred from previous sentences in the squence by one of the given rules of inference. To illustrate, the preceding four-line sequence is a proof for the argument:

$A \vee (B \cdot C), \sim A \therefore B$

As another example, a proof for the next argument:

$\sim (A \cdot B) \cdot C, (A \cdot B) \vee D \therefore D$

would be:

1. $\sim (A \cdot B) \cdot C$ Premise
2. $(A \cdot B) \vee D$ Premise
3. $\sim (A \cdot B)$ 1 rule 2
4. D 2,3 rule 1

It is easily seen that this sequence of lines satisfies the preceding definition for a proof of a sentential argument. When a proof for an argument is constructed, this shows that the argument is valid and that the conclusion is truth-functionally implied by the premises, since each of the rules is truth-functionally valid.

Obviously in order to construct proofs for all valid sentential arguments we need more than two rules. Since any valid argument pattern determines a rule, the following pattern:

$p \supset q, p \therefore q$

determines the following rule:

Rule 3:   From $p \supset q$ and p one can infer q.

This rule is called *modus ponens* and its use is illustrated in the following proof:

$A \supset (B \cdot A), A \therefore B$

1.	$A \supset (B \cdot A)$	P ("P" for "premise")
2.	A	P
3.	$B \cdot A$	1,2 by *modus ponens*
4.	B	3 by rule 2

The other rules which will be used to construct proofs will now be given. (The validity of each can be demonstrated by showing the validity of its corresponding argument pattern.) We list the rules by indicating both their names and convenient abbreviations for their names.

Truth-Functional Rules of Inference

1. Disjunctive Syllogism (DS): From $p \lor q$ and $\sim p$ one can infer q.
2. Simplification (Simp): From $p \cdot q$ one can infer p.
   From $p \cdot q$ one can infer q.
3. *Modus Ponens* (MP): From $p \supset q$ and p one can infer q.
4. *Modus Tollens* (MT): From $p \supset q$ and $\sim q$ one can infer $\sim p$.
5. Conjunction (Conj): From p and q one can infer $p \cdot q$.
6. Hypothetical Syllogism (HS): From $p \supset q$ and $q \supset r$ one can infer $p \supset r$.
7. Addition (Add): From p one can infer $p \lor q$.
8. Constructive Dilemma (CD): From $p \supset q$ and $r \supset s$ and $p \lor r$ one can infer $q \lor s$.

It must be stressed and carefully noted that in applying these rules we can only apply them to sentences that are not parts of more complex sentences. Thus, for example, the following is an erroneous application of Simp:

1. $(A \cdot B) \supset C$
2. A from 1 by Simp (erroneous)

Line 1 is a conditional sentence and not a conjunction and Simp must be applied to sentences which are conjunctions. Similarly, DS applies to disjunctions and the negation of another sentence which is one of the disjuncts of the disjunction, MP applies to conditionals and to a sentence which is the antecedent of the conditional, and so on. In other words, taking Simp as our example, Simp is read: "if one has a sentence (not a part of a sentence) which is a conjunction, one can infer the first conjunct (same for second conjunct)."

Why construct proofs for sentential arguments when truth table methods can easily establish the validity of such arguments? There are several reasons for doing this. Among them are the following four reasons: First, the intrinsic interest in any proof system for sentential arguments; second, the value of having several methods for showing validity in sentential logic; third, the fact that later when we come to predicate logic we will need to make use of the proof system in this chapter; and, finally, as indicated at the outset of this chapter, this method for establishing the validity of arguments corresponds more or less with the natural method. And one would expect a formal logic to attempt as much as possible to have and to expose methods which closely correspond to our intuitions.

Why include the above eight rules, plus the remaining twenty rules to be discussed, in a natural deduction system for sentential logic? First, all of these rules are rules which we often employ in reasoning, and they are easily seen to be valid. Second, we wish to have a set of rules which are complete. To say the deduction system made up of these twenty rules is *complete* is to say that it is powerful enough to validate all sentential arguments. These twenty rules constitute a complete system for sentential logic. (The proof of the completeness of this system is an exercise in exercise section 10.6.) Now it will be easily seen later that we have *more* than enough rules for a complete system. That is, we could omit some rules and still have a complete system. For example later we will see that in place of the rule RCP we could use eight other rules. But there is an advantage to having more rules than are needed, logically speaking. It makes proof construction easier. For example it is easier to use RCP—one rule—than a set of eight rules.

EXERCISES 7.1

A. Each of the following is a partially worked-out proof for an argument. Fill in the missing justifications.

1. 1. $A \supset \sim C$ P
    2. $D \supset E$ P
    3. $\sim \sim C \cdot A$ P
    4. A
    5. $A \vee D$
    6. $\sim C \vee E$
    7. $\sim \sim C$
    8. E

2. 1. $(\sim B \supset C) \cdot (C \supset E)$ P
    2. $\sim E$ P
    3. $C \supset E$

      4. ~C
      5. ~B ⊃ C
      6. ~ ~B
      7. ~C · ~ ~B
      8. ~E · (~C · ~ ~B)
   3. 1. A ⊃ [A · (B · ~C)]   P
      2. A   P
      3. A · (B · ~C)
      4. A
      5. B · ~C
      6. ~C
      7. ~C ∨ A
      8. [A · (B · ~C)] ∨ [~C ⊃ (B · ~B)]
   4. 1. A ⊃ B   P
      2. [E ⊃ (C ∨ D)] ⊃ (F · G)   P
      3. B ⊃ [E ⊃ (C ∨ D)]   P
      4. ~(F · G)   P
      5. ~[E ⊃ (C ∨ D)]
      6. A ⊃ [E ⊃ (C ∨ D)]
      7. ~A
   5. 1. A   P
      2. A ∨ B
      3. (A ∨ B) ∨ (C · ~D)
      4. [(A ∨ B) ∨ (C · ~D)] ∨ B
      5. {[(A ∨ B) ∨ (C · ~D)] ∨ B} ∨ (C ⊃ ~B)
   6. 1. [(A ∨ B) ∨ (~C ∨ ~D)] · E   P
      2. (A ∨ B) ∨ (~C ∨ ~D)
      3. ~(A ∨ B)   P
      4. ~C ∨ ~D
      5. ~ ~C   P
      6. ~D

B.   Construct proofs for the following:

   1. G ⊃ (S ⊃ U), G, ~U ∴ ~S
   2. N ⊃ M, M ⊃ D, M ⊃ P, ~P, M ∨ N ∴ D
   3. J ⊃ B, D ⊃ H, ~U ∨ (J ∨ D), ~ ~U ∴ B ∨ H
   4. P, (P ∨ R) ⊃ D ∴ P · D
   5. (D ⊃ F) · (C ⊃ F), D ∨ C, (F ∨ F) ⊃ E, E ⊃ G ∴ G
   6. T ⊃ (C · O), T · B, W ∨ F, (C ∨ D) ⊃ ~W ∴ F

C.   Construct proofs for the following arguments. Use the suggested
       capital letters as abbreviations for simple sentences in symbolizing the
       arguments.

1. If Alberta Peach goes to the movie tonight, she will be unhappy if the movie is not a mystery. She will go, she says, and the movie is a travelogue, not a mystery. So she will be unhappy. (*M, H, R*)
2. If Prof. Goodshot owned a gun, he would have used it if he saw the thief. He owned a gun but didn't use it. So he didn't see the thief. (*G, U, T*)
3. Either Gumdrop was elected or our leader failed and the township will suffer a depression. If Gumdrop was elected, there won't be a depression for the township. However, there will not not be a depression for the township, so our leader failed. (*G, L, T*)
4. Certainly Mrs. Freund and Mrs. Friendly would get along if their husbands would, and if one was an ethicist and the other a psychologist they would get along. But Freund is a psychologist and Friendly is an ethicist. So their wives will get along. (*Fr, Fi, H, E, P*)
5. Suppose no one claims the book you found, now that you have advertised it as lost. You cannot sell the books if you flunk ethics, even though you advertised it as lost and no one claims it. If Dr. Freund finds out you sold the book, you will flunk ethics; and he will. So you can't sell it. (*C, A, F, S, Fr*)
6. Either Dr. Freund and Dr. Friendly are crotchety or their wives are. If the men are crotchety, their dogs are. If their wives are crotchety, then their kids are. Therefore either their dogs or their kids are crotchety. (*Fr, Fi, W, D, K*)
7. If price controls are initiated, then inflation will cease. If either price controls are not initiated or spending increases, then the interest rates are raised. What goes up never comes down when it comes to inflation, so we face higher interest rates. (*P, I, S, R*)
8. If God is omnipotent then he exists. If he exists, then there is justice. If there is justice, provided God is omnipotent, then there is reason for optimism. So let's not be pessimistic. (*O, E, J, R*)
9. If the market rallies, then, provided that I am bold, I can make a profit. If the market does rally, then, if I make a profit, my stocks go up. The market will rally. Therefore if I am bold, then my stocks have nowhere to go but up. (*M, B, P, S*)

ANSWERS

A. 1. 3 Simp; 4 Add; 1,2,5 CD; 3 Simp; 6,7 DS.
    3. 1,2 MP; 3 Simp; 3 Simp; 5 Simp; 6 Add; 3 Add.
    5. 1 Add; 2 Add; 3 Add; 4 Add.

B. 1. 4. $S \supset U$ 1,2 MP. 5. $\sim S$ 4,3 MT.
    3. 5. $(J \vee D)$ 3,4 DS. 6. $B \vee H$ 1,2,5 CD.
    4. 3. $P \vee R$ 1 Add. 4. D 2,3 MP. 5. $P \cdot D$ 1,4 Conj.

6. 5. T 2 Simp. 6. $C \cdot O$ 5,1 MP. 7. C 6 Simp.
    8. $C \vee D$ 7 Add. 9. $\sim W$ 8,4 MP. 10. F 9,3 DS.

C. **1.** 1. $M \supset (\sim R \supset \sim H)$ P. 2. $M \cdot \sim R$ P. 3. M 2 Simp.
        4. $\sim R \supset \sim H$ 1,3 MP. 5. $\sim R$ 2 Simp. 6. $\sim H$ 4,5 MP.
    3. 1. $G \vee (L \cdot T)$ P. 2. $G \supset \sim T$ P. 3. $\sim \sim T$ P. 4. $\sim G$ 2,3 MT.
        5. $L \cdot T$ 1,4 DS. 6. L 5 Simp.
    5. 1. $\sim C \cdot A$ P. 2. $(F \cdot A \cdot \sim C) \supset \sim S$ P. 3. $Fr \supset F$ P.
        4. Fr P. 5. F 3,4 MP. 6. $F \cdot A \cdot \sim C$ 5,1 Simp, Conj.
        7. $\sim S$ 2,6 MP.
    8. 1. $O \supset E$ P. 2. $E \supset J$ P. 3. $(O \supset J) \supset R$ P.
        4. $O \supset J$ 1,2 HS. 5. R 3,4 MP.
    9. 1. $M \supset (B \supset P)$ P. 2. $M \supset (P \supset S)$ P. 3. M P.
        4. $B \supset P$ 1,3 MP. 5. $P \supset S$ 2,3 MP. 6. $B \supset S$ 4,5 HS.

Replacement Rules of Inference

In addition to the preceding eight rules of inference a set of rules determined by a set of valid biconditionals will be used to construct proofs. An example of such a biconditional is

$$p \equiv \sim \sim p$$

If a truth table were constructed for this biconditional, there would be a column of all **T**'s under the biconditional connective, thus confirming that p is logically equivalent to $\sim \sim p$. The rule determined by this logical equivalence is called Double Negation (abbreviated DN). The rule can be stated as follows:

Any sentence can be replaced with its double negation, and any doubly negated sentence can be replaced with the sentence.

Rules determined by logically equivalent formulas will be so understood that they can apply to sentences whether they occur alone or as parts of sentences. To put this in other terms, they can be applied to whole sentences (as the first eight rules can be applied) or they can be applied to parts of sentences (as the first eight rules cannot). To illustrate, each inference following is justified by DN;

1. $\sim \sim (A \cdot B)$ 1. $A \supset B$ 1. $\sim (\sim \sim A \cdot B)$
2. $A \cdot B$ 1 DN   2. $A \supset \sim \sim B$ 1 DN   2. $\sim (A \cdot B)$ 1 DN

Another biconditional which determines one of the replacement rules is

$$\sim(p \vee q) \equiv (\sim p \cdot \sim q)$$

The rule is called DeMorgan's Theorem (DeM), after the English mathematician and logician Augustus DeMorgan (1806–1871) who discovered the rule. The rule:

> The negation of a disjunction can be replaced with a conjunction by dropping the negation sign, replacing the disjunction with a conjunction, and negating each of the resulting conjuncts. And vice versa.

A closely related biconditional which determines a rule also called DeMorgan's Theorem is

$$\sim(p \cdot q) \equiv (\sim p \vee \sim q)$$

The rule is

> The negation of a conjunction can be replaced with a disjunction by dropping the negation sign, replacing the conjunction with a disjunction, and negating each of the resulting disjuncts. And vice versa.

Both versions of DeMorgan's rule are used in the following examples:

1. $\sim(A \vee B)$
2. $\sim A \cdot \sim B$ 1 DeM

1. $\sim[\sim A \cdot \sim(B \cdot C)]$
2. $\sim\sim A \vee \sim\sim(B \cdot C)$ 1 DeM

1. $\sim A \vee \sim(B \cdot C)$
2. $\sim[A \cdot (B \cdot C)]$ 1 DeM

Note that in the first example the first form of DeM is used. In the second example the second form of DeM is used. In the third example the second form of DeM is used in the vice-versa direction. The replacement rule called Commutation (Comm), determined by the following biconditionals:

$$(p \vee q) \equiv (q \vee p) \qquad\qquad (p \cdot q) \equiv (q \cdot p)$$

is:

> Any disjunction can be replaced with a disjunction in which the disjuncts change place. Same holds for conjunction.

The Commutation rule is used in the next example:

1.	$A \supset (B \cdot C)$	1.	$(A \cdot B) \supset (C \vee D)$
2.	$A \supset (C \cdot B)$ 1 Comm	2.	$(B \cdot A) \supset (D \vee C)$ 1 Comm
			(used twice)

We now list the equivalence rules that will be used in constructing proofs by listing the biconditionals which determine each rule.

Truth-Functional Replacement Rules

9. Double Negation (DN): $p \equiv \sim\sim p$

10. DeMorgan's Theorem (DeM): $\sim(p \vee q) \equiv (\sim p \cdot \sim q)$
    $$\sim(p \cdot q) \equiv (\sim p \vee \sim q)$$

11. Commutation (Comm): $(p \vee q) \equiv (q \vee p)$
    $$(p \cdot q) \equiv (q \cdot p)$$

12. Association (Assoc): $[(p \vee q) \vee r] \equiv [p \vee (q \vee r)]$
    $$[(p \cdot q) \cdot r] \equiv [p \cdot (q \cdot r)]$$

13. Distribution (Dist): $[(p \vee (q \cdot r)] \equiv [(p \vee q) \cdot (p \vee r)]$
    $$[p \cdot (q \vee r)] \equiv [(p \cdot q) \vee (p \cdot r)]$$

14. Contraposition (Contra): $(p \supset q) \equiv (\sim q \supset \sim p)$

15. Implication (Imp): $(p \supset q) \equiv (\sim p \vee q)$

16. Exportation (Exp): $[(p \cdot q) \supset r] \equiv [p \supset (q \supset r)]$

17. Tautology (Taut): $(p \cdot q) \equiv p$
    $$(p \vee p) \equiv p$$

18. Equivalence (Equiv): $(p \equiv q) \equiv [(p \supset q) \cdot (q \supset p)]$
    $$(p \equiv q) \equiv [(p \cdot q) \vee (\sim p \cdot \sim q)]$$

The following proof supplies an illustration of how some of these rules can be used in combination to provide a proof for an argument:

$A \supset B, C \supset B \therefore (A \vee C) \supset B$

1.	$A \supset B$	P
2.	$C \supset B$	P
3.	$\sim A \vee B$	1 Imp
4.	$\sim C \vee B$	2 Imp
5.	$B \vee \sim A$	3 Comm
6.	$B \vee \sim C$	4 Comm
7.	$(B \vee \sim A) \cdot (B \vee \sim C)$	5,6 Conj
8.	$B \vee (\sim A \cdot \sim C)$	7 Dist
9.	$(\sim A \cdot \sim C) \vee B$	8 Comm
10.	$\sim(A \vee C) \vee B$	9 DeM
11.	$(A \vee C) \supset B$	10 Imp

The proof of this argument is a difficult task. Notice especially line 8. It comes from 7 by using the first form of distribution (rule 13) but in going from line 7 to line 8 distribution goes from the right to the left with respect to the first form of rule 13. That is, we replace a sentence with the form $(p \vee q) \cdot (p \vee r)$ (line 7) with a sentence of the form $p \vee (q \cdot r)$ (line 8). In most uses of distribution one will find himself going from the left to the right in applying the rule. This proof deserves careful study. It is about as difficult a proof as one is likely to run into using only the preceding eighteen rules.

There are two rules of thumb that can be useful in constructing proofs for arguments. The first rule is to try to break down the compound sentences which occur in the premises. Let us illustrate this procedure on a full-blooded argument. Using suggested capital letters as abbreviations for simple sentences in the following argument:

> If the photograph resembles the girl, then she and the photographer will be disappointed. If the photograph does not resemble the girl, her guardian will refuse to pay; and, if that happens, the photographer will be disappointed. The photographer will not be disappointed. So the girl will be disappointed. (*P, S, O, H*)

one obtains

$$P \supset (S \cdot O), (\sim P \supset \sim H) \cdot (\sim H \supset O), \sim O \therefore S$$

How can one go about constructing a proof for this argument? The goal is to obtain *S*. *S* can be obtained from $S \cdot O$. $S \cdot O$ can be obtained from the first premise by detaching it from *P* using MP and *P*. *P* can be obtained from the first conjunct of the second premise by MT if we have *H*, and *H* can be obtained from the second conjunct of the second premise using MT with $\sim O$. And $\sim O$ is the third premise. Thus the proof goes:

1.	$P \supset (S \cdot O)$	P
2.	$(\sim P \supset \sim H) \cdot (\sim H \supset O)$	P
3.	$\sim O$	P
4.	$\sim P \supset \sim H$	2 Simp
5.	$\sim H \supset O$	2 Simp
6.	$\sim \sim H$	3,5 MT
7.	$\sim \sim P$	4,6 MT
8.	P	7 DN
9.	$S \cdot O$	1,8 MP
10.	S	9 Simp

The second rule of thumb is to try, if other things fail, to work back from the conclusion by transforming the conclusion using replacement rules. To illustrate, consider once again the example

$$A \supset B, C \supset B \therefore (A \vee C) \supset B$$

Using the equivalence rules we can transform the conclusion in various ways. Let us aim at decomposing the conclusion into two pieces since there are two premises. Here is such a transformation using some of the equivalence rules:

$(A \vee C) \supset B$
$\sim(A \vee C) \vee B$ Imp
$(\sim A \cdot \sim C) \vee B$ DeM
$(\sim A \vee B) \cdot (\sim C \vee B)$ Comm, Dist

Now it is relatively easy to see how one can obtain this transformed conclusion from the two premises: use Imp and Conj. This done, one can reverse the steps of the transformation and obtain the conclusion. This strategy is the one followed in constructing the proof for this argument.

In breaking down or atomizing compound sentences the rules which allow the elimination of statement connectives are DS, MP, MT, Simp, along with DeM, Equiv, and Idem. For example, DeM allows us to remove negation signs before parentheses. To demonstrate the validity of this argument:

$$\sim A \supset [\sim C \supset (D \supset H)], \; A \supset H, \; \sim(B \vee H), \; \sim C \therefore \sim H \supset \sim D$$

a good strategy is to eliminate connectives. Beginning with the removal of "$\sim$" in the third premise, using DeM one can obtain $\sim B$ and $\sim H$. From this point MT and MP can be used to obtain $D \supset H$ from which using Contra the conclusion is proven. The reader is to construct this proof as an exercise.

EXERCISES 7.2

A. Each of the following proofs is partially worked out. Fill in the missing justification.

    1.   1. $P \vee Q$ P
            2. $\sim\sim(P \vee Q)$
            3. $\sim(\sim P \cdot \sim Q)$
            4. $\sim\sim P \vee \sim\sim Q$
            5. $P \vee Q$
    2.   1. $(P \vee Q) \vee (R \cdot \sim S)$ P
            2. $P \vee [Q \vee (R \cdot \sim S)]$
            3. $[Q \vee (R \cdot \sim S)] \vee P$
            4. $Q \vee [R \cdot \sim S) \vee P]$
    3.   1. $Q \supset \sim R$ P
            2. $P \supset (Q \cdot R)$ P
            3. $\sim(Q \cdot R) \supset \sim P$
            4. $(\sim Q \vee \sim R) \supset \sim P$
            5. $\sim\sim(Q \supset \sim R) \supset \sim P$

6. $(Q \supset \sim R) \supset \sim P$

7. $\sim P$

4. 1. $\sim T$ P

    2. $P \supset [(Q \cdot S) \supset (T \vee R)]$ P

    3. $(S \cdot Q) \cdot P$ P

    4. $[P \cdot (Q \cdot S)] \supset (T \vee R)$

    5. $P \cdot (S \cdot Q)$

    6. $P \cdot (Q \cdot S)$

    7. $T \vee R$

    8. $\sim \sim T \vee R$

    9. $\sim T \supset R$

  10. R

5. 1. $P \cdot Q$ P

    2. $(P \cdot Q) \vee \sim (Q \vee P)$

    3. $(P \cdot Q) \vee (\sim Q \cdot \sim P)$

    4. $(P \cdot Q) \vee (\sim P \cdot \sim Q)$

    5. $P \equiv Q$

6. 1. $P \cdot Q$ P

    2. $\sim R \supset S$ P

    3. $(P \cdot Q) \cdot (\sim R \supset S)$

    4. $(P \cdot Q) \cdot (\sim \sim R \vee S)$

    5. $(P \cdot Q) \cdot (S \vee R)$

    6. $[(P \cdot Q) \cdot S] \vee [(P \cdot Q) \cdot R]$

7. 1. $P \equiv (Q \cdot R)$ P

    2. $[P \supset (Q \cdot R) \cdot [(Q \cdot R) \supset P]$

    3. $[\sim (Q \cdot R) \supset \sim P] \cdot [\sim P \supset \sim (Q \cdot R)]$

    4. $\sim \sim \{ [\sim (Q \cdot R) \supset \sim P] \cdot [\sim P \supset \sim (Q \cdot R)] \}$

    5. $\sim \{ \sim [\sim (Q \cdot R) \supset \sim P] \vee \sim [\sim P \supset \sim (Q \cdot R)] \}$

    6. $\sim \{ [\sim (Q \cdot R) \supset \sim P] \supset \sim [\sim P \supset \sim (Q \cdot R)] \}$

    7. $\sim \{ [(\sim Q \vee \sim R) \supset \sim P] \supset \sim [\sim P \supset (\sim Q \vee \sim R)] \}$

    8. $\sim \{ \sim [(\sim Q \vee \sim R) \supset \sim P] \vee \sim [\sim P \supset (\sim Q \vee \sim R)] \}$

    9. $\sim \sim [(\sim Q \vee \sim R) \supset \sim P] \cdot \sim \sim [\sim P \supset (\sim Q \vee \sim R)]$

  10. $[(\sim Q \vee \sim R) \supset \sim P] \cdot [\sim P \supset (\sim Q \vee \sim R)]$

8. 1. $(P \vee Q) \equiv (R \cdot S)$ P

    2. $[(P \vee Q) \cdot (R \cdot S)] \vee [\sim (P \vee Q) \cdot \sim (R \cdot S)]$

    3. $[(P \vee Q) \cdot (R \cdot S)] \vee \sim [\sim \sim (P \vee Q) \vee \sim \sim (R \cdot S)]$

    4. $\sim [\sim (P \vee Q) \vee \sim (R \cdot S)] \vee \sim [\sim \sim (P \vee Q) \vee \sim \sim (R \cdot S)]$

    5. $\sim [\sim (P \vee Q) \vee \sim (R \cdot S)] \vee \sim [(P \vee Q) \vee (R \cdot S)]$

    6. $[\sim (P \vee Q) \vee \sim (R \cdot S)] \supset \sim [(P \vee Q) \vee (S \cdot R)]$

    7. $[\sim (P \vee Q) \vee \sim (R \cdot S)] \supset \sim \{ [(P \vee Q) \vee S] \cdot [(P \vee Q) \vee R] \}$

B. Construct proofs for the following:

    1. $\sim \sim R \cdot S \therefore R \vee P$

    2. $Q \cdot (Q \supset R), P \vee \sim R \therefore P$

3. $(P \supset Q), (P \lor R), (R \supset Q) \cdot (\sim Q \lor S) \therefore S \cdot Q$
4. $(P \equiv \sim P) \cdot P \therefore S$
5. $(P \lor Q) \lor \sim R, (P \lor Q) \supset (S \cdot \sim Q), R \therefore P \cdot R$
6. $(P \supset Q) \lor R \therefore (P \cdot \sim Q) \supset R$
7. $(P \supset Q) \supset Q \therefore P \lor Q$
8. $C \equiv J, \sim J \therefore C \supset (E \lor \sim K)$

C. Using the suggested abbreviation for simple sentences, symbolize each argument following and construct a proof.

1. Although the flock would not be disturbed unless the wolf howled, it is false that either the wolf or the dog howled last night. So neither was the flock disturbed nor did the dog howl. (F, W, D)

2. If she wrote a good story, she will get it published. If she gets it published, she will not begin her vacation, but she will begin her novel. If she does not begin her vacation, she will not begin her novel. So she did not write a good story. (S, P, V, N)

3. Either it is not the case that either Perry or Melvin went to the party or it is true that both Sarah and Rachel did. I know Sarah did not go, so Melvin didn't. (P, M, S, R)

4. If I take geology and either political science or Spanish, then I will not work part time. But I will work part time and I will take political science. So I will not take geology. (G, P, S, W)

5. If she either swims or water skis, she'll get sunburned and thirsty. If she gets either thirsty or hungry, she'll want to borrow some money. She is swimming now, so she'll want to borrow some money. (S, W, B, T, H, M)

6. Football players are either large or not stupid or they are highly motivated. Football players are not large unless they are both stupid and not large. So if they are stupid, they are highly motivated. (L, S, H)

7. Conscientious students will either read the text or attend the lectures only if the instructor and the course are stimulating. The instructor, unfortunately, is a bore, so conscientious students do not read the text. (R, A, I, C)

8. If God were willing to prevent evil or unable to do so, he would be impotent; if he were able to prevent evil or unwilling to do so, he would be malevolent. Evil can exist only if God is either unwilling or unable to prevent it. There is evil. If God exists, he is neither impotent nor malevolent. Therefore God does not exist. (W, A, I, M, E, G)

9. If unemployment is sufficient for Agnew's defeat, then all that he did the first term is wasted. Therefore it is false that both his first term is not wasted and he is defeated. (U, A, F)

10. If working hours drop, then leisure and recreation will increase. If either leisure or wages increase, then people will be happy. Either wages will increase or working hours will drop. Therefore people will be happy. (*H, L, R, W, P*)

D. Construct proofs for the arguments found in Exercise 6.6.

ANSWERS

A. **1.** 1 DN; 2 DeM; 3 DeM; 4 DN.
   3. 2 Contra; 3 DeM; 4 Imp, DN; 5 DN; 1,6 MP.
   5. 1 Add; 2 DeM; 3 Comm; 4 Equiv.
   7. 1 Equiv; 2 Contra; 3 DN; 4 DeM; 5 Imp; 6 DeM; 7 Imp; 8 DeM; 9 DN.

B. **1.** 2. $\sim\sim R$ 1 Simp. 3. R 2 DN. 4. $R \vee P$ 3 Add.
   3. 4. $R \supset Q$ 3 Simp. 5. $Q \vee Q$ 1,2,4 CD. 6. Q 5 Taut.
   7. $\sim Q \vee S$ 3 Simp. 8. $\sim\sim Q$ 6 DN. 9. S 7,8 DS. 10. $S \cdot Q$ 9,6 Conj.
   5. 4. $\sim R \vee (P \vee Q)$ 1 Comm. 5. $\sim\sim R$ 3 DN. 6. $P \vee Q$ 4,5 DS.
   7. $S \cdot \sim Q$ 2,6 MP. 8. $\sim Q$ 7 Simp. 9. $Q \vee P$ 6 Comm.
   10. P 8,9 DS. 11. $P \cdot R$ 10,3 Conj.
   7. 2. $\sim(\sim P \vee Q) \vee Q$ 1 Imp. 3. $(\sim\sim P \cdot \sim Q) \vee Q$ 2 DeM.
   4. $(P \cdot \sim Q) \vee Q$ 3 DN. 5. $Q \vee (P \cdot \sim Q)$ 4 Comm.
   6. $(Q \vee P) \cdot (Q \vee \sim Q)$ 5 Dist. 7. $Q \vee P$ 6 Simp. 8. $P \vee Q$ 7 Comm.

C. **1.** 1. $(\sim F \vee W) \cdot \sim(W \vee D)$ P. 2. $\sim(W \vee D)$ 1 Simp.
   3. $\sim W \cdot \sim D$ 2 DeM. 4. $\sim W$ 3 Simp. 5. $\sim F \vee W$ 1 Simp.
   6. $\sim F$ 4,5 Comm, DS. 7. $\sim F \cdot \sim D$ 3,6 Simp, Conj.
   3. 1. $\sim(P \vee M) \vee (S \cdot R)$ P. 2. $\sim S$ P. 3. $\sim S \vee \sim R$ 2 Add.
   4. $\sim(S \cdot R)$ 3 DeM. 5. $(P \vee M) \supset (S \cdot R)$ 1 Imp.
   6. $\sim(P \vee M)$ 4,5 MT. 7. $\sim P \cdot \sim M$ 6 DeM. 8. $\sim M$ 7 Simp.
   5. 1. $(S \vee W) \supset (B \cdot T)$ P. 2. $(T \vee H) \supset M$ P. 3. S P. 4. $S \vee W$ 3 Add. 5. $B \cdot T$ 1,4 MP. 6. T 5 Simp. 7. $T \vee H$ 6 Add. 8. M 2,7 MP.
   7. 1. $(R \vee A) \supset (I \cdot C)$ P. 2. $\sim I$ P. 3. $\sim I \vee \sim C$ 2 Add.
   4. $\sim(I \cdot C)$ 3 DeM. 5. $\sim(R \vee A)$ 1,4 MT.
   6. $\sim R \cdot \sim A$ 5 DeM. 7. $\sim R$ 6 Simp.
   9. 1. $(U \supset A) \supset F$ P. 2. $\sim(\sim U \vee A) \vee F$ 1 Imp. 3. $(U \cdot \sim A) \vee F$ 2 DeM, DN. 4. $(U \vee F) \cdot (\sim A \vee F)$ 3 Comm, Dist. 5. $\sim A \vee F$ 4 Simp. 6. $F \vee \sim A$ 5 Comm. 7. $\sim(\sim F \cdot A)$ 6 DeM, DN.

Conditional Proof Rule

We now introduce a rule of inference which enables the convenient deduction of conclusions which have the form of conditionals.

Let Pr represent the conjunction of the premises of an argument. The new rule states that if from Pr plus some assumed premise p, one can infer q, then one can infer $p \supset q$ from Pr alone. This new rule may be represented as follows:

19.   Rule of conditional proof (RCP)

$$Pr$$
$$\begin{array}{l} \llcorner p \quad \text{assumed premise (AP)} \\ \quad \vdots \\ \quad q \\ \hline p \supset q \end{array}$$

The line going from the assumed premise and separating q from the conditional $p \supset q$ indicates that $p \supset q$ follows from Pr alone and that p has been taken out of the proof as a premise. An application of this rule follows:

$A \vee \sim B, \ \sim C \supset \sim A \therefore B \supset C$

1.	$A \vee \sim B$	P
2.	$\sim C \supset \sim A$	P
3.	B	AP
4.	$\sim \sim B$	3 DN
5.	$\sim B \vee A$	1 Comm
6.	A	4,5 DS
7.	$\sim \sim A$	6 DN
8.	$\sim \sim C$	2,7 MT
9.	C	8 DN
10.	$B \supset C$	3–9 RCP

The line separating line 9 from 10 in the preceding proof indicates that 10 comes from 1 and 2 alone (since lines 1 and 2 are the remaining premise lines in the sequence). The line from 3 separating line 9 from 10 serves the function of indicating that the assumed premise is out of the proof or has been *discharged* from the proof. Whenever an assumed premise is entered into a proof for a use of RCP (or for the other assumption-discharging rule to be discussed next), all the assumed premises must be discharged in order to have a proof for the argument in question. In the preceding example all the assumed premises have been discharged since line 3 is the only assumed premise; thus this just mentioned condition is satisfied in the preceding sequence. Since each of the nonpremise lines follow using one of the 18 rules and RCP, the preceding sequence is a proof for the argument.

In the preceding example only one assumed premise is used. But any number of assumed premises can be introduced into a proof, provided that every one is eventually discharged so that the conclusion of the argument being considered depends only on the given premises. The following is a typical example of the use of two assumed premises in a double use of RCP:

$$\sim C \supset (A \supset \sim B) \therefore A \supset (\sim C \supset \sim B)$$

1.	$\sim C \supset (A \supset \sim B)$	P
2.	A	AP
3.	$\sim C$	AP
4.	$A \supset \sim B$	1,3 MP
5.	$\sim B$	2,4 MP
6.	$\sim C \supset \sim B$	3–5 RCP
7.	$A \supset (\sim C \supset \sim B)$	2–6 RCP

This last proof indicates a useful strategy in constructing proofs that have conditional conclusions, namely, use RCP as often as possible. Generally speaking, the more assumed premises one can introduce into a proof, the easier it is to derive the conclusion.

That RCP is a valid rule can be shown as follows using an indirect proof: Let us continue to use *Pr* to represent the conjunction of the stated premises of the argument. Now consider:

(i) *Pr*
    p
  ∴*q*

(ii) *Pr*
    ∴*p* ⊃ *q*

Suppose (i) is valid but (ii) is not. If (ii) is not valid, then *Pr* can be **T** and the conclusion in (ii) **F**. In other words:

Pr **T**
∴*p* ⊃ *q*
  T **F**

But this contradicts our supposition that (i) is valid. Thus supposing (i) is valid and (ii) is not leads to a contradiction. So if (i) is valid, so is (ii). If from *Pr* and *p*, *q* validly follows, then *p* ⊃ *q* follows from *Pr* alone. And this is what the rule RCP states.

To shed some more light on RCP we could argue directly for the validity of the rule as follows: (i) is a valid argument pattern if and only if

(iii) $(Pr \cdot p) \supset q$

always comes out true on a truth-table analysis. Formulas which always come out true on a truth-table analysis are called *tautologies*. So (i) is valid if

(iii) is a tautology. Now (iii) is logically equivalent to:

(iv) $Pr \supset (p \supset q)$

So if (i) is valid so is (ii). What this tells us is that if we wish to derive $p \supset q$ from Pr, $p \supset q$ validly follows, if q validly follows from Pr and p. But this is the rule RCP. RCP says that if the consequent of a conditional validly follows from Pr plus the antecedent of the conditional, then the conditional validly follows from Pr alone.

EXERCISES 7.3

A.   Use RCP in constructing proofs for the following arguments:
1. $A \supset B \therefore A \supset (A \cdot B)$
2. $A \supset [(B \cdot C) \vee E], (B \cdot C) \supset {\sim} A, D \supset {\sim} E \therefore A \supset {\sim} D$
3. $(P \vee Q) \supset R, (S \vee T) \supset [(A \vee B) \supset P] \therefore S \supset (A \supset R)$
4. $P \supset R, ({\sim} P \vee R) \supset (S \supset Q) \therefore P \supset (S \supset Q)$
5. ${\sim} A \supset {\sim} B, A \supset C, B \vee D, D \supset E \therefore E \vee C$
6. $(J \vee R) \supset (D \cdot V) \therefore {\sim} J \vee D$
7. $U \supset {\sim}(V \vee W), (W \vee X) \supset U, {\sim} Z \supset (X \cdot {\sim} Y) \therefore V \supset Z$
8. $Q \equiv R \therefore {\sim} Q \equiv {\sim} R$

B.   Use RCP in constructing proofs for the following arguments. Use the suggested capital letters as abbreviations for sentences in symbolizing the arguments.

1.   The president will not lose his job unless the dean, who swings a lot of weight, objects to something the president does. The dean, who is a fair man, will object to an action of the president only if it is unjust. The president will not do anything unjust unless he is ignorant of the situation. So if the president does lose his job he will have acted in ignorance of the situation. (P, D, U, I)

2.   If Dr. Freund reads a paper, Dr. Friendly will criticize it. And if Dr. Friendly criticizes it, the criticism will not be both fair and amiable. The criticism will be fair, however. So if Freund reads the paper, the criticism will not be amiable. (Fr, Fi, F, A)

3.   If Brigette buys dinner, Zen pays the tip, and if Brigette does not buy dinner, they walk home. Also, if they walk home, Brigette is furious with Zen. So if Zen does not pay the tip, Brigette is furious with Zen. (B, Z, W, F)

4.   If Myrtle likes her new dress, she will buy five more just like it. If she buys five more just like the new one she will be broke—unless she does not like the new one. If she is broke, she will starve—unless she does not buy five dresses just like the new one. So if Myrtle likes her new dress, she will starve. (L, F, B, S)

5. If you are all ready, we will leave immediately, unless there is a flat tire. Either there is a flat tire or there is a hole in the street. I see you are all ready. So if there is not a flat tire, we will leave immediately. (R, L, F, H)

6. There are no wage slaves. So there are either wage slaves or happy job holders if and only if there are happy job holders. (W, H)

7. If Russia defeats China, then the U.S. troubles are over. If either the U.S. troubles are over or she gives up imperialism, then there will be a better world. Consequently, if Russia defeats China, then if the United States gives up imperialism, then if there is still a world, either there will be a better world or no human race. ($R. U, G, B, S, N$)

8. Students are either not motivated and bored or not motivated and mildly interested. If students are mildly interested, then if they make it to class, they are always disappointed. So if they are not disappointed, then they are either bored or they do not make it to class. (M, B, I, C, D)

9. If Bobby gets a Nikon for Christmas, he will have to take Photography 101 unless someone gives him the instruction book, too. It is not true that if Bobby is a good boy, then someone will give him the instruction book. But if Bobby is a good boy, he will get a Nikon for Christmas. Therefore, if he will indeed get his Nikon, he will take Photography 101. (N, P, I, G)

C. Again construct proofs for some of the exercises in 7.2 C; this time use RCP and see how much easier it is.

ANSWERS

A. **3.** 3. S AP. 4. A AP. 5. $S \lor T$ 3 Add. 6. $(A \lor B) \supset P$ 5,2 MP.
7. $A \lor B$ 4 Add. 8. P 6,7 MP. 9. $P \lor Q$ 8 Add. 10. R 9,1 MP.
11. $A \supset R$ 4-10 RCP. 12. $S \supset (A \supset R)$ 3-11 RCP.

6. 2. J AP. 3. $J \lor R$ 2 Add. 4. $D \cdot V$ 1,3 MP. 5. D 4 Simp.
6. $J \supset D$ 2-5 RCP. 7. $\sim J \lor D$ 6 Imp.

8. 2. $\sim Q$ AP. 3. $\sim R$ AP. 4. $(Q \supset R) \cdot (R \supset Q)$ 1 Equiv.
5. $Q \supset R$ 4 Simp. 6. $\sim Q$ 3,5 MT. 7. $\sim R \supset \sim Q$ 3-6 RCP.
8. $R \supset Q$ 4 Simp. 9. $\sim R$ 2,8 MT. 10. $\sim Q \supset \sim R$ 2-9 RCP.
11. $(\sim R \supset \sim Q) \cdot (\sim Q \supset \sim R)$ 7,10 Conj. 12. $\sim Q \equiv \sim R$ 11
Equiv.

B. **3.** 1. $(B \supset Z) \cdot (\sim B \supset W)$ P. 2. $W \supset F$ P. 3. $\sim Z$ AP. 4. $B \supset Z$
1 Simp. 5. $\sim B$ 3,4 MT. 6. $\sim B \supset W$ 1 Simp. 7. W 5,6 MP.
8. F 2,7 MP. 9. $\sim Z \supset F$ 3-8 RCP.

6. 1. $\sim W$ P. 2. $W \lor H$ AP. 3. H 1,2 DS. 4. $(W \lor H) \supset H$ 2-3
RCP. 5. H AP. 6. $W \lor H$ 6 Add, Comm. 7. $H \supset (W \lor H)$ 5-6
RCP. 8. (4) · (7) Conj. 9. $(W \lor H) \equiv H$ 8 Equiv.

9. 1. $N \supset (P \lor I)$P. 2. $\sim(G \supset I)$ P. 3. $G \supset N$ P. 4. NAP.
5. $P \lor I$ 1,4 MP. 6. $\sim(\sim G \lor I)$ 2 Imp. 7. $\sim \sim G \cdot \sim I$ 6 DeM.
8. $\sim I$ 7 Simp. 9. P 8,5 Comm, DS. 10. $N \supset P$ 4-9 RCP.

Reductio ad Absurdum **Rule**

Consider the following use of RCP, where again *Pr* represents the conjunction of premises of any argument and p represents the conclusion of any argument:

Pr	P
$\sim p$	AP
$\vdots$	
$q \cdot \sim q$	
q	Simp
$q \lor p$	Add
$\sim q$	Simp
p	DS
$\sim p \supset p$	RCP
$p \lor p$	Imp, DN
p	Taut

This example illustrates the following: If we enter the denial of the conclusion of any argument into a proof as an added premise and if from this and the given premises we can derive a contradiction, any sentence of the form $q \cdot \sim q$, then by using Simp, Add, and DS we can derive the conclusion. And having done this we can then use RCP, discharge $\sim p$, and then by Imp, DN, and Taut derive the conclusion from *Pr* alone. Thus, in general, if from a set of premises and the negation of the conclusion one can derive any contradiction, then the conclusion follows from the premises alone. This generalization can be stated as a new rule. It is called the *reductio ad absurdum* rule or rule of indirect proof and can be represented as follows:

20. Rule of *Reductio ad Absurdum* (RAA)

Pr	
$\sim p$	AP
$\vdots$	
contradiction	
p	

This rule, as the preceding example attempts to illustrate, can be dropped and the inference which we make with the rule can always be made with the preceding combination of rules in a RCP strategy. Thus, if we assume the validity of these rules, the validity of RAA is established. However, the addition of RAA is advantageous in that rather than follow the preceding rule combination, which makes use of eight rules, we can use the one rule, RAA, and there are times when a RAA strategy simplifies the construction of a proof. Also RAA is a familiar rule of inference used often, for example, in mathematics and philosophy, and thus worth a separate entry. Finally, where *Pr* is empty this rule is used in the *reductio* truth table test considered in the last chapter.

This new assumption discharging rule is especially helpful when one has a conclusion which is not a conditional and where one cannot determine how to derive the conclusion using the other nineteen rules. To illustrate:

$A \vee B, B \supset (C \cdot D), (C \vee A) \supset E \therefore E$

1.	$A \vee B$	P
2.	$B \supset (C \cdot D)$	P
3.	$(C \vee A) \supset E$	P
4.	$\sim E$	AP
5.	$\sim (C \vee A)$	3,4 MT
6.	$\sim C \cdot \sim A$	5 DeM
7.	$\sim A$	6 Simp
8.	B	1,7 DS
9.	$C \cdot D$	2,8 MP
10.	C	9 Simp
11.	$\sim C$	6 Simp
12.	$C \cdot \sim C$	10,11 Conj
13.	E	4–12 RAA

Note that once one assumes the negation of the conclusion in a RAA strategy, one aims at deriving *any* contradiction, for this will be sufficient to infer the denial of the assumed premises following RAA. For example, in the last illustration, one could also have derived $E \cdot \sim E$ as the contradiction.

Often it is useful to combine RCP and RAA in a proof strategy. Typically we find it useful to employ a RAA strategy within a RCP strategy when the conclusion is a conditional and difficulty would be encountered in deriving the consequent using just the first eighteen rules. Consider:

$A \supset (B \supset C), \sim D \supset (A \vee C), A \supset B \therefore D \vee C$

Noting that the conclusion can be transformed into $\sim D \supset C$, so let us assume $\sim D$ in a RCP strategy and then assume $\sim C$ in a RAA strategy.

$$
\begin{array}{lll}
1. & A \supset (B \supset C) & P \\
2. & \sim D \supset (A \vee C) & P \\
3. & A \supset B & P \\
4. & \sim D & AP \\
5. & \sim C & AP \\
6. & A \vee C & 2,4 \text{ MP} \\
7. & A & 5,6 \text{ Comm, DS} \\
8. & B \supset C & 1,7 \text{ MP} \\
9. & \sim B & 5,8 \text{ MT} \\
10. & B & 3,7 \text{ MP} \\
11. & B \cdot \sim B & 9,10 \text{ Conj} \\
12. & C & 5\text{--}11 \text{ RAA} \\
13. & \sim D \supset C & 4\text{--}12 \text{ RCP} \\
14. & D \vee C & 13 \text{ Imp, DN}
\end{array}
$$

RAA is introduced above as a short way to do what we can do with RCP and some other rules. But the validity of the rule can be shown in ways analogous to the arguments used to support the validity of RCP. First we can argue indirectly. Consider

(i) Pr (ii) Pr
      $\sim p$ $\therefore p$
     $\therefore q \cdot \sim q$

Suppose (i) is valid but (ii) is not valid. If (ii) is invalid, then Pr can be **T** and p**F**; but this contradicts supposing (i) is valid. For if Pr is **T** and p is **F**, then each premise in (i) is true and the conclusion is false. A direct argument for the validity of the RAA rule makes use of tautologies. (i) is valid if

(iii) $(Pr \cdot \sim p) \supset (q \cdot \sim q)$

is a tautology. (iii) is logically equivalent to

(iv) $Pr \supset [\sim p \supset (q \cdot \sim q)]$

So the consequent of (iv) validly follows from the antecedent if (i) is valid. So if Pr is **T**, $\sim p \supset (q \cdot \sim q)$ must also be **T**. Since $q \cdot \sim q$ is necessarily **F**, p must be **T**. What all this comes to is that if (i) is a valid argument pattern, then if Pr is **T**, then p must be **T**. In other words, (ii) is a valid argument pattern. RAA states that if a contradiction can be derived from Pr plus an assumed premise $\sim p$, then p validly follows from Pr alone.

EXERCISES 7.4

A. Using RAA and any of the other nineteen rules, construct proofs for the following arguments:

1. $B \supset A, \sim(A \cdot \sim C) \supset B \therefore A$
2. $\sim B \supset E, D \supset \sim E, \sim(\sim D \cdot \sim B) \therefore B$
3. $A \equiv \sim A, A \therefore B$
4. $A \therefore B \vee \sim B$
5. $R \vee (Q \cdot P), P \supset \sim R \therefore Q \vee \sim P$
6. $\sim(C \supset A) \cdot (B \cdot \sim G), (A \vee \sim C) \vee [(B \cdot E) \supset G] \therefore \sim E$

B. Using RAA and any of the other nineteen rules, construct proofs for the following arguments. Use the suggested capital letters as abbreviations for simple sentences.

1. Dr. Friendly, the ethics teacher, told Dr. Freund, the psychologist, "If you would keep the crabgrass out of your lawn, then if our kids got along, we could get along. Since our kids get along and we don't, I must conclude that you don't keep the crabgrass out of your lawn." (*C, K, W*)
2. Either Dierdre will become a movie star and either make a lot of money or have a big family, or she will become a movie star and either spend a lot of time playing golf or become a good actress. The only sure conclusion is, though, that she will become a movie star. (*D, M, F, G, A*)
3. If working hours drop, then leisure and recreation will increase. If either leisure or wages increase, then people will be happy. Either wages will increase or working hours will drop. Therefore people will be happy. (*H, L, R, W, P*)
4. Either McGovern is a Democrat and Kennedy is a Democrat or Humphrey is mad. Either Humphrey is not mad or Kennedy is a Democrat. So Kennedy is a Democrat. (*M, K, H*)
5. Either the rivers stay polluted or government and industry must join in cleaning up. If the rivers stay polluted, then vacation lands are ruined, and if vacation lands are ruined then industry joins in the cleanup. Therefore industry will finally join in the cleanup. (*R, G, I, V*)

C. For some of the arguments in 1 and 2 in this exercise section construct a proof not using RAA, but using the combination Simp, Add, DS, RCP, Imp, DN, and Taut.

D. Show that we could omit some other rules in the system by making use of a set of remaining rules, thus demonstrating again that the system of twenty rules has more rules than are needed.

ANSWERS

A. 4. 1. A P. 2. $\sim(B \lor \sim B)$ AP. 3. $(\sim B \cdot \sim \sim B)$ 2 DeM.
4. $B \cdot \sim B$ 3 DN, Comm. 5. $B \lor \sim B$ 2-4 RAA.

B. 3. 1. $H \supset (L \cdot R)$ P. 2. $(L \lor W) \supset P$ P. 3. $W \lor H$ P.
4. $\sim P$ AP. 5. $\sim(L \lor W)$ 4,2 MT. 6. $\sim L \cdot \sim W$ 5 DeM.
7. $\sim W$ 6 Simp. 8. H 7,3 DS. 9. $L \cdot R$ 1,8 MP.
10. $L \cdot \sim L$ 6,9 Simp, Conj. 11. P 4-10 RAA.

5. 1. $R \lor (G \cdot I)$ P. 2. $(R \supset V) \cdot (V \supset I)$ P. 3. $\sim I$ AP.
4. $V \supset I$ 2 Simp. 5. $\sim V$ 3,4 MT. 6. $R \supset V$ 2 Simp.
7. $\sim R$ 5,6 MT. 8. $G \cdot I$ 7,1 DS. 9. I 8 Simp.
10. $I \cdot \sim I$ 3,9 Conj. 11. I 3-10 RAA.

D. In place of MP we could use Imp. and DS.

Consistency of Premises

The RAA method of proof involves deriving a type of inconsistency, a contradiction, from a set of augmented premises. The procedure is of course unobjectionable even though the premises so augmented by the negation of the conclusion are an inconsistent set. One is, as it were, deliberately making use of a feature of inconsistent sentences to show that one sentence is logically implied by the others. Ordinarily, however, one is not interested in what can be inferred from inconsistent premises. Nevertheless since p, $\sim p \therefore q$ is a valid pattern, arguments with inconsistent premises are valid arguments. This pattern determines the rule that from any set of inconsistent premises one can infer any sentence. This rule is not altogether intuitive. It seems to some odd at first sight. However, a moment's reflection makes it clear that if the premises of an argument are inconsistent, then using rules which most find intuitively satisfactory, any sentence follows. To illustrate:

1.	p	P
2.	$\sim p$	P
3.	$p \lor q$	1 Add
4.	q	2,3 DS

Thus if one finds Add and DS intuitively satisfactory, intuition needs to adjust to the rule that from any set of inconsistent premises any sentence follows.

Let us call arguments which are valid and whose premises are consistent *demonstrative arguments*. These are arguments whose premises may all be true; they are consistent, so that proofs of these arguments show that necessarily if the premises are true the conclusion is true. Ordinarily those arguments which one would be inclined to consider as valid are candidates for demonstrative arguments.

If the premises of an argument can each be true, they are consistent; if they cannot, they are inconsistent. In order to distinguish demonstrative arguments from nondemonstrative arguments one must first determine whether or not the premises can all be true. If the consistency or inconsistency of a set of premises is exclusively a function of how simple sentences are related by statement connectives, then a procedure similar to the procedure followed in the short-cut truth table test can be used to determine consistency. To illustrate, suppose the following are premises of a sentential argument:

$$P \supset Q, \; \sim P \vee R, \; \sim R, \; \sim R \supset Q$$

Assign **T** to each premise and see if one can then make assignments to the simple sentences so each premise can indeed be **T**. Assigning **F** to R we find

$$P \supset Q, \; \sim P \vee R, \; \sim R, \; \sim R \supset Q$$
$$\textbf{F T T} \quad \textbf{T T F} \quad \textbf{T} \quad \textbf{T T T} \qquad (P \text{ must be } \textbf{F} \text{ and } Q \text{ must be } \textbf{T})$$

Each can be true. Suppose, though, we add this sentence $\sim R \supset \sim Q$. Since R is **F** and Q is **T**, $\sim R \supset \sim Q$ would be **F**. Thus with this addition the set of premises could not be true. This means that the five premises are inconsistent. An argument which has these five premises is not, then, a demonstrative argument.

It should again be stressed that for this method to work as a proof of consistency, the premises of the argument must be such that their consistency is exclusively a function of how simple sentences are related by statement connectives. For inconsistency can also arise because of the inner logical structure of simple sentences. For example, if these two sentences appeared as premises of an argument:

Mental illness is a crime.
Some mental illness is not a crime.

the premises would be inconsistent even though treated as whole sentences; **T** could be assigned to both. What this means is that even if we can assign **T** to each premise of an argument, treating each sentence as a unit, this does not insure that the premises are consistent. What it does insure is that the premises are consistent if their consistency is exclusively a function of how simple sentences are related by statement connectives. Analogously, to show that an argument is invalid by truth table methods insures its invalidity only if it is a sentential argument, for one can have valid arguments which are interpretations of invalid sentential argument patterns. For example, consider the following invalid pattern and the valid argument which is an interpretation of the pattern:

p	No mental illnesses are crimes.
$\therefore q$	Therefore no crimes are mental ill- nesses.

Though using this method does not insure the consistency for any set of premises, if the method shows inconsistency for any set of premises, then they are inconsistent. Analogously, if applying truth table methods to any argument shows validity then the argument is valid.

EXERCISES 7.5

A. Which of the following sets of sentences are consistent and which are inconsistent? For the nonsymbolized sentences use the suggested capital letters for simple sentences. If one of the sets is inconsistent in 4, 5 or 6 following, then from the set construct a proof with the set as premises and with this conclusion: Only gullible people are faithful spouses.

1. $P \equiv Q$
   $Q \cdot \sim P$

2. $\sim Q \vee R$
   $\sim R \cdot P$
   $\sim (\sim Q \cdot R)$

3. $A \vee B$
   $\sim B \supset \sim A$
   $\sim B \supset \sim A$
   $B \equiv A$
   $\sim A$

4. If Ed caught any fish they were either bluegills or crappies. If he used worms he did not hook bluegills and if he used minnows he caught crappies. He did have worms, though, and did not catch crappies. He did catch something, though. (F, B, C, W, M)

5. Albertine can check out another book if and only if she either pays her fine or pays for the late book. If she does not pay the fine she will flunk Ethics. She will pay for the book if and only if she does not pay the fine. (A, F, L, E)

6. If Allwet is a logician, then he is lazy and a fraud. If he is a fraud he will be exposed, unless he is not lazy. He will not be exposed and he is a logician. (A, L, F, E)

B. Construct a proof for all of the following arguments that have consistent premises.

1. $A \supset (B \vee C), \sim(\sim A \vee C), \sim B \therefore C$
2. $(A \cdot B) \supset (C \supset D), (E \supset \sim D), (B \cdot E) \therefore A \supset \sim C$
3. $A \supset (B \cdot \sim C), A \equiv D, (B \cdot C) \cdot \sim D, (A \vee C) \therefore B \supset D$
4. $A \supset (B \vee C), (C \cdot A) \supset E, \sim F \supset (\sim E \cdot \sim D) \therefore A \supset (B \vee F)$
5. $(T \supset V) \supset \sim V \therefore (T \vee \sim T) \supset \sim V$

C. For each of the following arguments construct a proof using the twenty rules, or prove it invalid using a truth table method. Test each set of premises for consistency. Use the suggested capital letters for simple sentences in symbolizing the arguments.

1. If you fish an Abdul, you will catch bass and not get caught in the weeds. But it is not the case that either you fish an Abdul and do not catch bass or you get caught in the weeds. So you will fish an Abdul and you will not get caught in the weeds. (*A, B, C*)
2. A house will sell only if it is correctly colored, and that house is correctly colored only if it has red or orange or yellow trim. I own the house. It has red trim. So it probably will sell. (*S, C, R, O, Y*)
3. Addie gets a poodle and an orangutan, if her rooster will die laughing. She gets a poodle but not the orangutan, if the rooster will not die laughing. So if she does not get a poodle, the rooster will die laughing if and only if she gets an orangutan. (*P, O, R*)
4. Either it is not the case that either nonsense occurs or language is perfect, or it is not true that language does not degenerate. So if either there is nonsense or language is perfect, then both either language is perfect or there is nonsense and language degenerates. (*N, P, D*)
5. If logic is not fun, then either neither humor exists nor whimsy exists or neither life is not serious nor does humor exist. So if humor exists then if life is not serious then logic is fun. (*L, H, W, S*)
6. Hitler is dead if and only if Eva is dead. If Hess is dead then Goebbels is dead. Either Hess is dead or Eva is not dead. Hence Goebbels is dead if Hitler is dead. (*H, E, HE, G*)
7. The masses are content provided that the media are doing their job. Either the media are doing their job or the vice-president is enraged. The president is not happy if and only if the masses are not content. So the vice-president is enraged, since the president is not happy. (*MA, ME, V, P*)
8. If you work hard, then your wages will be high, and if you do a good job, then your boss will be satisfied. So if either you work

hard or do a good job, then either your wages will be high or your boss will be satisfied. (*H, W, G, B*)

9. If either your wages are high or you do not do a good job then your boss will be pleased and not pleased. Thus if your wages are high, you do a good job. (*W, G, B*)

10. If I watch television or go to the movies then I will do no logic and will flunk the exam. If I don't watch television, then if I am happy, then I'm not happy; it is as simple as that. I will do my logic. So I'm not happy. (*W, G, L, F, H*)

ANSWERS

A. Only **2** and **5** are consistent sets.

B. Only **1** and **3** have inconsistent premises.

C. **2.** $(S \supset C)$, $C \supset (R \lor O \lor Y)$, R ∴ S invalid.

    8. 1. $(H \supset W) \cdot (G \supset B)$ P. 2. $H \lor G$ AP. 3. $W \lor B$ 1,2 CD. 4. $(H \lor G) \supset (W \lor B)$ 2-3 RCP.

    9. 1. $(W \lor \sim G) \supset (B \cdot \sim B)$ P. 2. W AP. 3. $\sim G$ AP. 4. $W \lor G$ 2 Add. 5. $B \cdot \sim B$ 1,4 MP. 6. G 3-5 RAA. 7. $W \supset G$ 2-6 RCP.

    10. 1. $(W \lor G) \supset (\sim L \cdot F)$ P. 2. $\sim W \supset (H \supset \sim H)$ P. 3. L P. 4. $\sim \sim H$ AP. 5. $(\sim W \cdot H) \supset \sim H$ 2 Exp. 6. $\sim (\sim W \cdot H)$ 4,5 MT. 7. $W \lor \sim H$ 6 DeM, DN. 8. W 4,7 DS. 9. $W \lor G$ 8 Add. 10. $\sim L \cdot F$ 9,1 MP. 11. $L \cdot \sim L$ 3,10 Simp, Conj. 12. $\sim H$ 4-11 RAA.

8

Traditional Syllogistic Logic

There are many simple, valid arguments for which the truth table methods and natural deduction method of the previous chapters are inadequate. An example of such an argument is the following:

All unemployed persons are lazy persons.
Some philosophers are unemployed persons.
Therefore some philosophers are lazy persons.

Using the methods for validation introduced in the preceding chapters, we symbolize this argument and find it to be an interpretation of the argument pattern p, q $\therefore r$. This argument pattern checks out invalid. There is in fact no valid sentential argument pattern from which one could obtain the preceding argument, for the validity of this argument is not exclusively a function of how simple sentences are related by sentence connectives. The argument is not a sentential argument. Rather the validity of the argument depends on the use of the words "all" and "some" and on the way in which "unemployed," "lazy," and "philosopher" are related by these words, as well as on the way the sentences are related. Thus to provide methods for testing such arguments, new methods are needed.

Categorical Sentences

Traditional syllogistic logic, begun with Aristotle (382–322 B.C.), is primarily concerned with techniques for establishing the validity of a certain class of nonsentential arguments. This class will be identified shortly. To begin, let us regard the preceding argument as an interpretation of the following nonsentential argument pattern:

All *M* are *P*.
Some *S* are *M*.
Therefore some *S* are *P*.

In this pattern the capital letters *M*, *P*, and *S* are used as variables for what are called general terms. Sentential variables *p*, *q*, and so on, are variables or placeholders for sentences; *M*, *P*, and *S* are to be variables or placeholders not for sentences but for general terms. Terms can be either singular or general. A *singular term* is a word or expression which can be true of only one individual; it denotes one individual. Proper names (e.g., "Socrates"), definite descriptions (e.g., "the philosopher who drank the hemlock"), and demonstrative expressions (e.g., "this" and "that") are examples of singular terms. *General terms* are words or expressions which can be truly said of more than one individual (e.g., "unemployed," "philosophers," and "lazy persons"). General terms may be true of no individuals (e.g., there are no winged horses, furry fish, or perfect husbands, so "winged horse," "furry fish," and "perfect husband" are true of no individuals). Such general terms are called *empty terms*. We can treat a wide variety of grammatically different expressions as general terms. Both substantive and adjective expressions can be treated as general terms. For example, "virtuous persons" and "virtuous" will both be possible interpretations of the new variables. Thus both "All men are virtuous persons" and "All men are virtuous" will be regarded as interpretations of "All *S* are *P*." In the same spirit verbs can be treated as general terms. Thus, for example, both "Some cats purr" and "Some cats are purring animals" will be regarded as interpretations of "Some *S* are *P*." Whether an expression can be singular or plural makes no difference with respect to general-termhood. For example, "No politician is wise" and "No politicians are wise" can both be regarded as interpretations of "No *S* is *P*" and "No *S* are *P*," respectively. In short, general terms are any expressions that can be true of one or more individuals.

Four ways of joining general terms in sentences have been studied in logic. These four ways are: "All *S* are *P*," "No *S* are *P*," "Some *S* are *P*," and "Some *S* are not *P*." These four sentence forms are patterns for what are called categorical sentences. A *categorical sentence* is any interpretation of one of these four sentence patterns. The four forms for categorical sentences are traditionally distinguished by the letters *A*, *E*, *I*, and *O*, as follows:

Universal affirmative	*A*:	All *S* are *P*.
Universal negative	*E*:	No *S* are *P*.
Particular affirmative	*I*:	Some *S* are *P*.
Particular negative	*O*:	Some *S* are not *P*.

A and *E* are said to be universal because sentences having either of these forms are used to make assertions about everything denoted by *S*. For example, if we replace *S* with "baby gorillas" and *P* with "timid thing," then the *A* and *E* sentences are

All baby gorillas are timid things.
No baby gorillas are timid things.

I and *O* are said to be particular because sentences having either of these forms are used to make assertions about at least one thing denoted by *S*, but not all; for example:

Some baby gorillas are timid things.
Some baby gorillas are not timid things.

E and *O* are said to be negative because sentences having these forms are used to deny something of the things denoted by the terms.

In ordinary discourse categorical sentences can be understood in different ways. For example, a sentence of the form "Some *S* are *P*" can be used to express: "More than one *S* but not all *S* are *P*." Or it can be used to express: "At least one *S* is *P*." *A* and *E* sentences are also ambiguous. For example, "All *S* are *P*" can be understood as the sentence "There are *S*'s and each of them is *P*" or it can be understood as the sentence "There is no *S* that is not *P*." If we wish to obtain methods to distinguish valid from invalid patterns made up of categorical sentence forms, then we must fix on some definite interpretation for *A*, *E*, *I*, and *O* sentences in order to remove such ambiguity.

I and *O* sentences are to be interpreted to mean that *there is at least one* thing *S* that has *P*, in the case of *I*, or does not have *P*, in the case of *O*. If an *I* sentence is true, then there is at least one thing *S* that has *P*, whereas if an *O* sentence is true, then there is at least one thing *S* that does not have *P*. Since if either *I* or *O* is true it follows that *there is* at least one thing, *I* and *O* are said to have *existential import*. The Venn diagrammatic method (John Venn, 1834–1923, British logician) of representing *I* and *O* sentences makes vividly clear how they are to be understood. Let two overlapping circles represent the individuals, if there are any, which are *S* and *P* as follows:

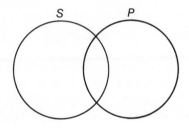

The part where the two circles overlap is the region in which individuals, if there are any, are both *S* and *P*. The other two regions contain the individuals, if there are any, which are *S* and not *P* and *P* and not *S*, respectively. Let *x* stand for *one* individual. "One individual is *S*" may be represented as follows:

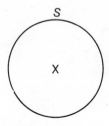

I and *O* sentences can now be represented by these overlapping circles:

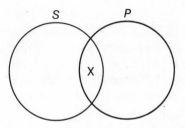

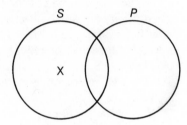

I: Some S are P   *O*: Some S are not P

A and **E** sentences will be interpreted to mean simply that there is no *S* that is not *P*, in the case of an **A**, and nothing is both an *S* and a *P*, in the case of an **E**. Overlapping circles can be used to make clear these interpretations. If a term is an empty term, let this be represented by *shading* the circle. Thus "centaur" may be represented as:

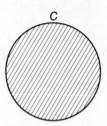

An area in a diagram that neither has an *x* nor is shaded—a white region—is one about which we lack information. That is, we do not know that an individual is denoted by the term represented by a white region, hence there is no *x* in it, nor do we know that the term is empty; thus there is no shading.

The interpretation of **A** and **E** sentences is thus made explicit in the following diagrams:

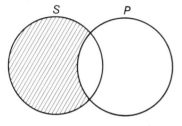

A: All S are P

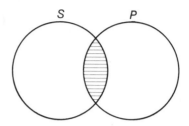

E: No S are P

Note that since an x is found in the diagram of **I** and **O**, they are said to have existential import. But since no x is found in the diagram for either **A** or **E**, **A** and **E** lack existential import. Thus if there are no S's or no P's this does *not* imply that **A** is false and **E** is false. As a matter of fact, if there are no S's we would shade the S region, so diagrammatically we have

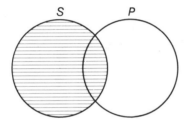

Note that in this last diagram both **A** and **E** have been diagrammed. Thus if S is an empty term both "All S are P" and "No S are P" are true.

EXERCISES 8.1

Classify the following sentences as **A**, **E**, **I**, or **O**. Which terms in the sentences are empty terms? How do the empty terms affect the truth value of the sentence in question?

1. All generals are clowns.
2. Some generals are clowns.
3. Some generals are not clowns.
4. No generals are clowns.
5. All square circles are unforgettable things.
6. All things identical with God are blessed.
7. Some unicorns have cloven hoofs.
8. All Italian Westerns are bloodbaths.

9. Some fascists are good company.
10. All perfect beauties are Americans.
11. Symbolic acts are never logical.
12. Nothing beats a good scream.
13. Some politicians have cloven hoofs.
14. Not all congressmen are powerless.
15. If you pay anyone enough, he can do it yesterday.

ANSWERS

1. *A.* 2. *I.* 3. *O.* 4. *E.* 5. *A.* 6. *A.* 7. *I.* 8. *A.*
9. *I.* 10. *A.* 11. *E.* 12. *E.* 13. *I.* 14. *I.* 15. *A.*

Empty terms: "square circles," "unicorns," perhaps "perfect beauties."
There is a way of understanding "doing something yesterday," so that it is
empty, but this, it seems, is not how to understand it in 15. Whether "things
identical with God" is an empty term is controversial. Exercise 5 is **T** and 7
is **F**.

Disguised Categorical Sentences

There are many variants of categorical sentences. The form "All *S* are *P*"
may be phrased, for example, as follows:

If anything is *S*, it is *P*. (If anything is a chess player then it is neurotic.)
Only *P* is *S*. (Only the rich are members of Volunteers for Good
   Government.)
None but *P* is *S*. (None but A students are honor graduates.)
S are *P*. (Whales are mammals.)
Each (Every, Any) *S* is *P*. (Every politician is pragmatic.)
S are always *P*. (Beautiful strangers are always welcomed.)
If it's an *S*, it's a *P*. (If it's a Junko, then it's made in Detroit.)
An *S* is a *P*. [A (The) Toyota is an inexpensive car.]

Similarly, *E* sentences can take different grammatical shapes. Each of the
following can be rephrased into the No *S* is *P* form:

There are no idealistic politicians.
Good students are not playboys.
If it is a bird, then it is not Superman.
None of the students survived logic.
Nothing is both round and square.
No one is both idealistic and a politician.
There is no substitute for trickery. (No things are substitutes for
   trickery.)

Correspondingly, for *I* each of the following may be phrased as "Some *S* are *P*":

> Honest politicians exist. (Some things are honest politicians.)
> An old lady came to class. (Some old ladies are members of the class.)
> Fish live in these waters. (Some fish are living in these waters.)
> College men read *Playboy*. (Some college men are readers of *Playboy*.)
> A few anthropologists are cute.

And here are some variants of *O*, for example:

> At least one congressman is not corrupt.
> All that glitters is not gold. (Some glittering things are not gold.)
> Not every black novel is stereotyped.

Of special interest is the treatment of singular sentences in syllogistic logic. A singular sentence is a sentence of the form *"a is S"* where *a* is a singular term. For example, each of the following is a singular sentence:

> Socrates is a man.
> The philosopher who taught Plato is snub-nosed.
> This student is not a poet.

Such sentences in syllogistic logic are treated as universal *A* when affirmative and as universal *E* when negative. To illustrate, the preceding three examples can be paraphrased as follows:

> All things identical with Socrates are men. (*A*)
> All things identical with the philosopher who taught Plato are snub-nosed. (*A*)
> No things identical with this student are poets. (*E*)

Unfortunately, there is no set of rules for paraphrasing any variant of a categorical sentence into an explicit categorical sentence. One must grasp the meaning of the sentence in context (or likely context, if the sentence is an exercise) and rephrase it into the proper categorical form. One must always be on the alert for irregularities of English. For example, sometimes "An *S* is *P*" is an *A* sentence, whereas sometimes it can be phrased as an *I* sentence. Consider: "A Volkswagen is inexpensive" ("All Volkswagens are inexpensive"). Sometimes an "All *S* are not *P*" is a particular. Consider: "All politicians are not dishonest" ("Some politicians are honest"). Sometimes "some" occurs in a universal sentence, as, for example: "Something is obscene only if it is inhuman" ("All obscene things are inhuman").

EXERCISES 8.2

Rephrase the following sentences into categorical sentences.

1. None but the brave deserve the fair.
2. Old soldiers never die.
3. Laugh and the world laughs with you.
4. All the world loves a lover.
5. Bureaucrats do virtually no work.
6. Political arguments are just noise.
7. Only students who do exercises pass logic.
8. Scarcely any poets showed up for the rally.
9. Illogical persons are despised.
10. Not every man has Portnoy's complaint.
11. There is no God but Allah.
12. God bless you.
13. Nixon is the one.
14. He believes.
15. Only Eve dated Adam.
16. You have nothing to worry about.
17. If she isn't here you can probably find someone just as good.
18. My boy, as you grow older, you'll find you can't burn the candle at both ends.

ANSWERS

1. All those who deserve the fair are brave persons.
3. All persons who laugh are persons with whom the world laughs.
5. All bureaucrats are persons who do little work.
7. All persons who pass logic are students who do exercises.
9. All illogical persons are despised persons.
11. All things identical with God are identical with Allah.
13. All things identical with Nixon are persons who are "the one" (whatever that is).
15. All those who dated Adam are things identical with Eve.

Syllogisms

A *syllogistic argument* is an argument in which a categorical sentence is the conclusion and two categorical sentences are premises, there being just three terms with each term appearing in two sentences. In traditional logic syllogistic arguments are the type of nonsentential argument to which the logical methods are applied. An example of a syllogistic argument is the following:

> No men are perfect.
> All Americans are men.
> Therefore no Americans are perfect.

The two premises are categorical sentences and the conclusion is a categorical sentence. There are just three terms, "Americans," "men," and "perfect things," and each term appears in two categorical sentences.

Traditionally the subject term of the conclusion is called the *minor term* of the syllogism, whereas the predicate term in the conclusion is called the *major term*. In the preceding example "Americans" is the minor term, whereas "perfect" or "perfect things" is the major term. The premise containing the minor term is called the *minor premise*, whereas the premise containing the major term is the *major premise*. In the preceding example the first premise is the major premise, whereas the second premise is the minor premise. The *middle term* of a syllogism is the term which occurs twice in the premises, "men" being the middle term in the example.

Traditionally, the form of the premises and the conclusion of a syllogism are indicated by a triple of letters, the first being the letter of the major premise, the second the letter of the minor premise, and the third the letter of the conclusion. Thus the form of the premises and conclusion of the preceding example can be indicated as **EAE**. In indicating the forms of the three categorical sentences that make up a syllogism (remember to put the letter for the major premise *first*), one is said to be indicating the *mood* of the syllogism.

The middle term of a syllogism may be situated in different places in a syllogism. The possible arrangements for the middle terms of a syllogism are called *figures*. The four possible arrangements for the middle term are

	Figure I		*Figure II*		*Figure III*		*Figure IV*	
Major premise:	*M*	*P*	*P*	*M*	*M*	*P*	*P*	*M*
Minor premise:	*S*	*M*	*S*	*M*	*M*	*S*	*M*	*S*
Conclusion:	*S*	*P*	*S*	*P*	*S*	*P*	*S*	*P*

Specification of mood and figure determines the form of a syllogism completely. Thus if a syllogism is an **EII** figure I, we know it has the following form:

> No *M* are *P*.
> Some *S* are *M*.
> Therefore some *S* are *P*.

Since every syllogism consists of three sentences which can have four different forms, there are sixty-four possible syllogistic moods, and since there are four different ways for a middle term to be situated, four possible figures, there are 256 possible syllogistic argument patterns.

A *valid syllogism* is a syllogism which is an interpretation of a valid syllogistic argument pattern. A syllogistic argument pattern is valid if and only if no matter what general terms replace S, P, and M, the result is a valid argument. For example, if we replace S, P, and M with "Greeks," "mortal," and "men," respectively in the valid **AAA**-I argument pattern, we obtain the valid argument:

All men are mortal.
All Greeks are men.
Therefore all Greeks are mortal.

The preceding definition for the validity of a syllogistic argument pattern stipulates that the pattern must yield a valid argument no matter what general term is substituted, whether the term is empty or not. Understanding "valid syllogistic argument pattern" in this way, how many valid patterns are there among the 256 possible syllogistic argument patterns? This problem has been solved in several ways (some of these ways are taken up later), and the result is that there are fifteen valid syllogistic argument patterns. They are

Figure I	Figure II	Figure III	Figure IV
AAA	**EAE**	**I A I**	**AEE**
EAE	**AEE**	**A I I**	**I A I**
A I I	**EIO**	**OAO**	**EIO**
EIO	**AOO**	**EIO**	

These fifteen patterns are all valid, and these fifteen are the only valid patterns.

In addition to these fifteen patterns, there are nine other patterns which deserve special mention. These nine forms only need a small reinforcing premise for them also to be valid. These additional premises take either of these three forms: "There are S"; "There are M"; or "There are P." These nine valid forms with the reinforcing premises follow:

Figure I	Figure II	Figure III	Figure IV	Added Premise
AAI, EAO	**AEO, EAO**	**EAO**	**AEO**	There are S.
		AAI	**EAO**	There are M.
			AAI	There are P.

To illustrate, the syllogism

> All folk music is simple.
> All folk music is honest.
> Therefore some honest things are simple.

is an interpretation of an **AAI**-III pattern which is not among the fifteen valid patterns. However if to **AAI**-III we add the premise "There are *M*," as indicated in the immediately preceding chart, then we have a valid pattern, namely,

> All *M* are *P*.
> All *M* are *S*.
> There are *M*.
> Therefore some *S* are *P*.

Of course, there is folk music. Thus rather than erroneously conclude that this argument is invalid, since it is not an interpretation of one of the fifteen valid syllogisms, we can certify it as valid since it is an interpretation of a valid reinforced syllogism.

To determine whether an argument is an interpretation of a valid syllogistic argument pattern, reinforced or not, the first step is to symbolize the argument. To symbolize a syllogism is to put the argument into explicit syllogistic form. This means rephrasing the sentences into explicit categorical sentences, if they are not already in this form, making sure that only three general terms occur, and arranging the premises so that the major premise comes first. Frequently arguments can have more than three terms and yet still be syllogisms since a term and its complement occur. If *S* denotes all things that are *S*, then non-*S* is said to be the *complement* of the term *S*. Thus the complement of "wealthy persons" is "nonwealthy persons" or "middle- or lower-income persons," the complement of "honest persons" is "non-honest persons" or "dishonest persons." Now consider the following argument:

> Wealthy persons are all dishonest, so philosophers are middle- or lower-income persons, for if philosophers are anything they are honest.

Taking the argument as it appears on the paper it contains five general terms: "wealthy persons," "dishonest persons," "philosophers," "middle- or lower-income persons," and "honest persons." However, two pairs are complementary, namely, the pair "wealthy persons" and "middle- or lower-income persons" and the pair "dishonest persons" and "honest persons." When complementary pairs occur, one of the terms can be eliminated, thus the preceding argument can be rephrased so that it contains only three general terms. One way to do this would be

> All wealthy persons are dishonest.
> No philosophers are dishonest.
> Therefore no philosophers are wealthy persons.

Another way would be

> No wealthy persons are honest persons.
> All philosphers are honest.
> Therefore no philosophers are wealthy persons.

Both of these ways, and there are still other ways to symbolize it, capture what is asserted; thus both ways are equivalent ways to rephrase the argument. The first paraphrase is an **AEE**-II (valid) whereas the second is an **EAE**-II (valid).

EXERCISES 8.3

Symbolize the following syllogisms. Which ones are interpretations of one of the fifteen valid syllogistic argument patterns? Are any of the arguments interpretations of valid reinforced syllogistic argument patterns?

1. No Mormon is a believer in predestination. No Unitarian is a believer in predestination. So Mormons are Unitarians.
2. Babies are illogical. Anyone who can't pass a test in logic is illogical. Therefore anyone who can't pass logic tests is a baby.
3. Don't be fooled. All conservative Republicans are really anarchists, for they basically favor a reduction in the power of the federal government, and so do the anarchists.
4. Some city bosses have to be pragmatists, for all city bosses are Democrats, and one has yet to meet a Democrat who isn't a pragmatist.
5. Every country is run by a small handful of powerful people. The U.S. is a country. Therefore the U.S. is run by a small handful of powerful people.
6. Dogma is the enemy of human freedom. No pragmatist is a dogmatist. So every pragmatist is a friend of human freedom.
7. Thou shalt not worship false gods. Wealth is a false god, so don't worship wealth.
8. Compromise is ethically unsavory and ugly. No politician can succeed without compromise. Hence every politician is ugly and unethical.
9. The senator says the war is a mistake. The enemy says the war is a mistake. So the senator is the enemy.
10. For the old to understand the young they must get younger. No one can ever get younger. Thus the old will never understand the young.

ANSWERS

2. All babies are illogical. All who can't pass a test in logic are illogical. Therefore all who can't pass a test in logic are babies. **AAA**-II (invalid.)

4. Valid. Interpretation of valid reinforced syllogistic pattern: **AAI**-I plus There are city bosses.

7. All acts of worshipping false gods are things you should not do. All acts of worshipping wealth are acts of worshipping false gods. Therefore all acts of worshipping wealth are things you should not do. **AAA**-I (valid).

10. All old persons who understand the young are those who have gotten younger. No persons are those who have gotten younger. Therefore no person is an old person who understands the young. **AEE**-II (valid).

Testing Syllogisms

As indicated in the last section, there are various methods by which one can determine which of the 256 syllogistic argument patterns are valid (other than by using the chart). Three of these methods will be discussed in this section.

Venn Diagrams

In the first section in this chapter a way to represent categorical sentences by using overlapping circles is discussed. The Venn diagram method for testing syllogisms employs this way of representing the categorical sentences of a syllogism. Since there are three and only three general terms in a syllogism, three circles are used. To test a syllogism one first draws *three* overlapping circles in this manner:

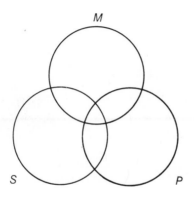

Next, each premise is diagrammed or represented in the same manner as it was represented in the first section. For example, if we were diagramming an **OAO**-III syllogism, we would diagram the **O** and **A** sentences as follows, diagramming the **A** premise first:

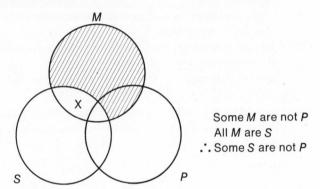

Some *M* are not *P*
All *M* are *S*
∴ Some *S* are not *P*

Finally, having inscribed the content of the two premises into the circles, we inspect the circles to see whether the content of the conclusion automatically appears in the circles as a result. If the conclusion has been diagrammed, the syllogism is valid; if it has not been diagrammed, the syllogism is invalid. In the preceding example, since "Some *S* is not *P*" has been automatically diagrammed in diagramming the two premises, the Venn diagram test for **OAO**-III shows it to be valid.

In using the Venn diagram test one should always diagram the universal (**A** or **E**) premise before the particular (**I** or **O**), as was just done in the example; otherwise one may find that he has to move the *x* after diagramming the universal. Also, in diagramming a particular sentence there may be alternative areas in which to place the *x*. For example, in diagramming **AII**-II, after diagramming the **A** premise, we have this situation:

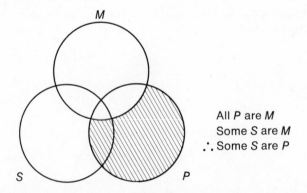

All *P* are *M*
Some *S* are *M*
∴ Some *S* are *P*

The second premise, "Some *S* are *M*," can be diagrammed by placing an *x* in the overlap area of the *M* and *S* circle or the overlap of the *M*, *P*, and *S* circle.

Since we do not wish to diagram any more than the content of the "Some *S* are *M*" premise in this argument context, and since nothing indicates in which overlap area the *x* is to go, we place it on the line as follows:

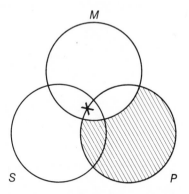

So placed, it indicates that nothing determines which overlap it is to go into, though by being on the line it indicates that it goes either in the one overlap area or the other.

To test a syllogism using Venn diagrams, first symbolize the argument (see last exercises), and, second, test the symbolized argument by letting the three circles represent the minor, major, and middle terms of the syllogism, and by diagramming in the content of the premises. Finally, see if the conclusion has been diagrammed. To illustrate, let us test the following syllogism for validity using the Venn diagram method:

> Georgia dates only boys that have long hair, and since Edgar doesn't have long hair, he can't get a date with Georgia.

Symbolized, we have:

> No things identical with Edgar (*E*) are boys with long hair (*B*).
> All Georgia dates (*G*) are *B*.
> Therefore no *G* are *E*.

Diagrammed:

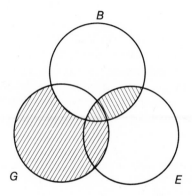

Since the conclusion automatically appears when the contents of the premises are diagrammed, the argument is valid.

As another illustration, exercise 6 from the last section of exercises, is symbolized:

> All dogmatists (*D*) are enemies of human freedom (*E*).
> No pragmatists (*P*) are *D*.
> Therefore no *P* are *E*.

Diagrammed:

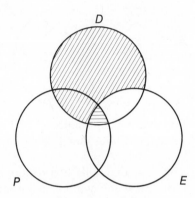

Since the conclusion "No *P* are *E*" does not appear when the contents of the two premises have been emptied into the diagram, the argument is invalid. This example may also be symbolized:

> No *D* are friends of human freedom (*F*).
> No *P* are *D*.
> Therefore all *P* are *F*.

An **EEA**-I invalid syllogism. Since different correct symbolizations of an argument are equivalent, the same results will be obtained when testing them.

Syllogistic Rules

To understand the syllogistic rule method for testing the validity of a syllogism, the notion of distribution must be introduced. A term is said to be *distributed* in a categorical sentence if the sentence is used to make an assertion about every object denoted by the term. Indications of what terms are distributed (indicated by circles) and are not distributed (no circles) in categorical sentences follow:

> **A**:   All Ⓢ are *P*.
> **E**:   No Ⓢ are Ⓟ
> **I**:   Some *S* are *P*.
> **O**:   Some *S* are not Ⓟ.

Thus, for example, *S* is distributed in "All *S* are *P*" since in asserting "All *S* are *P*" one is saying something about all the individuals denoted by *S*, namely, that they are *P*'s. In *O*, *P* is distributed, since in asserting "Some *S* are not *P*" one is saying that at least one thing that is *S* is not one of any of the individuals denoted by *P*.

If a syllogism satisfies each of the following five rules, it is valid, whereas if it fails to satisfy one or more of these rules (a syllogism can fail to satisfy more than one rule), then it is invalid:

Rule 1: The middle term must be distributed at least once.

Rule 2: If a term is distributed in the conclusion, it must be distributed in the premises.

Rule 3: At least one premise must be affirmative.

Rule 4: If either premise is negative, the conclusion must be negative.

Rule 5: If both premises are universal, then the conclusion cannot be particular.

Any of the fifteen valid syllogistic patterns can easily be seen to satisfy each of these rules, whereas any of the remaining 241 patterns can easily be seen to violate one or more of these rules.

If a syllogistic argument violates the first rule, it is traditionally said to be a *fallacy of undistributed middle term*. A fallacy, as we have seen, is an invalid argument which some may think valid. And since people may be persuaded that syllogisms with undistributed middle terms are valid when they are not, the term "fallacy" is used. The following is an example of a syllogism which commits this fallacy:

Bertrand Russell is an atheist, and all communists are atheists, so Bertrand Russell is a communist. (*AAA*-II)

The fallacy of undistributed middle term is another example of a formal fallacy. Arguments where this fallacy occurs are interpretations of patterns which are invalid but which closely resemble valid patterns, namely, the valid patterns where middle terms are distributed. Just as the fallacy of affirming the consequent resembles the valid pattern *modus ponens*, so, for example, an *AAA* syllogism which has an undistributed middle term resembles the valid *AAA* pattern—*AAA*-I.

If a syllogism violates the second rule, then it is said to be an instance of the *fallacy of illicit minor term* or *fallacy of illicit major term*, depending on whether the minor term is distributed in the conclusion and not in the premises (illicit minor) or the major term is distributed in the conclusion but not in the premises (illicit major). Illustrations of each fallacy in unsymbolized arguments follow:

You never get grapes from thorns. All thorny things are maddening. So no maddening things are grapes. (*EAE*-IV)

Symbolic acts are sometimes logical. Never are logical acts nutty. Thus some nutty things are not symbolic acts. (***IEO***-IV)

In the first argument "maddening things" is distributed in the conclusion but not in the second premise. In the second argument "symbolic act" is distributed in the conclusion but not in the first premise.

It is interesting to note that other rules can be derived from the preceding five rules. For example, this rule:

A syllogism cannot have only affirmative premises and a negative conclusion.

follows from rules 1, 2, and 5. Here is the proof: If the conclusion in our supposed valid syllogism is negative, then it cannot be an ***E*** statement. If it were an ***E*** and the syllogism were valid, then three terms would need to be distributed in the premises by rules 1 and 2. But then the premises could not be affirmative, one of them would have to be an ***E***. If the conclusion is an ***O*** statement, then for the syllogism to be valid two terms must be distributed in the premises, by rules 1 and 2. For two terms to be distributed in a pair of affirmative premises they must both be ***A*** statements. But by rule 5 no particular conclusion follows from two universal premises and thus an ***O*** cannot follow from two ***A*** premises. Since the negative conclusion is either an ***E*** or ***O*** and in each case the syllogism cannot be valid if the premises are both affirmative, the preceding rule is proved.

Inconsistent Triad Test

The advantage of the Venn diagram method for testing syllogisms is that it is intuitively satisfying. To test validity of a syllogism one empties into a diagram the logical content of each premise and checks to see if the conclusion makes its appearance. The advantage of the five rules method of testing the validity of syllogisms is that it provides one with a way to identify what goes wrong with a syllogism when it is invalid. The advantage of the next method for determining the validity of syllogisms, and the last, is that once it is mastered, applying it takes little time, for it makes use of the by now familiar *reductio ad absurdum* rule.

To understand this last method of testing the validity of syllogisms we must first see how categorical sentences can be reinterpreted as equations in the Boolean algebra of classes (see last section of this chapter for the identification of Boolean algebra). To achieve this reinterpretation, the letters S, P, and M are to be construed as variables for classes or sets rather than variables for general terms. Next, some elementary set terminology needs to be employed. The first such notion is that of *class complement*. An overbar on a class variable will be used to indicate the complement of that class. For example, the complement of the class S is $\bar{S}$. S is the class of things which are S, whereas $\bar{S}$ is the class of everything that is not S. $\bar{S}$ may be read as non-S. "Λ" will be used to indicate the empty set. Two sets are said to be identical if and only if they have the same members. Since any two empty sets must have the same members, namely, no members, all empty sets are identical, so one can speak of *the empty set* and let this be indicated by "Λ." The familiar sign for identity, "$=$," is introduced to express the identity between sets, and "$\neq$" is used to express the denial of identity. Finally we need to introduce the notion of the intersection of two sets. The *intersection* of two sets S and P is the area of overlap between S and P. The symbol "$\cap$" is used to designate set intersection. The intersection of sets S and P is thus represented by $S \cap P$. With this elementary set notation, the four categorical sentences can be expressed in this manner:

A: $S \cap \bar{P} = \Lambda$ **I**: $S \cap P \neq \Lambda$

E: $S \cap P = \Lambda$ **O**: $S \cap \bar{P} \neq \Lambda$

One can quickly confirm that what each of these expresses is just what is expressed when one uses circles to diagram the categorical sentences. For example, the circle diagrams for **A** and **O** are

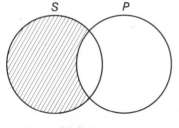

All S are P

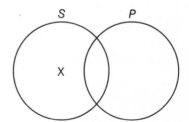

Some S are not P

Observing the diagram for "All S are P," the area that is both S and $\bar{P}$ is empty, i.e., shaded. $S \cap \bar{P} = \Lambda$ asserts just that, that the intersection of S and $\bar{P}$ is empty. Remember, to shade a circle is to indicate that the term in question is empty and that all empty terms designate the empty class, Λ. $S \cap \bar{P} \neq \Lambda$ asserts that the intersection of S and $\bar{P}$ is not empty, that there is at least one individual, one x, that is found in both S and $\bar{P}$. The diagram for "Some S are not P" expresses this.

The inconsistent triad test for syllogisms is a *reductio ad absurdum* argument which proceeds along these lines: First, translate the syllogism using this newly introduced set terminology. Second, replace "$=$" in the conclusion with "$\neq$," or replace "$\neq$" with "$=$," depending on whether an identity is asserted or denied. Third, determine the validity of the resulting syllogism by applying the following rule: A syllogism is valid if and only if with respect to the three equations:

1. There are two identities and one denial of identity.
2. One letter is common to both identities and a line is over one of them and only one of them, i.e., one and only one occurrence of this letter is complemented.
3. If a letter occurs complemented (uncomplemented) in the denial of identity, its other occurrence must be complemented (uncomplemented).

To illustrate, the following argument is tested using this method:

All friends are sympathetic.
No ghastly people are friends.
Therefore no ghastly people are sympathetic.

Translating the sentences into Boolean equations, we have:

$$F \cap \bar{S} = \Lambda$$
$$G \cap F = \Lambda$$
$$\therefore G \cap S = \Lambda$$

Replacing the conclusion with a denial of identity since it asserts identity, we have:

$$F \cap \bar{S} = \Lambda$$
$$G \cap F = \Lambda$$
$$\therefore G \cap S \neq \Lambda$$

The trio of equations contains two identities and one denial of identity, thus satisfying rule 1 above. The letter F appears in the two identities. However there is not a line over one of them, so rule 2 is not satisfied, and consequently, the argument is invalid. If there were a line over both occurrences of F, the argument would also fail rule 2. Rule 3 is also not satisfied since in the denial of identity, S is uncomplemented, but it is complemented in the first identity. Here is an argument that passes the test:

Everyone decries Machiavellian statecraft.
Those who decry such things are unrealistic.
Therefore everyone is unrealistic.

Using class terminology, we translate the argument:

$$P \cap \bar{D} = \Lambda$$
$$D \cap \bar{U} = \Lambda$$
$$\therefore P \cap \bar{U} = \Lambda$$

Replacing " = " with " ≠ " in the conclusion, we have two identities and one denial of identity, and D is common to both identities, with $\bar{D}$ occurring exactly once. And rule 3 is satisfied since P occurs uncomplemented and U is complemented in both occurrences. The argument, thus, is valid. Consider one more example:

> No Republicans are Democrats.
> Some wealthy men are not Democrats.
> Therefore some wealthy men are not Republicans.

This argument translates as

$$R \cap D = \Lambda$$
$$W \cap \bar{D} \neq \Lambda$$
$$\therefore W \cap \bar{R} \neq \Lambda$$

Replacing the conclusion with $W \cap \bar{R} = \Lambda$ we obtain the following results: Rules 1 and 2 are satisfied but rule 3 is not, for D occurs complemented in the denial of identity but uncomplemented in the first premise. Thus the argument is invalid.

These three methods for testing the validity of syllogisms are each complete and sound. To say a syllogistic method is *complete* is to say that it is powerful enough to establish as valid each valid syllogism. It is an easy though somewhat tedious exercise to prove that all fifteen valid syllogistic patterns come out valid using each method. It is also easy, though even more tedious, to prove that no invalid syllogistic pattern is valid by any of the methods, thus proving each method to be sound. To say a syllogistic method is *sound* is to say that it does not allow validation of an invalid syllogism.

EXERCISES 8.4

A. Symbolize the following syllogisms and test for validity using the Venn diagram test, the rule test, and the consistent triad test. Indicate the occurrence of any formal fallacies.

1. Every artist is an egotist, and some artists are poor, so some egotists are poor.
2. No Republicans are Democrats, so some Democrats are wealthy men, since some wealthy men are not Republicans.
3. No wealthy men are labor leaders, because no wealthy men are true liberals, and all labor leaders are true liberals.
4. All Supreme Court Justices are conservative. No teachers are Supreme Court Justices. So no teachers are conservative.
5. Tax reforms are harmful to business but good for the average man. Therefore everything harmful to business is good for the average man.

6. Every motivated ecologist is a socialist in disguise. Some socialists are Marxists; thus some motivated ecologists are Marxists.

7. Socialists support wealth redistribution. Most new-politics Democrats support wealth redistribution. So these Democrats are really socialists.

8. The great American dream is the glorious pursuit of happiness. Americans do not pursue happiness but rather work hard. Americans, thus, will never realize the great American dream.

9. Most bold cats are curious, so they die young, since curious cats die young.

10. One cannot step into the Great Lakes without a doctor urging immediate amputation. Godfrey Daniel made the mistake of putting his foot into the water near Detroit and so he is now in need of an amputation.

11. Billboards are the most nearly useless excrescence of industrial civilization. America is responsible for billboards, so America is responsible for this industrial waste.

B.   Answer the following questions by appealing to the five rules.

1. In what figure or figures can a valid syllogism distribute both major and minor term?

2. In what mood or moods can a syllogism with a particular conclusion be valid?

3. Can a valid syllogism have a term distributed in a premise and not distributed in the conclusion?

4. Which of the 256 possible syllogistic patterns are valid?

ANSWERS

A.   **6.**   Some socialists are Marxists. All motivated ecologists are socialists. Therefore some motivated ecologists are Marxists. *IAI*-I, invalid, fallacy of undistributed middle term.

8.   No realizers of the great American dream are hard-working persons. All Americans are hard-working persons. Therefore no Americans are realizers of the great American dream. *EAE*-II, valid.

10.   All persons who step into the Great Lakes are persons in need of amputation. All things identical with Godfrey Daniel are persons who step into the Great Lakes. Therefore all things identical with Godfrey Daniel are persons in need of amputation. *AAA*-I, valid.

B.   **3.**   No. If either *S* or *P* is distributed in the premises, then by rule 1 two terms are distributed. The conclusion cannot be an *E*. If it is an *A* then three terms must be distributed in the premises by rule 2. But this cannot be done unless there is a negative premise and thus the conclusion cannot be an *A* by rule 4. If it is an *I* for two terms to be distributed a premise must either be negative, violating rule 4, or both must be *A*, violating rule 5. If it is an *O* then three terms are distributed. To avoid using two negatives one has to be an *A* and the other an *E*, but this violates rule 5.

Immediate Inferences

Syllogisms confront us with relations between triples of categorical sentences. What are the relations between just pairs of categorical sentences? To begin with, *A* and *O* are mutual contradictories, that is, it is false that they can have the same truth value; in other words, $\sim(A \equiv O)$. The circle diagrams for *A* and *O* sentences reflect this; one simply denies the other. Similarly, *E* and *I* are mutual contradictories. Thus, for example, the following are valid argument patterns for *A* and *O*:

All *S* are *P*. ∴ ~Some *S* is not *P*.
~All *S* are *P*. ∴ Some *S* is not *P*.
Some *S* is not *P*. ∴ ~All *S* are *P*.
~Some *S* is not *P*. ∴ All *S* are *P*.

A and *E* may seem to some to be mutual contradictories, but this is not true. On the contrary, examples chosen at random are likely to show that both *A* and *E* can be false. This happens when, for example, *S* is taken as "students" and *P* is taken as "Christians." It is false both that all students are Christians and that no students are Christians. Whereas *A* and *E* are commonly both false, *I* and *O* are often both true. For example, it is true that some students are Christians and that some students are not Christians. It is less common that *A* and *E* can both be true and *I* and *O* can both be false, but this happens if *S* is taken as an empty term. Clearly if there is nothing that is *S*, then "Some *S* are *P*" and "Some *S* are not *P*" are both false. And if *A* and *E* are the contradictories of *I* and *O*, then "All *S* are *P*" and "No *S* are *P*" must both be true if "Some *S* are *P*" and "Some *S* are not *P*" are both false. The circle diagram for *A* and *E* verifies that both are true if *S* is an empty term, for recall that the following circles diagram *both A* and *E*:

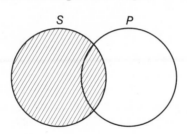

If **A** can be true while **I** is false, and if **E** can be true while **O** is false, then the following are *not* valid patterns:

All *S* are *P*.
Therefore some *S* are *P*.
No *S* are *P*.
Therefore some *S* are not *P*.

These logical relationships between **A**, **E**, **I**, and **O** sentences can be summed up in what is called the square of opposition:

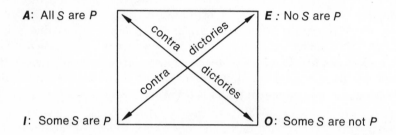

A: All *S* are *P*   **E** : No *S* are *P*

I: Some *S* are *P*   **O**: Some *S* are not *P*

When, however, one restricts interpretations of categorical sentence forms to nonempty terms, then other relationships exist between categorical sentences. If one supposes that there are *S* and there are *P*, then **A** and **E** cannot both be true, **I** and **O** cannot both be false, and if **A** is true, then **I** is true, and if **E**, then **O**. With this restricted interpretation the logical relationships between **A**, **E**, **I**, and **O** can be summed up in the following square of opposition:

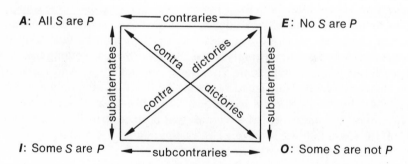

A: All *S* are *P*   contraries   **E**: No *S* are *P*

I: Some *S* are *P*   subcontraries   **O**: Some *S* are not *P*

Two sentences are *contraries* if both cannot be true, but both can be false, whereas two sentences are called *subcontraries* if both cannot be false but both can be true. **I** and **O** are said to be subalterns of **A** and **E**, respectively, meaning that if **A** is true, then **I** is true, and if **E** then **O**. Thus in addition to $\sim(\mathbf{A} \equiv \mathbf{O})$ and $\sim(\mathbf{E} \equiv \mathbf{I})$ these are valid if the interpretation for *S* and *P* is restricted to nonempty terms: $\sim(\mathbf{A} \cdot \mathbf{E})$, $\sim(\sim\mathbf{I} \cdot \sim\mathbf{O})$, $\mathbf{A} \supset \mathbf{I}$, and $\mathbf{E} \supset \mathbf{O}$.

There are other relationships between pairs of categorical sentences, and these are summarized by the following table:

	Converse	*Obverse*	*Contrapositive*
A: All *S* are *P*.	Some *P* are *S* (no empty terms)	No *S* are non-*P*.	All non-*P* are non-*S*.
E: No *S* are *P*.	No *P* are *S*.	All *S* are non-*P*.	Some non-*P* are not non-*S* (no empty terms).
I: Some *S* are *P*.	Some *P* are *S*.	Some *S* are not non-*P*.	None
O: Some *S* are not *P*.	None	Some *S* are non-*P*.	Some non-*P* are not non-*S*.

The *converse* of a sentence is formed by interchanging the subject and the predicate. As can be seen by the preceding table, **E** and **I** can be converted, but **O** cannot. If we suppose no empty terms, **A** implies **I** by subalternation and an **I** can be converted. So "All *S* are *P*" converts to "Some *P* are *S*" if neither *S* nor *P* is an empty term. The following is a valid argument pattern:

No *S* are *P*. ∴ No *P* are *S*.

since the conclusion is the converse of the premise and **E** sentences can be converted. On the other hand, the following is not valid:

Some *S* are not *P*. ∴ Some *P* are not *S*.

Such valid or invalid patterns can easily be read off the preceding table. To form the *obverse* of a categorical sentence, replace its predicate with its complement and change it from an affirmative to a negative or from a negative to an affirmative. As we see by the table, any categorical sentence can be obverted and one does not have to presuppose nonempty terms. Thus, for example, the following is a valid pattern:

All *S* are *P*. ∴ No *S* are non-*P*.

To form the *contrapositive* of a categorical sentence we interchange its subject and predicate and replace each term with its complement. Thus from the table we find that, for example, the following is valid if interpretations are limited to nonempty terms:

No *S* are *P*. ∴ Some non-*P* are not non-*S*.

E implies a corresponding **O** if no empty terms are involved and an **O** has a contrapositive.

A useful exercise in applying the immediate inferences is to be given a sentence and a set of other sentences with the same terms, the truth value of the first sentence, and then to determine the truth value of each member of the set, relying on the logical relationships between categorical propositions displayed in the preceding table and in the square of opposition. For example, given that the following is true:

The very wise can act like idiots. [All very wise persons (V) are persons who can act like idiots (P).]

What is the truth value of each of the following:

1.   Some non-P are not non-V.
2.   No V are non-P.
3.   All non-V are non-P.
4.   No non-P are V.
5.   No non-V are non-P.
6.   No V are P.
7.   Some V are P.
8.   Some V are not P.

Item 1 is **F** since its contrapositive contradicts the original sentence; 2 is **T** since it obverts into the original sentence. The contrapositive of 3 is "All P are V." Since from "All S are P" nothing follows about the truth or falsity of "All P are S," 3 is indeterminate. (We do not know that it is **T** or **F** given "All V are P" is **T**.) Item 4 obverts to "All non-P are non-V," which has as its contrapositive "All V are P," so 4 is **T** if the original sentence is **T**. Item 5 converts to "No non-P are non-V." The original sentence's contrapositive is "All non-P are non-V." Item 5 is thus the contrary of the original sentence. If we assume nonempty terms, 5 is **F**; otherwise it is indeterminate. Item 6 is **F** if we assume nonempty terms; otherwise it is indeterminate. Item 7 is **T** if we assume nonempty terms; otherwise it is indeterminate. Item 8 is the contradictory of the original sentence and is thus **F** whether we assume or do not assume nonempty terms.

EXERCISES 8.5

In each of the following exercises assume that S and P are not empty terms.

A.   Symbolize the following and convert those which can be converted:

1.   There is a Titus Mooney.
2.   Real insights are not to be found on television.
3.   There are men too gentle to live among wolves.
4.   Not all corporate leaders are above the law.
5.   A hungry poet is never a bum.

B. Symbolize the following and obvert each one:

1. Anyone will cheat in the name of profit.
2. Happy endings never occur.
3. The answer is mother's kisses.
4. Most popular novels are topical.
5. Hamlet is unemployable.

C. Symbolize the following and provide the contrapositive for those which have a contrapositive:

1. Billygoat Gruff has been in unsuccessful orgone analysis for nine years.
2. You go crazy pursuing visions.
3. Almost all contemporary experiences bring indigenous tensions.
4. Nothing will ever replace our disastrous prison system.
5. Unstructured talk of revolution is one way to avoid reality.

D. If "Americans never pick strong and able men for leaders" is true, what is the truth value of the following sentences? [Note: Let the sentence be symbolized "No persons picked for leadership by Americans are strong and able persons." (No *P* are *S*.) Also note that there are (we hope) strong and able persons.]

1. No non-*S* are *P*.
2. Some non-*S* are not non-*P*.
3. All non-*P* are non-*S*.
4. No *P* are non-*S*.
5. No non-*P* are non-*S*.
6. All *S* are *P*.
7. Some non-*S* are non-*P*.
8. All non-*S* are non-*P*.
9. Some *S* are not *P*.
10. No *P* are non-*S*.

ANSWERS

A. **5.** "No *H* are *B*" converts to "No *B* are *H*."

B. **5.** "No things identical with Hamlet (*H*) are employable (*E*)" obverts to "All *H* are non-*E*." Or "All *H* are unemployable" obverts to "No *H* are non-employable" or "No *H* are *E*."

C. **5.** "All *U* are reality-avoiding (*R*)" contrapositive is "All non-*R* are non-*U*."

D. **1.** False. **3.** False. **5.** Undetermined **7.** Undetermined (true if "No *P* are *S*" is false). **9.** True.

[Note in 5 that "No non-S are non-P" implies "Some P are not S" by contraposition. And "No P and S" implies "Some P are not S" by subalteration. But if "No P are S" is true, it does not follow that "No non-S are non-P" is true. Don't commit the fallacy of affirming the consequent!]

Syllogistic Chains (Sorites) and Enthymemes

Syllogisms can be set up in a chain fashion as follows:

P_1
P_2
$\therefore C_1$
P_3
$\therefore C_2$
$\vdots$
etc.

If one omits the intermediate conclusions the result is called a *sorites*. An example of a sorites taken from Lewis Carroll's *Symbolic Logic* is:

All babies are illogical.
No one is despised who can manage a crocodile.
Illogical persons are despised.
Therefore no babies can manage crocodiles.

The methods introduced in previous sections can be used to establish the validity of such syllogistic chains. The general procedure is this:

1. Symbolize the argument, being sure that you only have n number of terms, where n is the number of sentences in the sorites sequence. Do not count a term and its complement as one term.
2. Arrange the premise sentences so that each sentence has a term in common with the one that follows.
3. Supply the intermediate, unstated conclusions.
4. Test the validity of each syllogism in the chain.
5. The sorites is valid if and only if each syllogism in the chain is valid.

As illustration, this procedure is now applied to the preceding Carroll example. It is first symbolized:

All B are I.
No M are D.
All I are D.
Therefore no B are M.

Note that there are four terms. Arranging the chain following step 2 gives us:

All *B* are *I*.
All *I* are *D*.
No *M* are *D*.
Therefore no *B* are *M*.

The intermediate conclusion from the first two premises is "All *B* are *D*."
This gives us an **AAA**-I syllogism which can be confirmed as valid. The last
syllogism in the chain is the intermediate conclusion, the third premise and
the conclusion, i.e.,

All *B* are *D*.
No *M* are *D*.
Therefore no *B* are *M*.

This **EAE**-II checks out valid. Since each of the syllogisms in the chain is
valid, the sorites is valid.

As another example, consider this second sorites from Lewis Carroll:

Everyone who is sane can do logic.
No lunatics are fit to serve on a jury.
None of your sons can do logic.
Therefore none of your sons are fit to serve on a jury.

Symbolized:

All *S* are *L*.
No non-*S* are *F*.   converts and obverts to   All *F* are *S*.
No *Y* are *L*.
Therefore no *Y* are *F*.

Note two important things in this symbolizing. First, "sane" and "lunatic"
are taken to be complements; thus since *S* is put in for "sane," "non-*S*" is
put in for "lunatic." We need to do this to insure that we satisfy step 1.
Second, even with the complement we do not as yet satisfy step 1. We have
five terms and we must have only four terms, since there are four sentences
in the sorites sequence. So we must take out the complement. This is done by
converting and obverting the second premise to "All *F* are *S*." The
intermediate conclusion is, obviously, "All *F* are *L*" and the resulting two
syllogisms are both valid, so the sorites is valid.

Another form of argument to which the syllogistic methods can be applied
is the *enthymeme*. In the past "enthymeme" usually denoted a syllogism with
an unstated premise. Today, however, "enthymeme" is generally used to
denote any argument in which there is an unstated premise or premises
or conclusion. Enthymematic arguments usually arise because we do not

explicitly state in an argument what we take as common knowledge. For example, consider this enthymematic syllogism:

> Some of you are not conscientious students, for no really conscientious student is late for class two days in a row.

It has a missing minor premise which is not stated because in the context in which the argument is likely to occur—an unhappy instructor speaking after some students have come in late—it would be obviously understood as assumed. The argument with missing premise made explicit is:

> No student who is late for classes two days in a row is a conscientious student.
> Some students in this class have been late two days in a row.
> Therefore some students in this class are not conscientious students.
>   (***EIO***-I, valid).

A sorites, in fact, is an enthymeme, since the intermediate conclusions are unstated premises for a syllogism in the chain.

The conclusion of a syllogism may also be left unstated because it is obvious or, in some cases, the persuasive power of the argument may be enhanced if one lets the audience draw the conclusion. For example, a politician addressing a political rally says:

> Everyone who is easily influenced and who is unaware of the threat to our way of life needs to be *protected* from these insidious radical ideas. Some of the citizens of this country are easily influenced and ignorant of this threat, and so, unfortunately, are our children. The course of action is clear. (Pause) Thank you, my friends, for listening. (Applause)

The conclusion which is unstated is, of course: All children of ours are persons who need to be protected from radical ideas.

EXERCISES 8.6

A. The following examples or sorites are taken from Lewis Carroll's *Symbolic Logic*. Test each one for validity.

   1. All comets are wanderers in the zodiac.
   No terriers are wanderers in the zodiac.
   All curly-tailed creatures are terriers.
   Therefore no curly-tailed creatures are comets.
   2. No terriers wander among the signs of the zodiac.
   Nothing that does not wander among the signs of the zodiac is a comet.

Nothing but a terrier has a curly tail.

Therefore all creatures with curly tails are non-comets.

3. Which conclusion can be derived from the following premises:

All writers who understand human nature are clever.

No one is a true poet unless he can stir the hearts of men.

Shakespeare wrote *Hamlet.*

No writer who does not understand human nature can stir the hearts of men.

None but a true poet could have written *Hamlet.*

4. Find the conclusion here also:

No one takes in the *Times*, unless he is well-educated.

No Hedgehogs can read.

Those who cannot read are not well-educated.

5. When I work a logic example without grumbling, you may be sure that it is one that I understand.

These sorites are not arranged in regular order, like the examples I am used to.

No easy example ever makes my head ache.

I can't understand examples that are not arranged in regular order, like those I am used to.

I never grumble at an example, unless it gives me a headache.

What is the conclusion?

6. The only animals in the house are cats;

every animal is suitable for a pet that loves to gaze at the moon;

when I detest an animal I avoid it;

no animals are carnivorous, unless they prowl at night;

no cat fails to kill mice;

no animal ever takes to me, except what are in this house;

kangaroos are not suitable for pets;

none but carnivora kill mice;

animals that prowl at night always love to gaze at the moon.

I detest animals that do not take to me.

Therefore I always avoid a kangaroo.

B. Supply the missing premise or conclusion of each of the following enthymemes and test for validity.

1. All Athenians are corrupt because all men are corrupt.
2. Our poets should be honored because a real poet is rare.
3. Godfrey Daniel is a human being so Godfrey Daniel makes mistakes.
4. Since all Englishmen think the Commonwealth is something of world importance, when it isn't, you also think this.
5. This Broadway play is the best of the season since all the New York critics say it is.

Formal and Informal Fallacies

In this chapter and in Chapter 6 we have examined the most common formal fallacies. The four formal fallacies discussed in Chapter 6 are

1. Fallacy of affirming the consequent: $p \supset q, q \therefore p$.
2. Fallacy of denying the antecedent: $p \supset q, \sim p \therefore \sim q$.
3. Fallacy of invalid hypothetical syllogism: $p \supset q, r \supset q \therefore p \supset r$ or $p \supset q, p \supset r \therefore q \supset r$.
4. Fallacy of invalid dilemma: $p \supset q, r \supset s, q \vee s \therefore p \vee r$ or $p \supset q, r \supset s, \sim p \vee \sim r \therefore \sim q \vee \sim s$.

In this chapter we have examined the formal fallacies of distribution, namely

5. Fallacy of undistributed middle term.
6. Fallacy of illicit major.
7. Fallacy of illicit minor.

Formal fallacies such as these differ from informal fallacies, such as those discussed in Chapter 2, in that the former are incorrect arguments because of a faulty logical form and not because of ambiguities of language or inattention to the subject matter of the argument.

Illogical thinking occurs when people use arguments that are fallacious. One of the goals of a first course in logic is to provide some aids to being logical. One takes a step in this direction if one acquires the ability to sort out arguments as correct or incorrect, and, with respect to the incorrect arguments, identify occurrences of the common forms of formal or informal fallacies. The following exercise section tests this ability.

EXERCISES 8.7

For each argument below indicate whether it is correct or not. If it is correct, prove that it is correct. If it is incorrect, then indicate the fallacy (formal or informal) that occurs. Give reasons why you believe a fallacy occurs.

A. 1. Nothing is a horse unless it is a mammal. Nothing is a mammal unless it has a mammary gland, so nothing without a mammary gland is a horse.

2. Men, we will not win this game only if we go soft in the second half. But I know we're going to win, so we won't go soft in the second half.

3. If determinism holds, then man does not have free will. Man has free will. Hence determinism does not hold.

4. Aquinas' rational proofs for the existence of God are fallacious, for he was just trying to justify through reason what he already believed through faith.

5. God obviously exists. The reason is simple. If he did not exist, men would not believe all that is written in the Bible. But many men do believe everything that is written in the Bible, so God exists.

6. Every woman is an object, sexually speaking. No woman has a satisfactory feminine experience. So no sexual objects have satisfactory feminine experiences.

7. Machines are causally determined, so humans are machines since they are causally determined.

8. A fool can win your heart only if you are a bigger fool. A fool cannot win your heart. Thus you are not a bigger fool.

9. All working men are underpaid. So no underpaid people are people who like sales taxes.

10. When we die we either have an undisturbed sleep or we have the great pleasure of being with those we want to be with. Either way this is a gain, so death is a gain.

B.   1. Blacks are better athletes and entertainers than businessmen or lawyers. Look at Wilt Chamberlain and Richard Pryor.

2. The energy crisis is the fault of the Republicans; we never had one during a Democratic administration.

3. Georgia dates only boys that have tuxedos, and since Edgar doesn't have one, he can't get a date with Georgia.

4. You really should vote for this bill, Senator; our million-member union is in favor of it, and you are up for re-election this fall.

5. If I study I am likely to make good grades. If I do not study I can enjoy myself. Therefore either I will have good grades or I will enjoy myself.

6. He said they wanted men to fill potholes in the office of the Department of Highways. I think I'll apply for the job. I like to work indoors.

7. Jones is a very promising youth, but he has not fulfilled his promise. Only a liar does not keep his promise. So Jones must be a liar.

8. The Swedes are 90 percent Protestant. Uncle Gustav is a Swede. Therefore he is 90 percent Protestant.

9. All athletes are brawny. Charles is not brawny. Therefore Charles is not an athlete.

10. Some oil company ads are heavy handed, self-serving and sprinkled with half-truths. Asks one Mobil ad: "Are oil profits big? Right. Big enough? Wrong. So says the Chase Manhattan Bank." That is like asking a Volkswagen whether small cars have a future.

11. All departures from law should be punished. Whatever happens by chance is a departure from law. Therefore whatever happens by chance should be punished.

12. If enough food is produced to feed the expanding world population, then water and air will be polluted beyond the tolerable limit by the amount of fertilizers and insecticides that are required. If these fertilizers and insecticides are not used, not enough food will be produced on the land available and people will starve. So any way you look at it we face disaster.

13. It is no more necessary for there to be two political parties than that a man have two heads.

14. Of course there is a Santa Claus. But he doesn't bring any presents to children who don't believe in him.

15. I have never come across any argument for price controls that any sensible man could accept. So price controls can't work.

16. All attempts to end hostilities are efforts which should be approved by all nations. All of Cuba's present activities in Africa are attempts to end hostilities. So all of Cuba's actions in Africa should be approved by the United States.

ANSWERS

A. 1. valid syllogism   2. denying the antecedent   3. valid sentential argument.   4. *ad hominem* fallacy   5. valid sentential argument   6. illicit minor   7. undistributed middle term   8. denying the antecedent   9. illicit minor (enthymeme)   10. valid hypothetical syllogism

Boolean Algebra

To use the inconsistent triad test, categorical sentences are represented by taking S, P, and M to denote classes and by using the notions of class complement, identity, the empty set, and class intersection. As we have seen, the intersection of two classes A and B, symbolized $A \cap B$, is the class of things which A and B have in common. The portion enclosed by the heavy line in the following diagram in the two overlapping classes indicates the intersection of A and B:

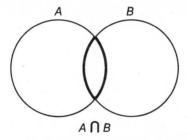

$A \cap B$

The class of things which belong to either one (or both) of two classes A and B is called their *union*, symbolized $A \cup B$. The union of A and B can be represented by the portion of two overlapping circles enclosed by the heavy line, as follows:

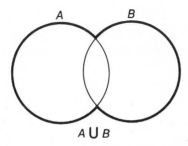

$A \cup B$

"Λ" is used to denote the empty set. The set which is the complement to "Λ," "$\bar{\Lambda}$," can be designated by the symbol "V." "V" is called the universal set, and it is identical with the complement of "Λ,", i.e., $V = \bar{\Lambda}$.

Boolean equations are identity equations using variables for classes, and the following constants: $\cup$, $\cap$, V, Λ and $^-$. We will use A, B, and C as variables for classes. Mathematicians are interested in those Boolean equations which come out true under every interpretation, where one obtains an interpretation by replacing the class variables with general terms. Boolean equations which come out true under every interpretation can be said to be *valid Boolean equations*.

The following are some valid Boolean equations:

1. $A \cap B = B \cap A$
2. $A \cap (B \cap C) = (A \cap B) \cap C$
3. $A \cap A = A$
4. $A \cap \Lambda = \Lambda$
5. $A \cap V = A$
6. $A \cup B = B \cup A$
7. $A \cup (B \cup C) = (A \cup B) \cup C$

8. $A \cup A = A$
9. $A \cup \Lambda = A$
10. $A \cup V = V$
11. $A \cap (B \cup C) = (A \cap B) \cup (A \cap C)$
12. $A \cup (B \cap C) = (A \cup B) \cap (A \cup C)$
13. $A \cap \bar{A} = \Lambda$
14. $A \cup \bar{A} = V$
15. $\bar{V} = \Lambda$

What is sometimes called the method of translation can be used for determining the validity of Boolean equations by truth tables. To use this method one first translates a Boolean equation into a sentential formula by using the following dictionary:

Boolean symbol	class variables	$\cap$	$\cup$	$-$	V	Λ	$=$
Translation	sentential variables	$\cdot$	$\vee$	$\sim$	$p \vee \sim p$	$p \cdot \sim p$	$\equiv$

For example,

$$[(A \cap B) \cup \bar{A}] = V$$

translates into

$$[(p \cdot q) \vee \sim p] \equiv (p \vee \sim p)$$

Valid Boolean equations translate into sentential formulas that are true no matter what truth values are assigned to the component variables. Such formulas are called *tautologous formulas*. If one constructs a truth table for a sentential formula and the result is a column of **T**'s under the main connective, the formula is a tautology. Invalid Boolean equations translate into nontautologous formulas. Thus to determine the validity of a Boolean equation, translate it into a sentential formula using the preceding dictionary, and use some truth table method to determine whether or not the sentential formula is a tautology. The last example translates into a non-tautologous sentential formula, so it is not a valid Boolean equation.

Each of the preceding fifteen numbered Boolean equations are valid and their validity can be demonstrated by using the translation method. For example, equation 1 translates into the tautology:

$$(p \cdot q) \equiv (q \cdot p)$$

Equation 4 translates into the tautology:

$$[p \cdot (p \cdot \sim p)] \equiv (p \cdot \sim p)$$

whereas 13 and 15 translate, respectively, into these tautologies:

$$(p \cdot \sim p) \equiv (p \cdot \sim p)$$
$$\sim(p \vee \sim p) \equiv (p \cdot \sim p)$$

As stated earlier, the inconsistent triad test for syllogisms is an application of the *reductio ad absurdum* rule. We assume the premises and deny the conclusion and see if we are left with the following inconsistent set of Boolean equations:

$$C \cap A = \Lambda$$
$$\bar{C} \cap B = \Lambda$$
$$A \cap B \neq \Lambda$$

We can now demonstrate that this set is inconsistent. Translating this trio following the dictionary, we have:

$$(p \cdot q) \equiv (p \cdot \sim p)$$
$$(\sim p \cdot r) \equiv (p \cdot \sim p)$$
$$\sim[(q \cdot r) \equiv (p \cdot \sim p)]$$

Conjoining these three sentential formulas and constructing a truth table for the resulting conjunction reveals that the conjunction is inconsistent.

EXERCISES 8.8

Prove that the remaining fifteen Boolean equations are valid by the translation method.

9

Predicate Logic

The arguments to which Venn tests and the other tests discussed in the last chapter apply are syllogisms. Syllogisms are examples of arguments whose validity is a function of how simple sentences are related by sentence connections and also a function of how terms are related by words such as "all" and "some." Let us call all such arguments *predicate arguments*. Predicate arguments differ from sentential arguments in that the latter are arguments whose validity is merely a matter of sentential structure—how simple sentences are related by sentence connectives. The reason for calling the former arguments "predicate arguments" will become clear as we move on.

Most predicate arguments are not syllogisms. Two examples of non-syllogistic predicate arguments are

Godfrey Daniel is alive.
Therefore something is alive.

Football is aggressive and authoritarian.
Therefore something is authoritarian.

It is immediately evident that if either argument is symbolized following the procedures found in the last two chapters, the resulting paraphrased argument is not an interpretation of either a valid argument pattern in sentential logic (Chapters 6 and 7) or a valid argument pattern in syllogistic logic (Chapter 8). On the other hand, it is also evident that each argument is valid. What this shows is that the methods of logic introduced up to this time have severe limitations.

Modern predicate logic or quantification theory, as it is sometimes called, encompasses virtually *all* argument forms. We begin with the techniques in predicate logic for exposing the inner logical structure of simple sentences.

Singular and General Sentences

Recall how singular sentences are treated in syllogistic logic. A singular sentence is a sentence with the form "*a* is . . ." where *a* is a singular term, a term true or possibly true of only one thing. Proper names, definite descriptions, and demonstrative expressions are all examples of singular terms. In syllogistic logic a singular sentence such as "Godfrey Daniel is alive" is treated as a universal affirmative, as follows: All things identical with Godfrey Daniel are alive. A less artificial way of treating such sentences is to replace the singular term "Godfrey Daniel" with a small letter, say, *g*, and replace the predicate "is alive" with a capital letter, say *A*. The sentence can then be expressed as *gA*. In this last example *g* is an abbreviation for the longer expression "Godfrey Daniel" and *A* is an abbreviation for the predicate "is alive." It is customary in logic to write this last sentence so that the predicate comes first, in this manner: *Ag*. Thus, following these new conventions, the singular sentences:

The current president is a Quaker.
This woman is unmarried.

would be symbolized:

Qc
~*Mt*

if we allow *Q* to abbreviate "is a Quaker," *c* to abbreviate "the current president," *M* to abbreviate "is married," and *t* to abbreviate "this woman."

Capital letters used in this way will be called *predicate constants*. Predicate constants are not variables, but are simply abbreviations for predicates. Small letters used in this way will be called *individual constants*. Individual constants are also not variables, but simply abbreviate singular terms.

Another kind of letter that is needed is called an *individual variable*. We will use *x* for an individual variable. An individual variable can be placed in the position where individual constants are found; for example: *Ax*, *Ox*, *Mx*. These examples read: "*x* is alive," "*x* is a Quaker," and "*x* is married." It is customary to speak of such expressions as *open sentences*. Open sentences are expressions which can become sentences in two ways. The first way is by replacing the individual variable with an individual constant. *Ax* becomes *Ag* upon replacing *x* by *g*. The fact that this *x* can be replaced with individual constants shows that it is a variable, in this case a place in which one can put names for individuals, thus the name "individual variables."

The second way to get a sentence from an open sentence such as Ax is to place one of the following expressions in front of it:

> Every x is such that
> Some x is such that

If we place the first expression in front of Ax we obtain:

> Every x is such that Ax.

which is the false sentence "Everything is alive." If we place the second expression in front of Ax we obtain:

> Some x is such that Ax.

which is a true sentence. These last two new expressions are called *quantifiers*. It will be convenient to have symbols which abbreviate these quantifiers. For this purpose we introduce two new logical constants:

> Universal quantifier: (x)
> Existential quantifier: $(\exists x)$

The first, (x), is an abbreviation for the expression "every x is such that." The second, $(\exists x)$, is an abbreviation for the expression "some x is such that." Sentences which begin with either prefix or a variation of it are called *general sentences*. **A**, **E**, **I**, and **O** sentences are all examples of general sentences. Nongeneral sentences are thus either singular sentences or compound sentences. Compound sentences are general or singular sentences connected by sentence connectives. Thus, for example, $(x)Ax \supset (\exists x)Ax$ is not a general sentence, but a compound sentence, whereas $(x)(Ax \supset Bx)$ is a noncompound general sentence.

Predicates can be sorted out as one-place predicates, two-place predicates, three-place predicates, and so on. Examples of one-place predicates are "x is alive," "x is a Quaker," and "x is married." These are called *one-place* predicates because only one individual variable is used to form the open sentence. Later it will be seen that it is necessary, if the logical structure of certain arguments is to be exposed, to expose in the symbolizing of sentences predicates which are n-place predicates where n is greater than 1. There is thus a need to take account of two-place predicates, three-place predicates, and so on. Here are some examples of such predicates, using y, z, and w as additional individual variables:

> Two-place predicates: x loves y, $x = y$, x is the brother of y, $x > y$
> Three-place predicates: x gave y to x, $x + y = z$, x is between y and z
> Four-place predicates: x is closer to y than z or w

In this chapter we will be primarily interested in the logic of one-place predicates, or monadic predicate logic.

Before turning to the exercises it is useful to note that there are other readings for the two quantifiers than those indicated in the preceding. With respect to the universal quantifiers, besides "every *x* is such that," it can be read: "for all *x*," "for every *x*," "for each *x*," "for anything *x*," "for all things *x*," "no matter which *x*," "everything *x* is such that," "any *x* is such that," "no matter which *x* you choose," and "for any *x*." The existential quantifiers can be read as: "some *x* is such that," "for some *x*," "there exists an *x* such that," "there is an *x* such that," "for at least one *x*," "at least one *x* is such that," "there are *x*'s which," and "there is at least one *x* such that."

EXERCISES 9.1

A. Symbolize the following sentences which are singular sentences (note: not every sentence is a singular sentence), using capital letters for predicates and small letters for singular terms. Be sure to place the singular term after the predicate.

  1. The Hunchback of Notre Dame is in the Menninger Clinic.
  2. Talmudic law forbids Jewish girls' writing about their fathers.
  3. The seven dwarfs are stock brokers.
  4. The Church created Christ.
  5. Cash can be made from trash.
  6. The brokers on Wall Street are racketeers.
  7. Otis B. Driftwood is parahuman.
  8. All God's chillun got guns.
  9. God cannot prevent evil.
  10. Rock and rhetoric is getting more popular.
  11. The Marx brothers are the kings of the comedy teams.
  12. Men cannot have deep friendships.

B. Turn each of the following open sentences into a sentence by first supplying an appropriate individual constant and, second, by prefixing each with one of the quantifiers. If possible, indicate the truth value of each resulting sentence.

  1. *x* will inherit what we do today.
  2. $x > 7$
  3. *x* is south west of New York.
  4. *x* rises in the east.
  5. *x* can never learn anything while in office.
  6. *x* is on the mat.

ANSWERS

A.   **8.**   not a singular sentence
 9. $\sim Pg$
 10.   not a singular sentence
 11. Km
 12.   not a singular sentence
B.   **1.**   "the children" **T**
 5.   "the president" **T? F?**

Categorical and Other General Sentences

In the last chapter, *I* and *O* categorical sentences were given the following interpretations:

I: Some *S* are *P*. Something is such that it is *S* and *P*.
O: Some *S* are not *P*. Something is such that it is *S* and not *P*.

In this chapter we will continue to interpret particular sentences in this way. If we prefix the open sentence $Sx \cdot Px$ with the existential quantifier, we obtain the sentence $(\exists x)(Sx \cdot Px)$, which reads: Some *x* is such that it is *S* and *P*. This is an exact paraphrase of an *I* categorical sentence. In turn, an *O* categorical sentence can be paraphrased: $(\exists x)(Sx \cdot \sim Px)$, which reads: Some *x* is such that it is *S* and not *P*. Since *A* and *O* are contradictories, the denial of an *O* is an *A*. Thus $\sim O$, that is, *A*, can be rendered:

$$\sim (\exists x)(Sx \cdot \sim Px) \quad \text{"It is false that some } x \text{ is such that it is } S \text{ and not } P\text{"}$$

Since an *E* is the denial of an *I*, an *E* sentence can be rendered:

$$\sim (\exists x)(Sx \cdot Px) \quad \text{"It is false that some } x \text{ is such that it is } S \text{ and } P\text{"}$$

Thus, in summary, we obtain the following:

A:	All *S* are *P*	$\sim (\exists x)(Sx \cdot \sim Px)$
E:	No *S* are *P*	$\sim (\exists x)(Sx \cdot Px)$
I:	Some *S* are *P*	$(\exists x)(Sx \cdot Px)$
O:	Some *S* are not *P*	$(\exists x)(Sx \cdot \sim Px)$

Universal and existential quantifiers are connected in meaning through negation. To deny $(\exists x)Sx$ is to say

There are no *S*.   Nothing is *S*.   *S* do not exist.

but these mean $(x) \sim Sx$. Thus

1. $\sim(\exists x)Sx$ is equivalent to $(x) \sim Sx$

The negation of $(x)Sx$ is

Not everything is an S.   There are things that are not S.

which is to say $(\exists x) \sim Sx$. Thus

2. $\sim(x)Sx$ is equivalent to $(\exists x) \sim Sx$

What this means is that the combination of symbols $\sim(\exists x)$ has the same meaning as $(x) \sim$, and the combination $\sim(x)$ has the same meaning as $(\exists x) \sim$. It follows that $(x)Sx$ has the same meaning as $\sim(\exists x) \sim Sx$, and $(\exists x)Sx$ has the same meaning as $\sim(x) \sim Sx$, recalling the double negation rule. That is,

3. $(x)Sx$ is equivalent to $\sim(\exists x) \sim Sx$
4. $(\exists x)Sx$ is equivalent to $\sim(x) \sim Sx$

(1) through (4) will be spoken of as the *Quantifier Negation rules.*
   Returning to the **A** sentence, it follows from these last rules that $\sim(\exists x)(Sx \cdot \sim Px)$ is equivalent to $(x) \sim (Sx \cdot \sim Px)$, which is equivalent to $(x)(Sx \supset Px)$. The **E** sentence $\sim(\exists x)(Sx \cdot Px)$, by quantifier negation rule 1, becomes $(x) \sim (Sx \cdot Px)$, and this can be transformed into $(x)(Sx \supset \sim Px)$. **A** and **E** are customarily symbolized in predicate logic in this way, namely:

   A: All S are P $(x)(Sx \supset Px)$
   E: No S are P $(x)(Sx \supset \sim Px)$

   This new notation allows us to symbolize a great many sentences other than categorical sentences. For example, in symbolizing "A woman wins an election if and only if she is good-looking," writing Wx for "x is a woman," Ix for "x wins an election," and Lx for "x is good-looking," and the sentence becomes $(x)[Wx \supset (Ix \equiv Lx)]$. As another example, "Some books are readable only if they are illustrated," writing Bx for "x is a book," Rx for "x is readable," and Ix for "x is illustrated," becomes $(\exists x)[Bx \cdot (Rx \supset Ix)]$. Finally, "Something is pleasant only if it is illegal, immoral, or fattening," writing Px for "x is pleasant," Ix for "x is illegal," Mx for "x is immoral," and Fx for "x is fattening," goes into $(x)[Px \supset (Ix \lor Mx \lor Fx)]$. Note that this last is a universal sentence, not a particular; thus English can again be misleading as to the logical structure of the sentence. Contrast this last sentence with "Something is valuable only if some people love God." In the sentence "Something is pleasant only if it is illegal, immoral, or fattening," the "it" after "only if" refers back to the "something." That is, it is asserted that if any x is pleasant, then x must be either illegal, immoral, or fattening.

In the last example there is no such connection. What follows "only if" is an independent sentence. In other words, the first sentence is a simple sentence, whereas the latter is a compound sentence. It is two simple sentences connected by the statement connective "if, then." With this in mind, and writing Vx for "x is valuable," Px for "x is a person," and Gx for "x loves God," the latter sentence is symbolized $(\exists x)Vx \supset (\exists x)(Px \cdot Gx)$.

Another pair of sentences similar to an earlier pair are:

If any senior fails logic, then he deserves to fail it.
If any senior fails logic, then every senior will.

The first is a general sentence, not a compound one. Writing Sx for "x is a senior," Fx for "x fails logic," and Dx for "x deserves to fail," the first is symbolized $(x)[(Sx \cdot Fx) \supset Dx]$, whereas the second is symbolized $(\exists x)(Sx \cdot Fx) \supset (x)(Sx \supset Fx)$. Another typical guideline in symbolizing is to be alert to conjunctions in general sentences which are really disjunctions. For example, "All that Karen buys for her boyfriends is gloves and hats," is properly paraphrased; "If Karen buys anything for her boyfriends, then it is *either* a glove or a hat." Obviously something cannot be both a glove and a hat.

Finally, it is well to note that we seldom assert general sentences with either of these forms:

$(x)(Sx \cdot Px)$
$(\exists x)(Sx \supset Px)$

We do not often assert sentences of the first form. It is rarely true that *all* the individuals which we are talking about have two interesting properties. For example, if one is talking about persons (or numbers), what two properties would be true of each and every person (or number)? We do not often assert sentences of the second form because they are too easily true. Using a quantification negation rule plus some truth-functional transformations, $(\exists x)(Sx \supset Px)$ is equivalent to $\sim(x)(Sx \cdot \sim Px)$. This sentence is true if at least one individual of the collection we are talking about does not have property S or at least one individual has property P. For example, some persons are not saints, so if "x is a person who is a saint" replaces Sx, then no matter what predicate is put in for Px, the resulting sentence is true.

EXERCISES 9.2

A. Symbolize the following sentences using the suggested capital letters for predicate letters and lower case letters for singular terms.

1. Brown is governor. (b: Brown, Gx: x is governor)
2. Brown is not president (Px: x is president)

3. It is not the case that if Brown is governor then he is president.
4. Every event has a cause. (*Ex*: *x* is an event, *Cx*: *x* has a cause)
5. Not every event has a cause.
6. No events have causes.
7. Some logic students are logical. (*Sx*: *x* is a logic student, *Lx*: *x* is logical)
8. Some logic students are not logical.
9. Not all logic students are logical.
10. Logic students are logical.
11. Logic students are not logical.
12. None but logic students are logical.
13. If some logic students are logical, then not all logic students are logical.
14. Some logic students are either logical or illogical.
15. Brown is illogical provided that not any logic student is logical.

B. Symbolize the following sentences using the suggested capital letters for predicate letters and lower case letters for singular terms.

1. Backgammon is not the only game people play. (*Bx*: *x* is backgammon, *Gx*: *x* is a game, *Px*: *x* is played by people)
2. No one who administers the machinery of a bureaucracy knows how it works. (*Px*: *x* is a person, *Ax*: *x* administers the machinery of a bureaucracy, *Kx*: *x* knows how it works)
3. Issues dealing with war and peace are too controversial to discuss. (*Ix*: *x* is an issue, *Cx*: *x* deals with war, *Px*: *x* deals with peace, *Tx*: *x* is too controversial to discuss)
4. Sophomores and juniors alone are admitted to the class. (*Sx*: *x* is a sophomore, *Jx*: *x* is a junior, *Ax*: *x* is admitted to the class)
5. Something is square if and only if it is not circular. (*Sx*: *x* is a square, *Cx*: *x* is a circle)
6. There is no president strong enough to collar the bureaucracy. (*Px*: *x* is a president, *Cx*: *x* can collar the bureaucracy)
7. Ecological crusaders are all seekers of social justice. (*Ex*: *x* is an ecological crusader, *Sx*: *x* is a seeker of social justice)
8. It is a wicked and perfidious act to cast out of one's body the soul which God has committed to it. (*Ax*: *x* is an act, *Cx*: *x* is casting out one's soul from his body, *Wx*: *x* is wicked, *Px*: *x* is perfidious)
9. Though Ho Chi Minh was a bad poet, he was a good organizer of society. (*a*: Ho Chi Minh, *Bx*: *x* was a bad poet, *Gx*: *x* was a good organizer of society)
10. Pollution can be eliminated only if each person reverts back to a pre-1900 way of life. (*P*: Pollution is eliminated, *Px*: *x* is a person, *Rx*: *x* reverts back to a pre-1900 way of life)

11. She'll find few admirers among locomotive greasers. (*Lx*: *x* is a locomotive greaser, *Ax*: *x* admires her)

12. When the starter shot, he hit a number of players. (*Px*: *x* is a player, *Hx*: *x* is hit by the starter gun)

13. Most of the exercises in texts are fascinating. (*Ex*: *x* is a text exercise, *Fx*: *x* is fascinating)

14. Hardly any horse would start at thirty below zero. (*Hx*: *x* is a horse, *Sx*: *x* starts at thirty below zero)

15. People are not all out of step with Abner. (*Px*: *x* is a person, *Ox*: *x* is in step with Abner)

16. Either she is dead or my watch has stopped.—Groucho Marx in *Day at the Races*, 1937. (*s*: she, *Dx*: *x* is dead, *g*: Groucho, *Wx*: *x* has a stopped watch)

17. Cameras are expensive if and only if they have superior lenses. Thus if there is a camera, then something is expensive if and only if something has a superior lens. (*Cx*: *x* is a camera, *Ex*: *x* is expensive, *Sx*: *x* has a superior lens)

18. Three years ago I came to Florida without a nickel in my pocket. Now I have a nickel in my pocket.—Groucho Marx in *The Cocoanuts*, 1925. (*g*: Groucho Marx, *Fx*: *x* came to Florida, *Wx*: *x* had a nickel, *Nx*: *x* has a nickel)

19. Americans will be led either by the president elected by a majority or by a disruptive and militant minority. (*Ax*: *x* is American, *Lx*: *x* is led by president, *Mx*: *x* is led by disruptive and militant minority)

20. If anyone is a saint, I'll be surprised. If everyone is a saint, I'll be surprised. (*Sx*: *x* is a saint, *I*; I'll be surprised)

ANSWERS

A. 2. $\sim Pa$
    4. $(x)(Ex \supset Cx)$
    6. $\sim (\exists x)(Ex \cdot Cx)$
    8. $(\exists x)(Sx \cdot \sim Lx)$
    10. $(x)(Sx \supset Lx)$
    12. $(x)(Lx \supset Sx)$
    14. $(\exists x)[Sx \cdot (Lx \vee \sim Lx)]$

B. 11. $\sim (\exists x)(Lx \cdot Ax)$? Perhaps it is a particular.
    12. $(\exists x)(Px \cdot Hx)$
    13. $(\exists x)(Ex \cdot Fx)$
    14. $\sim (\exists x)(Hx \cdot Sx)$? Perhaps it is a particular.
    15. $(\exists x)(Px \cdot Ox)$
    16. $Ds \vee Wg$

17. $(x)[Cx \supset (Ex \equiv Sx)] \therefore (\exists x)Cx \supset ((\exists x)Ex \equiv (\exists x)Sx)$
18. $Fg \cdot \sim Wg, Ng$
19. $(x)\{Ax \supset [(Lx \lor Mx) \cdot \sim (Lx \cdot Mx)]\}$
20. $(x)(Sx \supset I)$ or $(\exists x)Sx \supset I, (x)Sx \supset I$

Domains

When we use general sentences to make statements there are certain things that are referred to in making the statements. The sets of these things are called "domains." The most convenient way to identify a domain is in terms of a general sentence paraphrased using quantifiers. A *domain* is the set of objects over which the variables range. For example, if we paraphrase

(1)   All Greeks are mortal

as

(2) $(x)(Gx \supset Mx)$

we take as our domain the set of objects over which "x" ranges. The domain in this case is unrestricted—the set of all objects that make up the universe. We are saying with respect to any object in the universe that if it is a Greek, then it is mortal. However we may paraphrase (1) as

(3) $(x) Mx$

if we take the domain to be that set of objects that make up the class called Greeks. We are then saying, simply, that all Greeks are mortal.

We will use quantifiers and other logical terms to paraphrase arguments so as to make explicit their logical structure. Generally in symbolizing we take the domain to be all the objects in the universe, but sometimes it is more economical to pick out a more restricted domain. To illustrate, consider the following argument:

> All students are lugubrious.
> Some students are girls.
> Therefore some students are lugubrious girls.

To reveal the relevant logical structure of this argument we could symbolize it as follows:

$(x)(Sx \supset Lx)$
$(\exists x)(Sx \cdot Gx)$
Therefore $(\exists x)(Sx \cdot Gx \cdot Lx)$

where Sx: x is a student, Lx: x is lugubrious, Gx: x is a girl. But we will not do violence to the relevant logical structure of the argument if we restrict the domain of the variables and symbolize it as:

$(x)Lx$
$(\exists x)Gx$
Therefore $(\exists x)(Gx \cdot Lx)$

In the first case we take the universe to be the domain, while in the second case we take students to be the domain. In either case the relevant logical structure is exposed, and in both cases the result is a valid argument pattern. What in the end determines what domain one selects is how many predicates one must reveal in symbolizing in order to display the logical structure relevant to the validity or invalidity of the argument. The reader will see that the domain could not be restricted to girls or to lugubrious people.

EXERCISES 9.3

Paraphrase the following sentences using quantifiers. First use the universe as the domain, i.e., everything, then use a more restricted domain.

1. No honest taxpayers are rich doctors.
2. Anyone whose primary interest is money can't be a good college professor.
3. Most high school dropouts who are male end up in the army.
4. All who live by the sword die by the sword.
5. None but the brave deserve the fair.
6. All that glitters is not gold.
7. He jests at scars that never felt a wound.
8. He jests at instructors (who make mistakes at the board) who never had to do exercises before a class.
9. Every class at Arizona State that is either intellectually substantive or difficult has a low enrollment.
10. Any student who thinks he will fail or not get an A or a B in a class withdraws from that class at Arizona State.

ANSWERS

1. $(x)[(Tx \cdot Hx) \supset \sim (Rx \cdot Dx)]$ Tx: x is a taxpayer, Hx: x is honest
                                                          Rx: x is rich, Dx: x is a doctor
    $(x)[Hx \supset \sim (Rx \cdot Dx)]$ domain: taxpayers

Truth-Functional Expansion

The truth-functional expansion of general sentences enables one to grasp exactly what is asserted in a general sentence. Consider

(1) $(x)Fx$

and assume that "x" ranges over a finite set of n objects. Thus, in saying every x is F, one is saying of a finite number of x's that each is an F. (1) affirms that the predicate "F" is true of each of these x's. Let us suppose we have names for each of these individuals, and these names are: $a_1, a_2, \ldots, a_n$. Names for individuals in a domain are *individual constants*. (1) can now be expressed as a truth functional compound. It can be expressed as this finite conjunction:

$Fa_1 \cdot Fa_2 \cdot \ldots \cdot Fa_n$

So (1) says that a_1 is an F and a_2 is an F and . . . and a_n is an F. This, of course, is false if *any* of the a's is not an F. Next consider

(2) $(\exists x)Fx$

Let us also assume that x ranges over a finite set of objects. What (2) affirms is that the predicate "F" is true of at least one of these x's. Again using the above names for the x's, (2) can be expressed as this finite disjunction:

$Fa_1 \vee Fa_2 \vee \ldots \vee Fa_n$

This will be false only if none of the a's is an F. In general, universal or existential generalizations over finite domains can be expressed truth-functionally. However universal or existential generalization over infinite domains cannot be expressed truth-functionally, for it is impossible for there to be a disjunction made up of infinite numbers of disjuncts and a conjunction made up of infinite number of conjuncts. An example of a general statement about an infinite domain is

There is no greatest prime number

since there are an infinite number of numbers.

How truth-functional expansions can be an aid to understanding general statements can now be illustrated. Suppose we ask whether

(1) $(x)(Sx \cdot Px)$

is equivalent to

(2) $(x)Sx \cdot (x)Px$

One can see that they are by providing the following truth-functional expansion of (1)

(3) $(Sa_1 \cdot Pa_1) \cdot (Sa_2 \cdot Pa_2) \cdot \ldots \cdot (Sa_n \cdot Pa_n)$

and this expansion of (2)

(4) $(Sa_1 \cdot Sa_2 \cdot \ldots \cdot Sa_n) \cdot (Pa_1 \cdot Pa_2 \cdot \ldots \cdot Pa_n)$

(3) is equivalent to (4) by the truth-functional replacement rules commutation and association. On the other hand,

(5) $(\exists x)Sx \cdot (\exists x)Px$

expands into

(6) $(Sa_1 \vee Sa_2 \vee \ldots \vee Sa_n) \cdot (Pa_1 \vee Pa_2 \vee \ldots \vee Pa_n)$

while

(7) $(\exists x)(Sx \cdot Px)$

expands into

(8) $(Sa_1 \cdot Pa_1) \vee (Sa_2 \cdot Pa_2) \vee \ldots \vee (Sa_n \cdot Pa_n)$

One cannot use the truth-functional replacement rules to transform (6) into (8). Thus (5) is not equivalent to (7).

It should be noted that it can be shown that what is true here in finite domains is also true in infinite domains.

EXERCISES 9.4

Assuming a finite domain $(a_1, a_2, \ldots, a_n)$ provide truth-functional expansions for the following:

1. $(x) \sim Sx$
2. $\sim (\exists x)Sx$
3. $(x)Sx \supset (\exists x)Sx$
4. $\sim (\exists x)Sx \vee (\exists x) \sim Sx$
5. $(x)Sx \supset Sa$

ANSWERS

3. $(Sa_1 \cdot Sa_2 \cdot \ldots \cdot Sa_n) \supset (Sa_1 \vee Sa_2 \vee \ldots \vee Sa_n)$

Valid Argument Patterns

We can now form argument patterns using

Quantifiers
Predicate variables
Individual constants (names)
Truth-functional connectives

Examples of such patterns are:

$(x)Sx$ Sa $(\exists x)(Sx \cdot Px)$

$\therefore (\exists x)Sx$ $\therefore (\exists x)Sx$ $\therefore (\exists x)(Px \cdot Sx)$

At this juncture, the reader should be able to see that these are valid and the following are invalid patterns:

$(\exists x)Sx$ $(\exists x)Sx$ $(\exists x)(Sx \cdot Px)$

$\therefore (x)Sx$ $\therefore Sa$ $\therefore (x)(Px \supset Sx)$

We can explain the notion of valid patterns by describing first how one obtains an interpretation of a sentence in predicate logic. Consider:

Godfrey Daniel is fastidious.

This sentence may be regarded as a result of interpreting:

(1) Fa

where the domain is people, the predicate letter F is replaced with "is fastidious" and the individual constant "a" is replaced with the same "Godfrey Daniel." Next consider:

If anything is a number, then it is even.

This sentence may be regarded as the result of interpreting

(2) $(x)(Fx \supset Gx)$

where the domain is the universe, "x is a number" replaces "Fx" and "x is even" replaces "*Gx.*" Obviously we can provide different interpretations for (1) and (2). For example

2 is even

is an interpretation of (1), and

All men are mortal

is an interpretation of (2). It is also obvious that we can give an interpretation of a set of sentences in predicate logic. For example

$(x)(Fx \lor Gx)$
$\sim Fa$

can be given this interpretation:

Everything is either a gas or a solid.
This can is not a gas.

In general we give an interpretation of a sentence or set of sentences in predicate logic if and only if we

1. Select a domain of individuals *D*.
2. Replace predicate variables with predicates.
3. Replace individual constants (if there are any) with names of individuals of *D*.

A *sentence* in predicate logic is said to be *true under an interpretation* if the sentence obtained by the interpretation is true. Thus, for example,

$(x)Fx \supset Fa$

is true under this interpretation:

D: universe, *Fx*: *x* occupies space, *a*: Godfrey Daniel

Since

If everything occupies space, then Godfrey Daniel occupies space.

is true.

An *argument pattern* in predicate logic is *valid* if and only if no interpretation in any nonempty domain is an argument whose premises are true and whose conclusion is false. For example

Fa
$\therefore (\exists x)Fx$

is valid. No matter what interpretation is supplied for this pattern the result will never be an argument with a true premise and a false conclusion. (Methods to demonstrate that patterns are valid will be introduced later in this chapter.) On the other hand

Fa
$\therefore (x)Fx$

is invalid. An interpretation that proves this would be:

D: living persons
Fx: x is rich
a: Rockefeller

This interpretation yields the argument

Rockefeller is rich.
Therefore everyone is rich.

Here the premise is true, while the conclusion is false. An interpretation which proves this pattern

$(\exists x)Fx$
$(\exists x)Gx$
$\therefore (\exists x)(Fx \cdot Gx)$

to be invalid would be:

Domain: positive integers
Fx: x is odd
Gx: x is even

Under this interpretation we obtain

Some numbers are odd.
Some numbers are even.
Therefore some numbers are odd and even.

Consider next:

$$(x)(Fx \supset Gx)$$
$$(x)(Fx \supset Hx)$$
$$\therefore (x)(Gx \supset Hx)$$

Let the domain be arguments, Fx: x is sound, Gx: x is valid, and Hx: x has true premises. Under this interpretation we obtain:

Any sound argument is valid.
Any sound argument has true premises.
Therefore any valid argument has true premises.

This argument is invalid. Each premise is true but the conclusion is false since a valid argument can have false premises.

The above definition of validity for an argument pattern in predicate logic excludes the empty set as a domain. Why is this? If empty domains were admitted, then, for example, this valid pattern

(3) $(x)Fx$
      $\therefore (\exists x)Fx$

would *not* be valid. To show this we provide the following interpretation

D: winged horses
Fx: x is notorious

obtaining

Every winged horse is notorious.
Therefore some winged horse is notorious.

Now

$$(\exists x)Wx$$
$$(\exists x) \sim Wx$$

where Wx: x is a winged horse, are both false since there are no winged horses. To deny a false statement is to make a true statement. So

$$\sim (\exists x) \sim Wx$$

is true. Since $\sim (\exists x) \sim Wx$ is equivalent to $(x)Wx$ the premise of the above argument is true and the conclusion is false. Thus if we allow empty domains, we prove that (3) is invalid.

The definition for the validity of an argument pattern in predicate logic could be formulated so as to remove the nonempty domain restriction. In some versions of predicate logic this is done. But doing it would complicate the methods for determining validity. So to simplify the methods of predicate logic it is standard practice to just exclude empty domains in the definition of validity.

EXERCISES 9.5

Below are some invalid argument patterns. Provide interpretations for each which result in an argument that has all true premises and a false conclusion (thus proving the patterns are invalid).

1. $(\exists x)Sx, (\exists x)Px \therefore (\exists x)(Sx \cdot Px)$
2. $(x)(Sx \supset Mx), (x)(Px \supset Mx) \therefore (x)(Sx \supset Px)$
3. $(x)(Gx \supset Fx), (x)(Gx \supset Hx) \therefore (x)(Fx \supset Hx)$
4. $(\exists x)Fx \therefore (x)Fx$
5. $(x)Sx \supset (x)Px \therefore (x)(Sx \supset Px)$
6. $(x)(Sx \vee Px) \therefore (x)Sx \vee (x)Px$
7. $(x)(Sx \supset Px) \therefore (\exists x)(Sx \cdot Px)$
8. $\sim(x)Sx \therefore \sim(\exists x)Sx$
9. $(\exists x)Sx \cdot (\exists x)Px \therefore (x)(Sx \cdot Px)$
10. $(x)(Sx \vee Px) \therefore (x)Sx$
11. $(x)(Sx \supset \sim Px) \therefore (\exists x)(Sx \cdot \sim Px)$
12. $(x)(Sx \supset Mx), (x)(Mx \supset Px) \therefore (\exists x)(Sx \cdot Px)$

ANSWERS

2. Domain: everything, Sx: x is a cat, Mx: x is an animal, Px:x is a dog
6. Domain: positive integers, Sx: x is odd, Px: x is even
10. Domain: everything, Sx: x is physical, Px: x is mental
12. Domain: everything, Sx: x is a furry fish, Mx: x is a fish, Px: x is furry

Monadic Predicate Test

Truth expansion of general sentences in a finite domain of n individuals makes possible a truth table method for determining the validity of certain predicate argument patterns. Let us first identify these patterns. As noted earlier, predicates can be one-place, e.g., x is red; two-place, e.g., x loves y; three-place, e.g., x is between y and z; and so on. Argument patterns in predicate logic that contain no predicates other than one-place predicates are called *monadic predicate argument patterns*. It is for these patterns that it is possible to provide a truth table test.

To introduce this test method it is first useful to speak of the n-validity of a monadic predicate argument pattern. A monadic predicate argument pattern is n-valid if and only if its expansion in a domain of n individuals results in an argument such that the conclusion is a truth-functional consequence of the premises. To illustrate:

$$(\exists x)Sx \therefore (x)Sx$$

is 1-valid but it is not 2-valid. One can use a *reductio* test from Chapter 6 to verify that the first expansion below is a valid sentential argument pattern (the expansion of the argument pattern in a one-individual domain), whereas the second expansion is an invalid pattern (the expansion of the argument pattern in a two-individual domain):

$$Sa_1 \qquad Sa_1 \vee Sa_2$$
$$\therefore Sa_1 \qquad \therefore Sa_1 \cdot Sa_2$$

To take another illustration, the expansion of the following argument in a three-individual domain produces a sentential argument pattern whose validity can be easily determined by the *reductio* test, and it is 3-valid:

$$(x)Sx \cdot (x)Px \qquad (Sa_1 \cdot Sa_2 \cdot Sa_3) \cdot (Pa_1 \cdot Pa_2 \cdot Pa_3)$$
$$\therefore (x)(Sx \cdot Px) \qquad \therefore (Sa_1 \cdot Pa_1) \cdot (Sa_2 \cdot Pa_2) \cdot (Sa_3 \cdot Pa_3)$$

The method for determining the validity of monadic predicate argument patterns can now be stated in the form of a decision procedure for the validity of any monadic predicate argument. Here is the statement:

A monadic predicate argument pattern with n distinct predicate variables is valid if and only if its expansion in a 2^n individual domain results in a valid sentential argument pattern.

To illustrate, the following argument pattern is valid if and only if its expansion in a 2^1 domain is valid, since this argument contains one distinct predicate variable S.

$$(x)Sx$$
$$\therefore (\exists x)Sx$$

Its expansion in a 2^1-, or a two-individual, domain is:

$$Sa_1 \cdot Sa_2$$
$$\therefore Sa_1 \vee Sa_2$$

Applying the *reductio* test to this expansion, we find that truth-value assignments cannot be consistently made so that the premise comes out *T* and the conclusion *F*; thus the initial argument is established as valid. On the other hand, this next argument pattern,

$$(\exists x)(Sx \cdot Px), (\exists x)(\sim Sx \cdot Px) \therefore (x)Px$$

is valid if and only if its expansion in a 2^2-individual domain is valid, since this argument contains two distinct predicate variables, S and P. Its expansion in a 2^2-, or four-individual domain is:

$$(Sa_1 \cdot Pa_1) \vee (Sa_2 \cdot Pa_2) \vee (Sa_3 \cdot Pa_3) \vee (Sa_4 \cdot Pa_4)$$
$$(\sim Sa_1 \cdot Pa_1) \vee (\sim Sa_2 \cdot Pa_2) \vee (\sim Sa_3 \cdot Pa_3) \vee (\sim Sa_4 \cdot Pa_4)$$
$$\therefore Pa_1 \cdot Pa_2 \cdot Pa_3 \cdot Pa_4$$

Using the *reductio* test, we find that the expansion is not valid; truth assignments can be made so that each premise is true although the conclusion is false, so this argument pattern is not valid.

Expansions will show that the last argument pattern is 1-valid and also 2-valid; however, given a three-individual domain it shows itself to be 3-invalid. If an argument is invalid in an n domain, this is sufficient to establish its invalidity, for if an argument is valid, it follows that it is n-valid for any n. And an argument may be invalid in a 2^n-domain, where n is the number of distinct predicate variables it contains, yet be valid in a smaller domain, as just illustrated. However, if an argument is n-valid this is not sufficient to establish its validity unless n equals 2^k, where k is the number of distinct predicate variables found in the argument. For example, the last example is both 1-valid and 2-valid, but it is not valid.

Needless to say, this decision procedure for the validity of monadic predicate argument patterns is cumbersome to apply even when there are only two distinct variables and a moderately complex argument.

The idea behind this decision procedure is that if there are n distinct monadic predicates, and only those individuals are considered such that each of the properties either belongs or does not belong to each of the individuals, then, no matter how many individuals there are in a domain under consideration, the greatest number of logically possible different classes into which n monadic predicates can in principle sort things in such a way that each individual is in one and only one class, is exactly 2^n. For example, no matter how many individuals there are, if there are only two monadic predicates to consider, the greatest number of logically possible classes into which individuals can be sorted by their means in such a way that each individual is in one and only one class is 2^2, or 4. For example, suppose there are two monadic predicates, Sx and Px. The predicates will either be true of the individuals of the domain of discourse or not. The four possible classes into which all individuals in any domain will sort themselves out are

1. Things that have S and P.
2. Things that have S and $\sim P$.
3. Things that have $\sim S$ and P.
4. Things that have $\sim S$ and $\sim P$.

And this holds no matter what predicates replace the predicate variables. Thus if an argument pattern in monadic predicate logic with n distinct predicate variables is expanded in a 2^n domain and it is valid, then it is valid no matter what domain is supposed. The addition of individuals to the domain will not add any more classes, and the argument's validity is founded on the relationships of just these classes.

To test a monadic predicate argument for validity, a procedure similar to that for sentential arguments is followed. First, symbolize the argument. Second, treat the symbolized argument as if it were an argument pattern and apply the preceding method, or apply the method to the argument pattern of which it is an interpretation.

Consider a simple argument but one which raises a difficulty that we have not so far commented on:

> Someone is a recording star this year, so Baby Okra is a recording star this year.

Writing Rx for "x is a recording star this year," and b for "Baby Okra," we symbolize the argument:

$(\exists x)Rx$
$\therefore Rb$

This argument is valid if the argument pattern of which it is an interpretation—namely, $(\exists x)Sx \therefore Sa$—is a valid pattern. Using the preceding method, we expand the pattern in a two-individual domain. But what should be done with the individual constant b under such expansions? The answer is that such an individual constant becomes a name for an individual in the domain of discourse. Let a_1 be the name for one of the individuals in our two-individual domain and a_2 be a name for the others. And let a_1 be the name for b. The expansion of the last pattern in a two-individual domain is thus:

$Sa_1 \vee Sa_2$
$\therefore Sa_1$

and it tests out invalid; thus the original argument is invalid. In contrast:

> Anyone can beat Boris Spassky, so Bobby Fischer can beat Boris Spassky.

writing Bx for "x can beat Boris Spassky" and b for "Bobby Fischer," comes out: $(x)Bx \therefore Bb$. And in a two-individual domain, letting b be a_1, we get:

$$Ba_1 \cdot Ba_2$$
$$\therefore Ba_1$$

which tests valid; thus the argument is valid.

EXERCISES 9.6

A. Test the following argument patterns for validity using the *reductio* method. The argument patterns have been so selected that if they are invalid they are either 1- or 2-invalid, otherwise valid.

1. $(x)(Sx \cdot Px) \therefore (x)Sx \cdot (x)Px$
2. $(x)(Sx \supset Px) \therefore (x)Sx \supset (x)Px$
3. $(\exists x)(Sx \cdot Px) \therefore (\exists x)Sx \cdot (\exists x)Px$
4. $(x)(Sx \supset Px) \therefore (x)(Px \supset Sx)$
5. $(x)(Sx \supset {\sim}Px) \therefore (x)(Px \supset {\sim}Sx)$
6. $(x)Sx \cdot (x)Px \therefore (x)(Sx \cdot Px)$
7. $(x)(Sx \supset Px) \therefore (\exists x)(Sx \cdot Px)$
8. $(x)(Sx \supset Px) \therefore {\sim}(\exists x)(Sx \cdot {\sim}Px)$
9. $(x)Sx \vee (x)Px \therefore (x)(Sx \vee Px)$
10. $(\exists x)(Sx \cdot Px) \therefore (\exists x)Sx \vee (\exists x)Px$
11. ${\sim}(\exists x)(Sx \cdot Px) \therefore (x)(Sx \supset {\sim}Px)$
12. $(x)(Ex \supset Px), (x)(Sx \supset {\sim}Ex) \therefore (x)(Px \supset {\sim}Sx)$

B. Test the following arguments for validity. Each one is valid if not either 1- or 2-invalid. Use the suggested letters for predicates.

1. Everything is either a substance or a property. Actions are not substances. So actions are properties. (Sx: x is a subtance, Px: x is a property, Ax: x is an action)
2. Georgia dates boys if they have tuxedoes, and since Edgar doesn't have one, he can't get a date with Georgia. (Tx: x has a tuxedo, e: Edgar, Dx: x can get a date with Georgia)
3. One will make the dean's list if he doesn't go to movies and doesn't carouse. Since Edgar has never caroused and doesn't like movies, he will make the dean's list. (Dx: x makes the dean's list, Mx: x goes to the movies, Cx: x carouses, e: Edgar)
4. Some students are very intelligent but not very conscientious. Every student is only human, however. Students, of course, are not all very intelligent, but every girl is. And so some humans are not girls. (Sx: x is a student, Ix: x is intelligent, Cx: x is conscientious, Hx: x is human, Gx: x is a girl)

5. Members of Xi Xi are either screwballs or athletes. Since at least one Xi Xi is not an athlete, this means that at least one Xi Xi is a screwball. (Mx: x is a member of Xi Xi, Sx: x is a screwball, Ax: x is an athlete)

6. A man will catch bass in August if and only if he fishes at night or is phenomenally lucky. Ham Hanks catches bass in August, so Ham is very lucky. (Bx: x will catch bass in August, Fx: x fishes at night, Lx: x is phenomenally lucky, h: Ham Hanks)

7. No one who is a defendant will be convicted if he is innocent. Anyone who is tried is a defendant. Almost all who are not convicted are acquitted. Therefore if anyone is tried, he is acquitted if he is innocent. (Dx: x is a defendant, Cx: x will be convicted, Ix: x is innocent, Tx: x is tried, Ax: x is acquitted)

8. None of Audrey's suitors like any of her relatives but all of her suitors like all of her girl friends. Audrey does have a number of suitors. So there is someone who likes Audrey's girl friends but does not like her relatives. (Ax: x is Audrey's suitors, Rx: x likes Audrey's relatives, Gx: x likes Audrey's girl friends)

9. All of Miss Gee's boarders are fastidious students. If one of her boarders complains, he is justified in doing so. If a fastidious person doesn't have a room with a bed, he complains. There are boarders with no beds in their rooms. Therefore some boarders who are fastidious complain, and they are justified in doing this. (Bx: x is a boarder of Miss Gee, Fx: x is fastidious, Sx: x is a student, Cx: x complains, Jx: x is justified, Rx: x has a room with a bed)

10. Every number is either even or uneven, so every number is even or every number is uneven. Not every number is even, how absurd! Therefore every number is uneven. But how can this be? (Ex: x is even)

ANSWERS

A. Only **4, 7,** and **12** are invalid.

B. **1.** $(x)(Sx \lor Px)$, $(x)(Ax \supset {\sim}Sx)$ $\therefore (x)(Ax \supset Px)$ valid

    2. $(x)(Tx \supset Dx)$ $(Te \supset De) \cdot (Ta_2 \supset Da_2)$

        ${\sim}Te$ ${\sim}Te$

        $\therefore {\sim}De$ $\therefore {\sim}De$

    invalid: if Te is **F**, De is **T**, and both Ta_2 and Da_2 are **T**, expansion results in premises that are **T** and a **F** conclusion.

    9. $(x)[Bx \supset (Sx \cdot Fx)]$ $[Ba_1 \supset (Sa_1 \cdot Fa_1)] \cdot [Ba_2 \supset (Sa_2 \cdot Fa_2)]$

        $(x)[(Bx \cdot Cx) \supset Jx]$ $[(Ba_1 \cdot Ca_1) \supset Ja_1] \cdot [(Ba_2 \cdot Ca_2) \supset Ja_2]$

        $(x)[(Fx \cdot {\sim}Rx) \supset Cx]$ $[(Fa_1 \cdot {\sim}Ra_1) \supset Ca_1] \cdot [(Fa_2 \cdot {\sim}Ra_2) \supset Ca_2]$

$(\exists x)(Bx \cdot \sim Rx)$ $(Ba_1 \cdot \sim Ra_1) \vee (Ba_2 \cdot \sim Ra_2)$
$\therefore (\exists x)(Bx \cdot Fx \cdot Cx \cdot Jx) \therefore (Ba_1 \cdot Fa_1 \cdot Ca_1 \cdot Ja_1) \vee (Ba_2 \cdot Fa_2 \cdot Ca_2 \cdot Ja_2)$
valid
Arguments 2, 6, 7, and 10 are the only invalid arguments.

Rules for Predicate Logic

In this section a natural deduction system for monadic predicate logic is given. We have studied a natural deduction system for sentence logic in Chapter 7. It consists of rules used to derive conclusions from premises. To have a natural deduction system for predicate logic we need to add to the rules found in Chapter 7. We need to add rules reflecting the logic of quantifiers. A satisfactory system of rules for predicate logic should fulfill two conditions: It should be sound and complete. To say the system is *sound* is to say that in applying the rules one will not validate an invalid monadic predicate argument. To say the system is *complete* is to say that the system is powerful enough to validate *all* valid monadic predicate arguments. In beginning logic one does not take up the proofs for the soundness and completeness of a system for predicate logic. (In the next chapter proofs are given for the soundness and completeness of a system for sentential logic. Since there are a finite number of valid syllogisms, one can in a tedious way easily prove that the various methods introduced in Chapter 8 for syllogistic logic are sound and complete.) Also in beginning logic, predicate logic is generally restricted to sound and complete methods for determining the validity of monadic predicate logic. In this section we will present such a sound and complete method.

The system for predicate logic makes use of two groups of rules. First we take over all the eighteen rules plus RCP and RAA from Chapter 7. In addition four new rules will now be added. In predicate logic the validity of arguments depends not only on how sentences are related by truth-functional connectives, but on the inner structure of general and singular sentences. So a second group of rules is needed which relates to the part played by the inner structure of simple sentences in a valid argument.

As an aid to introducing the four new rules, consider each of the following arguments and its corresponding argument pattern:

Everyone is weak.	(1)	$(x)Fx$
Therefore Godfrey Daniel is weak.		$\therefore Fa$
Godfrey Daniel is weak.	(2)	Fa
Therefore someone is weak.		$\therefore (\exists x)Fx$
Godfrey Daniel is weak.	(3)	Fa
Therefore everyone is weak.		$\therefore (x)Fx$

Someone is weak.   (4) $(\exists x)Fx$
Therefore Godfrey Daniel is weak. $\therefore Fa$

Now the four new rules will correspond to these four patterns. At first, this seems surprising, because although it is easily seen that (1) and (2) are valid patterns and can be easily proved valid by the truth table procedure outlined in the last section, (3) and (4) are not valid patterns and can be proved so by the method of the last section or by counterexamples. However if the "a" in (3) is such that *in the context of a proof* we can replace "a" with the name for any of the individuals in the domain of $(x)Fx$, then the conclusion would follow. Furthermore if the "a" in (4) is such that in the context of a proof "a" is the something that is an F, then the conclusion of (4) would logically follow. Rules corresponding to (3) and (4) will thus be formulated with restrictions so that they will function in this valid way in the context of a proof.

We begin, first, with rules corresponding to valid pattern (1) and valid pattern (2). The first rule allows us to proceed from what is true of each of a number of things to what is true of one of the things. The rule is *Universal Instantiation* and is:

UI: From a universally generalized sentence one can derive any of its instances.

To understand this rule we must make clear exactly what is to count as an instance of a general sentence. An *instance* of a general sentence is obtained by dropping the quantifier and uniformly replacing *all* occurrences of the quantified variable with occurrences of any individual constant within the domain. To illustrate consider the general sentence

$(x)(Fx \cdot Gx)$

The following are instances

$Fa \cdot Ga$
$Gb \cdot Gb$

while the next are not

(1) $Fa \cdot Fb$
(2) $Fx \cdot Fa$

In the first group a single individual constant replaced x in each occurrence of x after (x) was dropped. In (1) more than one individual constant was used. In (2) a single constant was used but it did not replace *all* the occurrences of the quantified "x" after the quantifier was dropped.

This rule can now be used in validating predicate arguments. To illustrate consider the following argument:

All humans are failures.
All failures are rejected by God.
Godfrey Daniel is human.
Therefore Godfrey Daniel is rejected by God.

The derivation of the conclusion is as follows:

1. $(x)(Hx \supset Fx)$ P
2. $(x)(Fx \supset Rx)$ P
3. Ha P
4. $Ha \supset Fa$ 1 UI
5. $Fa \supset Ra$ 2 UI
6. $Ha \supset Ra$ 4,5 HS
7. Ra 3,6 MP

UI was properly applied on lines 4 and 5, since each line is an instance of the corresponding general sentence. This derivation illustrates the basic strategy in constructing proofs in a natural deduction system for predicate logic. First the quantifiers are dropped. Then the conclusion is obtained as a truth-functional consequence using rules from Chapter 7. In other derivations where the conclusion is a general statement, quantifier rules will be available to add on quantifiers.

Although UI is a simple rule it is subject to two misapplications. The first is illustrated next:

1. $(x)(Fx \supset Gx)$ P
2. $Fa \supset Gx$ 1 UI (erroneous)

Here line 2 is not an instance of 1 since not all occurrences of x in the general sentence are replaced with "a." The second misapplication is illustrated below:

1. $\sim(x)Fx$ P   1. $(x)Fx \supset Ga$ P
2. $\sim Fa$ 1 UI   2. $Fa \supset Ga$ 1 UI
           (erroneous)   (erroneous)

The error in these cases is that UI is applied not to a universal generalization but to part of a compound sentence which contains a universal generaliza-tion. UI cannot be applied to a negation of a universal sentence. (The reader can verify that the first argument is invalid by this interpretation: D: women, a: Marie Curie, Fx: x is Nobel prize winner.) In the second argument UI is erroneously applied to a universal sentence which is the antecedent of a conditional sentence. (That this argument is invalid is shown by this interpretation: D: electorate, a: Godfrey Daniel, Fx: x votes for Godfrey Daniel, Gx: x is elected.) The rule UI may be applied correctly only to independent universal general sentences, not to universal general sentences that are parts of compound sentences.

The second rule allows the adding of an existential quantifier. The rule corresponds to:

Fa
$\therefore (\exists x)Fx$

It is the rule that what is true of a particular individual is true of some individual (that is, at least one individual). It is called *Existential Generalization* and can be formulated as follows:

EG: From a sentence containing an individual constant one may derive any existential generalization of that sentence.

The application of EG will consist in introducing an existential quantifier and replacing all *or some* occurrences of the individual constant in the sentence with the variable of the quantifier. For example from:

$Fa \cdot Ga$

one can infer

$(\exists x)(Fx \cdot Gx)$

or one can infer

$(\exists x)(Fx \cdot Ga)$

The validity of the second inference can be demonstrated by using the truth table method discussed in the previous section of this chapter. Since we wish the rules for monadic predicate logic to be complete, that is, have the power of validating all valid monadic predicate arguments, we need to allow for only some occurrences of the constant being replaced by the variable of the quantifier.

The following is a proof using EG along with UI and some truth-functional rules.

Godfrey Daniel is happy and famous.
If anyone is famous or glamorous, then he is well known.
Therefore someone is happy and well known.

1.	$Hd \cdot Fd$	P
2.	$(x)[(Fx \lor Gx) \supset Wx]$	P
3.	$(Fd \lor Gd) \supset Wd$	2 UI
4.	Fd	1 Simp
5.	$Fd \lor Gd$	4 Add
6.	Wd	3,5 MP
7.	Hd	1 Simp
8.	$Hd \cdot Wd$	7,6 Conj
9.	$(\exists x)(Hx \cdot Wx)$	8 EG

This proof illustrates the full basic strategy in constructing proofs. First, drop the quantifiers. Second, obtain the conclusion without quantifiers by truth-functional inference. Finally, add on the quantifier to obtain the conclusion. The reason for introducing the individual constant d, rather than, say, a, when dropping the quantifier from premise line 2 is that if we put in d when we drop the quantifier from line 2 we are able to derive line 8 and thus (by EG) obtain the conclusion. This shows that sometimes one must be alert to exactly which individual constant will work in a proof when using UI. However, in using UI it is permissible to use any individual constant.

EG can also be misapplied. For example

Godfrey Daniel is not Arabian.
Therefore no one is Arabian.

1.	$\sim Ad$	P
2.	$\sim (\exists x)Ax$	2 EG (erroneous)

As with UI (and each of the four rules) EG cannot be applied to part of a compound sentence if the system of rules is to be sound.

The third rule is *Existential Instantiation*. Consider the following valid argument:

Every war is unjust.
Some things are wars.
Therefore some things are unjust.

Since this is a valid argument we want to be able to construct a proof for it since we want our system of predicate logic to be complete. How would such a proof develop? Consider

1.	$(x)(Wx \supset Ux)$	P
2.	$(\exists x)Wx$	P
3.	$Wa \supset Ua$	1 UI
4.	Wa	2____
5.	Ua	3,4 MP
6.	$(\exists x)Ux$	5 EG

The third rule will be the justification for line 4. Here is the rule:

> Preliminary EI: From an existentially quantified sentence, one can derive any of its instances.

Restrictions need to be attached to EI so that in the context of a proof the rule is valid.
    To begin with, consider:

> $(\exists x)Fx$
> Ga
> $\therefore (\exists x)(Fx \cdot Gx)$

(This can be seen to be an invalid pattern with: D: positive integers, a: 6, Fx: x is odd, Gx: x is even.) Thus the following proof is erroneous:

1.	$(\exists x)Fx$	P
2.	Ga	P
3.	Fa	1 EI (erroneous)
4.	$Fa \cdot Ga$	2,3 Conj
5.	$(\exists x)(Fx \cdot Gx)$	4 EG

To block this erroneous use of EI we now add the first restriction:

> EI Restriction One: In applying EI do not use an individual constant that appears in any premise of the argument.

Since on line 3 "a" is used and "a" appears in premise 2, line 3 is a violation of restriction one. Next consider:

> Something is square.
> Something is not square.
> Therefore something is square and not square.

and this erroneous proof:

1.	$(\exists x)Sx$	P
2.	$(\exists x)\sim Sx$	P
3.	Sa	1 EI
4.	$\sim Sa$	2 EI (erroneous)
5.	$Sa \cdot \sim Sa$	3,4 Conj
6.	$(\exists x)(Sx \cdot \sim Sx)$	5 EG

To block line 4 we now introduce the second restriction:

> EI Restriction Two: In applying EI do not use an individual constant that has been introduced into the proof by an earlier application of EI.

Since "*a*" is introduced in line 3 by EI, the application of EI on line 4 is a violation of this second restriction on EI. Finally, consider

Something is an odd number.
Therefore 2 is an odd number.
1. $(\exists x)Ox$ P
2. Oa 1 EI (erroneous)

To block this application of EI we introduce the last restriction on EI:

EI Restriction Three: In applying EI do not use an individual constant that appears in the conclusion.

Since "*a*" appears in the conclusion of the last erroneous proof this use of EI violates restriction three.

Although it is now clear why one needs three restrictions, why, with these three restrictions, is the EI rule valid in the proof context? The reason is this: Making sure that the individual constant, which replaces occurrences of x when the existential quantifier is removed, does not appear in premises or conclusion or was not introduced by EI insures that it is a name in the proof context of whatever thing it is that makes $(\exists x)Fx$ true. To illustrate a correct application of EI in a proof:

Some students are disciples.
Every disciple loves his master.
Therefore some students love their master.
1. $(\exists x)(Sx \cdot Dx)$ P
2. $(x)(Dx \supset Lx)$ P
3. $Sa \cdot Da$ 1 EI
4. $Da \supset La$ 2 UI
5. La 3,4 Simp, MP
6. $Sa \cdot La$ 3,5 Simp, Conj
7. $(\exists x)(Sx \cdot Lx)$ 6 EG

The final rule allows us to add a universal quantifier under certain restrictions. Although

Fa
$\therefore (x)Fx$

is not valid there are contexts where one can validly infer from what is true of a to what is true of all individuals in the domain. To illustrate:

All babies are illogical.
Illogical persons are despised.
Therefore all babies are despised.

1. $(x)(Bx \supset Ix)$ P
2. $(x)(Ix \supset Dx)$ P
3. $Ba \supset Ia$ 1 UI
4. $Ia \supset Da$ 2 UI
5. $Ba \supset Da$ 3,4 HS
6. $(x)(Bx \supset Dx)$ 5 ____

Line 6 follows from 5 in the context of the proof. The reason for this is that what is true of a is true of all the members of the domain. For we can apply UI to 1 and 2 with respect not only to a, but to $a_1, a_2, a_3, \ldots, a_n$ where these are the members of the domain.

The rule that will justify line 6 is called *Universal Generalization*. It is useful to state the rule and then list the restrictions necessary to make the rule a sound rule.

> Preliminary UG: From a sentence containing an individual constant one can derive the universal generalization of that sentence.

Here by the universal generalization of a sentence containing an individual constant is understood the sentence obtained by replacing uniformly *all* occurrences of the constant with occurrences of a variable, and prefixing to the result a universal quantifier *binding* all occurrences of the variable. Line 6 is a universal generalization of line 5. Below are some examples that are *not* universal generalizations of line 5:

$(x)(Ba \supset Dx)$
$(x)Bx \supset Dx$

In the first, not all occurrences of "a" are replaced with "x." In the second, although all occurrences of "a" are replaced with "x" the absence of parentheses indicates that the quantifier does not affect the final occurrence of "x." The quantifier, as we will say, binds Bx, but not Dx. For the quantifier to bind a variable it must come within the *scope* of the quantifier where the scope is indicated by parentheses. Just as in

$\sim p \cdot q$

where the conjunction does not come under the scope of "$\sim$," so in

$(x)Bx \supset Dx$

Dx does not come under the scope of (x). And as in

$\sim (p \cdot q)$

where the conjunction does come under the scope of "~," so in line 6, $Bx \supset Dx$ is made to come under the scope of (x) by using parentheses.

Two restrictions must be placed on UI to assure its soundness in proof context. Consider

1.	*Fa*	P
2.	$(x)Fx$	1 UG (erroneous)

This is an incorrect application of UG. (This is easily demonstrated with this interpretation: D: positive integers, a: 1, Fx: x is odd.) To block this erroneous application of UG we add the following restriction:

> UG Restriction One: The individual constant which is replaced by a variable in the application of UG may not appear in any premise.

Since both RCP and RAA are carried over as rules in this system this restriction also must apply to *assumed* premises if the system is to be sound. (This also applies to Restriction One for EI.) If this restriction did not also apply to assumed premises the following could take place:

1.	$\sim(x)Fx$	P
2.	*Fa*	AP
3.	$(x)Fx$	2 UG (erroneous)
4.	$(1) \cdot (3)$	1,3 Conj
5.	$\sim Fa$	2–4 RAA
6.	$(x)\sim Fx$	5 UG

(The invalidity of the argument pattern is demonstrated by this interpretation: D: positive integers, Fx: x is odd.) Although line 3 violates the first restriction on UG, line 6 is a correct application of UG. Once the assumed premise is *discharged* we count the individual constant as no longer appearing in the premise. To illustrate:

Everyone is either Marxist or Capitalist.
No Arab is a Marxist.
Therefore all Arabs are Capitalists.

1.	$(x)(Mx \lor Cx)$	P
2.	$(x)(Ax \supset \sim Mx)$	P
3.	*Aa*	AP
4.	$Aa \supset \sim Ma$	2 UI
5.	$\sim Ma$	3,4 MP
6.	$Ma \lor Ca$	1 UG
7.	*Ca*	5,6 DS
8.	$Aa \supset Ca$	3–7 RCP
9.	$(x)(Ax \supset Cx)$	8 UG

In this proof we have applied UG in going from line 8 to line 9. Though "a" appears in an assumed premise, line 3, line 3 has been discharged, is out of the proof, by the time UG is applied to line 8. In this proof context any individual in the domain can be named by a constant in an AP. That is, for each individual a, a_1, a_2, a_3, . . . in the domain we would obtain

$Aa \supset Ca$
$Aa_1 \supset Ca_1$
$Aa_2 \supset Ca_2$
etc.

by successively assuming Aa, Aa_1, Aa_2, etc. Thus we can validly infer 9 from 8, for "a" in this context functions like any constant where UG can be applied. It so functions in this proof context that what is true for "a" is true for all the individuals in the domain.

The second restriction on UG is

UG Restriction Two: The individual constant is not introduced into the proof by EI.

The motivation for this restriction is illustrated as follows:

Something is solid.
Therefore everything is solid.
1. $(\exists x)Sx$ P
2. Sa 1 EI
3. $(x)Sx$ 2 UG (erroneous)

The final versions of the four rules together with their restrictions are as follows:

UI: From a universally quantified sentence one can derive any of its instances.

EG: From a sentence containing an individual constant one can derive the existential quantification of that sentence.

EI: From an existentially quantified sentence one can derive any of its instances.

  R1.   Do not use an individual constant that appears in any premise of the argument.

  R2.   Do not use an individual constant that has been introduced by EI.

  R3.   Do not use an individual constant that would appear in the conclusion.

UG: From a sentence containing an individual constant one can derive the universal quantification of the sentence.

R1. Do not apply UG with respect to individual constants which appear in a premise.

R2. Do not apply UG with respect to an individual constant introduced by E1.

In constructing proofs it is sometimes useful to use quantification negation rules (QN rules). The QN rules are the following:

1. $\sim(\exists x)Sx$ is equivalent to $(x)\sim Sx$.
2. $\sim(x)Sx$ is equivalent to $(\exists x)\sim Sx$.
3. $(x)Sx$ is equivalent to $\sim(\exists x)\sim Sx$.
4. $(\exists x)Sx$ is equivalent to $\sim(x)\sim Sx$.

The use of a QN rule is illustrated by this proof:

It is false that some animals do not have souls.
Fido is an animal.
Therefore Fido has a soul.

1.	$\sim(\exists x)(Ax \cdot \sim Sx)$	P
2.	Aa	P
3.	$(x)\sim(Ax \cdot \sim Sx)$	1 QN
4.	$\sim(Aa \cdot \sim Sa)$	3 UI
5.	$\sim Aa \vee Sa$	5 DeM, DN
6.	Sa	2,5 DS, DN

The four quantifier rules are for monadic logic. In order for the rules to be valid for relational logic—logic of nonmonadic predicates—further restrictions would be needed for the rules. For example, we would need to block the following:

1.	$(x)(\exists y)Fxy$	P
2.	$(\exists y)Fay$	1 UI
3.	Faa	2 EI (erroneous)
4.	$(\exists x)Fxx$	3 EG

That this is an invalid argument pattern is demonstrated by: D: positive integers, Fxy: $x < y$. The premise reads, on this interpretation:

For every number x there is a number y such that $x < y$.

That is: For every number some number or other is greater than it. But the conclusion reads, on this interpretation:

Some number is greater than itself.

This, of course, is impossible.

Relational logic is beyond the scope of a first course in logic, so we will stop at this point in our account of predicate logic. But it is worth noting that there are arguments whose validity depends on relational predicates. An example is:

All circles are figures.
Therefore all who draw circles draw figures.

The premise can be represented in our previous way of symbolizing as $(x)(Cx \supset Fx)$ and we can represent the conclusion as $(x)(Dx \supset Ix)$ with Cx as "x is a circle," Fx as "x is a figure," Dx as "x draws a circle," and Ix as "x draws a figure." But symbolized this way the conclusion has no connection with the premise. What is needed is to expose the two-place predicate "x draws y." Such predicates—that is, nonmonadic predicates—are relational predicates. With Rxy as the relational predicate "x draws y," the preceding argument can be symbolized:

$(x)(Cx \supset Fx)$
$\therefore (x)[(\exists y)(Cy \cdot Rxy) \supset (\exists y)(Fy \cdot Rxy)]$

To construct a proof for this argument some additional restrictions would need to be added to the four predicate rules. From "Someone loves everyone"

1. $(\exists x)(y)Lxy$

"Everyone is loved by someone or other" follows, symbolized:

2. $(y)(\exists x)Lxy$

However, the converse is not valid. But without new restrictions on the quantification rules a "proof" could be constructed for $(2) \therefore (1)$. To see that (1) follows from (2) but not conversely, note that if someone loves everyone, then it follows that everyone is loved by someone or other, but if everyone is loved by someone or other, it does not follow that someone loves everyone. If we suppose that at least everyone loves himself, then it is true that everyone is loved by someone or other, but it may not be true that someone loves everyone. To aid in understanding, it is useful to expand (1) and (2) in a limited domain, say, of two individuals, and see what each asserts. The expansion of these formulas in a two-individual domain is, respectively:

1'. $(y)La_1y \lor (y)La_2y$
   $(La_1a_1 \cdot La_1a_2) \lor (La_2a_1 \cdot La_2a_2)$
2'. $(\exists x)Lxa_1 \cdot (\exists x)Lxa_2$
   $(La_1a_1 \lor La_2a_1) \cdot (La_1a_2 \lor La_2a_2)$

In a two-individual domain, where "x loves y" is Lxy, the first says that either a_1 loves a_1 and a_2, the two individuals in the domain, or a_2 loves a_1 and a_2. In other words, some one individual loves everyone in the domain. The second says either one or the other individual in the universe loves a_1 and either one or the other of the individuals in the domain loves a_2; in other words, every individual in the domain is loved by someone or other. For example, if a_1 loves a_1 and a_2 loves a_2, then the second is true, whereas for the first to be true some one individual must love both a_1 and a_2.

Two restrictions need to be added to the four rules in order for them to be valid for relational logic. The first restriction is added to EI and is:

EI Restriction Four: In applying EI do not use a constant that appears in the existential generalization to which EI is being applied.

This restriction blocks the erroneous inference discussed earlier as indicated below:

1. $(x)(\exists y)Fxy$ P
2. $(\exists y)Fay$ 1 UI
3. Faa 2 EI (violates EI restriction four)
4. $(\exists x)Fxx$ 3 EG

The second restriction is added to UG and the reason for its addition can be illustrated by the following erroneous application of UG:

1. $(y)(\exists x)Fxy$ P
2. $(\exists x)Fxa$ 2 UI
3. Fba 3 EI
4. $(y)Fby$ 4 UG (erroneous)
5. $(\exists x)(y)Fxy$ 5 EG

That line 5 does not follow from line 1 is verified by this interpretation: D: positive integers, Fxy: $x > y$. To block such erroneous inferences the restriction below is added to UG:

UG Restriction Three: UG may not be applied to a constant which appears together in a relational singular sentence with a constant introduced by EI.

A relational singular sentence is a singular sentence made up of nonmonadic or relational predicates and constants.

EXERCISES 9.7

A. Indicate which of the following lines are not valid and explain why.

    1. 1. $(x)(Fx \cdot Fx)$ P
           2. $(Fa \cdot Fb) \supset Fc$ P
           3. $Fa \cdot Fb$ 1, UI
           4. Fc 2,3 MP

    2. 1. $\sim(\exists x)Fx$ P
           2. $\sim Fa$ 1, EI
           3. $(x)\sim Fx$ 2, UG

    3. 1. $(x)(Sx \cdot Px)$ P
           2. $Sa \cdot Pa$ 1, UI
           3. $(x)Sx \cdot Pa$ 2, UG
           4. $(x)Sx \cdot (x)Px$ 3, UG

    4. 1. $(x)(Sx \supset Px)$ P
           2. $Sa \supset Pa$ 1, UI
         ┌3. Sa AP
         │ 4. Pa 2,3 MP
         └5. $(x)Px$ 4 UG
           6. $Sa \supset (x)Px$ 3–5 RCP
           7. $(x)Sx \supset (x)Px$ 6, UG

    5. 1. $(x)(Fx \cdot Gx) \supset Ha$ P
           2. $(\exists x)(Fx \cdot Gx)$ P
           3. $Fa \cdot Ga$ 2, EI
           4. $(x)(Fx \cdot Gx)$ 3, UG
           5. Ha 1,4 MP

    6. 1. $(\exists x)(Fx \cdot Gx)$ P
           2. $(\exists x)(Fa \cdot Gx)$ 1, EI
           3. $\sim(x)\sim(Fa \cdot Gx)$ 2, QN
           4. $\sim(x)(\sim Fa \vee \sim Gx)$ 3, DeM
           5. $\sim Fa \vee \sim Gb$ 4, UI
           6. Fa P
           7. $\sim Gb$ 5,6 DS

    7. 1. Fa P
           2. $(x)Hx$ P
           3. Ha 2, UI
           4. $Fa \cdot Ha$ 1,3 Conj
          5. $(x)(Fx \cdot Hx)$ 4, UG

    8. 1. $(\exists x)(Fx \cdot Gx)$ P
           2. Ha P
           3. $Fa \cdot Ga$ 1, EI
           4. Fa 3, Simp
          5. $Ha \cdot Fa$ 2,4 Conj
          6. $(\exists x)(Hx \cdot Fa)$ 5, EG

9. 1. $(x)Fx$ .... P
  2. $\sim(\exists x)Gx$ .... AP
  3. $(x)\sim Gx$ .... 2, QN
  4. $\sim Ga$ .... 3, UI
  5. Fa .... 1, UI
  6. $Fa \cdot \sim Ga$ .... 4,5 Conj
  7. $(x)(Fx \cdot \sim Gx)$ .... 6, UG
  8. $\sim(\exists x)Gx \supset (x)(Fx \cdot \sim Gx)$ ... 2–7 RCP

10. 1. $(x)[Bx \equiv (Fx \vee Lx)]$ .... P
  2. $(\exists x)\sim Fx$ .... P
  3. Bh .... P
  4. $Bh \equiv (Fh \vee Lh)$ .... 1, UI
  5. $Fh \vee Lh$ .... 3,4 Equiv, MP
  6. $\sim Fh$ .... 2, EI
  7. Lh .... 5,6 DS
  8. $(\exists x)Lx$ .... 7 EG
  9. $\sim(\exists x)Lx$ .... AP
  10. $(\exists x)Lx \cdot \sim(\exists x)Lx$ ... 8,9 Conj
  11. $(\exists x)Lx$ .... 9–10 RAA

B. Derive the conclusion from the premises of the following symbolized arguments.

 1. $(x)(Dx \supset Ex), (\exists x)(Fx \cdot \sim Ex) \therefore (\exists x)(Fx \cdot \sim Dx)$

 2. $(x)[(Ax \vee Bx) \supset Cx], (\exists x)(Ax \cdot Dx) \therefore (\exists x)Cx \cdot (\exists x)Dx$

 3. $(x)(Fx \cdot Gx) \therefore (x)Fx \cdot (x)Gx$

 4. $(x)(Gx \supset Ex), (x)(Wx \supset \sim Sx), (\exists x)(Wx \cdot \sim Ex) \therefore (\exists x) \sim (Gs \vee Sx)$

 5. $(x)[(Ix \vee Jx) \supset (Kx \cdot Lx)] \therefore (x)(Ix \supset Lx)$

 6. $(x)(Tx \supset Ux), (x)[(Ux \cdot Tx) \supset Vx] \therefore (x)[Tx \supset (Tx \cdot Vx)]$

 7. $(x)[(Fx \vee Gx) \supset Hx], (x)[Hx \supset \sim (Ix \cdot Jx)], (\exists x)(Fx \cdot Jx) \therefore (\exists x)(Fx \cdot \sim Ix)$

 8. $(x)(Sx \supset Px) \therefore (x)Sx \supset (x)Px$

 9. $(x)(Sx \vee Px), (x)(Ax \supset \sim Sx) \therefore (x)(Ax \supset Px)$

 10. $(x)[(Sx \cdot Px) \supset \sim Mx], (x)[Px \supset (Mx \vee Rx)] \therefore (x)(Sx \supset Px) \supset (x)(Sx \supset Rx)$

C. Symbolize the following arguments using the suggested predicate letters. Then for each derive the conclusion from the premises.

 1. Even though every war is unjust, some wars are understandable, so unjust but understandable things do exist. (Wx: x is a war, Jx: x is just, Ux: x is understandable)

 2. All babies are illogical. No one is despised who can manage a crocodile. Illogical persons are despised. Therefore no babies can manage crocodiles. (*Bx*: *x* is a baby, *Lx*: *x* is logical, *Mx*: *x* can manage a crocodile, *Dx*: *x* is despised)

3. Everyone who goes to a university either takes courses or drops out. Anyone who takes courses works hard. Anyone who drops out is drafted. So provided that a person goes to the university, he works hard or is drafted. (*Ax*: *x* attends a university, *Tx*: *x* takes courses, *Dx*: *x* drops out, *Wx*: *x* works hard, *DRx*: *x* is drafted)

4. Everyone who is sane can do Logic. No lunatics are fit to serve on a jury. None of your sons can do Logic. So none of your sons are fit to serve on a jury. (*Sx*: *x* is sane, *Lx*: *x* can do Logic, *Fx*: *x* is fit to serve on a jury, *Yx*: *x* is your son)

5. There are courageous men, but only vile things are men, so it is false that nothing is both courageous and vile. (*Mx*: *x* is a man, *Cx*: *x* is courageous, *Vx*: *x* is vile)

6. He did not take the crown. Therefore it is certain he is not ambitious. (enthymene) (*a*: he, *Tx*: *x* takes the crown, *Ax*: *x* is ambitious)

7. Everything is spiritual. Something is spiritual if and only if it is divinely created. There is something which is such that it is either not divinely created or explainable. So there is something that is spiritual and explainable. (*Sx*: *x* is spiritual, *Dx*: *x* is divinely created, *Ex*: *x* is explainable)

8. None but the brave deserve the fair. Only college professors are brave. So the fair are deserved only by college professors. (*Bx*: *x* is brave, *Dx*: *x* deserves the fair, *Sx*: *x* is a college professor)

9. Everyone that asketh receiveth. Most of us receive very little. Therefore some of us cannot be asking. (*Px*: *x* is a person, *Ax*: *x* asks, *Rx*: *x* receives)

10. Everyone wants law and order. So some want freedom and law and order just in case they want freedom, and any who do not want law and order should see the vice-president. (*Lx*: *x* wants law, *Ox*: *x* wants order, *Fx*: *x* wants freedom, *Sx*: *x* should see the vice-president)

11. Some piano players play poorly and some piano players are not accomplished, for every pianist is a piano player. And some pianists do not play well and some pianists are not accomplished. (*Px*: *x* plays the piano, *Wx*: *x* plays well, *PIx*: *x* is a pianist, *A*: *x* is accomplished)

12. Everything is in space and time, so everything is in space and everything is in time. (*Sx*: *x* is in space, *Tx*: *x* is in time)

13. Every substance is extended, thus if everything is substance then everything is extended. (*Sx*: *x* is a subtance, *Ex*: *x* is extended)

14. Everything is physical or mental. If anything is mind, then it is not physical. Thus if anything is mind then it is mental.

15. Not all students who are deserving are both intelligent and hardworking. So if all students are intelligent, then there are some students who are deserving and not hardworking. (*Sx*: *x* is a student, *Dx*: *x* is deserving, *Ix*: *x* is intelligent, *Hx*: *x* is hardworking)

D. Some of the following arguments are valid. Some are invalid. Validate those arguments which can be validated using truth-table methods or the natural deduction system for monadic predicate logic found in this chapter. *Note*: some arguments may be nonmonadic predicate arguments.

1. Edgar hates anyone who believes there will be a tax increase. Henry believes there will be one, so Edgar hates Henry.

2. Either Henry is not in favor of a tax cut or there is something wrong with his thinking. If the GNP is down, then Henry is in favor of a tax cut. Thus there is not anything wrong with his thinking only if the GNP is not down.

3. Anyone who feels there will be a tax cut has something wrong with his thinking. Only a few narrow-minded businessmen feel there will be a tax cut. Therefore some narrow-minded businessmen have something wrong with their thinking.

4. If there is a tax cut, no one will be happy if the national debt is increased. And if the debt is not increased, expenditures will be decreased. Expenditures have increased and so there will not be a tax cut.

5. All circles are figures. Therefore anyone who draws a circle draws a figure.

6. If anyone feels there will be a tax cut, there is either something wrong with his thinking or he knows no political philosophy. Henry feels there will be a tax cut, so if there is nothing wrong with his thinking, he knows no political philosophy.

7. Every businessman feels there will be a tax cut, although some feel it will not come right now. Thus, if businessmen feel there will be a tax cut, they feel it will not come right now.

8. If prices are high, there will not be a tax cut. Either Henry wants a tax cut or prices are high. If Henry wants a tax cut, no one else does. However, some others do want a tax cut. So there will not be a tax cut.

9. Anyone who is in favor of a tax cut is not worried about the federal debt. Each businessman is either in favor of a tax cut or is not worried about the federal debt. Some, of course, are in favor of a tax cut. So some are not worried about the debt.

10. If someone is not in favor of a tax cut, he is not wealthy and not a businessman. If he is not in favor of reducing the federal debt, he

is not in favor of a tax cut. Thus, everyone who is either a businessman or wealthy is in favor of reducing the federal debt.

11. The authors responsible for this text are experimental logicians. If no experimental logicians are known to the profession, then no professors are experimental logicians. Thus if any professor is an author responsible for this text, then some experimental logicians are known to the profession.

12. $2 + 3 = 5$; therefore $5 = 2 + 3$.

ANSWERS

A. 1. UI (erroneous), line 3 is not an instance of line 1.
   4. Both uses of UG (erroneous).
   6. UI (erroneous), UI applied to component of a compound sentence, not to whole sentence. Also EI and DeM.
   8. EI (erroneous), violates restriction 3 on EI, since "a" appears in premise.
Only **9** has no errors.

B. 3. 2. $Fa \cdot Ga$ 1 UI. 3. Fa 2 Simp. 4. Ga 2 Simp. 5. $(x)Fx$ 3 UG. 6. $(x)Gx$ 4 UG. 7. $(x)Fx \cdot (x)Gx$ 5,6 Conj.
   5. 2. Ia AP. 3. $(Ia \lor Ja) \supset (Ka \cdot La)$ 1 UI. 4. $Ia \lor Ja$ 2 Add. 5. $Ka \cdot La$ 3,4 MP. 6. La 5 Simp. 7. $Ia \supset La$ 2–6 RCP. 8. $(x)(Ix \supset Lx)$ 7 UG.

C. 3. $(x)(Ax \supset (Tx \lor Dx))$, $(x)(Tx \supset Wx)$, $(x)(Dx \supset DRx) \therefore (x)(Ax \supset (Wx \lor DRx))$. Take Aa as AP in RCP strategy. Later use CD.
   7. $(x)Sx$, $(x)(Sx \equiv Dx)$, $(\exists x)(\sim Dx \lor Ex) \therefore (\exists x)(Sx \cdot Ex)$. From the first two premises after UI obtain Da by Equiv and MP, then Ea by DS after EI premise 3.
   10. Try for Oa and $\sim Oa$ and then get Sa by RAA in deriving second conjunct of conclusion.
   11. $(x)(PIx \supset Px)$, $(\exists x)(PIx \cdot \sim Wx)$, $(\exists x)(PIx \cdot \sim Ax) \therefore$ $(\exists x)(Px \cdot \sim Wx) \cdot (\exists x)(Px \cdot \sim Ax)$. Apply UI to the first premise twice, once with a then a_1. Put in a when EI second premise (doing this first) and a_1 when EI the third premise (doing this second).

D. 1. $(x)(Bx \supset Hex)$, $Bh \therefore Heh$ valid
   3. $(x)(Fx \supset Wx)$, $(\exists x)(Nx \cdot Fx) \therefore (\exists x)(Nx \cdot Wx)$ valid
   6. $(x)[Fx \supset (Hx \lor \sim Px)]$, $Fh \therefore \sim Hh \supset \sim Ph$ valid
   8. $P \supset \sim T$, $H \lor P$, $H \supset N$, $\sim N \therefore \sim T$ valid
   10. $(x)[\sim Tx \supset (\sim Wx \cdot \sim Bx)]$, $(x)(\sim Rx \supset \sim Tx) \therefore (x)[(Bx \lor Wx) \supset Rx]$ valid

Only **2**, **4**, and **8** are sentential arguments. Only **1**, **5** and **12** are relational predicate arguments. All the rest are monadic predicate arguments.

10

Axioms

The application of logic to mathematics, physics, and other disciplines is often made by means of an axiom system. Certain statements about the subject matter of the discipline are taken as unproved, as fundamental assumptions; these are the axioms. From these axioms theorems are generated by showing that the theorems validly follow from the axioms in the same way that one might show that a conclusion of an argument validly follows from some set of premises. In other words, when a discipline is developed by formulating axioms, what validly follows from the axioms or is logically implied by the axioms is counted as theorems.

The axiomatic method is often used within logic itself. An example of the use of the axiom method for sentential logic will be studied in this chapter. The axiom system will have valid sentential formulas for axioms. Valid sentential formulas are formulas composed of sentence variables and connectives which come out true no matter what truth value is assigned to the sentence variables. These formulas are dubbed tautologies earlier on. Using a pair of rules of inference, we will prove theorems from the axioms. The axioms and rules will be so selected that the theorems will be tautologies and every tautology will be a theorem. One of the major interests in this chapter will be to outline proofs that only tautologies are theorems of this axiom system and that every tautology is a theorem.

Examples of some familiar tautologies are

$$p \vee {\sim}p \qquad\qquad p \supset (p \vee q)$$
$$p \supset p \qquad\qquad p \equiv {\sim}{\sim}p$$
$${\sim}(p \cdot {\sim}p) \qquad\qquad (p \supset q) \equiv ({\sim}q \supset {\sim}p)$$

Tautologies such as these are examples of what are called truths of logic. There are other kinds of truths of logic beside tautologies. And, interestingly, tautologies and some other kinds of truths of logic can be proved using the methods of Chapters 7 and 9. Before describing the axiom system for sentential logic to be studied in this chapter, we shall briefly illuminate these last remarks.

Truths of Logic

A truth of logic is a certain kind of formula. Formulas in logic are formed out of the following expressions: sentence connectives, quantifiers, variables for sentences, predicates, and individual variables and constants, in addition to a constant not discussed here, the relation of identity. Some of these formulas are such that they come out true no matter how they are interpreted. (Remember an interpretation for such formulas is given when a domain is supplied, predicate letters replace the predicate variables, "true" or "false" replace sentential variables, and names for individuals in the domain replace any individual constant.) Others have the property that they will come out false under any interpretation, whereas others will come out true or false on interpretation. A *truth of logic* is a formula in logic which comes out true under all interpretations. In other words, truths of logic are simply valid formulas of logic. Some examples of such truths are

$(p \cdot q) \supset p$ $(p \cdot q) \equiv (q \cdot p)$

$(x)Sx \supset (\exists x)Sx$ $[(\exists x)Sx \lor (\exists x)Px] \supset (\exists x)(Sx \lor Px)$

$(x)(x = x)$ (not discussed) $(\exists x)(y)Fxy \supset (y)(\exists x)Fxy$

Methods from previous chapters can in fact be used to verify that a formula (not using the sign for identity "$=$") is a truth of logic. With respect to sentential formulas such as the first pair above, truth table methods can be used to verify that they are tautologies. And every tautology is a truth of logic. Also the proof method of Chapter 7 can be used to establish that each is a truth of logic. Here is how it can be done for the first formula:

1. $p \cdot q$ AP
2. p 1 Simp
3. $(p \cdot q) \supset p$ 1–2 RCP

Notice that in this proof no premise is used. The first line is an *assumed* premise and each of the other lines follows by one of the rules from Chapter 7. Also note that all the assumed premises have been discharged by the time one gets to line 3. Generalizing from this example, it can be said that a proof of a truth of logic using Chapter 7 rules is obtained when in a no-premise proof all the assumed premises have been discharged. In connection with the set of rules from Chapter 7, such proofs will be proofs for tautologies, for the last lines of such proofs are tautologies. To illustrate, the following are two more proofs of tautologies:

$$
\begin{array}{lll}
1.\ \sim(p \lor \sim p) & & \text{AP} \\
2.\ \sim p \cdot \sim\sim p & & \text{1 DeM} \\
3.\ p \cdot \sim p & & \text{2 DN, Comm} \\
\overline{4.\ p \lor \sim p} & & \text{1–3 RAA}
\end{array}
$$

$$
\begin{array}{lll}
1.\ p & & \text{AP} \\
2.\ q & & \text{AP} \\
3.\ p \cdot q & & \text{1,2 Conj} \\
4.\ q \supset (p \cdot q) & & \text{2–3 RCP} \\
\overline{5.\ p \supset [(q \supset (p \cdot q))]} & & \text{1–4 RCP}
\end{array}
$$

There are two basic strategies in obtaining proofs for tautologies. Deny the desired tautology, as the proof for $p \lor \sim p$ above illustrates, or, if the tautology is a conditional, assume the antecedent of the condition in a RCP proof, as the first and third proofs illustrate.

In the proof system for predicate logic found in Chapter 9, no-premise proofs can be constructed in which all the assumed premises are discharged. Such proofs will give truths of logic from predicate logic. For example, the proof for one of the preceding predicate formulas is

$$
\begin{array}{lll}
1.\ (x)Sx & & \text{AP} \\
2.\ Sa & & \text{1 UI} \\
3.\ (\exists x)Sx & & \text{2 EG} \\
\overline{4.\ (x)Sx \supset (\exists x)Sx} & & \text{1–3 RCP}
\end{array}
$$

In constructing proofs for valid predicate formulas, strategies are followed that are similar to those followed in constructing proofs for tautologies.

When using the rules from Chapters 7 or 9 in constructing no-premise proofs, a *theorem* is the last line of a no-premise proof when all the assumed premises have been discharged by RCP or RAA. Theorems in these systems are truths of logic or valid logical formulas.

We have remarked that what is a theorem of an axiom system in mathematics, physics, or other disciplines is what validly follows or what is logically implied by the axioms. It can now be said that some set of axioms A logically implies some statement S if and only if $A \supset S$ is a logical truth. And a conditional is a logical truth if and only if it is an interpretation of a truth of logic. The same obtains for the validity of an argument. A set of premises Pr logically implies some conclusion C if and only if $Pr \supset C$ is a logical truth.

This notion of a logical truth needs further clarification. Any sentence which is an interpretation of a truth of logic or a valid formula in logic is a *logical truth*. Examples of logical truths are

Mr. Nixon is a Quaker or it is false that he is a Quaker.
If all bachelors are married, then some bachelors are married.
Every number is identical with itself.

Logical truths are expressed by sentences that we say are true. But such sentences are true because and only because of the arrangement of the logical terms in the sentences, logical terms being the logical constants: sentence connectives, quantifiers, and identity. As is sometimes said, logical truths are true sentences whose truth follows from the pattern of logical words. Such truths may be contrasted with sentences, such as:

Mr. Nixon is a Quaker.
Not all bachelors own waterbeds.

which are true but are such that their truth does not follow just from the pattern of the logical words they contain. Indeed, the first sentence does not contain any logical words. They are factual or contingent sentences whose truth depends on facts, on what is the case.

Some sentences can be transformed into logical truths by virtue of the meaning of some of the nonlogical words they contain. For example, since "bachelor" means "unmarried adult male," the sentence "All bachelors are unmarried" can be transformed into "All unmarried adult males are unmarried." This last sentence is a logical truth, since it is an interpretation of the following valid formula of predicate logic: $(x)[(Sx \cdot Px \cdot Mx) \supset Sx]$. Such sentences, sentences which can be transformed into logical truths, along with logical truths, are commonly called *analytic sentences*. Nonanalytic sentences are called *synthetic sentences*. Analytic sentences are thus interpretations of valid logical formulas or are sentences which can be transformed into interpretations of valid logical formulas by use of intensional definitions for some or all of the nonlogical words they contain. *Logical falsehoods* are interpretations of inconsistent formulas in logic— formulas which come out false under all interpretations—or are sentences which can be transformed into interpretations of inconsistent formulas by the use of intensional definitions. Examples of logical falsehoods are

It is false that if some bachelors are married then some married persons are bachelors.
Some bachelors are married.

EXERCISES 10.1

A. Using the natural deduction system of Chapters 7 and 9, prove the following as theorems.

1. $p \supset p$
2. $p \supset (p \lor q)$
3. $p \supset {\sim}{\sim}p$
4. ${\sim}(p \cdot {\sim}p)$
5. $(p \supset q) \equiv ({\sim}q \supset {\sim}p)$

6. $(x)(Sx \cdot Px) \supset [(x)Sx \cdot (x)Px]$
7. $\sim(\exists x)Sx \supset (x)\sim Sx$
8. $[(x)Sx \lor (x)Px] \supset (x)(Sx \lor Px)$
9. $[(\exists x)Sx \lor (\exists x)Px] \equiv (\exists x)(Sx \lor Px)$
10. $(\exists x)(y)Fxy \supset (y)(\exists x)Fxy$

B. Which of the following are logical truths and which can be transformed into logical truths by using definitions? Are there any logical falsehoods?

1. If everyone contradicts himself, then so does Gummo.
2. If something is red and something is colored, then something is red and colored.
3. My paternal grandfather had at least one child.
4. The sun rises in the east.
5. Either he came with Aloyce or he did not come with him.
6. No one can travel thirty miles in three seconds.
7. If $x > y$, then $\sim(y > x)$.
8. The most un-American thing in America in its day was the House Committee on Un-American Activities. (Truman, *Memoirs*)
9. The cat is on the mat, but I don't believe it.
10. He said that he was sitting perfectly still.

ANSWERS

A. 4. Begin with $\sim\sim(p \cdot \sim p)$ as AP in a RAA strategy.
    5. First prove $(p \supset q) \supset (\sim q \supset \sim p)$, then its converse, and then use Equiv. Prove by using $p \supset q$ as AP in RCP strategy, then $\sim q \supset \sim p$ as AP in RCP strategy.
B. 1. Logical truth.   3. Can be transformed into logical truth.
    5. Logical truth.   8. Neither analytic nor a logical falsehood.

Axioms for Sentential Logic

The axiom systems for sentential logic to be studied in this chapter will have the structure of any axiom system. What are the elements found in every axiom system whether it is logic, mathematics, physics, or any other discipline? First, there is the *vocabulary*. The vocabulary of an axiom system is made up of the expressions that can be combined to form sentences about the subject matter of the system. For sentential logic the vocabulary consists of sentential variables, connectives, and parentheses used for purposes of punctuation. Second, there are rules determining how the expressions making up the vocabulary are put together so as to form syntactically correct sentences. Such strings are called *well-formed formulas*. Third, there are the *axioms*. Generally these axioms are synthetic sentences about the subject matter of the discipline in the case of nonlogical axiom systems. These sentences are selected as axioms because of their powers to generate theorems. They are used like premises in logically deriving conclusions which are the theorems of the system. Fourth, there are the *truths of logic* that are used or presupposed in the derivations of the theorems. And, finally, there are the *theorems*. If the axioms are indeed true and if the derivation of theorems is done by using truths of logic, then the theorems must be true. Frequently some of the expressions are defined in terms of expressions which are not defined, namely, the *primitive expressions*. In the axiom system for sentential logic "~" and " v " will be taken as primitives, whereas the other familiar connectives will be defined in terms of them. There are several reasons for having defined expressions (and thus limiting the primitive expressions), and some of these will become apparent as we progress.

The system presented here for sentential logic is the one found in Bertrand Russell and Alfred North Whitehead's early classic treatise on symbolic logic, *Principia Mathematica*. This axiom system will be called *PM*, after Russell and Whitehead's book.

The vocabulary for PM is

1. Sentential variables: $p, q, r, \ldots$.
2. Sentential connectives: ~ and v .
3. Parentheses: ( ).

These elements are combined into a proper string or well-formed formula, abbreviated wff, when the formula satisfies the following rules, called *formation rules*:

1. A sentential variable is a wff.
2. Any wff preceded by ~ is a wff.
3. Any wff followed by v followed by a wff, the whole enclosed in parentheses, is a wff.

These rules can be restated by allowing P and Q to be variables for any wffs. $p, q, r, \ldots$ are variables for sentences; capitals P and Q are variables for sentential formulas. Using these new variables, we can restate the formation rules in this manner:

1. Any sentential variable is a wff.
2. If P is a wff, then $\sim P$ is a wff.
3. If P and Q are wffs, then $(P \vee Q)$ is a wff.

The preceding set of rules provides a decision procedure for determining whether a string is made up of the vocabulary of PM is or is not a wff. To illustrate, consider $[\sim(p \lor p) \lor p]$. By the rules we determine the following:

> p is a wff by rule 1.
> $(p \lor p)$ is a wff by rule 3 since p is a wff and parentheses are used.
> $\sim(p \lor p)$ is a wff by rule 2 since $(p \lor p)$ is a wff.
> $[\sim(p \lor p) \lor p]$ is a wff by rule 3 since both disjuncts are wffs and the whole is enclosed by parentheses.

Thus the original formula is a wff. On the other hand, $p \lor \sim p$ fails to be a wff, for though p is a wff by rule 1, and $\sim p$ is a wff by rule 2, the disjunction of the two is not a wff, since the whole has not been surrounded by parentheses. It will be convenient, however, to eliminate some of these parentheses. The outer parentheses do not do any work, so the convention will be adopted now of dropping all outer parentheses. The last clause of rule 3 is needed, however, in order to avoid ambiguous formulas such as $p \lor q \lor p$, and to make possible the negation of compound formulas.

It goes without saying that what up to this time we have naturally regarded as wffs in sentential logic are wffs, and what we have naturally rejected as some kind of nonsense, for example, $p \lor \lor q$ are clearly not wffs under the rules. These formation rules plus the convention for reducing the number of parentheses more or less match our logical intuition for the well-formedness of sentential formulas that we have relied on but have not made explicit until now.

In PM "$\sim$" and "$\lor$" are taken as the primitive expressions with the other familiar sentence connectives introduced by these definitions:

> D1: $P \supset Q$ is defined as $\sim P \lor Q$
> D2: $P \cdot Q$ is defined as $\sim(\sim P \lor \sim Q)$
> D3: $P \equiv Q$ is defined as $(P \supset Q) \cdot (Q \supset P)$

When theorems are derived in PM, one line is sometimes the result of another line *by definition*. That is, a given formula is changed or transformed by using one of these definitions. Examples of such definitional transformations are

$$\sim(p \lor p) \lor p \qquad\qquad \sim\sim[\sim p \lor \sim(p \cdot q)]$$
$$(p \lor p) \supset p \quad \text{by D1} \qquad\qquad \sim[p \cdot (p \cdot q)] \quad \text{by D2}$$

Note that in the definitions P and Q are variables for wffs. Thus in the first definitional transformation, $(p \lor p)$ goes in for P in D1, whereas p goes in for Q; and in the second transformation p goes in for P of D2, whereas $(p \cdot q)$ goes in for Q. Note also that the force of "is defined as" is to be understood as declaring that any interpretation of what is found on one side of the "is defined as" can be replaced with what is found on the other side whether it is a whole formula or part of a formula. In using D2 in the second illustration, replacement is made with respect to *part* of the formula.

The axioms of PM are the following five tautologies which are written in the form of conditionals to make them easier to understand. If they were written using only the primitive connectives, it would be harder to grasp their significance.

A1: $(p \vee p) \supset p$
A2: $p \supset (q \vee p)$
A3: $(p \vee q) \supset (q \vee p)$
A4: $(p \supset q) \supset [(r \vee p) \supset (r \vee q)]$
A5: $[p \vee (q \vee r)] \supset [q \vee (p \vee r)]$

There are two rules of inference in PM, a rule corresponding to *modus ponens*, rule 1, abbreviated R1, and a rule of substitution, R2:

R1:   If $P \supset Q$ and P, then Q may be inferred.
R2:   Any wff may be substituted for any variable in a formula, provided that the substitution is made for every occurrence of that variable.

We are already familiar with *modus ponens* and how we can infer a line from previous lines by using it. R1 is this rule. R2 is a rule of substitution and allows us, for example, to make the following inferences:

$(p \vee p) \supset p$	$q \supset (p \vee q)$	$p \supset p$
$(\sim p \vee \sim p) \supset \sim p$	$r \supset (q \vee r)$	$(p \cdot q) \supset (p \cdot q)$

In the first, $\sim p$ is substituted for p, which we indicate in this manner: $p/\sim p$, best read "p is supplanted by $\sim p$." The second has q/r and p/q in two simultaneous applications of R2. In the third the compound $(p \cdot q)$ is substituted for every occurrence of p in $p \supset p$. Note that we can substitute any wff, simple or compound, as long as the substitution is made for single, individual, sentential variables and as long as this is done uniformly. Consequently, for example, the following are *not* correct applications of R2:

$p \supset p$		$p \supset p$	
p	$p \supset p/p$ (erroneous)	$p \supset q$	p/q (erroneous)

A *proof in PM* is defined as any sequence of wff formulas such that each one is either an axiom or follows from previous lines by one of the rules or by definition. The last line of a proof is a *theorem of PM*. Illustrations of proofs for some theorems make up the next section.

It is desired that PM have certain properties. The most important property is that it be consistent. An axiom system such as PM is consistent in the sense of being *negation consistent* if for any wff P, P and $\sim P$ are not both derivable, that is, are not both theorems of PM. The importance of this property arises because, in PM, any instance of $P \supset (\sim P \supset Q)$ is a theorem.

Thus if P and $\sim P$ are both theorems, then Q is a theorem by two applications of R2. And since Q is any wff, it follows that any wff of PM is a theorem if PM is not negation consistent. Needless to say, an axiom system in which any wff is a theorem is a useless system.

Another important property is completeness. PM is complete in the sense of *semantically complete* if every acceptable formula, in this case, every tautology, is a theorem of the system. We wish PM to be such that all truths of logic, i.e., all tautologies, found among the wffs are theorems of PM.

A third important property is soundness. PM is sound if every theorem is a truth of logic, i.e., a tautology in this case. A system is sound if every theorem is an acceptable wff, whereas a system is semantically complete if every acceptable formula is a theorem. Outlines of proofs for the consistency, completeness, and soundness of PM follow the next section.

A less important property that is desirable for certain purposes is independence. The axioms of a system are *independent* if no member of the axiom set is derivable from the other members. Interestingly, A5 is not an independent axiom; it can be derived as a theorem in PM from the other four axioms. That the fifth axiom was dependent was not known to Russell and Whitehead and was subsequently shown to be derivable from the first four axioms by the logician Paul Bernays. The method of showing that a formula is independent is closely related to the method of proving PM negation consistent, as we shall see.

EXERCISES 10.2

A. Which of the following are correct definitional transformations?

1. $\sim p \supset q$
   $p \lor q$
2. $\sim(\sim p \supset q)$
   $\sim(\sim\sim p \lor q)$
3. $\sim(p \cdot q)$
   $\sim\sim(\sim p \lor \sim q)$
4. $p \lor q$
   $\sim(\sim p \cdot \sim q)$
5. $\sim(p \equiv q)$
   $\sim[(p \supset q) \cdot (q \supset p)]$
6. $\sim p \supset p$
   $p \lor p$
7. $\sim(p \lor \sim\sim q)$
   $\sim p \cdot \sim q$
8. $\sim\sim(\sim p \lor \sim\sim q)$
   $\sim(p \cdot \sim q)$

B. Which of the following are correct applications of R2?

1. $(p \lor p) \supset p$
   $(p \lor p) \supset r$
2. $p \supset (p \lor q)$
   $p \supset (p \lor p)$
3. $p \supset (p \lor q)$
   $p \supset \{p \lor [(p \lor p) \supset p]\}$
4. $p \supset (p \lor q)$
   $q \supset (q \lor p)$
5. $(p \lor p) \supset p$
   $p \supset p$

ANSWERS

A. Only **1, 4, 6**, and **7** are not correct definitional transformations.
B. Only **2, 3**, and **4** are correct applications of R2.

Some Theorems of PM

Some theorems of PM will be proved in this section to illustrate what proofs are in PM and how they are devised. At the right side of each line in a proof sequence the justification for the line will be given, even though this does not enter in the definition for a proof in PM. If, for example, 5, 6 R1 is found to the right of a line, this will mean that the line is obtained by an application of R1 to lines 5 and 6. If 8 R2 p/q is found to the right of a line, this will indicate that this line is obtained from line 8 by an application of R2, in which every occurrence of p is supplanted by q. The proofs of early theorems in an axiom system are often difficult, and the following proofs deserve careful study. "T" is used as an abbreviation for "theorem," and each theorem following is given a number.

T1. $p \supset (q \supset p)$
   1. $p \supset (q \vee p)$ A2
   2. $p \supset (\sim q \vee p)$ 1 R2, $q/\sim q$
   3. $p \supset (q \supset p)$ 2 D2

The first line is an axiom, A2. The second line comes from line 1 by R2, replacing q with $\sim q$. The third line comes from line 2 by definition for $\supset$, D2. Note that this sequence of lines satisfies the definition for a proof in PM. Each line is either an axiom or comes from previous lines by a rule or definition. The last line of a proof is a theorem. Line 3 is the last line and is T1; thus a proof for T1 is constructed. This proof illustrates one of the strategies for proving a theorem, namely, *substitution*. One tries to obtain the desired theorem by making substitutions in axioms and using the definitions.

T2. $(p \supset q) \supset [(r \supset p) \supset (r \supset p)]$
   1. $(p \supset q) \supset [(r \vee p) \supset (r \vee q)]$ A4
   2. $(p \supset q) \supset [(\sim r \vee p) \supset (\sim r \vee q)]$ $r/\sim r$
   3. T2   2 D1

In this proof by substitution the justification has been shortened. Since $r/\sim r$ indicates an application of R2, and since we will understand an application of R2 to apply to the previous line unless otherwise stated, the justification for line 2 can be simply $r/\sim r$. The same will hold for definition.

T3. $[p \supset (q \supset r)] \supset [q \supset (p \supset r)]$
   1. $[p \vee (q \vee r)] \supset [(q \vee (p \vee r)]$ A5
   2. $[\sim p \vee (\sim q \vee r)] \supset [\sim q \vee (\sim p \vee r)]$ $p/\sim p, q/\sim q$
   3. T3   D1

Another substitution strategy.

T4. $(p \supset q) \supset [(q \supset r) \supset (p \supset r)]$
   1. $\{(q \supset r) \supset [(p \supset q) \supset (p \supset r)]\} \supset T4$ T3, $p/q \supset r$,
                                                $q/p \supset q, r/p \supset r$
   2. $(q \supset r) \supset [(p \supset q) \supset (p \supset r)]$ T2, $p/q, q/r, r/p$
   3. T4   1,2 R1

Further abbreviations are entered with the preceding proof for T4. First, a previously proved theorem (with certain substitutions) is introduced as line 1. This is not part of what is called a proof in PM. However, one could replace this introduction of T3 with the preceding three-line sequence for T3 and then, using R2, obtain the first line of this proof for T4. Thus putting in a previously proved theorem (with or without applications of R2) is a way to shorten a proof. Strictly speaking, T3 at the justification point for line 1 should read: "At this point put in proof for T3."

The strategy used in proving T4 is sometimes called *detachment*. It may happen that by substitution in an axiom or previously proved theorem one can obtain a line of the form $P \supset Q$ where Q is the desired theorem. If, now, P is a previously proved theorem or an axiom or a substitution instance of either, then by R1, the rule of detachment or *modus ponens*, one can obtain Q. In the proof of T4, T4 is found to be the consequent of T3 if appropriate substitutions are made. T2 with the indicated substitutions is the antecedent when the indicated substitution on T3 is made. Thus, by R1 on lines 1 and 2, line 3 or theorem T4 is obtained.

T5. $p \supset p$
   1. $(p \vee p) \supset p$ A1
   2. $p \supset (q \vee p)$ A2
   3. $p \supset (p \vee p)$ q/p
   4. $(p \supset q) \supset [(q \supset r) \supset (p \supset r)]$ T4
   5. $(3) \supset [(1) \supset (6)]$ $q/p \vee p, r/p$
   6. T5   3,1,5 R1(2)

Note that in this proof the detachment method is used. However, two previous axioms or theorems are needed to detach the inner consequent of line 5.

T6. $p \vee \sim p$

This proof is left for the reader. (Hint: use A3, T5, and D1 in a detachment strategy.)

T7. $p \supset \sim\sim p$

This problem is also left for the reader. (Hint: use substitution and D1 on T6.)

T8. $\sim\sim p \supset p$
1. $p \supset \sim\sim p$ — T7
2. $\sim p \supset \sim\sim\sim p$ — $p/\sim p$
3. $(p \supset q) \supset [(r \vee p) \supset (r \vee q)]$ — A4
4. $(2) \supset (5)$ — $p/\sim p, q/\sim\sim\sim p, r/p$
5. $(p \vee \sim p) \supset (p \vee \sim\sim\sim p)$ — 2,4 R1
6. $p \vee \sim p$ — T6
7. $p \vee \sim\sim\sim p$ — 5,6 R1
8. $(p \vee q) \supset (q \vee p)$ — A3
9. $(p \vee \sim\sim\sim p) \supset (\sim\sim\sim p \vee p)$ — $q/\sim\sim\sim p$
10. $\sim\sim\sim p \vee p$ — 7,9 R1
11. T8 — D1

T9. $(p \supset q) \supset (\sim q \supset \sim p)$
1. $(q \supset \sim\sim q) \supset [(p \supset q) \supset (p \supset \sim\sim q)]$ — T2 $p/q, q/\sim\sim q, r/p$
2. $q \supset \sim\sim q$ — T7 p/q
3. $(p \supset q) \supset (p \supset \sim\sim q)$ — 1,2 R1
4. $(\sim p \vee \sim\sim q) \supset (\sim\sim q \vee \sim p)$ — A3, $p/\sim p, q/\sim\sim q$
5. $(p \supset \sim\sim q) \supset (\sim q \supset \sim p)$ — D1
6. $(3) \supset [(5) \supset (7)]$ — T4, $p/p \supset q,$ $q/p \supset \sim\sim q,$ $r/\sim q \supset \sim p$
7. T9 — 3,5,6 R1(2)

The last proof is shortened by entering needed axioms and theorems with the desired application of R2, the rule of substitution.

T10. $(\sim q \supset \sim p) \supset (p \supset q)$

This proof is left to the reader and it is a difficult proof. [Hint: use T9 to obtain: $(\sim q \supset \sim p) \supset (\sim\sim p \supset \sim\sim q)$. If one can now obtain: $(\sim\sim p \supset \sim\sim q) \supset (p \supset q)$, then with T4 one can obtain T10. One can obtain this last needed formula as follows: from T4, R2, T7, and R1 obtain $(\sim\sim p \supset \sim\sim q) \supset (p \supset \sim\sim q)$, and from T2, R2, R1, T8 obtain $(p \supset \sim\sim q) \supset (p \supset q)$, then use T4.]

T11. $p \supset [q \supset (p \cdot q)]$

1. $(\sim p \vee \sim q) \vee \sim (\sim p \vee \sim q)$	T6
2.	D2
3.	A3, T4, R1
4.	A5, R1, R2
5.	D1
6.	A3, T4, R1, R2
7.	D1

It is left to the reader to supply the sequences of formulas for the proof of T11. Note that the indicated substitution is omitted to further shorten the proof. Also several steps have been collapsed into one line for lines 3, 4, and 6.

T12. $p \equiv \sim\sim p$

1. $p \supset \sim\sim p$	T7
2. $\sim\sim p \supset p$	T8
3. $(1) \cdot (2)$	T11, R1
4. T12	D3

T13. $(p \supset q) \equiv (\sim q \supset \sim p)$

The proof of T13 is left to the reader. It is easy and is like the proof of T12 but uses T9 and T10.

T14. $p \equiv p$

The proof of theorems is made easier by the use of what are called *derived rules*. When a derived rule is used to prove a theorem, one can forego its use and prove the theorem using the primitive, nonderived rules, plus the axioms of PM. Thus the use of a derived rule does not increase the class of theorems of PM. In fact the use of a derived rule produces an abbreviated proof, similar to those obtained when theorems are introduced as lines in proofs.

The first derived rule is justified by T4, and is

DR1. If $P \supset Q$ and $Q \supset R$, then we may infer $P \supset R$.

The next derived rule that is useful to have is justified by T11:

DR2. If P and Q, then we may infer $P \cdot Q$.

The first rule is a transitivity of implication rule, whereas the second rule is a rule of conjunction. The final derived rule is justified by a set of theorems, most of which we have not derived, and is a rule which allows us to replace one formula with another under certain circumstances. Let P and Q be formulas in PM, let P_M be a formula with one or more occurrences of M, and let Q_N be a formula which results from replacing one or more occurrences of M in P_M with N, then:

DR3. If $M \equiv N$ is a theorem, then from P_M we may infer Q_N.

This rule is applicable whenever we have proved a theorem of the form $M \equiv N$. T12, T13, and T14 have this form. Thus since T12 is a theorem, in any formula we can add double negations or remove them, using T12 plus DR3. DR3 plus T12 gives us in effect a double negation rule for PM. Some applications of these derived rules follow. The listed but unproved theorems are left as exercises for the reader.

T15. $(p \cdot q) \equiv \sim(\sim p \vee \sim q)$ (DeMorgan's Theorem)

T15 is easily proved using D2 plus T14.

T16. $(p \vee q) \equiv \sim(\sim p \cdot \sim q)$ (DeMorgan's Theorem)
 1. $\sim(\sim p \cdot \sim q) \equiv \sim(\sim p \cdot \sim q)$ T14
 2. $\sim\sim(\sim\sim p \vee \sim\sim q) \equiv \sim(\sim p \cdot \sim q)$ D2
 3. $(p \vee q) \equiv \sim(\sim p \cdot \sim q)$ 2 T12, DR3

T17. $(p \vee q) \equiv (q \vee p)$ (Commutation)
 1. $(p \vee q) \supset (q \vee p)$ A3
 2. $(q \vee p) \supset (p \vee q)$ A3
 3. $(1) \cdot (2)$ 1,2 DR2
 4. T17   D3

T18. $(p \cdot q) \equiv (q \cdot p)$ (Commutation)
T19. $[p \vee q) \vee r] \equiv [p \vee (q \vee r)]$ (Association)
T20. $[(p \cdot q) \cdot r] \equiv [p \cdot (q \cdot r)]$ (Association)
T21. $[p \vee (p \cdot r)] \equiv [(p \vee q) \cdot (p \vee r)]$ (Distribution)
T22. $[p \cdot (q \vee r)] \equiv [(p \cdot q) \vee (p \cdot r)]$ (Distribution)

EXERCISES 10.3

A.   Derive the underived theorems through T14 not using any derived rules.
B.   Use any rules and derive the underived theorems T15 through T22.

Consistency of PM

An axiom system is negation consistent if for no wff, P, P and $\sim P$ are both derivable. A proof of the consistency of PM cannot proceed by attempting and failing to derive the negation of some formula already derived, for our failure may be due to our lack of ingenuity. Thus, though we might show the system to be inconsistent in this manner, if it is consistent, we would not show the system to be consistent.

The proof of consistency for a system can be a relative proof, one in which we suppose the consistency of some other system. For example, assuming algebra consistent, we prove the consistency of geometry by translating each theorem of geometry into algebraic truths. Or the proof of the consistency of a system can be a nonrelative or absolute proof where the proof does not assume the consistency of another system. For PM a relative proof would be possible via assuming the consistency of Boolean algebra, but an absolute proof for the consistency of PM will now be given. The proof of consistency is a proof about the system and is on that account sometimes called a *metalogical* result. The proof cannot be formulated within PM, and the assertion that PM is consistent is not a theorem of PM, since only formulas made up of strings of the vocabulary can be theorems. Similar remarks apply to proofs of independence and completeness. In each case the results are about the axiom system—not theorems derivable from the axioms.

In outline, the proof of the consistency of PM consists of the following steps:

1. Show that each axiom of PM is a tautological formula.
2. Show that being a tautology is an hereditary property with respect to the two rules. In other words, show that if either rule is applied to tautologous formulas, the inferred formula is a tautology.
3. Given 1 and 2, every theorem of PM is a tautology, since a theorem is the last line of a sequence of formulas, each of which is either an axiom or follows by one of the rules. In other words, given 1 and 2, PM is sound.
4. If PM is sound, every theorem is a tautology. Thus, for no formula P are both P and $\sim P$ theorems, for both P and $\sim P$ cannot be tautologies. Thus PM is negation consistent.

As can be seen by this proof outline, the demonstration of 1 and 2 is sufficient to show that PM is negation consistent. That every axiom is a tautology can easily be demonstrated using standard truth table procedures. This leaves us with the need to prove that each rule of PM passes on the property of being a tautology.

Rule 1, *modus ponens*: If P and $P \supset Q$ are both tautologies, then Q is a tautology.

Suppose that P and $P \supset Q$ are both tautologies but Q is not. If Q is not a tautology, then Q can be **F** while P and $P \supset Q$ are both true. But this contradicts our assumption that $P \supset Q$ is true—that is, a tautology. Therefore if P and $P \supset Q$ are both tautologies, so is Q.

Rule 2, rules of substitution: (left as an exercise).

Since each axiom is a tautology and this property is hereditary with respect to R1 and R2, each theorem is a tautology (PM is sound). If each theorem is a tautology, then for any P both P and $\sim P$ cannot be theorems, for P and $\sim P$ cannot both be tautologies. Thus PM is consistent.

A variation of this proof shows that there is at least one wff that is not a theorem of PM. p is such a formula since p is not a tautology, and steps 1 and 2 establish that each theorem is a tautology. If at least one formula is not a theorem of PM, then PM is consistent. For if PM were not consistent, then every wff would be a theorem of PM. This is shown by noting that $p \supset (\sim p \supset q)$ is a theorem of PM; thus by R2 any substitution instance of this theorem is a theorem of PM. Consequently, if PM is not consistent, then for some P both P and $\sim P$ are theorems, and thus q is a theorem. And if a single sentential variable such as q is a theorem, then by R2 any wff is a theorem. But since p is not a theorem PM is consistent. It should be noted that a system is said to be *absolutely consistent* if and only if at least one wff of the system is not a theorem of the system. Since p is not a theorem of PM, PM is absolutely consistent.

EXERCISES 10.4

A. In connection with the proof of consistency give an example of a tautology and an inconsistent formula, and show that their nature does not change by the use of R2 in supplanting variables with

1. $\sim p$
2. $p \cdot (q \cdot r)$
3. $(q \cdot \sim q)$
4. $p \vee \sim p$

B. Prove that the rule of substitution passes on the property of being a tautology if the formula to which it is applied is a tautology.

C. Prove that PM plus $p \supset q$ as an additional axiom is negation inconsistent.

Independence of the Axioms of PM

Let *P* be one of the axioms of PM. Let PM – *P* be PM with the omission of *P*. Then *P* is independent of the other axioms of PM if and only if there is no proof in PM – *P* of *P*; that is, *P* is not a theorem of PM – *P*. It is easy to see how one can establish that an axiom is not independent of the other axioms of PM. Simply prove it as a theorem from the other axioms. A5 is an example of an axiom which is not independent. It can be derived as a theorem using A1 through A4 plus the two rules. But it perhaps is not obvious how one goes about establishing that an axiom of PM is independent. The failure to prove it from the other axioms is not sufficient because one may not be ingenious enough. (Most likely any initial attempt on the reader's part to prove A5 from A1 through A4 will fail. Try to do it.) The method used in proving consistency of PM can, however, be used in proving independence.

In the proof of consistency we found a property that the axioms have (being tautologies) and that is hereditary when applying the two rules. The property of being a tautology accrues to the axioms because of the familiar truth table interpretation for the statement connectives. Suppose that a different interpretation for the connectives is given, so that axioms 2, 3, and 4 have a new property; it is hereditary with respect to the rules, and it is a property which axiom 1 lacks. Then axiom 1 cannot be derived from the 2nd, 3rd, and 4th axioms; otherwise it would have the property. This interpretation cannot be the standard one for the connectives, since the standard one results in the axioms' all having the property of being tautologies. The interpretation may seem strange, but if it provides a property true of A2, A3, and A4, but not true of A1, and a property that is passed on by the rules, then it does the job—namely, it aids in establishing the independence of A1.

Rather than the standard tables for the two primitive connectives, suppose the following interpretation, where 0, 1, and 2 can be understood in any way one wishes:

p	~*p*		*p*	*q*	*p* ∨ *q*
0	1		0	0	0
1	0		1	0	0
2	2		2	0	0
			0	1	0
			1	1	1
			2	1	2
			0	2	0
			1	2	2
			2	2	0

On this interpretation we obtain the following table for A1, rewritten using only the primitive connectives:

p	$\sim(p \vee p) \vee p$
0	1 0 0
1	0 1 0
2	1 0 2

Note the occurrence of a 2 in the last column, the column under the main connective of A1. The rest of the axioms come out 0 under this new interpretation, that is, they come out 0 no matter whether their components are 0, 1, or 2. For example, with respect to A2:

p	q	$\sim p \vee (p \vee q)$
0	0	1 0 0
1	0	0 0 0
2	0	2 0 0
0	1	1 0 0
1	1	0 0 1
2	1	2 0 2
0	2	1 0 0
1	2	0 0 2
2	2	2 0 0

A2, A3, and A4 are, we may say, 0 formulas. A1 is not a 0-formula. Being a 0-formula is a property which is passed on by the rules of PM (as the reader can verify), just as the property of being a tautological formula is passed on. Thus, A1 cannot be derived from A2, A3, and A4 using R1 and R2. Note that since A5 is not independent, no nonstandard interpretation of the connectives will possibly provide a property true of A1 through A4, not true of A5, and hereditary with respect to the rules. Note also that to prove either A2, A3, or A4 independent, which they are, an interpretation other than the preceding and other than the standard one is necessary.

EXERCISES 10.5

1. Prove the independence of A2 from A1, A3, and A4.
2. Show that $[(p \supset q) \cdot q] \supset p$ is not a theorem of PM.
3. Derive A5 from PM minus A5.

ANSWERS

1. The independence of A2 from A1, A3, and A4 can be demonstrated by using the following interpretations:

~			∨	0	1	2	3
0	3		0	0	0	0	0
1	2		1	0	3	0	3
2	1		2	0	0	3	3
3	0		3	0	3	3	3

2. Standard interpretation for statement connectives works.

Completeness of PM

Systems can be said to be complete if all the acceptable wffs are theorems of the system. In PM, wffs can be sorted out into three classes: tautologous formulas, contingent formulas, and inconsistent formulas. The formulas we want for PM are only those in the first class. In most nonlogical systems wffs sort themselves out so that for any formula either it or its negation is counted as an acceptable formula. For example, in mathematics, given any wff, either it or its negation is regarded as a truth of mathematics. For such systems to be complete, for every wff P, either P or $\sim P$ is a theorem. Such systems are said to be *negation complete*. Though PM is complete, it is not negation complete, for given any contingent formula, neither it nor its negation is a theorem of PM, since we proved earlier that PM is sound and every theorem is a tautology. However, PM is complete, since all its acceptable wffs are theorems. This is sometimes spoken of as *semantic completeness*. Clearly if a system is negation complete, it is semantically complete, but a system such as PM can be semantically complete and not be negation complete.

The first proof of semantic completeness for sentential logic was given by Emil Post in 1920 for the system PM. A bare outline of a variation of Post's proof follows.

There is an effective method for transforming any formula of PM into a standard form called *conjunctive normal form*, abbreviated CNF. To define a CNF, let a *single formula* be either a sentential variable or a negative of a sentential variable. Let an *elementary disjunction* be a formula of the form

$$P_1 \lor P_2 \lor \ldots \lor P_n$$

where P's are single formulas. An elementary disjunction is a string of disjuncts where the disjuncts are single formulas. We will count every single formula as being in CNF and every elementary disjunction as being in CNF. Thus, the following are all examples of formulas in CNF:

$$p \qquad \sim p \qquad p \lor p \qquad \sim p \lor q \lor r$$

Note that the first two are also elementary disjunctions when $n = 1$. When elementary disjunctions are conjoined together the result will also count as a CNF. Thus any formula with the form:

$$P_1 \cdot P_2 \cdot P_3 \ldots P_n$$

where the P's are elementary disjunctions is in CNF. The standard case of CNF *is* conjunctions of elementary disjunctions. The following are both examples of formulas in CNF:

$$(p \vee {\sim}p) \cdot (r \vee {\sim}r \vee p) \qquad\qquad p \cdot (p \vee r \vee {\sim}p)$$

Any formula in PM can be transformed into a CNF by using the rule of replacement (DR3), definitions, and the following biconditional theorems: DeMorgan's theorems, Double Negation, Association, Commutation, and Distribution. Each of these biconditionals is a listed theorem of PM, and let us assume that each is proved either in the text or as an exercise. Any formula can be transformed into a CNF by following this four-step procedure:

1. Use D1 and D3 to obtain a formula containing only the connectives "$\vee$," "$\cdot$," and "$\sim$."
2. Use DeM and DN to remove all negations outside parentheses.
3. Use DN to remove all double negations.
4. Use distribution theorems as many times as necessary to produce a CNF.

To illustrate, the following formula is transformed into CNF:

$$p \supset (q \supset p)$$
$${\sim}p \vee ({\sim}q \vee p)$$

Ignoring the parentheses, we have an elementary disjunction, thus a CNF. As another illustration:

$$p \supset [q \supset (p \cdot q)]$$
$${\sim}p \vee [{\sim}q \vee (p \cdot q)]$$
$${\sim}p \vee [({\sim}q \vee p) \cdot ({\sim}q \vee q)]$$
$$({\sim}p \vee {\sim}q \vee p) \cdot ({\sim}p \vee {\sim}q \vee q)$$

Theorems for each of the preceding biconditionals are found in PM. Let P be any formula and P' its conjunctive normal form. For any formula P we can obtain

$$P \equiv P$$

as a theorem of PM, since $p \equiv p$ is a theorem of PM. By using the preceding biconditionals plus the rule of replacement, we can obtain as a theorem in PM for any P

$$P \equiv P'$$

These results can be summed up as follows:

I. If P is a wff in PM, then there is a wff in PM, P' in CNF such that $P \equiv P'$ is a theorem of PM.

Formulas in CNF are such that they can be divided like other formulas into three sets: tautologous formulas, contingent formulas, and inconsistent formulas. Every tautological CNF has a distinctive feature. It is that for *each* elementary disjunction there occurs a sentential variable in one place and the negation of that variable in another place. To illustrate, the preceding two formulas which are transformed into CNF are tautologies and their CNF satisfy this characteristic. In the first we have just an elementary disjunction where p and $\sim p$ occur. In the second we have a conjunction of two elementary disjunctions, and in the first elementary disjunction p and $\sim p$ occur, whereas in the second elementary disjunction q and $\sim q$ occur.

By following another simple procedure any tautological CNF can be proven as a theorem in PM, given the following theorems:

a. $p \vee \sim p$
b. $p \supset (p \vee q)$
c. $p \supset [q \supset (p \cdot q)]$

plus Commutation and Association. The procedure is this: First prove each of the elementary disjunctions by using (a) and (b) above. Second combine the elementary disjunctions using (c). Finally use Comm and Assoc as often as necessary to obtain the desired CNF. To illustrate, we prove the tautological CNF of $p \supset [q \supset (p \cdot q)]$:

1. $p \vee \sim p$	a.
2. $(p \vee \sim p) \vee \sim q$	1 b.
3. $\sim p \vee \sim q \vee p$	2 Comm, Assoc (dropping parentheses)
4. $q \vee \sim q$	a.
5. $(q \vee \sim q) \vee \sim p$	4 b.
6. $\sim p \vee \sim q \vee q$	5 Comm, Assoc (dropping parentheses)
7. $(3) \cdot (6)$	3, 6 c.

Theorems (a), (b), and (c) plus Commutation and Association allow us to prove any tautological CNF. Thus:

II. Every tautologous CNF is a theorem of PM.

The proof that PM is semantically complete now easily follows from (I) and (II). If every tautologous wff in CNF is a theorem of PM, and with respect to any wff P and its CNF P', $P \equiv P'$ is a theorem, then it follows that:

Every tautologous wff of PM is a theorem of PM (PM is semantically complete).

EXERCISES 10.6

A. Follow the four step procedure and transform the following formulas into CNF:

1. $p \supset (\sim p \supset q)$
2. $p \equiv (p \lor q)$
3. $(p \supset q) \cdot (\sim q \supset \sim p)$
4. $[(p \supset q) \cdot (q \supset r)] \supset (p \supset r)$
5. $(p \cdot q) \equiv \sim(\sim p \lor \sim q)$

B. For each of the above formulas in CNF, indicate which are tautologies, and derive them as theorems of PM using theorems a, b, c, and Comm and Assoc.

C. How can you prove that the natural deduction system for sentential logic (Chapter 7) is semantically complete?

D. How can the procedures involved in exercises A and B above be used to provide an automatic procedure for proving any theorem in PM?

E. Another set of axioms for sentential logic is Lukasiewicz' 1924 set:

$(p \supset q) \supset [(q \supset r) \supset (p \supset r)]$
$p \supset (\sim p \supset q)$
$(\sim p \supset p) \supset p$

The rules of inference are again *modus ponens* and substitution. The same definitions are supposed. Show that the axiom system is sound, consistent, independent, and complete.

ANSWERS

A. 4. $[(p \supset q) \cdot (q \supset r)] \supset (p \supset r)$
$[(\sim p \lor q) \cdot (\sim q \lor r)] \supset (\sim p \lor r)$
$\sim[(\sim p \lor q) \cdot (\sim q \lor r)] \lor (\sim p \lor r)$
$[\sim(\sim p \lor q) \lor \sim(\sim q \lor r)] \lor (\sim p \lor r)$
$[(p \cdot \sim q) \lor (q \cdot \sim r)] \lor (\sim p \lor r)$
$\{[(p \cdot \sim q) \lor q] \cdot [(p \cdot \sim q) \lor \sim r]\} \lor (\sim p \lor r)$

$$\{[q \lor p) \cdot (q \lor \sim q)] \cdot [(\sim r \lor p) \cdot (\sim r \lor \sim q)]\} \lor (\sim p \lor r)$$
$$(\sim p \lor r \lor q \lor p) \cdot (\sim p \lor r \lor q \lor \sim q) \cdot (\sim p \lor r \lor \sim r \lor p) \cdot$$
$$(\sim p \lor r \lor \sim r \lor \sim q)$$

a tautology.

C. Give a relative proof assuming PM complete by showing that the deductive powers of PM are matched in the natural deduction system. Another way is proof that (I) and (II) also hold for the natural deduction system.

D. Any derivable formula can be transformed into CNF. Its CNF can be obtained as a theorem following B. The procedure of obtaining the CNF is then reversed, thus obtaining the original formula.

E. Adopt proofs used for PM. For simplicity's sake suppose any needed tautology is proved.

THE LOGICAL STRUCTURE
OF SCIENCE

II

Science and Hypotheses

Inductive Logic

An argument is a set of two or more statements and a claim. The claim is that one of the statements, the conclusion, follows from the other statements, the premises. Arguments can be sorted into two very general classes according to the nature of the argument claim. If the claim is that it is impossible for the premises to be true and the conclusion false the argument is deductive. Almost all the examples of arguments in Part 2 are deductive arguments. If the claim of the argument is that the premises, if true, provide evidence for thinking the conclusion is likely true, the argument is an inductive argument. Earlier we discussed four types of inductive arguments. First: inductive generalizations from samples. Here is an example:

All the recessions since World War Two have been moderate.
Therefore the next recession will be moderate.

Second: analogical inductions, for example:

My neighbor's VW diesel Rabbit gets over 45 miles per gallon in the city.
Therefore my diesel Rabbit is likely to get over 45 miles per gallon in the city.

And in the introductory chapter brief mention is made of inductive arguments in which a hypothesis is constructed on the basis of evidence, and of inductive arguments which generalize on the basis of mathematical probability. An example of the former is:

The automobile induces a peculiar state of mind. For example, the man who with a benign smile holds the door for a woman when they are on foot, gives her a blast of the horn when she does not get out of the way quickly enough in the pedestrian crossing. The possession of a ton and a half of steel instills in modern man the same destructive instincts that a club instilled in the caveman. So man's civilized behavior is just veneer.

Here is an example of the latter:

> A distinguished stock analyst says Kodak may not appreciate in the coming year, since it appreciates two years out of five in the long run. Therefore there is 40 per cent chance that the stock will appreciate in the coming year.

Both deductive and inductive arguments can be divided into correct and incorrect arguments. A deductive argument is correct when it is valid. An argument is valid when it is impossible for the premises to be true and the conclusion false. An inductive argument is correct when the premises, if true, justify the inductive claim. The study of *deductive logic* is the study of rules and methods to determine the validity of deductive arguments. Some of these methods are considered in Part 2. The study of *inductive logic* is the study of rules and methods for assigning probabilities to the conclusions of inductive arguments when the premises are assumed to be true. Inductive logic is the attempt to answer this question: How does one determine how likely a conclusion is on the basis of the evidence cited in the premises? It may be that one or more of these types is just a subtype of another. Unfortunately no one has yet produced an adequate formulation of the rules of scientific inductive logic. In fact, inductive logic is in much the same state as deductive logic was before Aristotle. Setting up rules to determine inductive strength is so difficult that some philosophers are convinced it is impossible.

Why is a system of inductive logic so difficult? Some of the difficulties can be seen in trying to construct a system of scientific induction by simply having this one rule:

> Rule I: For an argument of the form
> N per cent of the observed A's have been B's.
>   Therefore the next observed A will be a B.
>   assign the probability of $N/100$ to the conclusion.

The rule may seem adequate on first reading. Suppose we have landed on Mars and are observing the birds. We see hundreds of ducks and find that ninety percent are blue. The probability that the next one we see will be blue is obviously $90/100$; that is, chances are nine out of ten that the next duck will be blue.

But this rule as a system of induction is inadequate.[1] First, consider again some of the examples of inductive arguments in the introductory chapter of this text. Specifically recall the two pairs of arguments in the section on Correct Inductive Arguments in Chapter 1: (1) and (2) and (3) and (4). It is intuitively clear for each pair that the second is stronger than the first and the fourth is stronger than the third. For example, if all of two million remelads have been found to be green, it is far more likely that all remelads are green than if only 10 remelads have been examined and have been found to be green. Yet the rule assigns the same probability to (1) and (2), and the same to (3) and (4).

Second: It is not always possible to infer that the next A that is observed will certainly be a B when only one A has been observed. But consider:

> This logic text is easy.
> Therefore the next logic text that I examine will be easy.

Rule I assigns the probability 1, that is, certainty, to the conclusion and that is obviously incorrect. It *is* possible to correctly infer, with certainty, that the next A you see will be a B, even though you have only seen one A. This is possible when you are certain that the A you see is a sample which is exactly like the remainder of the A's. Rule I treats all cases in the same way, however. Here is one common sort of case in which an inference is made on the basis of (what amounts to) one sample.

For example, when farmers take their wheat to the elevator the buyer has a problem in determining the quality of the whole truckload of wheat. The buyer may have his tester take a portion of grain from the front of the load, a portion from the back, one half way down, and two on each side from the bottom. The tester then dumps all of this into a sack, shakes it, and takes out a handful. The quality of the wheat is determined on the basis of this handful of wheat. The tester, as we can see, makes this inference:

(i)   The handful (A) is of quality x.
Therefore the whole load is of quality x.

This inference has the form of:

(ii)   An A is B.
Therefore all A's are B.

Here again this inference is correct—if the procedure described is followed. What prevents this from being an instance of the hasty generalization

---

[1] For a discussion of the inadequacies of this rule as a system of inductive logic see Chapter Three of Brian Skyrms, *An Introduction to Inductive Logic* (Belmont: Dickenson Publishing Co., Inc., 1966).

fallacy? The tester has taken care to make sure that the handful is representative of the whole. If he had not, if he had just reached in the truck and
taken a handful and inferred the quality of the truckload from the quantity of
the handful, then (i) would, possibly, be incorrect, since it is not an
uncommon practice to "stack" such loads. The single handful may not be
representative of the quality of the load for other reasons. In general,
sampling inferences with the form of (ii) are correct depending on whether A
is representative of all A's—in our example, whether the handful is
representative of the truckload. However, what determines whether A is
representative depends on the particular context or circumstance.

Third, Rule I applies to one kind of inductive argument, namely, generalizations from samples. Rule I leaves us in the dark about the other kinds of
inductive arguments, for example, inductive arguments in which a hypothesis is made on the basis of evidence.

Though no one has yet proposed an inductive logic, nevertheless there are
important elements that any inductive logic will need to consider. Some of
these elements will be discussed in this part of the text. The elements we
have chosen to discuss are these:

(1)   What in science is an inductive argument in which a hypothesis is
made on the basis of evidence?

(2)   What evidence counts as rational grounds for concluding that a
hypothesis in science is satisfactory?

(3)   What factors lead to the abandonment of hypotheses in science?

(4)   What methods do we use to determine rationally that A causes B?
When a conclusion of an inductive argument is that A causes B,
how do we determine the correctness of the argument so as to
avoid the false cause fallacy?

(5)   How do explanations in science differ?

(6)   How do we determine whether an explanation is a scientific
explanation or a psuedoscientific explanation?

(7)   What is the logic of probability? How is the logic of probability
related to inductive conclusions made on the basis of mathematical probability?

In the remainder of this chapter we consider issues (1) and (2). In the next
chapter (3) and (4) are discussed. Topics (5) and (6) are taken up in the next
to the last chapter, and in the last chapter we consider issue (7).

Theoretical Aim of Science

It is not uncommon to distinguish the practical aim of science from the
theoretical aim. The *practical aim* of science is the application of scientific

knowledge. (It is generally assumed that such an application is in the interest of man.) All of us, of course, see the results of this application and feel the impact of this application on our lives. It is easy to make a list of applications of scientific knowledge which affect our lives. For example, all these things are made possible through the application of scientific knowledge: X-ray machines, nuclear power plants, automobiles, television, computers, insecticides, the new drugs and medicines, rockets, and plastics.

This knowledge is attained by men seeking and finding empirically testable explanations for certain observed phenomena. The body of statements which makes up established explanations is what is called *scientific knowledge*. The *theoretical aim* of science is to achieve such explanations. People sometimes speak of the "ideal of science." This generally is used to mean the attainment of systematic explanations of the whole field of experience by displaying what is observed as exemplifying the operation of a single, interrelated system of laws or principles. The theoretical aim of any particular science is the explanation of distinguishable classes of phenomena. The theoretical aim of the sciences collectively is to attain, as far as possible, the ideal of science.

We will now examine four famous episodes from the history of science in order to describe clearly what a scientific explanation, or hypothesis, is, how scientists come upon scientific hypotheses, how hypotheses differ (logically) from one another, and how they are tested and justified. In addition we will examine the roles of induction and deduction in each of the four episodes.

Four Episodes from the History of Science

Torricelli's Hypothesis

For ages people have known (P_1) that to drain a liquid from a barrel there needs to be an opening near the bottom and one at the top of the barrel, and (P_2) that if one sucks up liquid in a tube and closes the top with his finger, the liquid will not run out.[2] In the Middle Ages these phenomena, P_1 and P_2, were explained in terms of the notion of a "full universe." This hypothesis involved the principle that "nature abhors a vacuum." The first phenomenon (P_1) is explained by the hypothesis in this way: if water flows out of the bottom without there being a hole for air to get in, a vacuum will result. But by the principle ("nature abhors a vacuum") this is impossible. Thus, one needs an opening to let in the air. We can easily see how the "full universe" hypothesis also explains the second phenomenon.

---

[2] It will be convenient for us to refer to statments describing phenomena such as the two cited above by the letter *P*.

In Galileo's *Dialogues Concerning Two New Sciences*, published in 1638, he notes that (P_3) a suction pump (like those in roadside parks) will not raise water more than a certain height. Galileo's student, Torricelli, was struck by this and asked "Why?" Torricelli hypothesized that the earth is surrounded by a "sea of air." He argued that if the earth were surrounded by a "sea of air" and if air had weight, then there would be an air pressure on all objects submerged in this sea of air, exactly as there is water pressure below the surface of the ocean. If this hypothesis is true, then P_3 is explained—the pump creates a vacuum in the tube so that there is no atmospheric pressure in the top of the tube to oppose that pressing down on the water outside the tube. The water rises to a certain height because the pressure forces it to do so. We can also see how Torricelli's hypothesis explains P_1 and P_2.

Torricelli found that the limit to which water can be made to rise is 34 feet. If this hypothesis is correct, then it can be deduced (P_4) that mercury, which is fourteen times heavier than water, can be made to rise in a tube (or held up in a tube) only about 30 inches (see outline of deduction at end of this chapter). Around 1643 Torricelli performed an experiment which verified this prediction. He took a glass tube over 30 inches long which was closed at one end, filled it with mercury, placed his finger over the opening, inverted the tube, submerged the bottom (open) end in a dish of mercury, and removed his finger. The mercury dropped until the column was about 30 inches high. A vacuum was created thereby in the top of the tube. This verification of a deduction from his hypothesis also went against the "full universe" hypothesis, since the empty space in the tube was a vacuum "created by nature."

Other statements were also deduced from the hypothesis. For example, if we live in a sea of air which exerts a pressure, then (P_5) the pressure should diminish as we rise to the "surface." If the pressure so diminishes, then the height of a mercury column should decrease as the column is carried up a mountain. Blaise Pascal in 1648 had his brother-in-law carry an inverted tube of mercury up the Puy-de-Dome in southern France. The experiment was repeated five different times, with the same result—the column went down as the brother-in-law climbed. Also an observer at the bottom of the mountain watched a tube during the experiment and found that the level remained unchanged. Pascal had thus verified P_5.

Notice these features about the preceding episode. For years people had known P_1 and P_2. The explanation for P_1 and P_2 which was thought to be satisfactory was the "full universe" hypothesis. Generally, a *hypothesis* in science is an explanation or *proposed* explanation for phenomena. Torricelli was *struck* by P_3 because the "full universe" hypothesis did not adequately explain P_3. This is often what leads to the formulation of a hypothesis—some phenomenon is noted because it does not fit in with the commonly held explanations of things; the new hypothesis is formulated to explain this and the old relevant phenomena. Torricelli asked what would explain P_1, P_2, and P_3. His "sea of air" hypothesis was his answer to this question. He then proceeded to test his hypothesis. The way he and others went about this was to deduce other P's from the hypothesis and see if they were true. For example, as was noted, P_4 and P_5 were deduced and tested. In the course of this testing it was noticed that the old "full universe" hypothesis did not provide an adequate explanation for these P's.

Also this feature should be noticed: if one were to ask, "What justification is there for Torricelli's hypothesis?" or, "Why is Torricelli's hypothesis true?" the justification would take (at least up to Pascal's time) more or less this form:

> Torricelli's hypothesis explains the known P's connected with the matter to be explained.
> If Torricelli's hypothesis is true, then certain other P's are true.
> By experiment it is found that these P's are true.
> The competing hypotheses cannot adequately explain these P's.
> Torricelli's hypothesis does not conflict with what is known to be true.
> Therefore Torricelli's hypothesis is true.[3]

This argument is an *inductive* argument. The nature of such arguments and how they differ from other inductive arguments will be considered in the last section of this chapter.

William Harvey's Hypothesis

In 1628 William Harvey announced his hypothesis that the blood in the human body circulates from the heart, which is a pump, through the arteries to the veins and back to the heart through the veins.

What led Harvey to this hypothesis? To answer this, we must first understand the theory about the blood system which Harvey's hypothesis replaced. For it was, as we will now see, the inability of the existing theory to explain certain discovered facts (P's) about the blood system which led to Harvey's hypothesis.

Aristotle taught that blood was composed in the liver from the digested foods. From there it was carried to the heart by the great vein, the vena cava, then pumped back through the vena cava and its branches to the members of the body. The Alexandrian physicians Erasistratus and Herophilus added to this theory the assumption that, while the veins carried blood, the arteries

[3] The use of "true" here should not be taken as an indication that we have taken sides in the controversy over the complex issue in the philosophy of science: Do the theoretical terms employed in science refer to entities in the way in which terms like "sticks" and "stones" do? Theories *are* commonly said to be true, so we use the word "true" here without intending that this should be taken as entailing the view that the answer to the question is affirmative. For a good general description of these views and issues, see Nagel's *The Structure of Science*, Chap. 6, and for detailed treatments see the works cited in the footnotes of this chapter.

carried a subtle kind of air, or vital spirit. The Greek physician Galen
discovered, however, that the arteries were not mere airpipes, but that they
contained blood. The accepted theory in the sixteenth century, often called
the Galenic view, was as follows (see figure).

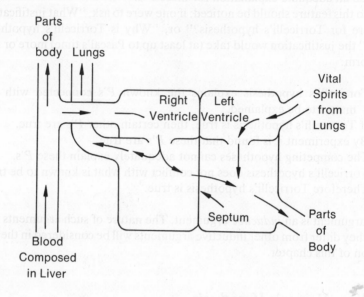

First, the blood is composed from the digested food in the liver; some of
this blood goes through the veins to nourish parts of the body. Most of it
passes up the great vein of the body, the vena cava, to the right ventricle of
the heart. Some of this blood is squeezed up what is now recognized as the
pulmonary artery (though it was thought at that time to be a vein) into the
lungs for its nourishment and then it goes to other parts of the body. The rest
of the blood passes through the septum (the thick wall dividing the heart into
two chambers or ventricles). There the blood is mixed with "vital spirits"
from the air which comes down from the pulmonary vein (which was thought
to be an artery). This blood then goes through the aorta artery to the parts of
the body. Second, there is no connection between the veins and the arteries.
Blood gets to the arteries from the veins by passing through the septum.
Third, the blood neither lies stagnant nor does it circulate through either the
veins or the arteries. The blood is like a stream with thousands of places
where it empties. Those holding the Galenic view even spoke of the "ebb
and flow" of the blood.

In the sixteenth century three discoveries were made which Harvey saw
were incompatible with the Galenic theory. First, in 1543, Vesalius, a
professor of surgery in Padua, probed the septum but was unable to find a
passage. But having faith in the Galenic theory his reaction to this was,

"none of these pits penetrate (at least according to sense) from the right ventricle to the left; therefore indeed I was compelled to marvel at the activity of the Creator of things, in that the blood should sweat from the right ventricle to the left through passages escaping the sight."[4]

Second, in 1553 Servetus found the blood passes from the pulmonary artery to the pulmonary vein *through* the lungs. And third, Harvey's teacher, Fabricius, noticed the system of *valves* in the veins which give free passage of blood *toward* the heart, but obstruct it from flowing *away* from the heart.

Harvey saw that the hypothesis which would explain all these phenomena would be: the blood passes through the veins to the right ventricle of the heart, is pumped into the lungs through an artery, passes from the lungs into a vein, flows back into the heart, out through an artery to the parts of the body, and back again through the veins—in short, the blood circulates through the veins and arteries.

This hypothesis explains all the known facts (P's), whereas the Galenic theory and others considered do not. Furthermore, this hypothesis explains in a more satisfactory way the known fact that the heart pumps into the arteries, in the space of half an hour, more that the whole of the blood in the body. According to the Galenic hypothesis, all this blood was constantly being composed in the liver from the juices of the food. How could this be? According to Harvey's hypothesis, the blood being pumped out is the same blood which comes in; this explains where the great quantities of blood come from. Thus the fact that Harvey's hypothesis explained the known P's, whereas the Galenic theory and other considered hypotheses did not, provided good grounds for Harvey's hypothesis.

Harvey's explanation can be directly tested; that is, we can observe the blood, veins, and so forth to see whether his hypothesis is true. But he could not directly test it. For one thing, Harvey did not have microscopes with which to see the blood passing from the arteries, through the capillaries, to the veins. So he indirectly tested his hypothesis. For example, he studied the blood systems of living animals and found they all corresponded to his hypothesis about the blood systems of human beings; he found support for his hypothesis in the facts observed in diseases—for example, organisms can quickly spread through the entire body once they enter the blood stream; and examining the veins of the arm, he showed that the limb is swollen with blood when the veins are compressed, and emptied of blood when the arteries are compressed. These are P's which we would expect if Harvey's hypothesis were true. The discovery of these P's provided strong additional grounds in support of Harvey's hypothesis—strong enough to make Harvey's the accepted theory.

The same features noted in connection with the Torricelli episode are found here. There is, however, one difference which for our considerations is

---

[4] A. R. Hall, *The Scientific Revolution* (Boston: Beacon, 1957), p. 139.

most important. Both Harvey's and Torricelli's hypotheses were indirectly tested, whereas Harvey's hypothesis could have been and was eventually directly tested. Torricelli's hypothesis, on the other hand, cannot be directly tested. What is meant here by "*indirectly testing* a hypothesis" is "deducing *P*'s from the hypothesis and then checking to see if the *P*'s are true." To *test* a hypothesis *directly* is to observe the things referred to by the terms in the hypothesis and see if in fact they are related as they are related in the hypothesis.[5] As was indicated, if Harvey had had the equipment, he could have directly tested his hypothesis. He could have, in a word, seen the blood circulating in the way he thought it did. But one cannot see the sea of air or feel the pressure of a normal atmosphere. The testing of such a hypothesis must be indirect. The difference between direct and indirect testing and the difference between the two kinds of hypotheses will become clearer as we examine the last two episodes.

Newton's Corpuscular Theory of Light

Since 300 B.C. it has been known that light travels in a straight line and that light refracts. If a beam of light is passed through an opening toward a dark background, this phenomenon will occur:

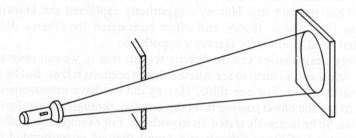

If the light did not travel in a straight line, the white area on the dark background would either be larger or smaller. Light, when it passes through a glass plate or when it passes from the air through water, refracts, as

---

[5] Some philosophers take the view that knowledge about things such as hearts, stones, and tables is to be analyzed in terms of knowledge about sensations, or sense data. In this view hearts, tables, and measuring instruments are inferred, nonobservable entities in the same way that elementary particles and other theoretical entities are inferred, nonobservable entities. Now, though this choice may be unfortunate, we have chosen not to concern ourselves with these questions in this elementary treatment of the nature of scientific statements and how they are related to observed facts. So "observable facts" is here understood to refer to all those things which we ordinarily take to be observable. (Statements designated by the letter *P* are assumed to contain nonlogical terms which refer only to observable things—objects, events, and so on.)

illustrated here:

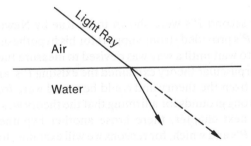

The dotted line shows the path the light would take if it were not refracted.

In 1666 Newton reproduced another familiar phenomenon connected with light. Here is Newton's own description of what he did:

> In the year 1666 (at which time I applied myself to the grinding of optick glasses of other figures than spherical) I procured me a triangular glass prism, to try therewith the celebrated phenomena of colours. And in order thereto, having darkened my chamber, and made a small hole in my window-shuts, to let in a convenient quantity of the sun's light, I placed my prism at its entrance, that it might thereby be refracted to the opposite wall. It was at first a very pleasing divertisement, to view the vivid and intense colours produced thereby.

Newton's explanation of this phenomenon was that white light is a mixture of corpuscles of different kinds. The prism separates these corpuscles. The separate corpuscles belong to different colors. The glass of the prism exerts a force which causes the separation of the corpuscles of light.

The hypothesis that light is made up of corpuscles which behave according to the laws of motion governing all bodies is called the corpuscular theory of light. As we have seen, it explains the prism phenomenon. In addition, it explains why light travels in a straight line and why it refracts. The light source emits particles of light which travel along straight lines as a bullet would do. Light refracts when it hits a substance like water because the water exerts a force which changes the direction of the particles. This hypothesis also explains why light reflects off, say, a mirror. The corpuscles bounce as an elastic ball thrown against a wall bounces.

Additional *P*'s follow from the corpuscular theory. (Just *how* they follow will not be explained in detail.) For example, if all the beams of the separate colors resulting from the light's passage through the prism were passed through a second prism, it follows from the theory that white light would again appear. Also if a beam of the separated, homogeneous light, were passed through a prism, the theory says that the same color would result since the corpuscles cannot be split any further. Last, from the theory it follows that light, when it reaches water after traveling in the air, will increase its speed, since the water exerts a force which changes its direction.

The first and second P's were shown to be true by Newton. This direct testing of these P's provided strong support for his hypothesis. The testing of the third P had to wait until a way was devised to measure the speed of light. But since the corpuscular theory explained the existing P's, and since the P's which followed from the theory and could be tested were found to be true, this provided strong grounds for affirming that the theory was true. But as we will see in the next chapter, there arose another hypothesis which also explained these P's and which, for reasons we will examine, took the place of the corpuscular theory.

Rumford's Hypothesis That Heat Is Motion

When two bodies are brought into contact, one of a higher temperature than the other, eventually they will reach the same temperature. The picture of heat "flowing" from one body to another as water flows from a high level to a lower level is suggested here. But one finds, for example, that a piece of iron weighs no more when it is red hot than when it is ice cold. If heat is conceived of as a substance which "flows," then it is weightless. For a time it was thought that heat was such a substance.

This weightless heat-substance was called *caloric*. The caloric theory of heat was the theory which assumed the existence of such a substance. This hypothesis explains a wide range of P's. For example, it explains why two bodies of different temperatures reach the same temperature when brought into contact with each other. It explains why substances expand when heated, and a number of other phenomena.

But there are some commonly known phenomena that it is difficult for the caloric theory to explain. Heat can be created by friction, say, by rubbing two sticks together. But we think that a substance is something which can be neither created nor destroyed (conservation of matter). Can the caloric theory explain how heat can be created by friction? Defenders of the theory thought it could without denying the principle of the conservation of matter. The sticks rubbing against each other changes some property of the wood. This change in the wood produces a change in specific heat or heat capacity of the wood—it goes *down*.[6] Thus the unchanged quantity of heat produces a higher temperature.

It happens that there are simple methods for determining the specific heat of a substance. It is easy to take two identical pieces of wood and induce heat

---

[6] A pound of water, for example, has a greater heat capacity or specific heat than a pound of mercury, since less heat is needed to raise the temperature of mercury one degree than to raise the temperature of the water one degree.

in the one by friction and in the other by contact with a radiator. If the two pieces of wood then have the same specific heat, it looks as if either the assumption that heat is a substance or the assumption that substance cannot be created would have to be given up.

Such an experiment was performed more than one hundred and fifty years ago by Count Rumford. Here is his own account:

It frequently happens, that in the ordinary affairs and occupations of life, opportunities present themselves of contemplating some of the most curious operations of Nature; and very interesting philosophical experiments might often be made, almost without trouble or expense, by means of machinery contrived for the mere mechanical purposes of the arts and manufactures.

I have frequently had occasion to make this observation; and am persuaded, that a habit of keeping the eyes open to every thing that is going on in the ordinary course of the business of life has oftener led, as it were by accident, or in the playful excursions of the imagination, put into action by contemplating the most common appearances, to useful doubts, and sensible schemes for investigation and improvement, than all the more intense meditations of philosophers in the hours expressly set apart for study.

Being engaged, lately, in superintending the boring of cannon, in the workshops of the military arsenal at Munich, I was struck with the still more intense Heat (much greater than that of boiling water, as I found in my experiment) of the metallic chips separated from it by the borer....

From whence comes the Heat actually produced in the mechanical operation above mentioned?

Is it furnished by the metallic chips which are separated by the borer from the solid mass of metal?

If this were the case, then, according to the modern doctrines of latent Heat, and of caloric, the capacity ought not only to be changed, but the change undergone by them should be sufficiently great to account for all the Heat produced.

But no such change had taken place; for I found, upon taking equal quantities, by weight, of these chips, and of thin slips of the same block of metal separated by means of a fine saw and putting them, at the same temperature (that of boiling water), into equal quantities of cold water (that is to say, at the temperature of $59\frac{1}{2}°F$.) the portion of water into which the chips were put was not, to all appearance, heated either less or more than the other portion, in which the slips of metal were put.

And, in reasoning on this subject, we must not forget to consider that most remarkable circumstance, that the source of the Heat generated by friction, in these Experiments, appeared evidently to be *inexhaustible*.

It is hardly necessary to add, that anything which any *insulated* body, or system of bodies, can continue to furnish *without limitation* cannot possibly be a *material substance*; and it appears to me to be extremely difficult, if not quite impossible, to form any distinct idea of anything, capable of being excited and communicated, in the manner the Heat was excited and communicated in these Experiments, except it be MOTION.

Rumford was, as he says, struck by the amount of heat produced in the boring of the cannon. Here was a phenomenon which he noticed because of its apparent conflict with the caloric theory.[7] Rumford then noticed the explanation the caloric theory gives for this phenomenon. That is, he noticed that according to the caloric theory it must be the case that the heat capacity changes. He then performed the simple experiment with the chips which, as we see, falsified the statement which follows from the caloric theory.

In the final paragraphs of Rumford's account we find his hypothesis. What would explain the known phenomena connected with heat? Some of these are, for example: two bodies of different temperatures acquire the same temperature when in contact, most substances expand when heated, heat is produced by friction, and the amount of heat generated by friction is, as Rumford says, apparently "inexhaustible." (This fourth phenomenon, by the way, would be difficult to explain by the caloric theory.) Rumford's answer was that one should conceive of heat as motion (kinetic theory of heat)[8] rather than as a substance.

Using this and the other episodes as examples we will now elaborate the distinction between the two kinds of hypotheses encountered (those which can only be indirectly tested and those which can be directly and indirectly tested) and the nature of the justification for affirming a hypothesis (inductive arguments).

Empirical and Theoretical Hypotheses

Both Newton's and Rumford's hypotheses are like Torricelli's in that they can only be indirectly tested. Hypotheses like these are often called

---

[7] Often important basic observations take place because of the observer's knowledge of some theory. Charles Darwin wrote, "How odd it is that anyone should not see that all observation must be for or against some view, if it is to be of any service." Karl Popper writes, "the belief that we can start with pure observations alone, without anything in the nature of a theory, is absurd; as may be illustrated by the story of the man who dedicated his life to natural science, wrote down everything he could observe, and bequeathed his priceless collection of observations to the Royal Society to be used as inductive evidence. This story should show us that though beetles may profitably be collected, observations may not.

"Twenty-five years ago I tried to bring home the same point to a group of physics students in Vienna by beginning a lecture with the following instructions: Take pencil and paper; carefully observe, and write down what you have observed!" They asked, of course, *what* I wanted them to observe. Clearly the instruction, 'Observe!' is absurd. (It is not even idiomatic, unless the object of the transitive verb can be taken as understood.) Observation is always selective. It needs a chosen object, a definite task, an interest, a point of view, a problem." [Karl R. Popper, *Conjectures and Refutations* (London: Routledge and Kegan Paul, 1963), p. 46. © Karl R. Popper 1963. Used by permission of Routledge and Kegan Paul Ltd. and K. R. Popper.]

[8] The kinetic theory of heat assumes that objects are made up of an enormous number of particles or *molecules* moving in different directions, colliding with each other, and so forth. There is an average speed of the molecules of any given substance. Heat is the motion of the molecules. The heat of an object thus increases as the average speed of the molecules increases.

theoretical hypotheses, whereas hypotheses like Harvey's that can be tested directly are called *empirical hypotheses* (or experimental hypotheses). These terms are intended to emphasize three related differences:

First, empirical hypotheses state that certain relationships exist between observable things or features of things.[9] Theoretical hypotheses state that certain relationships exist between unobservable things or features of things. For example, Harvey's hypothesis involves observable things and processes: the blood in the veins, the flow of the blood towards the heart, and so forth. Newton's hypothesis involves light corpuscles, whereas Rumford's involves molecules. Both light corpuscles and molecules are unobservable. They are commonly called *theoretical entities*. *Second*, empirical hypotheses can be directly tested, whereas theoretical hypotheses can only be indirectly tested. *Third*, empirical hypotheses can be affirmed (as inductive generalizations) on the basis of statements which refer to the observable things or features of things to which the terms in the generalization refer, whereas theoretical hypotheses are only affirmed on the basis of different and varied statements.

This third difference is explained and illustrated by comparing the justification one might give for Harvey's empirical hypothesis with the justification one might give for Torricelli's, Newton's and Rumford's hypotheses. If one were to set out to determine whether Harvey's hypothesis was true he would examine several human beings. The form of the justification would thus be (ignoring present-day knowledge):

> Individual 1 has blood which circulates.
> Individual 2 has blood which circulates.
>   ⋮
> Individual *n* has blood which circulates.
> Therefore, in humans, blood circulates.

(In this case, perhaps only one premise would be necessary—see the next section.) In contrast, the justification of Torricelli's and Rumford's hypotheses, at one time in the history of science, took more or less the following form (for Newton's justification, premise 4 was missing):

> 1. The hypothesis explains the relevant phenomena.
> 2. If the hypothesis is true, then certain phenomena (will) occur.
> 3. By experiment it is found that these phenomena do occur.

---

[9] To make this clearer, we would say that observable criteria can be given for each of the nonlogical terms—for example, "flood," "pendulum," "tornado"—of an empirical hypothesis, while this cannot be done for the nonlogical terms—for example, "sea of air," "atom," "magnetic field," "gene"—of theoretical hypotheses. (Characteristics which when present in something constitute a justification for calling that thing *X*, are criteria for the word *X*. See Chapter 3). It should be noted that, in general, the relations between theoretical and empirical hypotheses are very complex, and our simplified presentation of the relations between them is not wholly accurate on that account. See P. K. Feyerabend's "Explanation, Reduction, and Empiricism," *Minnesota Studies in the Philosophy of Science*, Volume III.

4. The competing hypotheses cannot adequately explain these phenomena.
5. The hypothesis is compatible with existing knowledge.
   Therefore the hypothesis is true.

Depending on the time (in the history of science), and the hypothesis, and the phenomena to be explained, there will be found certain variations among the premises which constitute good grounds for affirming a theoretical hypothesis. For example, sometimes the hypothesis itself can be deduced from (or explained by) an established theoretical hypothesis. If so, this fact would provide an additional premise in the justification of the hypothesis. (The form of justification for hypotheses introduced to explain established hypotheses also takes a somewhat different form.) When (1) through (5) are true of a hypothesis, the hypothesis is sometimes said to be, using Karl Popper's term, *corroborated*. Ordinarily, when a hypothesis is corroborated it is spoken of as "established." Corroborating a hypothesis differs from indirectly testing a hypothesis since indirect testing is only what is involved in premises 2 and 3. Also, if a hypothesis cannot be directly tested, it is desirable, if not necesssary, that it be corroborated. However, if it can be directly tested, then corroboration is superfluous.

Though the words "hypothesis," "theory," and "law" are used in a number of different ways in science, very often the distinctions can be understood in this way: A general statement or collection of statements when first introduced to explain relevant phenomena is called a *hypothesis*. When the statement or collection is made up of empirical statements which are verified by testing, they are called laws (*empirical laws*). When the statement or collection is made up of theoretical statements which have been corroborated, the collection is called a *theory*. And when the statement or collection achieves wide corroboration, these statements are called laws (*theoretical laws*). Examples of empirical laws are the following:

Lead melts at 327°C.
Orbiting objects follow elliptical paths.
The angle of reflection of a light ray is equal to the angle of incidence.
Reduced taxes lead to increased business investments.
When water in an open container is heated it evaporates.
The velocity of sound is greater in less dense gases than in more dense ones.
Children of blue-eyed parents are blue-eyed.

These laws are clear instances of empirical laws, and even though it is not possible to state (nonarbitrarily) what is observable and what is not, one can give obvious instances of theories which involve references to nonobservable objects, properties, and phenomena. Thus the law explaining the sun's radiation as the result of nuclear fission and laws about the behavior of electrons and other elementary particles—in fact the whole set of laws pertaining to atomic phenomena—are theoretical laws. Also laws pertaining to the role of the DNA molecule in heredity and the growth of an organism, laws (if the statements are acceptable as laws) pertaining to the ego–id conflict, and laws about the shape and action of fields of force are strictly theoretical laws.

To some extent all theories are tentative, and to stress this in the following chapters, we will sometimes refer to the statements of a theory as *assumptions*. Some theories, such as those of the atom and of the gene, are continually undergoing revision, while other theories, such as those of Torricelli and Rumford, are relatively secure from such modification (except as revisions of atomic theory, for example, make it necessary to modify Rumford's original idea). Psychoanalytic theory is an example of a theory which postulates theoretical entities—the id, ego, superego—and which is extremely controversial, especially in the details of the theory; it thus will in all probability be revised and modified to a great extent as time goes on.

Induction and Deduction

Two types of inductive arguments occur in these episodes. The first type is generalization from samples. Pascal, for example, had his brother-in-law carry the barometer up the mountain several times before concluding that the height of the mercury decreases as the altitude increases. Part of Pascal's justification for the general statement—barometers fall when their altitude increases—thus was

1. The first time the barometer was taken up the mountain (that is, its altitude increased) it fell.
   Each time the barometer was taken up the mountain (that is, its altitude increased) it fell.
   Therefore barometers fall when their altitude increases.

Often one test is sufficient to warrant such a conclusion. For example, the testing of the P that homogeneous light stays the same when passed through a prism did *not* involve this kind of argument:

2. The first homogeneous light passed through the first prism remained the same.
   The second homogeneous light passed through the second prism remained the same.
   The nth homogeneous light passsed through the nth prism remained the same.
   Therefore homogeneous light when passed through a prism remains the same.

The testing of this generalization took just one carefully conducted experiment. Newton took great care to be sure that he was experimenting with an accurate, pure prism and he realized that the conditions under which he experimented were such that no accidental factors could influence the results. Thus he was justified in making the generalization from just one experiment.

Arguments such as Pascal's have this form (often called *induction by enumeration*):

A_1 is B.

A_2 is B.

$$\vdots$$

A_n is B.
Therefore all A's are B.

Empirical hypotheses can be confirmed as inductive generalizations from observable states of affairs.

A second type of inductive argument occurs in these episodes. It is an inductive argument in which a hypothesis is affirmed on the basis of evidence. In these episodes we have encountered arguments of this form:

The hypothesis explains the relevant phenomena.
If the hypothesis is true, then certain P's are true.
By experiment it is found that these P's are true.
The competing hypotheses cannot adequately explain these P's.
The hypothesis is compatible with existing knowledge.
Therefore the hypothesis is true.

Such arguments are examples of inductive arguments in which a hypothesis is affirmed on the basis of evidence.

Some have thought that hypotheses in science are arrived at solely through inductive inferences of the first kind. This view is sometimes called *inductivism* (Karl Popper's term). Inductivism can be understood as either the view that scientific hypotheses are *discovered* by, for example, inductive enumeration or the view that this is true and, in addition, scientific hypotheses are *justified* by, for example, inductive enumeration. Supposing the four episodes examined are representative of the context of discovery and justification of scientific hypotheses, it can be concluded that inductivism is, on the whole, mistaken. For, considering the context of discovery, the hypotheses were not discovered by inductive enumeration. That is, it was not the case, for example, that A's were observed followed by B's and this occasioned the formulation of a hypothesis (A's are B). For, first, three of the hypotheses contain terms which refer to unobservables. And, second, and more importantly, the hypotheses were arrived at by answering the question: Why do such-and-such phenomena occur? As it is sometimes put, hypotheses are "the free creation of the mind" (Einstein's favorite characterization). However, there are certain controls on this creation—not just *any* hypothesis reasonably explains a given set of related phenomena. What controls such "creations" is such things as one's general knowledge and knowledge of the particular subject matter. Turning to the context of justification, it has been argued that though empirical hypotheses are or can be justified by, for example, induction by enumeration, theoretical hypotheses cannot. Justification of theoretical hypotheses involve the complex inductive argument which we here are calling corroboration.

Another mistaken belief that some have held is that inductive inferences are the only kinds employed in science. But deduction is also employed in all four episodes. In each case certain P's were deduced from the hypotheses and then tested.

For example, in relating Torricelli's adventure we spoke of a deduction that he made. In outline, it may have been something like this:

Hypothesis: (a) The sea of air exerts a constant pressure in all directions at a given altitude.

Data: (b) The pressure exerted downward by air pressure will sustain 34 feet of water in a tube which is open at one end and closed at the other, filled with water, inverted, and set in a container of water. This is equivalent to the statement that a suction pump will only draw water 34 feet. [(b) means that the pressure exerted downward by the water in the tube, that is the weight, is matched by the air pressure, preventing the rise of the water level of the container into which the tube empties.]

(c) Since mercury is fourteen times as heavy as water, a calculation will show that the same air pressure will sustain a thirty-inch column of mercury in a tube.

Conclusion: (d) Therefore only a thirty-inch column of mercury will be sustained.

This outline bears little resemblance to the formal deductions of Part II. Nevertheless, the similarities exist and the form of Torricelli's inference is a deduction. The hypothesis and the data form premises and, given numerous definitions and conventions, the deduction could be formalized in such a way that the rules of inference of Part II (plus others not discussed) and the transformations of mathematics would yield the conclusion.

We may briefly describe here four main areas in which deduction plays a role in science.

First, deductive arguments are often given in response to requests to explain some phenomenon or law. These can only be given with established laws as premises, or as some of the premises. An example is the explanation of why, in terms of Torricelli's law, about 30 inches of mercury is sustained in the present-day barometer.

Second, deductive arguments are utilized in checking the consistency of theories and their compatibility with other theories. A theory is forthwith rejected if it is self-contradictory, and it is ordinarily regarded with suspicion if there is a logical incompatibility between it and another established theory. Later we will discuss examples illustrating this.

Third, deductions, as we have already seen, are utilized in deriving testable consequences (P's) from theories or hypotheses. The techniques of psychoanalysis, for example, are based on consequences of Freud's theories and provide some verification of them. The supposition that light travels faster in water than it does in air is a consequence of Newton's theory of light. The consequences of a theory can be regarded as predictions. Thus, by deduction, Newton was able to predict that light would travel faster in water than it does in air, and Torriccelli was able to predict that air pressure will sustain only thirty inches of mercury.

Fourth, deductions also figure—in complex ways—in the *applications* of science; in plotting the trajectory of an orbital flight; in the development of new vaccines, new varieties of wheat, new advertising techniques; in the invention of labor-saving devices and countless other things. These, however, are in the province of the applied sciences: engineering, agronomy, preventive medicine, horticulture, and so on.

EXERCISES 11.1

Consider each of the following passages in terms of these questions: What phenomena (P's) are to be explained? What hypotheses are employed to explain them? Are the hypotheses empirical or theoretical? Are there any competing hypotheses? What verification or corroboration is to be found or could be found for the hypotheses?

1. In a series of postmortem examinations of tubercular rats, Johannes Fibiger, a pathologist of the University of Copenhagen, found three that suffered from stomach cancers. This was strange, since rats rarely suffer from tumors of the stomach. Fibiger made a visit to the dealer who had been supplying him with these rats, and on questioning found that those sent to his laboratory had all come from a sugar refinery. Was there anything peculiar about this refinery which could account for the unusually large percentage of stomach-cancerous mice from this spot? He investigated the place and found nothing unusual except a high infestation with cockroaches, which formed a fairly large part of the diet of its rats. Could he find some connection between roaches, rats, and cancer? Cancer as a disease of filth had been spoken about for years, and

vermin were said to be responsible for the so-called "cancer houses," private homes from which emerged many a human cancer victim of the same family.

Fibiger planned a controlled experiment. He collected thousands of the refinery roaches and fed them to rats from another breeding establishment. The rats enjoyed this strange treatment, and for three years—that was the normal life span of his rodents—Fibiger remained sceptical. Then they died, and one by one he opened them up. To his astonishment, he found many stomach cancers. Fibiger made a careful microscopic study of the growths. He discovered in every case they had formed around a parasitic worm, the same worm to which the roach had been host before it was fed to the rat. The larva of the worm coiled up in the muscles of the rat, later developing into an adult worm in the animal's stomach. Around this the tumerous growth had appeared. Fibiger had actually for the first time produced artificial cancer in a laboratory animal. (BERNARD JAFFE, *Outposts of Science*)

2. On the 7th of January 1610, at one o'clock in the morning, when he directed his telescope to Jupiter, he observed three stars near the body of the planet, two being to the east and one to the west of him. They were all in a straight line, and parallel to the ecliptic, and they appeared brighter than other stars of the same magnitude. Believing them to be fixed stars, he paid no great attention to their distances from Jupiter and from one another. On the 8th of January, however, when, from some cause or other, he had been led to observe all the stars again, he found a very different arrangement of them: all the three were on the west side of Jupiter, *nerarer one another than before*, and almost at equal distances. Although he had not turned his attention to the extraordinary fact of the mutual approach of the stars, yet he began to consider how Jupiter could be found to the east of the three stars, when but the day before he had been to the west of two of them. The only explanation which he could give of this fact was, that the motion of Jupiter was *direct*, contrary to astronomical calculations, and that he had got before these two stars by his own motion.

In this dilemma between the testimony of his senses and the results of calculation, he waited for the following night with the utmost anxiety; but his hopes were disappointed, for the heavens were wholly veiled in clouds. On the 10th, two only of the stars appeared, and both on the east of the planet. As it was obviously impossible that Jupiter could have advanced from west to east on the 8th of January, and from east to west on the 10th, Galileo was forced to conclude that the phenomenon which he had observed arose from the motion of the stars, and he set himself to observe diligently their change of place. On the 11th, there were still only two stars, and both to the east of Jupiter; but the more eastern star was now *twice as large as the other one*, though on the preceding night they had been perfectly equal. This fact threw a new light upon Galileo's difficulties, and he immediately drew the conclusion, which he considered to be indubitable, '*that there were in the heaven three stars which revolved round Jupiter, in the same manner as Venus and Mercury revolved round the sun.*' On the 12th of January, he again observed them in new positions, and of different magnitudes; and, on the 13th, he discovered a fourth star, which completed the *four* secondary planets with which Jupiter is surrounded.

(SIR DAVID BREWSTER, *The Martyrs of Science*)

3. It was thought at the time of Francesco Redi that there was "spontaneous generation." Supposed evidence for this was the appearance of worms on meat after a few days. Redi observed that not only worms appear but also small objects (he called them "eggs" though they are pupae) and many flies appear. Redi wrote: "Having considered these things, I began to believe that all worms found in meat were derived from the dropping of flies and not from the putrefaction of the meat." He then tested his hypothesis by eliminating the flies. First he sealed meat in a glass, and then he covered the galss with "fine Naples veil" which would not allow flies to enter. Even after many days no worms were seen, though in an open glass the meat had become wormy.

(Adapted from JAMES B. CONANT, *Science and Common Sense*)[10]

4. Pasteur, during his work on lactic acid fermentation, wrote:

"One knew that ferments originated from the contact of albuminous substances with oxygen gas. One of two things must be true, I said to myself; either ferments are organized entities and they are produced by oxygen alone, considered merely as oxygen, in contact with albuminous materials, in which case they are spontaneously generated; or if they are not of spontaneous origin, it is not oxygen alone as such that intervenes in their production, but the gas acts as a stimulant to a germ carried with it or existing in the nitrogenous or fermentable materials."

Pasteur then passed air through a red-hot tube and into a sterilized flask containing fermentable material. The material did not ferment. On the other hand, when ordinary air was put into the flask the material fermented.

But one who held that fermentation is produced by oxygen alone and not from germs in the air could also have accounted for the results of these experiments.

Pasteur then placed his solution in flasks, sealed the flasks, and heated them. When he broke the tips of the flasks in the country, eight out of seventy-three showed signs of fermentation. When he broke twenty of them on a glacier (the Mer de Glace), only one showed such signs, while when he broke others in his room in the inn at Chamonix, ten out of

[10] James B. Conant, *Science and Common Sense* (New Haven: Yale University Press, 1961).

thirteen showed signs of fermentation. Air could thus enter many flasks and not cause fermentation.

5. From the lecture notes of Professor Samuel Williams, the Hollis Professor of Mathematics and Natural Philosophy at Harvard from 1780–1788:

    Take some combustible substance and let it be inflamed or set fire: In this state inclose it in a vessel containing a small quantity of atmospherical air. Effect: The combustion will continue but a short time and then cease. Part of the combustible substance is reduced to ashes and the other part remains entire. And the air appears to be changed and altered. . . . Here then we have a representation of what the chemists call phlogiston and of the air's being loaded with it. In the confined air the combustible matter continues burning until the air becomes loaded with something that prevents any further combustion. And being confined by the closeness of the vessel, whatever the matter be with which the air is loaded, it is confined within the vessel and cannot escape. . . .

    It seems, therefore, from this experiment that phlogiston must be a real substance, and that the air is loaded or saturated with it. For what can the inclosing the combustible matter in the phial do but to prevent the escape or dispersion of some real substance? And is it not evident that so long as the air can receive this substance from the combustible matter so long the body will continue burning; and that as soon as the air is saturated and can receive no more of the phlogiston, the combustion must cease for no more phlogiston can escape or be thrown out from the burning body. And therefore when fresh air is admitted to receive phlogiston, the combustion will again take place. . . . And hence are derived the phrases of phlogisticated and dephlogisticated air. By phlogisticated air is intended air which is charged or loaded with phlogiston, and by dephlogisticated air is meant air which is free from phlogiston; or which does not contain this principal element of inflammability.

6. In 1772 Antoine Lavoisier wrote this note and sent it to the French Academy: "About eight days ago I discovered that sulfur in burning, far from losing weight, on the contrary gains it; . . . it is the same with phosphorus; this increase of weight arises from a prodigious quantity of air that is fixed during the combustion and combines with the vapours.

    "This discovery, which I have established by experiments that I regard as decisive, has led me to think that what is observed in the combustion of sulfur and phosphorus may well take place in the case of all substances that gain in weight by combustion and calcination; . . ."[11]

    Lavoisier's explanation is that something from the air, or the air itself, is absorbed in combustion.

[11] *Ibid.*, pp. 176–77.

His classic experiment to support his theory is:

"Mercury heated in common air produces a red material (an oxide, we would say, a 'calx' to the chemists of the eighteenth century). In a closed space about one-fifth of the air disappears in this process. The red material weighs more than the metal from which it was formed. Therefore something has disappeared from the air and combined with the metal. The red material, the oxide or calx, is next strongly heated in an enclosed space with the sun's rays brought to a focus by a large lens or 'burning glass,' a gas is evolved, and the metal regenerated. The new gas is the 'something' which disappeared from the original air, for the amount is the same, and the calx has lost weight in the right amount. The new gas (oxygen) mixed with the residue from the first experiment yields a mixture which is identical with common air."[12]

7. Avogadro (and some of his contemporaries) were impressed by the quantitative relationship that had been found to hold when *gaseous* elements combine. Here we are considering not weight but volumes of gases, let it be carefully noted. One illustration will suffice. If a mixture of hydrogen gas and oxygen gas is exploded by a spark, the following relationship is found to hold: 1 volume of oxygen + 2 volumes of hydrogen = 2 volumes of water vapor. (Any units of volume, for example cubic feet, may be used to express this relation.) The relation between volumes is very simple: 1 to 2 to 2. Other gaseous elements were likewise found to combine in a volume relationship expressed by *small whole numbers*.

Avogadro made two assumptions to account for the whole-number relationship between the *volumes* of gaseous elements which combine to form compounds. The first was that *equal volumes of gases under the same conditions of temperature and pressure contain the same number of particles*. The second was that the particles of hydrogen and oxygen are each composed of *two* atoms united together.

With the aid of these assumptions Avogadro accounted for all the known facts about chemical reactions between gases and was led to the conclusion that the water molecule was composed of two atoms of hydrogen and one of oxygen, that is, it is to be represented by H_2O.[13]

8. Botanists have been trying for nearly a century to discover the process by which plants shed their leaves. One of the first clues that attracted their attention was the fact that some plants develop a distinct layer of cells at the base of the leaf stalk and leaves then break off at that point. But the so-called "separation layer" proved to be a false clue. Many plants have no such layer, and many others have one but their leaves do not separate at that place.

. . .

[12] Ibid., pp. 189–90.
[13] Ibid., pp. 200–201.

The two major parts of a leaf are the flat blade and the stalk by which the blade is attached to the plant stem. . . . When the blade of a leaf is cut off, the remaining leaf stalk soon separates and drops from the stem. . . . The first substantial hint as to the internal mechanism controlling fall came when it was found that even if only a tiny piece of the leaf blade was left on the stalk, the leaf would stay on the stem just as long as if it had a complete blade. This indicated that the substance in the blade that prevented the fall of the leaf must be active in very minute amounts. . . .

The hormone was soon identified. It is the plant growth substance, auxin. The substance, as a later investigator found, not only kept debladed coleus leaves growing but delayed their fall. . . . The general conclusion was that auxin produced in the leaf blade moves down into the leaf stalk, and there inhibits leaf fall in direct relation to how much auxin there is. This conclusion was confirmed in a qualitative way for the leaves of other plants and for a number of kinds of fruits. . . .

The control of leaf fall by auxin seemed to be completely clear. It was, in fact, *too* clear. . . .

While thinking over this theory of leaf fall, I was struck by the odd circumstance that each leaf seemed to be acting as an independent entity. The theory implied that the fall of a leaf depended only on how much auxin was coming into its stalk from its own blade. Now in most cases we know of, the behavior or development of one part of a plant is subject to inhibitions and stimulations from other parts of the plant. One therefore had to suspect the completeness of the hypothesis that leaf fall was totally independent of influence from the rest of the plant. Furthermore, while the hypothesis seemed to explain what prevented leaves from falling, it left unclear what causes them to fall when they do.

With these thoughts in mind, we planned some experiments to try to detect influences from the rest of the plant. These involved trials of various patterns in deblading the leaves of a plant. Coleus leaves grow in pairs, the two members of each pair coming from opposite sides of the stem. The usual practice had been to deblade one of each pair, leaving the "sister" leaf intact as a control. Now, if the fall of each leaf was controlled independently within itself, it should be immaterial in what pattern the leaves up the stem were debladed, or how many of them were. But experiments showed that the pattern of deblading did make a consistent, though small, difference in the time of leaf fall, and that when *all* the leaves (except those in the bud at the apex of the stem) were debladed, the fall was strikingly slowed down!

The most obvious conclusion was that the presence of intact leaves in some way speeded the fall of debladed leaves. Indeed their presence accelerated the fall even of old leaves that were not debladed, for when the blades were removed from all the younger leaves, the old ones remained no longer than they would have otherwise.

It seemed, then, that leaf blades produced not only a substance (auxin) which inhibits falling but also a substance which speeds falling. What might this substance be? The most likely candidate was ethylene. This ingredient of illuminating gas has long been known to cause trees' leaves to fall, and recently it has been learned that some ethylene is naturally present in plant tissues; it is emitted by ripening fruit and by leaves. However we were unable in an extensive series of experiments to find any evidence that ethylene from leaves speeded leaf fall.

Although we scoured the research literature, we could find no other leads that proved fruitful. We therefore decided to look more closely at the experimental plants. It was then we noticed something we should have seen before. In every experiment we had left untouched the tiny leaves in the apical bud at the top of the stem. And every treatment that speeded the fall of leaves lower on the stem had at the same time accelerated the growth of the apical leaves. We now noticed a clear correlation between this growth and the time of the debladed leaves' fall. They fell just when the bottom leaves of the apical bud above them reached a length of 70 or 80 millimeters. Fast leaf fall seemed to be closely tied up with the presence just above of leaves 70 to 80 millimeters long.

When a leaf reaches this size it attains its maximum production of auxin. It was beginning to look as if the primary cause of speeded leaf fall was auxin production by the apical bud leaves above the debladed leaves. Further analysis indicated that the presence of intact leaves lower on the stem speeds leaf fall indirectly by speeding the growth of these apical leaves.

This view was confirmed by the following experiment. Many plants were prepared in which the young leaves were debladed and the older leaf pairs left intact. As in earlier experiments, the presence of the older leaves low on the stem speeded the fall of the debladed leaves above them, so long as the apical bud was left intact. But when the apical bud was cut off, the debladed leaves in that set of plants fell much more slowly. If, however, synthetic auxin was applied in place of the cut-off bud, the debladed leaves fell as fast as if the bud were on. Thus the experiments confirmed our surmise that auxin from the apical bud speeds the fall of debladed leaves.

These experiments, along with others which there is not space to describe, show that the fall of leaves is controlled by an "auxin-auxin balance." Auxin both slows and speeds leaf fall. So long as a leaf's own blade produces enough auxin to overcome the effect of auxin coming from younger leaves above, the leaf will stay on the plant. But as soon as its production of auxin drops to less than the critical rate—because of old age, too much shade, insect attack or deblading—the auxin from the younger, more rigorous leaves above causes the leaf to fall. Such a system has obvious adaptive value. The old and infirm are shed by the action of a hormone from the young and vigorous.

(WILLIAM P. JACOBS, "What Makes Leaves Fall")[14]

9. If one puts a small dish of sugar water near a beehive, the dish may not be discovered for several days. But as soon as one bee found the dish and returned to the hive, more foragers come from the same hive. In an hour hundreds may be there.

Why is this? It seems that the first bee must pass on a message to the other bees.

To discover how the message is passed on we conducted a large number of experiments, marking individual bees with colored dots so that we could recognize them in the milling crowds of their fellows and building a hive with glass walls through which we could watch what was happening inside. Briefly, this is what we learned. A bee that has discovered a rich source of food near the hive performs on her return a "round dance." (Like all the other work of the colony, food-foraging is carried out by females.) She turns in circles, alternately to the left and to the right. This dance excites the neighboring bees; they start to troop behind the dancer and soon fly off to look for the food. They seek the kind of flower whose scent they detected on the original forager.

The richer the source of food, the more vigorous and the longer the dance. And the livelier the dance, the more strongly it arouses the other bees. If several kinds of plants are in bloom at the same time, those with the most and the sweetest nectar cause the liveliest dances. Therefore the largest number of bees fly to the blossoms where collecting is currently most rewarding. When the newly recruited helpers get home, they dance too, and so the number of foragers increases until they have drained most of the nectar from the blossoms. Then the dances slow down or stop altogether. The stream of workers now turns to other blossoms for which the dancing is livelier. The scheme provides a simple and purposeful regulation of supply and demand.

(KARL VON FRISCH, "Dialects in the Language of the Bees")[15]

---

[14] William P. Jacobs, "What Makes Leaves Fall?" in *Plant Life: A Scientific American Book* (New York: Simon and Schuster, 1957). Reprinted with permission. Copyright © 1957 by Scientific American, Inc. All rights reserved.

[15] Karl von Frisch, "Dialects in the Language of the Bees," in *Scientific American*, Vol. 207, No. 2, August 1962.

ANSWERS

2. The relevant phenomena are the varying positions of the "fixed stars" in relation to Jupiter. The first (empirical) hypothesis was that the motion of Jupiter was direct—across the two stars. This was shown to be absurd by the situation on the 10th. So a second hypothesis was entertained— that the "fixed stars" were not fixed, that they revolved about Jupiter. The second hypothesis was confirmed by subsequent observations.

12

Crucial Experiments and Mill's Methods

In the last chapter we examined several examples of inductive arguments in science where an hypothesis is affirmed on the basis of evidence. As a rough guideline we concluded that such arguments are correct when the hypothesis is corroborated. In this chapter we will first consider the logic involved in giving up hypotheses in science. Next we will outline some of the methods that are used to correctly infer from evidence that A is the cause of B.

Crucial Experiments and Empirical Hypotheses

Empirical hypotheses are from time to time falsified. The Galenic theory about the behavior of the blood is an example of an empirical hypothesis which was falsified. Eventually by observation it was seen that all the statements which make up the theory were false, for example, the statements that the blood is produced in the liver and that there is no connection between the veins and arteries.

Another example of a falsified empirical hypothesis is the belief, held around 1890, that air consists only of nitrogen and oxygen. Rayleigh found that nitrogen removed from air was slightly heavier than nitrogen removed from other sources. The difference was one part in a thousand. The explanation seemed simple: nitrogen prepared from air is not pure nitrogen. Rayleigh and others then employed various methods for removing hydrogen, and isolated a residue gas which was about 1 percent of the weight of the nitrogen. This gas was called argon. The hypothesis that air consists only of nitrogen and oxygen was falsified by Rayleigh's experiment.

Experiments which falsify empirical hypotheses are often called *crucial experiments*. As we will see shortly, there is another group of experiments connected with theoretical hypotheses also called crucial experiments. These experiments are related to theoretical hypotheses in a way different from the way in which Rayleigh's experiment was related to the nitrogen–oxygen hypothesis.

In preparation for the discussion which follows it should be noted that in these two episodes singular observation statements (for example, this liver does not produce blood, and this sample of air contains argon) logically entailed the falsity of the empirical hypothesis. That is, to take the second example, this is a valid argument:

> This representative sample of air contains nitrogen, oxygen, and argon.
> Therefore it is false that air consists only of nitrogen and oxygen.

Crucial Experiments and Theoretical Hypotheses[1]

Can theoretical hypotheses be falsified in the way in which empirical hypotheses can? At first sight it would seem that they too can be falsified in a relatively direct fashion. Statements (P's) which can be directly tested are deducible from a theoretical hypothesis (H). Suppose on experimentation it is found that such a P is false. Does it not necessarily follow that the theoretical hypothesis is false? For, it seems, what we have here is a simple instance of the valid argument form called *modus tollens*:

1. H implies P.
    Not-P.
    Therefore not-H.

But (1) simplifies certain important logical and semantic features found in most scientific contexts. When these are made clear it can be seen that a falsified P which is deduced from the theory does not necessarily entail the falsity of the theory.

Logical Features

From the caloric theory—the theory that heat is a weightless substance—as we have seen in the last chapter, this P was deduced: If a body changes its temperature through friction, then its specific heat must change. The experiment which Count Rumford performed showed there is no change in

[1] The account of crucial experiments found here conforms (more or less) to P. Duhem's view found in *The Aim and Structure of Physical Theory*. An important and serious criticism of this view is found in some of the essays by Adolf Grunbaum, for example, "The Duhemian Argument," in *Philosophy of Science*, Vol. 27, 1960.

specific heat when a body changes its temperature through friction. Did this experiment falsify the caloric theory? There are two things to note here. First, the deduction of this P from the theory involved the assumption (among other assumptions) that matter can be neither created nor destroyed. And, second, the theory is made up of more than one assumption. Thus the relevant structure of this deduction is this:

$[(A_1, A_2, \ldots, A_n)$ and $D]$ implies P.
P is false.
Therefore $[(A_1, A_2, \ldots, A_n)$ and $D]$ is false.

where the A's stand for the assumptions of the theory H, and D stands for the nontrivial assumption or assumptions needed, in addition to the theory, to make the *formal* deduction. An example of a D would be the assumption that matter can be neither created nor destroyed. Another example would be the use of non-Euclidian geometry rather than Euclidean geometry to arrive at a deduction. Now it should be noted that if a conjunction of statements is said to be false, as the above conclusion has it, then it logically follows only that at least one of the statements in the conjunction is false. One or more of the assumptions which make up D may be false or one or more of the assumptions which make up H may be false. From the fact that P is falsified, in any case, it does not necessarily follow that the theory is false.

Generally, if the assumption or assumptions of D are not well established relative to the body of assumptions which make up the theory, an assumption or assumptions which make up D are given up rather than the theory. Consequently, the effect, in such cases, of a falsified P which is deduced from the theory is that the theory is left intact. On the other hand, when the D is established, then one or more of the assumptions of the H must be modified or abandoned or the theory must be given up. This brings us to an important semantic issue.

Semantic Features

How is the phrase "X theory" (where a name such as "caloric," "corpuscular," or "molecular" replaces the X) used in science? If what is called X theory is a certain set of specific assumptions, and if *each* of these assumptions is necessary in order to call a set of statements "X theory," then if the D is established and if a P which is deduced from the theory is falsified, the result must be the abandonment of X theory. For if a P which is deduced from the theory is falsified, then either an assumption (or assumptions) must be modified or abandoned, and thus the theory abandoned, or an assumption (or assumptions) of D must be modified or abandoned. But generally the name of a theory is not used in this way. How it is used can be illustrated schematically as follows: Certain assumptions are necessary to call a set of statements X theory, but the remaining assumptions are not. Suppose what is called X theory is made up at one time of these four assumptions: A_1, A_2, A_3, and A_4. Let us suppose A_1 is necessary, in that if that were given up we would not call A_2, A_3, A_4, plus any other assumptions, X theory. But if either A_2, A_3, or A_4 were given up we would call what is left, plus certain other assumptions, X theory, since it is still essentially like the old set of assumptions. There are, let us imagine, cases where we would be in doubt whether to call a set—say, A_1 and A_2, plus other assumptions, without A_3 and A_4—X theory. The consequences of this use of X theory is that certain assumptions can be modified or abandoned, and we would still speak of the set of assumptions as X theory. (An illustration of this is found in the next section.)

In summary, the falsification of a P or P's deduced from a theoretical hypothesis with the help of nontrivial subsidiary assumptions D do not entail the falsity of the hypothesis—that is, the falsity of one or more of the essential assumptions of the theory. Rather, the falsification of such P's entails the falsity of the conjunction of assumptions which made up the H and D. Thus no observation statement (or statements) entails that a theory is false, whereas observation statements can entail that an empirical hypothesis is false.

What accounts for this difference between theories and empirical hypotheses can easily be seen. To deduce a singular observation statement from a statement contained in an empirical hypothesis, often all that is needed is a singular statement as in this example:

Air is composed only of oxygen and hydrogen.
This X is a representative sample of air.
Therefore this X is composed only of oxygen and hydrogen.

And if the conclusion here is false, it logically follows that the first premise, the empirical hypothesis, is false (assuming the particular premise to be true). But to deduce an observation statement from a theory involves employing all or most of the assumptions of the theory, plus the assumptions in D (plus singular propositions if a singular observation statement is to be deduced). It is this impossibility of deducing observation statements from particular statements of the theory which accounts for the logical impossibility of a falsified P which is deduced from the theory implying the falsity of a theory.

"Death Blows"

Many times in the history of science falsified P's have, as it is often put, "dealt death blows" to the theoretical hypotheses from which they were derived. Rumford's experiment is often described as having dealt a death blow to the caloric theory. Now if his experiment did not entail the falsity of the theory, what is meant by saying that it dealt it a death blow? A theory is *dealt a death blow* when, first, a *P* which is deduced from it is falsified; second, all the assumptions involved in the *D* are well established; and third, certain assumptions of the theory other than the *essential* assumptions are regarded as well established. The result of falsifying such a *P* will be the abandonment of the theory—that is, the abandonment of the essential assumption(s) of the theory. An experiment which determines whether a *P* related to an *H* in this way is true is called a *crucial experiment*. There are thus two kinds of crucial experiments: those which falsify or do not falsify an empirical hypothesis and those which deal or do not deal a death blow to a theoretical hypothesis. Rumford's experiment was a crucial experiment of the second kind.

Let us consider another classical example of a crucial experiment which dealt a death blow to a theory. Recall Newton's corpuscular theory of light, discussed in the last chapter. The theory, it will be remembered, describes light as made up of particles that are emitted from light sources. The theory also supposes that these particles are attracted and repelled according to Newton's laws of motion for bodies. For example, the particles which make up water attract the light particles from the air when the distance between the water particles and light particles is small. These assumptions explain why light travels in a straight line, why it reflects and refracts, the prism phenomenon—in short, they explain all the then known light phenomena. The theory also implies the following consequence: the index of refraction of light passing from one medium into another is equal to the velocity of the light particle within the medium it penetrates, divided by the velocity of the same particle in the medium it leaves behind. (We will not try to review all the assumptions and steps employed to deduce this *P* from Newton's hypothesis.) From this proposition a second one follows: light travels faster in water than in air.

The testing of this deduced *P* had to wait until the speed of light could be measured. When means were devised for such a measurement, the experiment was performed by Foucault and he found that the light was propagated less rapidly in water than in air. Some thought that this experiment condemned once and for all the corpuscular theory of light. In a sense this is true, and in a sense this is not true. It did deal a "death blow" to the corpuscular theory of light; no scientist since then has regarded light as merely a collection of corpuscles. But the theory, we recall, is made up of *several* assumptions. One or more of these must be given up or changed in the light of Foucault's experiment. However, the assumption which might need modification so that the theory is compatible with Foucault's experiment need not *necessarily* be the assumption that light is made up of projected corpuscles. If this were retained in the modified theory, we would speak of it as the same theory. But since the other assumptions which *could* be given up or modified were regarded as more or less established, Foucault's experiment dealt the death blow.

When a theory is to be modified in the face of disconfirmed P's, and when it is to be abandoned, and when one should stop modification and abandon a theory in the face of disconfirmed P's is all a matter of extreme complexity, ordinarily, and involves factors not subject to general rules.

Fact of the Cross

Suppose there there are two rival theoretical hypotheses for the same group of phenomena. And suppose from H_1 (a given hypothesis), P_1 follows and from H_2 not-P_1 follows. In addition, let us imagine that the testing of P_1 is a crucial experiment for both theories. That is, no matter what the outcome of the test, one of the theories will be dealt a death blow. The result of the test, consequently, will be that one theory will be abandoned and the other will be corroborated and thus will be the accepted theory. Newton called such an experiment a "fact of the cross," borrowing this expression, as he says, from the crosses which at an intersection indicate the various roads.

Actually Foucault's experiment was thought to be an experiment of this kind. For at the time there were two competing theories about the nature of light—Newton's corpuscular theory and Huygens' wave theory. Huygens' wave theory supposed that light consisted of waves propagated within ether. The wave theory, as was the case with Newton's hypothesis, explained all the then known light-phenomena. But a consequence of the wave theory was that light travels more quickly in air than in water. The result of Foucault's experiment was the abandonment of the corpuscular theory and an acceptance of the wave theory.

Some have not only thought that experiment and observation can demonstrate the falsity of a theory but have argued that observations can demonstrate the truth of a theory. In fact Jean Arago, the celebrated French astronomer, wrote as if he believed the Foucault experiment demonstrated that Huygens' theory was true and Newton's false. As we have already seen, the results of experiments cannot entail the falsity of theory, though they can deliver the theory a death blow. And it is easy to see how some, having *modus tollens* in mind, might have thought that observations do entail the falsity of a theory. But what led some to think that experiments could demonstrate the certainty of a theory? The explanation seems to be this: If, it is argued, we enumerate all the theoretical hypotheses which can explain a set of phenomena, and if by experiment all are shown to be false but one, then this remaining hypothesis must be certain. Now this argument presupposes the following questionable assumptions: First, that there is a single theoretical explanation for a set of phenomena; second, that observation statements do entail the falsity of a theory; and, third, that it is possible to enumerate all the possible hypotheses which explain a set of phenomena. Since Arago seems to have thought that light must either be made up of particles or be a wave, he believed that Newton's theory and Huygens' theory exhausted the possible explanations for light phenomena. Since he believed that Foucault's experiment demonstrated the falsity of Newton's theory, we can see why he thought that this experiment demonstrated the certainty of Huygens' theory.

Summary

Observation statements do entail the falsity of empirical generalizations but do not entail the falsity of theories.

A theory can conflict with observation—that is, consequences can be deduced from the theory which conflict with observation. But such deductions involve the use of many or most of the assumptions in the theory plus certain subsidiary assumptions. Theories, however, can receive death blows from the results of experiments. A theory is dealt a death blow when (1) an observation statement that is deduced from it is falsified by experimental observation, (2) all the assumptions involved in the D (assumptions needed for the derivation in addition to those which make up the hypothesis) are established, and (3) certain assumptions of the theory other than the essential assumptions are regarded as well established.

EXERCISES 12.1

A. In each of the following passages:

What hypotheses or competing hypotheses are found?
Are the hypotheses theoretical or empirical?
Are they tested?
Does any test establish a hypothesis or deal a "death blow" to a hypothesis?
What is the effect of the test or tests?

1. In the early nineteenth century the German geologist Abraham Werner propounded the geological theory called "Neptunism." The theory was offered as an explanation of rock formations. Werner held that at one time the earth was covered by an ocean. All the rock strata had been deposited by processes of crystallization, chemical precipitation, or mechanical sedimentation.

   "First of all came the primitive rocks, such as granite, which had crystallized out of the primeval ocean: these were entirely devoid of fossils. Then came the transitional rocks such as the micas and the slates, containing a few fossils, which had been precipitated from the ocean. Next there were the sedimentary rocks, richer in fossils, such as coal and limestone, formed by the deposition of solids from the waters. Finally there were the derivative rocks, such as sand and clay, which were derived from the others by a process of weathering. Werner thought that volcanoes were due to coal catching fire underground, the heat generated melting the neighbouring rocks, and forcing the eruption of volcanic lava from time to time. Thus, for Werner, heat was not an important geological force: volcanic action due to burning coal was a late and subsidiary rock-forming agency, appearing only after the main strata had been laid down."[2]

One of the shortcomings of this theory was the lack of an explanation for the disappearance of the ocean after the rock strata had been formed. James Hutton, an amateur scientist of Edinburgh, put forward a theory which employed only geological forces which are in operation today. The interior of the earth, Hutton held, was composed of molten lava, the solid surface of the earth serving as a containing vessel, which was closed apart from the volcanoes that served as safety valves. From time to time, he thought, the molten rock escaped through cracks just beneath the earth's surface and tilted up the overlying sedimentary strata. The molten rock then solidified to form the crystalline rocks, such as basalt and granite, thus giving the mountains with their crystalline cores and sedimentary sides.

. . .

"Werner's followers argued against Hutton, first, that molten rock would not become crystalline on solidification but would be glassy like lava, and secondly, that some rocks, like limestone, would decompose if subject to heat. Hall observed in a glass factory at Leith that if molten glass were allowed to cool very slowly it became crystalline and opaque, whilst if it were cooled more quickly it became glassy and transparent. He presumed that molten rock would behave in a similar way, and accordingly he obtained some lava from Vesuvius and Etna, and melted it in the blast furnace of an iron works. As he had expected, the molten rock became crystalline, like basalt, when allowed to cool slowly, and glassy, like lava, when cooled rapidly. Hall showed further that if limestone were heated in a closed vessel, it did not decompose as the Neptunists thought, but melted and became marble on cooling as Hutton suggested."[3]

During the period between 1790 and 1830 the study of fossils in rocks was begun. Fossil remains of land animals of different ages

---

[2] Reprinted from *Main Currents of Scientific Thought*, by S. F. Mason, by permission of Abelard-Schuman Ltd. and Routledge and Kegan Paul Ltd. All rights reserved. Copyright 1953.

[3] Ibid., pp. 325–336. Used by permission.

were found in different rock layers. This gave new support to Hutton's theory. Some Neptunists responded by claiming that the agents of these formations were a *series* of catastrophic floods.

Around 1819 Sedgwick and Murchison studied the early rocks containing no fossils in coal mines and the like. They concluded that this rock was formed by the solidification of molten rock, not by crystallization from water.

2. Those who believed that microorganisms could arise *de novo* without parents, did in fact accept that life was continually being created anew from inanimate matter. This belief came to be known as the doctrine of spontaneous generation. . . .

Among the many other types of experiments that Pasteur designed to rule out spontaneous generation, one is worth some emphasis by virtue of its very simplicity and decisiveness and because it finally silenced his opponents and settled the issue—at least for the time being. A fermentable fluid was put into a flask, the long neck of which was then heated and drawn into the form of an S tube (hence the name "swan-neck flask"). When the liquid was boiled, the vapor forced the air out through the orifice of the neck. As the fluid became cool again, the air slowly returned to the flask, but was washed in the moisture that condensed in the curves of the neck after heating was interrupted. Under these conditions, any dust or particle carried by the air was trapped in the neck, and the fluid in the flask remained clear, sterile. However, when the neck of the flask was broken, and the unwashed air allowed to come into contact with the fluid, then microscopic life immediately began to develop.

Despite the spectacular success of these experiments, there were still unforeseen difficulties to overcome. They arose from the fact, then unknown but now well understood, that certain species of bacteria form heat-resistant spores. In some of the early experiments these spores persisted in the fluid that was presumed to have been sterilized by heating, and when they germinated, they gave rise to bacterial growth even though access to outside air had been prevented. These difficulties arising from the presence of heat-resistant spores were eventually overcome, and Pasteur was able to prepare his swan-neck flasks in such a manner that the broth remained sterile in them all.

In Pasteur's words, "Never will the doctrine of spontaneous generation recover from the mortal blow of this simple experiment."

(RENÉ DUBOS, *Pasteur and Modern Science*)[4]

---

[4] From *Pasteur and Modern Science*, by René Dubos, copyright © 1960 by Educational Services, Inc. Reprinted by permission of Doubleday & Company, Inc., and Heinemann Educational Books Ltd., London.

3. When something, say a match, burns, it appears that something is released from the match. According to a theory of combustion formulated by two German chemists, Becher and Stahl, in the 17th and 18th centuries, when a substance was burnt "phlogiston" was said to escape in the form of fire and flame.

One application of the "phlogiston" theory was eventually to lead chemists into much confusion and to help to bring about its downfall. It arose in this way. When a metal, such as copper or lead, is sufficiently heated, it turns into a powdery substance and its metallic properties are lost. (The same thing happens in the familiar rusting of iron, but there without the application of heat.) The chemists of that time explained this by saying that a metal, when heated, lost its "phlogiston", leaving the powdery residue, which they called a calx. They knew that if this calx was heated afresh with charcoal, it was converted back again into metal; and charcoal, since it would burn away almost entirely, was held to be very rich in "phlogiston." The heating of the calx with charcoal had therefore restored enough "phlogiston" to the calx to reconstitute the original metal. Thus a metal was a compound of its calx and "phlogiston;" and the process of heating a metal to give it calx, called calcination, was a decomposition, a kind of combustion in which "phlogiston" escaped from the metal.

It was known, on the other hand, that, when a metal was calcined, the weight of the residual calx or powder was greater than the original weight of the metal taken. But how could the weight increase, since something material, namely "phlogiston," had been lost from the substance of the metal? In answer to this, some of the chemists who accepted the "phlogiston" theory were driven to suppose that "phlogiston" did not gravitate as other matter, but levitated—that it naturally rose upwards to the heavens whereas other substances naturally tended to fall to the earth—that it had a negative weight, as we might say.

(DOUGLAS McKIE, "The Birth of Modern Chemistry")

Antoine Lavoisier, the founder of modern chemistry, believed that air plays an important part in combustion. He believed that in combustion things combine with air and that this explains why the calx has greater weight. Lavoisier in a famous experiment succeeded in separating hydrogen and oxygen from the air. He noted that things would burn in the presence of oxygen but not with hydrogen. He then reasoned that when hydrogen burns it should, according to his theory, combine with oxygen. All attempts by Lavoisier and others failed until Cavendish found that when hydrogen burns, water is produced. After this experiment the phlogiston theory was gradually abandoned.

(Also see the experiment described in exercise 6 of the last chapter.)

There were attempts to modify the phlogiston theory in the face of these experiments. According to the modified theory, when metal is heated it turns to pure earth and its phlogiston goes into the air. The earth then combines with water from the air to form calx.

4. When the moon is on the horizon it looks bigger than when it is high in the sky (zenith moon). However in photographs its image is the same size. This is also true of the image in the eye.

Two explanations have been advanced for this: the apparent-distance theory and the angle-of-regard theory. According to the first theory, the moon looks bigger because it seems further away. Any object seen through filled space, such as the horizon moon, is perceived as being more distant than an object just as far away but seen through empty space, such as the zenith moon. It is well known that an observer perceiving two equal images and receiving sensory information that one object is farther away than the other, correctly sees the farther to be larger. According to the second theory the moon looks smaller because the viewer raises his eyes or head to look at it.

Some years ago Edwin G. Boring subjected the apparent-distance theory to what he considered a critical test. He asked people to judge the relative distance of the zenith and horizon moons. Most said the horizon moon seemed nearer. He then had subjects match moons of the same size on a screen. Those they saw at eye level they said were larger.

In 1957 Lloyd Kaufman and Irvin Rock investigated the phenomenon. They devised an optical apparatus which simulated the moon against the sky. With the use of this instrument they found that the horizon moon looks larger whether or not the eyes are raised. The moon in the same region of the sky was the same whether or not the eyes were elevated. They concluded that Boring's findings on eye elevation were peculiar to the methods he employed.

In Kaufman and Rock's words: "We therefore turned to the apparent-distance theory. Boring had rejected it because his subjects said that the horizon moon appeared to be nearer than the zenith moon. But, we wondered, did they really see the horizon moon as nearer? Or were they judging it to be nearer precisely because it looked bigger, effectively turning the reasoning upside down? In that case the reported distance would be a secondary phenomenon, an artifact of the very illusion it was supposed to test. To check this possibility we showed our subjects pairs of artificial moons of different diameters and instructed them to compare their relative distances. Whenever the zenith moon was larger, the subjects said it was nearer than the horizon moon; when it was smaller, they said it was farther away."

Kaufman and Rock then made additional experiments to confirm that the horizon moon looks larger only because it is seen over terrain. After this they showed the moon looks larger when it is seen over a more distant horizon, and that the illusion increases with the degree of cloudiness. When the horizon was inverted, the moon looked smaller. They also found that the framing-effect one gets in cities enhances the size of the horizon moon. Last, they showed that color has no effect on the illusion.

Kaufman and Rock concluded from all this that they had "tested" the apparent-distance theory and "provided evidence that it is correct."

(Taken from LLOYD KAUFMAN and IRVIN ROCK, "The Moon Illusion")[5]

B.   Again review exercises at the end of the last chapter and analyze them, in so far as possible, in the way the above were analyzed.

ANSWERS

2.   One hypothesis was that life could arise from inanimate matter by spontaneous generation. The other was that microorganisms were responsible for the appearance of life in fluids (for example). In this case the hypothesis was, at the time, theoretical, but it had consequences which could be empirically observed. The experiments proved that the first hypothesis was false, leaving the second as the only plausible alternative. This was the effect of the experiment—a "death blow" to the first hypothesis.

Mill's Methods

The usual inductive techniques employed to establish (and sometimes discover) causal connections have come to be known as *Mill's methods*. They are called this because John Stuart Mill was one of the first to formulate them and give them names. Mill wrote that these inductive inferential methods were the "mode of discovery and proving laws of nature." Mill thought that the business of science was to discover the causes of things. He also thought that his methods were used to discover causal connections and to establish causal connections. The discovery of causes of things, however, is but one part of the activities of science. The primary theoretical aim of science is to

[5] Lloyd Kaufman and Irvin Rock, "The Moon Illusion," in *Scientific American*, Vol. 207, No. 1, July 1962.

explain phenomena. However, Mill's methods are sometimes employed in the discovery of causal connections or functional relations between two or more factors. In addition, and more important, they are generally employed to establish causal and functional connections, especially in the social sciences. Some commentators on Mill's writings believe that he had only the social sciences in mind when he formulated his methods.

Method of Agreement. Imagine that there is some phenomenon P which interests us, and we would like to know its cause. Let the antecedent factors be represented by capital letters. And let "→" express "is followed by." If we find:

$$A\ B\ C \to P$$
$$A\ D\ E \to P$$

this provides grounds, Mill says, for asserting that A is the cause of P.[6] Mill calls an inductive inference of this kind the *method of agreement.* Mill writes in this respect:

> If two or more instances of the phenomenon under investigation have only one circumstance in common, the circumstance in which alone all the instances agree is the cause (or effect) of the given phenomenon.
> (JOHN STUART MILL, *A System of Logic*)

The example Mill gives of the employment of this method is:[7]

> Instances in which bodies assume a crystalline structure are found to have been preceded by instances which have in common only one antecedent, namely, the process of solidification from a fluid state. This antecedent, therefore, is the cause of the crystalline structure.

Method of Difference. If we find this:

$$A\ B\ C \to P$$
$$B\ C \to \text{not-}P$$

This provides grounds for our saying, Mill tells us, that A is the cause of P. Mill called this inference the *Method of Difference.* According to Mill:

> If an instance in which the phenomenon under investigation occurs, and an instance in which it does not occur, have every circumstance in common save one, that one occurring only in the former; the circumstance in which alone the two instances differ is the effect, or the cause, or an indispensable part of the cause of the phenomenon.
> (MILL, *A System of Logic*)

---

[6] All arguments which have premises which satisfy these "methods" are instances of inductions of the kind A, discussed in the last chapter. The use of the letters A, B, C, and D in this and the following formulations of Mill's methods are not meant to suggest that just this many factors are involved. There may be more—or fewer.

[7] The phrasing of this example is taken from L. S. Stebbing, *A Modern Introduction to Logic*, 2nd ed. (London: Methuen, 1933), p. 334.

Mill's example is:[8]

> A man in the fullness of life is shot through the heart; he is wounded and dies. The wound is the only circumstance that is different; hence, his death is caused by the wound.

Joint Method of Agreement and Difference. If we find this:

$A\ B \rightarrow P$
$A\ C \rightarrow P$
$B\ C \rightarrow \text{not-}P$
$B \rightarrow \text{not-}P$
$C \rightarrow \text{not-}P$

we have grounds for saying A is the cause of P. Mill called this the *Method of Agreement and Difference.* And we can see why: the inductive inference involves both of the first two methods. He wrote:

> If two or more instances in which the phenomenon occurs have only one circumstance in common, while two or more instances in which it does not occur have nothing in common save the absence of that circumstance, the circumstance in which alone the two sets of instances differ is the effect, or the cause, or an indispensible part of the cause, of the phenomenon.
>
> (MILL, *A System of Logic*)

Method of Residues. Suppose we know that A, B, and C together is the cause of a, b, and c. Suppose by using the preceding techniques we find that A is the cause of a and B is the cause of b. This provides grounds, according to Mill, for saying that C is the cause of c. Mill calls this inference the *Method of Residues.* He writes:

> Subduct from any phenomenon such part as is known by previous inductions to be the effect of certain antecedents, and the residue of the phenomenon is the effect of the remaining antecedents.   (MILL, *A System of Logic*)

Many commentators believe that the Method of Residues is in no sense an inductive method, even in the sense in which Mill usually understood this phrase.[9] Often this method is omitted in descriptions of Mill's methods.

Method of Concomitant variations. Last, if some modification of, say, A without any modifications of B and C always results in a modification of P, this provides grounds for saying A is the cause of P. Mill calls this inference the *Method of Concomitant Variations.* He writes:

[8] The phrasing of this example is taken from Stebbing, op. cit.
[9] Cf. Stebbing, op. cit., p. 333.

> Whatever phenomenon varies in any manner whenever another phenomenon varies in some particular manner, is either a cause or an effect of that phenomenon, or is connected with it through some fact of causation.
>
> (MILL, *A System of Logic*)

Mill thought that this method was to be used to establish causal connections when the other four could not be used. He thought, for example, that to establish a causal relation between the earth's movement and the movement of a pendulum one must use this last method.

The inductive methods are illustrated in this simple, imagined example: Once upon a time a farmer noticed that where he had put manure earlier in the season, the plants were excellent in all of the various places on his land where he put the manure (method of agreement). He also noticed that in those places where he had not put manure the plants were not doing as well as in the manured places (method of difference). He concluded that manure is responsible for the excellent plants (method of agreement and difference). This judgment was further confirmed when he noticed that where the quality of the crops was high this was directly proportional with the amount of manure he had dropped (method of concomitant variations)—supposing, of course, he didn't drop too much.

Let us now examine two real-life examples in which Mill's inductive techniques are employed. In the first example the techniques are employed to support the claim that two factors are causally related, while in the second example the methods are employed to disprove such a connection.

Mill's techniques are employed from time to time to test deductions from theoretical hypotheses. Pascal's testing of a deduction from the "sea of air" theory, discussed in the last chapter, employed such techniques. From the "sea of air" hypothesis it followed that the pressure of the air diminishes as we rise. The barometer measures the pressure of air. Thus we should find that mercury in a barometer goes down as the barometer is raised in its altitude. To test this, he employed (1) induction by enumeration, (2) the method of difference, and (3) the method of concomitant variation. First he found:

1. A_1 (Climbing up the mountain) $\rightarrow D$ (dropping of mercury in barometer)

   $A_2 \rightarrow D$

   $\vdots$

   $A_5 \rightarrow D$

Second, Pascal had friends watching a barometer at the side of the mountain while his brother-in-law made the climbs. He found this:

2. $A\,B\,C\,P$ (shared conditions) $\rightarrow D$

   $B\,C\,P \rightarrow$ not-D

Finally, the brother-in-law noticed that the mercury changed as he climbed, that is:

3. Changes in $A \to$ changes in D

From (1), (2), and (3) Pascal concluded that mercury in a barometer goes down as the barometer is raised.

Here is the second example. An economist, Dr. Luigi Laurenti, conducted studies of the relation of property value to racial integration in housing. The purpose of this study was to find out if this widely held belief is true: property values fall significantly when Negro or other non-white families move into a previously all-white neighborhood. The first paragraph below, taken from a magazine article of Dr. Laurenti's work, summarizes a 1961 study; the rest of the passage, also taken from the article, concerns a study in 1955.[10]

> Dr. Laurenti analyzed over a five-year period the sales of 10,000 homes in San Francisco, Oakland, and Philadelphia. As Negroes, Japanese, Chinese, Filipino, or Mexican families began moving into a white neighborhood, Dr. Laurenti went to work. First, he selected another neighborhood as similar as possible to the first one, with the exception that it never did become integrated. Then he amassed facts and figures on the values of the homes in both areas for the period of a year before the first minority family moved in to a point five years later. After comparing the prices in both neighborhoods, Dr. Laurenti found: In 40% of the comparisons, there was *no* difference in property values before and after the neighborhood became integrated; in 45% of the comparisons, property values *rose* anywhere from 5 to 26%; in only 15% of the cases did property values drop, and then only by 5 to 9%.
>
> .   .   .
>
> In 1955 with the help of expert appraisers and brokers in the areas to be studied, he carefully matched all-white areas with racially mixed areas of up to 70% non-white populations. A total of 39 neighborhoods were compared to discover price differences. And, as mentioned earlier, sales data were collected for a period well before the first non-white family moved in, as well as for several years after mixed occupancy. Let's take a closer look at one of the test neighborhoods studied.
>
> Oceanview, in San Francisco, is typical. Until January, 1948 this was an all-white neighborhood. Oceanview covers 20 blocks in the Ocean Avenue district near San Francisco's southern city limits. Except for some light commercial development along one main street, the use of land is entirely residential. The 600 homes are mostly single-family, owner-occupied. They are mostly of frame construction, with exteriors finished in stucco, and have five rooms. It generally is a younger neighborhood, 70 percent of its homes having been built since 1940. The homes have been well kept by their owners, many of whom are of Irish and Italian backgrounds.

[10] Joanne Gemar, "Property Values and Race" in *The Californian*, June 1962, pp. 14–15. Copyright 1962, *The Californian*. Used by permission.

Dr. Laurenti then located another neighborhood closely comparable to Oceanview in all of the important price-determining respects, except that it has remained all white. In choosing Sunnyside, which is a short way north-east of Oceanview, he found some increase in size—30 blocks with 850 homes— but no significant difference. In the age, type and market value of the homes, in the general topography and pattern of land use, in the relationship to the center of the city, shopping areas and transportation facilities, in the income class and social status class of the occupants, Oceanview and Sunnyside were very much alike.

After the first non-whites, a Negro family, moved into Oceanview in January, 1948, others followed suit. By the end of the year there were 10 Negro families. Several years later Negro occupancy had reached 100 families (about 18% of the population of Oceanview).

Both Oceanview and Sunnyside rose steadily in value during the 24-quarter observation period. At the beginning, houses were selling in Oceanview for $10,112, in Sunnyside for $9,747. Six years later homes in Oceanview were selling for $11,446, an increase of 13.2%. At the same time, Sunnyside homes were selling for $10,865, an increase of 11.5%. So, there was no appreciable difference. Neither the fact of Negro occupancy not the extent of their moving in seemed to affect real estate values.

One after another, the other 37 neighborhoods studied revealed the same conclusions. And it remained true whether the number of non-whites stayed low, around 3% of the population, or whether it became heavy, up to 70%.

In the 1961 study the hypothesis is tested by employing the methods of difference and agreement. If the hypothesis were true, then Dr. Laurenti should find:

1. San Francisco neighborhood: I (integration) $\rightarrow LPV$ (lower property values)
   Oakland neighborhood: $I \rightarrow LPV$
   Etc.

[Since each of the communities differed, (1) would be an application of the method of agreement.]

2. Neighborhood 1: $I\,A\,B\,C$ (factors in common) $\rightarrow LPV$
   Neighborhood 2: not-$I\,A\,B\,C \rightarrow$ not-LPV

But, as we see, practically no detrimental effect on property values resulted, and most of the time a rise in values took place. That is, (1) and (2) were not found to be the case.

In the second study the methods of difference and agreement are used in the same way with the same results. For example, if the hypothesis were true, then we would expect:

3. Oceanview: $I\,B\,C$ (significant factors in common) $\rightarrow LPV$
   Sunnyside: Not-$I\,A\,B\,C \rightarrow$ not-LPV

As Dr. Laurenti reported, this was not found to be the case. In addition, no relation was found between the increase of minority families and property values. If there were a connection, then it is likely that concomitant variation should have been seen—that is, property values should have decreased as the number of minority families increased.

Mistakes can obviously occur in employing these deductive techniques. Employing one, two, or all the methods does not necessarily insure that the conclusion is established. For example there is the story of the scientific drinker who on:

> Monday, drinks scotch and soda → being drunk
> Tuesdays, drinks bourbon and soda → being drunk
> Wednesday, drinks rum and soda → being drunk
> $\vdots$

and concludes that it is the soda he must quit drinking if he is to keep from being drunk. The drinker has here employed the method of agreement and has mistakenly concluded that the soda is the cause of his being drunk. If he had employed the method of difference he would not have made this mistake. Sometimes, however, the employment of several inductive methods can lead to mistakes. For example, the story is told that in the New Hebrides the natives believe that lice keep a person healthy. They observe that almost all healthy natives have lice, whereas sick natives generally do not have lice. As we can see, they employ both simple enumeration and the method of difference and agreement. The arrow here means "concomitant with."

1. Person 1: L (lice) → H (good health)
   $\vdots$
   Person n: $L \rightarrow H$
2. Person 1: $L\,A\,B\,C \rightarrow H$
   Person 2: $\quad A\,B\,C \rightarrow$ not-H
3. Person 1: $L\,A\,B\,C \rightarrow H$
   Person 2: $L\,D\,E\,F \rightarrow H$

(where A, B, C, ... would be things such as age, sex, weight, diet, occupation, living conditions, and the like). From (1), (2), and (3) they conclude that lice keep a person healthy. As we can easily see, they have committed the false cause fallacy. The presence of lice is not the cause of health; rather, lice, being leeches, naturally survive best on healthy hosts. The mistake the natives make is thinking in (2) that all the relevant factors to health are the same except L, or that there is no common relevant factor other than L in (3).

Suppose in the Oceanview–Sunnyside example some factor was present in Sunnyside that was not in Oceanview, and this factor caused the Sunnyside values not to rise as they would have if it had not been there. For example, suppose property taxes for some reason were greatly increased in Sunnyside. Under these conditions one would be unjustified in concluding that I had no effect on LPV from the findings that

Oceanview: $I\,A\,B\,C \to$ not-LPV
Sunnyside: not-$I\,A\,B\,C \to$ not-LPV

where, as we remember, $A\,B\,C$ stand for such things as age, type, and market value of the homes, topography and pattern of land, relationship to the center of city, shopping areas, and so forth. Dr. Laurenti, as we saw, took precautions against such a mistake. First, he took care to see that no such factor was present. In addition, he studied not one pair but a number of pairs of such communities.

This naturally raises these questions: "How can one tell that all *possible* relevant factors are the same in using the method of difference?" "How can one tell, when using the method of agreement, that there is no common relevant factor but the one in question?" and so forth. Here again no general rules can be set down. What is relevant will depend on the particular case. And knowledge of what is relevant in the particular case comes as a result of training, study, and experience. Thus, the employment of Mill's techniques does not insure that an inductive inference is correct. A correct inference results not only from the employment of the techniques, but also from proper consideration of the relevant factors. Without the relevant factors being properly considered, the employment of the techniques is not grounds for assurance that the inductive inference is correct.

EXERCISES 12.2

Indicate whether any of Mill's methods are being used in the following:

1. Christian Eijkman, a Dutch doctor, originally thought that beri-beri is caused by a bacillus. He had noticed, however, that the hens in the courtyard of the prison at which he worked acted as did the human prisoners who had beri-beri. That prompted the thought: could the hens' illness and that of the prisoners have the same cause? For the two had one thing in common: their food. The prisoners were fed almost entirely on polished rice and the hens lived on what the prisoners threw out of their barred windows into the yard. Eijkman next inquired how things were in other prisons, and found that some had many cases of beri-beri and others scarcely any. And what about the diet, was that the same? No. In the prisons with much beri-beri it was the same as in that of which Eijkman was in charge: polished rice. In those with few or no cases, the prisoners were given unpolished rice, which was cheaper. Thus, the actual discovery was made.

Eijkman published a report of his observations. This attracted little attention, so he continued experimenting with animals to test his ideas. He took two lots of hens; to one he gave husked rice, to the other unhusked rice. The hens that had had the husked rice contracted the same nervous paralysis he had seen before: the others remained healthy.

The next question Eijkman had to ask himself was: what is the difference between polished rice and unpolished rice? The silvery husk that the merchant removed to make the rice look more attractive and enable him to charge a higher price also contained the germ of the rice-grain; thus in this germ or husk there must be some stuff, the lack of which caused beri-beri in those fed exclusively on such rice. This important conclusion went unheeded until, years later, a young Pole, Kasimir Funk, learned of it, dug out the reports and experimented on pigeons. He succeeded in extracting from the rice husks those substances of whose presence Eijkman had been convinced, and which could prevent beri-beri. Thus he proved that Eijkman was right. Funk called these substances vitamins.

(Adapted from Hugo Glaser, *The Road to Modern Surgery*)

2. In a New York experiment drab wooden telephone booths in a ferry terminal were replaced by new aluminum and glass booths. Revenue doubled. From this it was concluded that the booths tempt people to stop and telephone on impulse.

3. In the period from the early 1920s to 1960 the consumption of tobacco products in the United states rose about 30 percent. Significantly, the rise was due to the use of cigarettes. The use of tobacco in other forms actually declined. During this same period death rates from all infectious diseases declined rapidly except for the death rates from lung cancer. Deaths from lung cancer in the United States climbed from 4,000 in 1935 to 36,000 in 1960. Painstaking studies have clearly shown that the increase in lung cancer is real and not attributable to improved diagnosis.

It was known for some time that lung cancer could result from prolonged and heavy occupational exposure to certain industrial dusts and vapors. This led to the hypothesis that the increase in lung cancer was due to increased exposure of the human population to air contamination of some sort. The factor involved had to be widespread and not confined to any particular occupational group. (In all countries with adequate mortality statistics lung cancer was found to have increased.) Three factors that met the requirements were: fumes from the combustion of solid and liquid fuels, dust from asphalt roads and the tires of motor vehicles, and cigarette smoking.

A number of studies were made comparing the smoking habits of lung cancer patients with the smoking habits of individuals free of the disease. The findings in all the investigations were remarkably similar. Lung cancer is an extremely rare cause of death among nonsmokers, except for those who have had prolonged and heavy occupational exposure to certain dusts and fumes. The death rate from lung cancer was very low for men who had never smoked, it increased with the amount of cigarette smoking, and it was very high for men who smoked two or more packs of cigarettes a day. For those who smoked 40 or more cigarettes per day the death rate from lung cancer per 100,000 man-years was 214. 143.9 was the figure for those who smoked 20 to 39 cigarettes a day, and 3.4 for those who never smoked. It was also found that the relative death rate from all causes increases with the degree of inhalation from cigarettes.

(Adapted from E. CUYLER HAMMOND, "The Effects of Smoking")[11]

4. In the part of William Wells' investigations which are related, in his words, below, he used little bundles of wool weighing 10 grains each for collecting dew.

"I now proceed to relate the influence which several differences in the situation have upon the production of dew.

"One general fact relative to the situation is, that whatever diminishes the view of the sky, as seen from the exposed body, occasions the quantity of dew, which is formed upon it, to be less than would have occurred if the exposure to the sky had been complete.

"*Experiment with elevated board*—I placed, on several clear and still nights, 10 grains of wool upon the middle of a painted board, ... elevated 4 feet above the grass-plot, by means of four slender wooden props of equal height; and at the same time I attached, loosely, 10 grains of wool to the middle of its under side. The two parcels were, consequently, only an inch asunder, and were equally exposed to the action of the air. Upon one night, however, I found that the upper parcel had gained 14 grains in weight, but the lower only 4. On a second night, the quantities of moisture, acquired by like parcels of wool, in the same situations as in the first experiment, were 19 and 6 grains; on a third, 11 and 2; on a fourth, 20 and 4, the smaller quantity being always that which was gained by the wool attached to the lower side of the board.

"*Experiment with hollow cylinder*—I placed, upright, on the grass-plot, a hollow cylinder of baked clay, the height of which was $2\frac{1}{2}$ feet, and diameter 1 foot. On the grass, surrounded by the cylinder, were laid 10 grains of wool, which, in this situation, as there was not the least wind, would have received as much rain as a like quantity of wool exposed to the sky. But the quantity of moisture obtained by the wool surrounded by the cylinder was only a little more than 2 grains, while that acquired by 10 grains of fully exposed wool was 16. . . .

[11] E. Cuyler Hammond, "The Effects of Smoking," in *Scientific American*, Vol. 207, No. 1, July, 1962.

"*Other varieties of situation*—Dew, however, will in consequence of other varieties of situation, form in very different quantities, upon substances of the same kind, although these should be similarly exposed to the sky.

"(1) In the first place, it is requisite, for the most abundant formation of dew, that the substance attracting it *should rest on a stable horizontal body of some extent*. Thus, upon one night, while 10 grains of wool, laid upon the raised board, increased 20 grains in weight, an equal quantity, suspended in the open air, $5\frac{1}{2}$ feet above the ground increased only 11 grains, notwithstanding that it presented a greater surface to the air than the other parcel. On another night, 10 grains of wool gained on the raised board 19 grains, but the same quantity suspended in the air, on a level with the board, only 13; and a third, 10 grains of wool acquired, on the same board, $2\frac{1}{2}$ grains of weight, during the time in which other 10 grains, hung in the air, at the same height, acquired only half a grain."

In other experiments. Wells varied the substances on which the wool lay and in still others placed the wool in various positions during different weather conditions.   (WILLIAM WELLS)

5. Puzzled by the fact that hens were refractory to anthrax, he (Pasteur) wondered whether this might not be explained by their body temperature, which is higher than that of animals susceptible to this disease. To test this hypothesis, he innoculated hens with anthrax bacilli and placed them in a cold bath to lower their body temperature. Animals so treated died the next day, showing numerous bacilli in their blood and organs. Another hen was similarly infected and maintained in the cold bath until the disease was in full progress, and then taken out of the water, dried, wrapped, and placed under conditions that allowed rapid return to normal body temperature. *Mirabile dictu*, this hen made a complete recovery. Thus a mere fall of a few degrees in body temperature was sufficient to render birds almost as receptive to anthrax as were rabbits or guinea pigs.   (RENÉ DUBOS, *Pasteur and Modern Science*)[12]

6. In the spring of 1881 a veterinarian named Rossignol succeeded in enlisting the support of many farmers of the Brie district, near Paris, to finance a large-scale test of anthrax immunization.

In the experiment, twenty-four sheep, one goat, and six cows were inoculated on May 5 with five drops of a living attenuated culture of anthrax bacillus. This is vaccination—a technique for specifically increasing the resistance of the body to an inimical agent. On May 17 all these animals had been re-vaccinated with a second dose of a less attenuated culture. On May 31 all the immunized animals were infected with a highly virulent anthrax culture, and the same culture was injected as well into twenty-nine normal animals: twenty-four sheep, one goat, and four cows. When Pasteur arrived on the field on the second day of

---

[12] Op. Cit., pp. 138–39.

June he was greeted with loud acclamation. All the vaccinated sheep were well. Twenty-one of the control sheep and the single goat were dead of anthrax, two other control sheep died in front of the spectators, and the last unprotected sheep died at the end of the day. The six vaccinated cows were well and showed no symptoms, whereas the four control cows had extensive swellings at the site of innoculation and febrile reactions. The triumph was complete.

(RENÉ DUBOS, *Pasteur and Modern Science*)[13]

7. I observed that plants not only have a faculty to correct bad air in six or ten days by growing in it, as the experiments of Dr. Priestly indicate, but that they perform this important office in a complete manner in a few hours; that this wonderful operation is by no means owing to the vegetation of the plant, but to the influence of the light of the sun upon the plant. . . . I found that this operation of the plants is more or less brisk in proportion to the clearness of the day and the exposition of the plants; diminishes towards the close of the day, and ceases entirely at sunset; that this office is not performed by the whole plant, but only the leaves and the green stalks. . . .   (JAN INGEN-HOUSZ, 1779)

8. Infants at a nursery in a home for delinquent girls and infants in a foundling home were studied. The nursery over a period of time produced normal healthy children, while the foundling home produced children whose development was greatly retarded, who were very susceptible to infection and illness of every kind, and whose mental health deteriorated rapidly while at the foundling home. The infant mortality rate at the foundling home was extremely high compared to that of the nursery. Dr. Spitz noted the similarities and differences in the environments and treatment of the two groups of infants.

Similarities:

1. Housing condition—much the same—large, pleasant quarters.
2. Food—in both institutions excellent.
3. Clothing—practically the same.
4. Medical care—in the home the children were regularly visited by a physician; in the nursery the children received professional care only when they appeared to need it.
5. Background—the background of the delinquent girls was probably worse than that of the mothers of the children in the home. The latter were often normal women who were unable to support their children. On admission, however, roughly the same level of health was enjoyed by each group of babies.

Differences:

1. Toys—the children in the nursery were provided with more than those in the home—the latter often had none.

---

[13] Ibid., pp. 118–119.

2. Visual Radius—in the nursery the children can see through the windows, other children, etc. In the home the cribs were enclosed by sheets on three sides—the other faced a featureless corridor.

3. Radius of Locomotion—in both cases this consists of the bed, which is adequate for an infant. But in the home, owing to a lack of stimulation, apparently, the babies lie supine for many months and a hollow is worn into their mattress, inhibiting their movements.

4. Personnel—in the home there is a head nurse and five assistant nurses for forty-five babies. Each is competent, conscientious, and is a "baby loving" woman, but each baby has the attention of a nurse only about one-eighth of the time it is awake. In the nursery each child is cared for by his own mother. And due to the nature of penal institutions of this kind, the baby provides the sole outlet of the mother's affection and is the only source of prestige, and so on, so that even more care and attention is given to these babies than babies normally receive.

(It seems evident from these observations, that the continuous care that a mother normally provides her baby, and the nature of that care is of essential importance in the mental and physical health of an infant.)
(RENÉ SPITZ, *The Psychoanalytic Study of the Child*)[14]

ANSWERS

1. Method of Agreement. The symptoms of the illness in the chickens and the men are similar. The food is the same for the chickens and the men, but nothing else (that is a possible cause of ill-health) is the same. Therefore, by the method of agreement, the food causes the illness. Also, in prisons in which men are healthy, the rice they eat was not polished, but in the prisons in which the men had beri-beri, the rice was unhusked. No other difference seemed relevant. So by the method of difference the absence of the husk caused beri-beri. The experiment with the chickens confirmed this.

7. The variation of the amount of light affects the operation of plants in correcting bad air. The more light the more brisk the operation and the less light the less brisk. So, by the method of concomitant variation it is, indeed, the operation of the plants which causes the air to become clean.

[14] An account of observations of Dr. René Spitz in *The Psychoanalytic Study of the Child*, Vol. 1, 1945.

13

Patterns of Scientific Explanation

As was indicated earlier, the primary theoretical function of scientific activity is the explanation of phenomena. In the first part of this chapter are found six examples of scientific explanations. Our interest will be to see in what way they are similar and in what way they differ from each other. In the last part of the chapter we will see how these six examples of genuine scientific explanations differ from explanations which appear to be scientific but which on analysis can be seen to be pseudoscientific explanations. The reader should not judge that the six examples exhaust the *kinds* of explanations found in the sciences.

We will find it useful to refer to what is explained as the *explicandum* and refer to the statements which function as the explanation as the *explicans*. Thus, according to this convention, the parts of an explanation are:

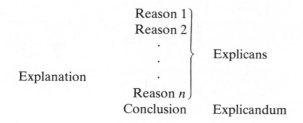

Deductive Explanations

A *deductive explanation* is one in which the explicandum is a logically necessary consequence of the explicans. This type of explanation is commonly regarded as the ideal form of explanation when the explicans contains universal generalizations. Thus it is thought by many that efforts should be made to make all explanations in science conform to this ideal.

In (1) and (2) below are found two explanations[1] which accord with this ideal, though certain trivial assumptions would have to be formulated so that the explicandum in each would be a formal logical consequence of the explicans. In these two examples we find what are called *universal generalizations* in each of the explicans. For example, in (1) the explicans fully formulated would contain this statement: All the planets revolve around the sun. In (2) we find Galileo's empirical law concerning falling bodies—$D = AT^2/2$—and Newton's theoretical law—the change of motion is proportional to the motive force impressed and is made in the direction of the right line in which that force is impressed. As we can see, Galileo's law states something about how *all* falling bodies will always behave, and Newton's law does the same thing for moving bodies.

1. According to the Ptolemaic view of the solar system (the dominant view in the Middle Ages), the Earth, Venus, and the Sun were thought to be related in this way:

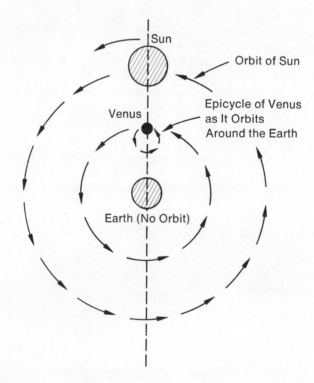

---

[1] For a fuller treatment of these explanations, see I. Bernard Cohen's *The Birth of a New Physics* (New York: Anchor Books, 1960), pp. 81 f., pp. 117 f.

The center of the epicycle orbit of Venus was thought to be permanently aligned between the center of the Earth and the center of the Sun. Venus thus would move around the Earth with the Sun.

In 1609 Galileo heard a report about an instrument called the telescope and succeeded in constructing "so excellent an instrument that objects seen by means of it appeared nearly one thousand times larger and over thirty times closer than when regarded with our natural vision." He turned the instrument toward the heavens and made a number of discoveries which dealt a death blow to the Ptolemaic system and supported the Copernican system (which maintained among other things that the planets, including Earth, orbited around the Sun).

One such discovery was that Venus exhibits phases. That is, at one time Venus appears as a complete circle, then it is seen as a crescent, then a half circle, and then as a crescent, and so forth. The phases can be illustrated as follows:

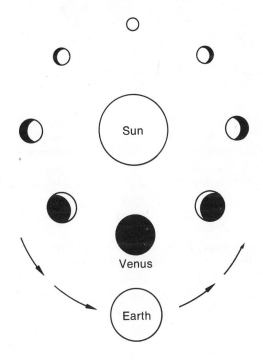

In addition, the disc displays different sizes during the phases.

What would explain these phases of Venus? As one can see, the Ptolemaic picture of the relation between the Earth, Venus, and the Sun does not explain it. In fact Galileo's discovery is in conflict with this system. The phases predicted from the Ptolemaic system are these:

with little difference in apparent size and Venus never seen as a full disc. Venus would not display a complete sequence of phases to observers on the Earth. However since the Earth and Venus both orbited around the Sun with Venus (Venus, of course, completing its orbit sooner than the Earth) between the Earth and the Sun, these phases would be predicted:

This corresponds to Galileo's observation. Copernicus' hypothesis thus explains the observed phases of Venus, whereas the Ptolemaic hypothesis does not.

2. If a sailing ship is standing still and a stone is dropped from the top of a mast, it will fall to the foot of the mast. Will the stone fall to the foot of the mast if the stone is dropped while the ship is moving at a constant speed? Many would say it would fall somewhere behind the foot of the mast. If the ship were moving very fast it would fall farther behind the mast than if it were moving slowly. However, this does not happen; the stone will fall to the foot of the mast no matter what the speed of the ship is, so long as its speed is constant. Why is this?

Here briefly is the explanation which Newton gave: According to the law of inertia, every body preserves its state of rest, or uniform motion, unless it is compelled to change that state by an external force. The stone at the moment of release was traveling at the speed the ship was—let us imagine, 10 feet a second. If the stone continued on a straight line and did not fall, it would be related to the ship in this way:

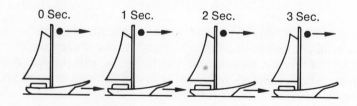

0 Sec.   1 Sec.   2 Sec.   3 Sec.

According to Newton's second law of motion, if a force is to slow down the speed of the stone, it must act from the direction opposite to the one in which the stone is moving:

In the case of the stone dropping from the mast, resistance from the air is such a force, but its effects are negligible. The stone, however, is a free falling body and the force of gravity will pull it toward the earth's center. But since this force does not act in the direction that the stone is moving, but is, rather, perpendicular to the path of the stone, it will not affect its forward motion. Thus no matter how high the mast is, and no matter how fast the ship is traveling, if the ship is traveling at a constant speed, the stone will land at the same place it would if the ship were standing still.

What in essence has happened here is that from two laws of motion this general statement was seen to follow: "Objects dropped from a body (onto the same body) moving uniformly will hit the same place they would if the body were standing still." If a few trivial assumptions were made explicit, the explanation would be seen to have this form:

$$
\text{Deduction} \quad
\left.
\begin{array}{l}
\text{Law 1} \\
\text{Law 2} \\
\vdots \\

\end{array}
\right\} \qquad \text{explicans}
$$

General Statement   explicandum

This general statement was thought of in terms of an example—the ship, mast, and stone—for clarity.

Let us suppose that in a particular case a stone dropped from a 114-feet-high mast on a ship hits the foot of that mast. The ship, let us suppose, is traveling at a constant speed of 10 feet a second. The stone hits the foot of the mast in three seconds. One might ask, "Why does the stone hit the foot of the mast in three seconds?"

Galileo discovered that the distance covered by free falling bodies is computed by this law:

$$D = \tfrac{1}{2}AT^2,$$

where D is distance, A is 32 ft./sec.^{2}, and T is time. Taking this law plus the law of inertia and the second law of motion together with what are called initial conditions—the mast is 114 feet high, the ship is traveling at a constant speed of 10 feet a second, and so on—it could be deduced that the stone would hit the foot of the mast in three seconds. To diagram the application of these laws:

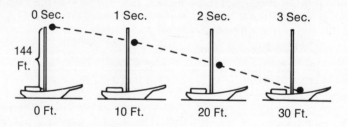

The form of the explanation would be this:

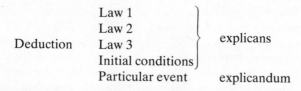

In this example the question "Why?" was asked of a particular event, and the answer took the form of a deduction from laws and a statement of initial conditions, such as, "the ship is traveling at a constant speed of 10 feet a second," and "the mast is 114 feet high." If we had started with the laws and initial conditions and deduced this particular event, this would be an example of a *prediction*.

Probabilistic Explanations

Many explanations in the sciences are not deductive explanations. These nondeductive explanations are sometimes called *probabilistic explanations*. Generally such explanations take this form:

$$\left.\begin{array}{l} \text{Probabilistic generalities} \\ \text{Statements of initial conditions} \end{array}\right\} \text{explicans}$$

$$\text{Singular statement} \qquad \text{explicandum}$$

A singular statement treats of some particular event, person, and so on. A *probabilistic generality* is a generality which is not stated with strict universality but has forms such as: "Most X's are Y's" or "Generally X is Y." Probabilistic generalities *can* occur in deductive explanations since the distinction between deductive and probabilistic explanations is a distinction based on the way the explicans is related to the explicandum. In a probabilistic explanation the relation is nondeductive. The distinction between probabilistic and deductive explanations has nothing to do with whether the explanation is true or just "probable," as this word is commonly used.

Such a probabilistic explanation will now be considered. It is an explanation of this event: the disappearance of many competing daily newspapers between 1920 and 1962.

In 1920 there were 552 cities with competing daily newspapers. In 1962 there were fewer than 60. Why has this happened? Ben Bagdikian, the chief Washington correspondent of *The Providence Journal*, gave this explanation:[2] The greatest part of the total cost of the daily papers is paid for not by their readers, who barely support the cost of delivery, but by advertisers, who pay 75 to 80 percent of the total. The prime concern of the advertiser is the cost of getting one line of advertising into the hands of one reader. Thus they will generally advertise with the paper which charges attractive rates. Since the cost of production is about the same, normally, for a large paper as it is for a small paper (the big cost is in the composing room), the larger papers can give lower rates. This results in money flowing to the larger papers without collusion, etc. The result is an almost irresistible trend to monopoly, which explains the fact that in 1920 there were 552 cities with competing dailies whereas today there are fewer than 60. This explanation can be distilled even further as follows:

Generally between 1920 and 1962 advertisers' money has gone to the larger papers.
Generally is a paper cannot get advertisers it cannot survive.
The smaller papers have generally not gotten the advertisers' dollar.　　　　explicans

Smaller papers died between 1920 and 1962.　　　　explicandum

Note that this explicandum is not a deductive consequence of these probabilistic generalizations (or of other appropriate probabilistic or singular statements which we might add to the explicans).

Historical Explanations

In the following example a particular event which happened in the past is explained—the U.S.S.R. built during a particular space of time only a fraction of the nuclear delivery system which they could have built. The explanation, as we will see, takes the form of explaining the *reasons* or motives the leaders of the U.S.S.R had in doing this.

[2] Cf. Ben Bagdikian, "Why Dailies Die," in *The New Republic*, Vol. 146, April 1962.

In 1961 Robert McNamara, the Secretary of Defense of the United States, said the United States nuclear strike force consisted of 17,000 intercontinental bombers, 1,000 medium-range bombers, several dozen operational ICBMs, 80 Polaris missiles in submarines, 300 carrier aircraft armed with nuclear warheads, and 1,000 land-based supersonic fighters with nuclear warheads. Semiofficial estimates from Washington gave the U.S.S.R. some 50 ICBMs, 150 intercontinental bombers, and some 400 medium-range bombers which cannot cover the United States as the United States nonintercontinental aircraft can cover Russia.

According to a statement of Senator Stuart Symington, the U.S.S.R. in 1961 had only 3.5 percent of the number of ICBMs predicted in 1956 and only 19 percent of the bomber strength predicted in 1956. If the U.S.S.R. had the capacity to build such a large nuclear delivery system, why, up to late 1961, had it built such a small system (supposing the semiofficial figures and Senator Symington's sources are correct)?

P. M. S. Blackett, a British physicist and military analyst, provided this *possible* explanation:[3] Blackett says that to understand the possible motives behind Soviet defense policy it is necessary to consider the history of the growth of nuclear weapon power. From 1947 to 1954, during the period of the United States' monopoly or overwhelming numerical superiority, the United States' defense policy was to destroy Soviet cities in the event of a war. From the U.S.S.R.'s point of view, land forces were the only available counter to this. "The answer to the threat of nuclear attack was the threat of taking over Europe on the ground." The United States' strategy of massive retaliation became less and less plausible as the Soviet nuclear stockpile grew. You cannot threaten an enemy with a nuclear attack when you know he can level an attack against you. The advent of the ICMB, which is difficult to destroy in flight, increased the stalemate. Two contrasting military theories evolved in response to this situation. The first was minimum deterrence, that is, the possession of a force adequate only for retaliatory attack and highly invulnerable to the first strike attack because of being either underground or hidden. The second was maximum deterrence (or counterforce), that is, the development of a force which could wipe out an enemy without his being able to retaliate substantially, so that if it ever became obvious that an attack was imminent, an attack could be launched before the aggressor's attack. Since, for one thing, the U.S.S.R. could disperse and keep secret its ICBM bases, and since an enormous military bill is a burden for a developing country like the U.S.S.R., they followed the first theory and produced a fraction of the delivery system they could have produced.

---

[3] Cf. P. M. S. Blackett, "Steps Toward Disarmament," in *Scientific American*, Vol. 206, No. 34, April 1962.

Blackett's explanation can be summarized as follows:

> The Soviet leaders believed that a minimum deterrent force, given the vastness of their land and secrecy, would provide an adequate deterrent and be less a burden on the economy than a maximum deterrent force.

> Therefore during 1956–61 the U.S.S.R. built only a fraction of the nuclear delivery system which they could have built.

This explanation is a historical explanation. And since the explicans gives the reasons why a person or persons acted in a certain way, it is often called a *reason-explanation*.

An issue of importance and interest raised concerning historical explanations is: Do historical explanations contain implicit assumptions dealing with probabilistic generalities? No explicitly stated probabilistic generality is to be found in the preceding historical explanation. However, those who see such generalities implicit in such explanations would argue that a statement like the following is supposed in the explicans: Generally when people believe a plan is possible and the alternative to it involve burdens not involved in this plan (and sometimes such plan must be followed), people choose this plan. If such generalities are implicit, then reason-explanations in history would have a closer similarity to the earlier examples than they would have without such generalities.

Not all historical explanations or explanations in the other social sciences, for example, sociology and economics, deal with the reasons for a person or persons doing some act. Often, to take one example, the social scientist is interested in the causes which led up to some state of affairs, for example, the Renaissance, or some particular event, for example, the stock market drop on Blue Monday.

Functional Explanations

In the human bloodstream there are about 7,000 white blood cells per cubic millimeter (the leucocytes and the lymphocytes). The leucocytes are formed in the red bone marrow in the same region where red cells arise. They are constantly being formed and disintegrated. Why does the blood contain leucocytes? When they are markedly reduced in number an individual becomes quite susceptible to infections. Great reduction in numbers is fatal. Their primary function is thus to defend the body against infection. They defend against infection by engulfing and destroying the invading organic particles.

In this example the question was asked, "Why are there leucocytes in the blood?" To ask this question, in this context, is to ask for the *function* of leucocytes in the blood. In turn, to ask for their function in this context is to ask for their role in maintaining life in the human body. Or, to put it another way, given a system S (the human body) and a state B (the state of being a living organism), in asking for the function of X (leucocytes) we want to know how X is related to maintaining S in state B.

There are three interesting aspects of functional explanations. First, to give a functional explanation for some X, one must be able to describe both S and B. Second, since in areas other than biology (even in physics) one is able to describe S's and the corresponding B's, functional explanations for X's can be given in other sciences. Third, functional explanations are, ordinarily, genuine explanations. (The notion of a "genuine explanation" is discussed in the next section.)

Empathetic Explanations

Here is what is now generally regarded as the classic example of an empathetic or, as it is sometimes called, a meaningful explanation: Max Weber in his book *The Protestant Ethic and the Spirit of Capitalism*, makes the observation that "business leaders and owners of capital, as well as the higher grades of skilled labour, and even more the higher technically and commercially trained personnel of modern enterprises, are overwhelmingly Protestant." He then employs Mill's Methods and concludes that the explanation for this is to be sought not only in the historico-politico-economic situations, but in the character of Protestant beliefs.

Weber begins his explanation by analyzing the attitude toward life or philosophy of life which those men have who are responsible for modern capitalism. He calls this attitude toward life "the Spirit of Capitalism." According to Weber, the spirit of capitalism is, first, the attitude that it is one's duty or ethical obligation to increase his profits; second, the attitude that profits are an end in themselves (at least in this life), that is, they are no longer sought as a means for satisfaction of material needs or for leisure; and, last, the attitude which seeks profits rationally, systematically, and legally. We can easily see how men with this attitude toward life would direct their activity toward money making.

He then analyzes the attitude toward life which often emerged from early Protestantism. He calls these psychological consequences "Protestant Asceticism." This attitude can be summarized as the belief that one's work is the task set by God—thus the fulfillment of this task is the highest form of moral activity—and the belief that good works are an indispensable sign of salvation. But by "good works" was meant a *life* of good works. "There was no place for the very human Catholic cycle of sin, repentance, atonement, release, followed by renewed sin." Only by a fundamental change, as Weber says, in the whole meaning of life at every moment and in every action could the effects of salvation be *proved*.

It is not hard for us to see how Weber thinks Protestant asceticism leads to the Spirit of Capitalism, especially if we believe, as Weber does, that many Protestants believed that the attainment of wealth, as a fruit of labor, was a sign of God's blessing. In support of this belief Weber cites (along with other statements) statements made by Protestant clergy. For example, Richard Baxter wrote, "If God shows you a way in which you may lawfully get more than in another way (without wrong to your soul or to any other), if you refuse this, and choose the less gainful way, you cross one of the ends of your calling, and you refuse to be God's steward, and to accept His gifts and use them for Him when He requireth it: you may labour to be rich for God, though not for the flesh and sin." Weber argues that today the spirit of capitalism exists generally without religious basis—"the idea of duty in one's calling prowls about in our lives like the ghost of dead religious beliefs." Most acquire this attitude not primarily through the church but through the existing economic and cultural order. The structure of Weber's explanation is shown in this simplified presentation of his argument:

1. Protestantism (C) developed individuals who had the attitude toward life called "Protestant Asceticism" (Vc).
2. We all understand *from our own experiences* how Vc leads to the attitude toward life called 'The Spirit of Capitalism" (Ve).
3. Individuals who had Ve were primarily responsible for the development of modern capitalism (E).

Therefore we can understand why E developed under conditions C.

This explanation connects C with E by way of psychological states Vc and Ve. A person is said to understand the connection between C and E (and thus see the explanation for C being connected with E) only insofar as he can understand from his own experience how Vc is connected with Ve. It is this feature which has led some to call such explanations *empathetic* or *meaningful explanations*. Such explanations employ what has been called "the operation called 'Verstehen'." This "operation" needs to be performed in order to understand premise (2) and see that it is true (supposing that it is true).

A much simpler example of an empathetic explanation is this: An investigator of the low marriage rates in a farm area finds that in this area the farmers have had a series of crop failures. He performs "verstehen" and comes up with this explanation:

1. Crop failures (C) produce feelings of insecurity (Vc).
2. From our own experiences we know that Vc leads to a fear of new commitments (Ve).
3. Ve would lead to low marriage rates (E).

Therefore we see why E occurs under conditions C.

Sometimes "verstehen" can be employed to suggest some C. Someone might ask, "Why E?" The answer would take this form: If Ve, then E. If Vc, then Ve. If C, then Vc. So it would seem that C is what explains the occurrence of E.

Four points need to be noticed about empathetic explanations: First, premises like (1), (2), and (3) cannot occur in explanations in the physical sciences for the obvious reason that inanimate and certain organic objects do not have such psychological states. In this sense empathetic explanations are unique to the social sciences. However, in each of the sciences certain subject matter is treated which is not found in any other science. Second, whether or not C is the cause of the primary variable related to E can be tested. In our second example the investigator might find that in the farm area there have been few if any eligible men. This would falsify the supposition that crop failures account for low marriage rates. Third, a social scientist does not have to have experienced himself the connection between Vc and Ve, $C—Vc$, and $Ve—E$ to know that there are such connections. Fourth, many philosophers of science see the value of "verstehen" as simply suggesting to the investigator a C and E relation.

Summary

Using a line to separate premises from conclusion, the typical form taken by explanations of the sciences is either:

	Universal Law (s)	Universal Law 1
		Universal Law 2
Deductive	Statement of initial conditions	.
		.
		Universal Law n
	Particular event	Universal generality
or:		
	Probabilistic generalities	
Nondeductive	Statements of initial conditions	
	Singular statement	

Examples 1, 2, and 3 fit into one of these patterns. The question whether historical and functional explanations fit a pattern is a controversial issue. Empathetic explanations, whether or not they fit a pattern, suggest possible relationships between certain C's and E's. All of the explicans in the six examples could be tested, though the test procedures would show certain variations.

It should again be pointed out that the six examples do not exhaust the various kinds of explanations found in the sciences. Nor should it be concluded that the different sciences *necessarily* provide a certain *type* of explanation—that is, that explanations in the biological sciences are necessarily functional. The sort of explanation—of a given phenomenon or historical event or of a group of such things—that is *possible* in the context of a science depends primarily on the stage of the development of that science into a formally organized body of knowledge and, indirectly, of course, on the knowledge available in that science.

EXERCISES 13.1

Classify each of the following as: deductive explanation; probabilistic explanation; teleological explanation; historical explanation; empathetic explanation; none of these. Justify your classification.

1. Why are tornadoes so destructive? A tornado destroys property and causes loss of life because the low pressures lead to the explosion of closed buildings and vehicles and the strong winds blow away whatever lies in their path.

    The reasons for the explosions are well known. The pressure in a tornado may cause a drop of atmospheric pressure by 8 percent or more in a matter of seconds. Suppose the pressure inside a house is normal atmospheric, about 15 pounds per square inch. If a tornado moves over the house, the pressure outside may suddenly drop by 8 percent to 13.8 pounds per square inch. Since the pressure inside the house will drop fairly slowly, especially if all the doors and windows are closed, the force on each square inch of wall and ceiling may amount to 1.2 pounds or about 170 pounds per square foot. If the house had a ceiling space 20 by 40 feet in area, the force exerted on the roof would be about 68 tons. This suddenly applied force can blow the roof off the house as if an explosion had occurred. This is especially true for dwellings, because in most houses the roof is held on mainly by its own weight. And it is evident, too, that few walls will survive 170 pounds of force per square foot.

    The strong winds associated with the tornado are capable of picking up and moving the entire house. Cars, trucks, trailers, and other heavy objects are frequently carried away. The velocity of these winds has been estimated at 500–700 miles per hour.

    (Adapted from Louis J. Battan, *The Nature of Violent Storms*)
2. How is light energy converted into chemical energy? Nature set herself the task to catch in flight the light streaming towards the earth, and to store this, the most evasive of all forces, by converting it into an

immobile form. To achieve this, she has covered the earth's crust with organisms, which while living take up the sunlight and use its force to add continuously to the sum of chemical difference.

These organisms are the plants: the plant world forms a reservoir in which the volatile sun rays are fixed and ingeniously laid down for later use; a providential economic measure, to which the very physical existence of the human race is inexorably bound.

(Julius Robert von Mayer, 1845)

3. Why does great display of wealth no longer occur in the United States? John Galbraith in his book *The Affluent Society* gives this explanation:

Such display is now passé. There was an adventitious contributing cause. The American well-to-do have long been curiously sensitive to feat of expropriation—a fear which may be related to the tendency for even the mildest reformist measures to be viewed, in the conservative conventional wisdom, as the portents of revolutions. The depression and especially the New Deal gave the American rich a serious fright. One consequence was to usher in a period of marked discretion in personal expenditure. Purely ostentatious outlays, especially on dwellings, yachts, and females, were believed likely to incite the masses to violence. They were rebuked as unwise and improper by the more discreet. It was much wiser to take on the protective coloration of the useful citizen, the industrial statesman, or even the average guy.

However, deeper causes were at work. Increasingly in the last quarter century the display of expensive goods, as a device for suggesting wealth, has been condemned as vulgar. The term is precise. Vulgar means: "Of or pertaining to the common people, or to the common herd or crowd." An this explains what happened. Lush expenditure could be afforded by so many that it ceased to be useful as a mark of distinction. A magnificent, richly upholstered, and extremely high-powered automobile conveys no impression of wealth in a day when such automobiles are mass-produced by the thousands. A house in Palm Beach is not a source of distinction when the rates for a thousand hotel rooms in Miami Beach rival its daily upkeep. Once a sufficiently impressive display of diamonds could create attention even for the most obese and repellent body, for they signified membership in a highly privileged caste. Now the same diamonds are afforded by a television star or a talented harlot. Modern mass communications, especially the movies and television, insure that the populace at large will see the most lavish caparisoning on the bodies not of the daughters of the rich but on the daughters of coal miners and commercial travelers, who struck it rich by their own talents or some facsimile thereof. In South America, in the Middle East, to a degree in socialist India, and at Nice, Cannes, and Deauville, ostentatious display by the rich is still much practiced. This accords with expectations. In these countries most people are still, in the main, poor and unable to afford the goods which advertise wealth. Therefore ostentation continues to have a purpose. In not being accessible to too many people it has not yet become vulgar.

(JOHN KENNETH GALBRAITH, *The Affluent Society*)[4]

4. In the early 1930's, while the world struggled to escape from the great depression that was shaking capitalism to its foundations, the classically trained economists wrestled to fit facts to orthodox theory. Public policy was in disarray. Classical theory had taught that when demand fell, prices and wages should fall and resources would once again be employed. But the actual effects of the drastic fall in prices on farmers was a disastrous fall in income! . . .

Gardiner Means and other economists were struck by the fact that some prices were more classical than others, that while farm prices had fallen sharply, many industrial prices—those in the great corporate industries—had fallen very little. Working for the Department of Agriculture, Means studied the behavior of 74 prices. This led him to his second major advance, the notion of administered prices.

There are, he found, two principal kinds of prices. One price is set in competitive markets and changes frequently in response to changes in demand. The other is set by administrative action and held constant for varying periods of time, despite changes in demand. Farm prices are typical market prices. Cement prices are typically administered.

In an administered market, an increase in demand leads to an increase in output. When demand falls, as it did during the great depressions, the price is largely held and output is slashed. This characteristic of rigid prices, Means concluded, was the basic cause of the depression's depth. As demand fell, output instead of price was cut; men were thrown out of work, and their loss of income further reduced total demand.

(BERNARD NOSSITER, "The World of Gardiner Means,"
The New Republic, May 7, 1962)

5. Consider the pre-Civil War clash of convictions on slavery in the United States. By and large, the prevailing opinion in the North was that slavery was morally wrong, and in the South that it was morally right. In the debate that raged in those days, both sides appealed to the highest moral authority in support of their respective views. Such a clear-cut division of moral sentiments on geographical lines is most remarkable. It could not have happened by chance and must be explained.

Today most of us would accept the explanation that the different convictions derived from the existence of different institutions. Slavery

---

[4] John Kenneth Galbraith, *The Affluent Society* (Boston: Houghton Mifflin Co., 1958), pp. 91–93. Copyright © 1958 by John Kenneth Galbraith. Used by permission.

was a fact in the South. It was woven into the very fabric of southern life. Therefore, a disturbance of slavery meant for southerners a profound change in their way of life. Under the supposition that man usually resists profound changes of established ways (except when the established ways become unbearable), we see that the southern support of slavery was understandable.

But the Marxists wish to delve deeper. . . .

Underlying the clash of conceptions of what is morally right, according to the Marxists, were the clashing economic interests of the ruling classes of the North and South, respectively. In the South, the ruling class, that is, the owners of the large plantations, derived their incomes and therefore their power, by exploiting agricultural labor. In those days, agricultural labor required no skill and could best be controlled if the laborers were kept in complete ignorance. Slavery, therefore, filled the bill. In the North, however, a new ruling class was emerging—the industrialists, who controlled the means of production in manufacture. Now the increasing importance of machinery made slave labor unfit in factories. The industrial worker had to be at least somewhat literate. More than that, he had to be motivated in a way that a slave could not be. Finally, it was in the interest of the manufacturer to have a fluid labor force, a labor market, a reservoir, from which labor could be recruited and on which it could be dumped when not needed. . . . the industrialist did not buy the whole worker; he bought only the worker's labor. . . .

An ambition to extend the industrial system to the South would therefore be coupled with a conviction that slavery must be replaced by a free labor force. Since high sounding ideals are easier to defend (to oneself as well as to others) than economic self-interest, it is easy to see how the real aim, freedom of contract, became translated quite sincerely into "freedom of person."

(ANATOL RAPOPORT, *Fights, Games and Debates*)[5]

6. Freud in his *A General Introduction to Psychoanalysis*, recounts how he was called upon to explain why a fifty-three year old happily married woman had *delusions of jealousy*. A young girl, clearly out of jealousy, sent a letter to the woman telling that another young girl was having an affair with her husband. Though the woman clearly saw the accusation was false, she was prostrated by the letter. She suffered as much as she would have if the charges were well-founded. What caused this suffering?

---

[5] Reprinted from *Fights, Games and Debates* by Anatol Rapoport by permission of the University of Michigan Press. Copyright © by the University of Michigan 1960. All rights reserved. Published in the United States of America by the University of Michigan Press and simultaneously in Toronto, Canada by Ambassador Books Limited.

Freud found out that the letter was provoked by the patient herself. She had said to the young lady, who was then her housemaid, that nothing could be more awful than to hear that her husband was having an affair. During the interview with the patient, Freud found that she had an infatuation for her son-in-law which she was not fully aware of, and she disguised it as harmless tenderness.

From these two observations, Freud provided this explanation for the woman's illness: such a monstrous infatuation was an impossible thing and could not come to her conscious mind. Some sort of relief had to be found since it "persisted" and "unconsciously exerted a heavy pressure." ". . . the simplest alleviation lay in that mechanism of displacement which so regularly plays its part in the formation of delusional jealousy. If not merely she, the old woman that she was, were in love with a young man, but if only her old husband too were in love with a young mistress, then her torturing conscience would be absolved from infidelity." Relief came to her by her "projecting" her own state of mind onto her husband.

7. When the group norms are no longer binding or valid in an area or for a population subgroup—. . . deviant behavior becomes more frequent. . . . In a stable community a child is born and raised in a context of established norms which are supported by a social concensus. He tends to interiorize these norms, and they contribute to the establishment of his psychological field of needs, goals and motivations. Generally, the child acts to satisfy his needs in a manner which has the approval of society. If he acts in a deviant fashion, formal and informal controls—including his own ego with its interiorized norms— act to deter the child from further deviant conduct. Unstable community conditions and the consequent weakening of social controls that are congruent with the dominant culture provide fertile ground for the emergence of variant norms and group standards.

(BERNARD LANDER, *Towards an Understanding of Juvenile Delinquency*)[6]

8. Why does it appear that man will not always dominate the planet? In the words of Edward Drinker Cope, the great American naturalist: "The highly developed, or specialized types of one geological period have not been the parents of the types of succeeding periods but . . . the descent has been derived from the less specialized of preceding ages." The highly and narrowly adapted flourish, but they move in a path which becomes ever more difficult to retrace or break away from as their adaptation becomes perfected. Their proficiency may increase, their numbers may grow. But their perfect adaptation, so necessary for

[6] Bernard Lander, *Towards an Understanding of Juvenile Delinquency* (New York: Columbia University Press, 1954).

survival, can become a euphemism for death. Man's specialization has introduced a new kind of life into the universe—one capable within limits of ordering its own environment and transmitting that order through social rather than biological heredity. Nevertheless his physical modifications appear to be at an end, or close to an end, and sooner or later, Cope's law of the unspecialized will have its chance once more. (Adapted from LOREN C. EISELEY, *"Is Man Here to Stay?"*)[7]

9. To understand how chelation works we must examine the nature of a chemical bond. According to the modern theory of valence, the atoms in a molecule are bound together by electrons, the charged particles that surround every atom. The bond may be established in one of two ways. An atom may transfer one of its electrons to its neighbor. In that case the atom that loses the electron also loses its electrical neutrality and becomes positively charged, while the atom that receives the electron becomes negatively charged. These two "ions" then are held together by the electrical attraction of their opposite charges. The other way in which two atoms may be bound together is by sharing a pair of electrons—as if two persons were held together by a pair of ropes that belonged not exclusively to either individual but to both together. This is called a covalent bond: the chemist represents it by a single line joining the two atoms. Usually each of the two joined atoms supplies one of the two binding electrons. But sometimes one atom supplies both, and that kind of link is called a co-ordinate bond. The chemist's symbol for such a bond is an arrow pointing toward the atom which has received the electrons. Now a chelate ring is simply a group of atoms linked into a ring with one or more co-ordinate bonds. The atoms that donate the electrons are usually oxygen, nitrogen or sulfur; the acceptor atom, grasped in the claw of arrows, is nearly always a metal. In such a ring the metal atom is gripped more firmly than if it were merely attached to atoms in independent molecules. Another way of saying this is that a metal atom is much more prone to unite with two donor atoms in a ring-forming molecule than with the same atoms in two separate molecules. The mechanics of the situation make clear why this is so. To become attached to two separate molecules, the metal atom must capture a donor atom in each molecule separately, and this depends on chance contacts. But when the metal atom becomes attached to one end of a molecule that can form a ring around it, it easily links up with the other end, for the latter is tethered and cannot range far ahead.   (HAROLD F. WALTON, "Chelation")[8]

---

[7] Loren C. Eiseley, "Is Man Here to Stay?" in *Scientific American Reader* (New York: Simon and Schuster, 1953), pp. 483–489.

[8] Harold F. Walton, "Chelation" in *New Chemistry* (New York: Simon and Schuster, 1957). Reprinted with permission. Copyright © 1957 by Scientific American, Inc. All rights reserved.

10. We know that the substances extracted from plants ferment when they are abandoned to themselves, and disappear little by little in contact with the air. We know that the cadavers of animals undergo putrefaction and that soon only their skeletons remain. This destruction of dead organic matter is one of the necessities of the perpetuation of life.

If the remnants of dead plants and animals were not destroyed, the surface of the earth would soon be encumbered with organic matter, and life would become impossible because the cycle of transformation . . . could no longer be closed.

It is necessary that the fibrin of our muscles, the albumin of our blood, the gelatine of our bones, the urea of our urine, the ligneus matter of plants, the sugar of their fruits, the starch of their seeds . . . be progressively converted into water, ammonia and carbon dioxide so that the elementary principles of these complex organic substances be taken up again by plants, elaborated anew, to serve as food for new living beings similar to those that gave birth to them, and so on *ad infinitum* to the end of the centuries.

(RENÉ DUBOS, *Pasteur and Modern Science*)[9]

11. The theory [Clark L. Hull's Learning Theory] is introduced by an anecdotal experiment. The subject is a six-year-old child who likes candy and is hungry for it. While she is out of the room a piece of her favorite candy is hidden under the edge of the center book in the lower shelf of a bookcase of several shelves. She is brought into the room, told there is candy hidden under one of the books, and asked if she wants to try to find it. She does, so she proceeds to look for the candy, after which she is told that she must replace each book after looking under it, and that she may eat the candy when she finds it. She finds the candy after spending 210 seconds and examining 37 books. The next time she goes right to the lower shelf, and it takes her only 87 seconds and she looks under only 12 books. The next time she finds the candy under the second book examined, and it has taken her only 11 seconds. The next time she doesn't do so well. She starts at the other end of the shelf and works back. The authors speculate that she either was just lucky the time before, or introduced some other notion as a result of her previous experience with hiding games, such as, "He'll probably change the place now that I know it." Thereafter she continues to do better until on the ninth and tenth trials she goes right to the correct book and gets the candy.

According to some psychologists, there are four facts in learning: drive, cue, response, and reward. A *drive* is a strong stimulus which impels to action. The child's drives were a complex of hunger, a cultivated appetite for candy, and secondary drives related to social participation and social approval. Responses are elicited by *cues*. Cues

---

[9] René Dubos, op. cit., pp. 74–75.

determine "when he will respond, where he will respond, and which response he will make." The child was given a great many cues. She was told that the candy was under a book, and that she would be permitted to eat it when she found it. Drive impels the individual to *respond* to certain cues. Only if the response occurs can it be rewarded and learned, and one of the tasks of training is so to arrange the situation that the desired response will occur. The little girl was impelled to begin picking up books by her appetite for candy and her knowledge that candy was to be found under a book. Responses made to cues in the presence of drives will be learned if they are *rewarded*. If they are not rewarded, the tendency to repeat them will be weakened. Rewards produce reduction in drives; drive-reduction is, in fact, what makes them rewarding. That is why it is rewarding to be relieved from pain, to drink when thirsty, to eat when hungry. In the case of the little girl, eating the candy was rewarding.

(Adapted from ERNEST L. HILGARD, *Theories of Learning*)

12. The reasons why religion is necessary is apparently to be found in the fact that human society achieves its unity primarily through the possession by its members of certain ultimate values and ends in common. Although these values and ends are subjective, they influence behavior, and their integration enables the society to operate as a system. Derived neither from inherited nor from external nature, they have evolved as a part of culture by communication and moral pressure. They must, however, appear to the members of the society to have some reality, and it is the role of religious belief and ritual to supply and reinforce this appearance of reality. Through belief and ritual the common ends and values are connected with an imaginary world symbolized by concrete sacred objects, which world in turn is related in a meaningful way to the facts and trials of the individual's life. Through the worship of the sacred objects and the beings they symbolize, and the acceptance of supernatural prescriptions that are at the same time codes of behavior, a powerful control over human conduct is exercised, guiding it along lines sustaining the institutional structure and conforming to the ultimate ends and values.

(KINGSLEY DAVIS and WILBERT E. MOORE, "Some Principles of Stratification") in *American Sociological Review*, Vol. 10.

13. What is the nature of the forces that hold together the protons and neutrons in an atomic nucleus? In 1935 the Japanese physicist Hideki Yukawa suggested that a new kind of field, consisting of quanta of energy which might take the form of particles of a certain mass, might account for these forces. He pointed out that electrical and gravitational forces, the two chief forces previously known, could be explained in terms of the emission and reabsorption of light quanta and gravitational quanta respectively. Since the nuclear forces were of a

completely different type—not only more powerful but acting over much smaller distances than electrical or gravitational forces—it seemed reasonable to Yukawa to introduce a new type of field which would be responsible for the nuclear forces.... Yukawa estimated that the mass of the field quanta exchanged between two nucleons would be about 200 to 300 times that of the electron. He called these field quanta mesons. The mesons were thought of as the nuclear glue binding together the neutrons and protons in the nucleus. Since there were three types of equally strong bonds in the nucleus (neutron-proton, proton-proton, and neutron-neutron) it was assumed that there would be three kinds of mesons, namely, positive, negative, and neutral.   (ROBERT E. MARSAK, "The Multiplicity of Particles" in *Scientific American Reader*, 1953)

ANSWERS

2. Functional. A system, roughly earth's environment, is maintained in a certain state, characterized by the abundance of certain chemicals, by the actions of plants exposed to sunlight.

3. Wealthy people in the United States came to realize that there were reasons why they should not ostentatiously display their wealth. One was that such a display would incite the masses to violence. The more significant reason was that everyone could afford what used to be the properties of the wealthy only. So, for these reasons the ostentatious display of wealth has declined. This is a historical explanation.

9. Clearly a causal explanation.

Genuine and Pseudoscientific Explanations

In this section conditions will be suggested which will enable us to distinguish genuine scientific explanations such as those considered in the first section, from pseudoscientific explanations such as biological entelechy theories, historical determinism, and astrology. The method employed in arriving at these conditions is this: We will first examine some suggested criteria for distinguishing genuine from pseudoexplanations. We will see how they do demarcate many clear-cut genuine explanations from clear-cut pseudoexplanations, but we will find that there are a significant number of clear-cut genuine explanations which are not properly demarcated from pseudoexplanations (and vice versa) by these criteria. We will then *suggest* a set of conditions which, on the whole, seem to set off clear-cut examples of genuine explanations from clear-cut examples of pseudoexplanations. The section will end up with suggestions for those additional conditions which will distinguish genuine scientific explanations which are satisfactory, such as the kinetic theory of heat, and the molecular theory of matter, from those genuine scientific explanations which are unsatisfactory such as the Ptolemaic theory, the caloric theory, and the Galenic theory.

It will be profitable to make mention of the distinction between genuine scientific explanations, pseudoscientific explanations, and nonscientific explanations. A nonscientific explanation is an answer to a why-question, as are scientific and pseudoscientific explanations. But in a nonscientific explanation both the question and the explanation fall outside the area of scientific why-questions and answers. Such questions and answers are sometimes found in such areas as the arts and religion. Often one indication of the fact that they do fall outside the area of scientific why-questions and answers is the impossibility of there being a conflict between these answers and statements in the sciences, but we will not elaborate this point. When, however, an explanation is represented as being in the area of science, then the question can be asked whether the explanation is a genuine scientific explanation or a pseudoscientific explanation.

Unsatisfactory Criteria of Demarcation

How does one tell, generally, when an explanation which is represented as scientific is a genuine explanation and when it is a pseudoscientific explanation? We will begin our reply to this question by considering three unsatisfactory criteria for distinguishing genuine from pseudoscientific explanations. The reason these criteria are unsatisfactory, as we will see, is not that they do not distinguish *some* genuine explanations from some pseudoscientific explanations, but that they exclude from the class of genuine explanations a number of generally recognized genuine explanations and include a number of generally recognized pseudoscientific explanations.

1. An explanation is genuine if the general statements in the explicans are arrived at by induction.

Some have supposed that the difference between a genuine scientific and a pseudoscientific explanation consists in whether the general statements in the explicans were arrived at by induction. By "induction" is meant arguments of the first kind discussed in Chapter 11, that is, arguments, for example, of this form:

A_1 is B
A_2 is B
$\vdots$
A_n is B
$\therefore A$ is B

If the general statements of the explicans were arrived at by induction, then the explanation is a genuine scientific explanation; and if the general statements were not arrived at by induction, then the explanation is a pseudoexplanation.

This criterion clearly will not do. As we have seen, most explanations for phenomena, empirical laws, and theoretical laws, are each originally arrived at as a "free creation of the mind." That is, they are a response to the question: What explains such-and-such phenomena, or law (or laws)? Thus if (1) were the criterion for demarcation, most theoretical explanations and many empirical explanations would fall into the class of pseudoexplanations.

> 2. An explanation is genuine if the general statements in the explicans are established by induction.

Generally empirical laws are established by induction, but theoretical hypotheses are not established by induction (in the above sense), but rather through what we have called corroboration. Thus (2) is an unsatisfactory criterion of demarcation, since theoretical explanations under this criterion would be classed as pseudoscientific explanations. However, if we understood "induction" to cover any inference from evidence for a generality to the generality itself, then (2), in substance, would mean that empirical hypotheses, to be genuine, must be tested, and theoretical hypotheses must be corroborated to be genuine. Understood in this way, is (2) a satisfactory criterion for demarcation? Hypotheses have been corroborated at one time and later abandoned because new phenomena or laws were uncovered, consequences from the theory were seen to conflict with observation, and so on. If (2) were the demarcation criterion, then it would follow that many hypotheses and theories in science were at one time genuine and later became pseudoexplanations. In addition, since the possibility exists that the present-day established or corroborated theory might undergo substantial change or even be abandoned at some future time, it is possible that all the presently established theories are pseudoscientific explanations, if (2) is the criterion. This criterion is thus clearly inadequate since our paradigm examples of explanations which we call genuine are those which are regarded in this way or are abandoned. Similarly, explanations like Newton's corpuscular theory of light and the Galenic theory of blood circulation are clear-cut cases of genuine scientific explanations even though they have been given up or falsified.

> 3. An explanation is genuine if there is observational verification of the statements in the explicans.

It has been suggested that one can tell the difference between a scientific and a pseudoscientific explanation by noticing whether the statements which make up the explicans can be verified by observation.

This criterion is also unsatisfactory. First, even explicans of some explanations which are regarded as pseudoexplanations can be verified by observation. For example, consider this explanation:

> When external influences tend to reduce or raise the bodily temperature of an organism, various bodily mechanisms come into play to return the temperature to normal.
> Why?
> Explanation: Homeostasis capacity of the organism.

This explanation is regarded as a pseudoexplanation, since "homeostasis" is a word used to refer to the process described in what is to be explained. It is what is called a circular explanation. However, by observation it can be verified that the human body has homeostasis capacity.

Second, (3) is unsatisfactory because, while empirical explanations can be verified by observation, no theoretical explanation can be verified or directly tested by observation. If (3), then, were our criterion for demarcation, theoretical explanations would be ruled out of the class of genuine scientific explanations, since by not being verified by observation they fail to fulfill (3).

4. An explanation is genuine if and only if falsifiability of the statements in the explicans is possible.

One can, it has been suggested, demarcate genuine from pseudo-explanations by seeing whether the statements in the explicans are falsifiable. If they are falsifiable, then the explanation is a genuine scientific explanation. If they are not falsifiable, then it is a pseudoexplanation.

The above is the criterion of demarcation suggested by the distinguished philosopher of science, Karl Popper. Popper writes:[10]

> Thus the problem which I tried to solve by proposing the criterion of falsifiability was neither a problem of meaningfulness or significance, nor a problem of truth or acceptability. It was the problem of drawing a line (as well as this can be done) between the statements, or systems of statements, of the empirical sciences, and all other statements—whether they are of a religious or of a metaphysical character, or simply pseudo-scientific. Years later—it must have been in 1928 or 1929—I called this first problem of mine the '*problem of demarcation*.' The criterion of falsifiability is a solution of this problem of demarcation, for it say that statements or systems of statements, in order to be ranked as scientific, must be capable of conflicting with possible, or conceivable, observations.

[10] Karl R. Popper, *Conjectures and Refutations* (London: Routledge and Kegan Paul, 1963), p. 39. © Karl R. Popper, 1963. Used by permission of Routledge and Kegan Paul Ltd. and K. R. Popper.

Popper is saying that in order to be classed as scientific, the statements in the explicans must be capable of conflicting with *possible* or *conceivable* observations. It is easy to misunderstand this criterion. Popper is not saying that an explanation must be false or probably false or possibly false to be ranked as scientific. He is saying that it must be *capable* of conflicting with *conceivable* observation. To make this clear, consider the statement "The sky is blue," which happens to be true today. This statement is thus *not* probably false or even possibly false, for it happens to be true that the sky is blue today. However, one could easily conceive of observations one could make today which would falsify the statement "The sky is blue." Thus the statement is true, but it is also falsifiable, as Popper uses this word. Examples of statements which are not falsifiable would be: "The universe is shrinking in such a fashion that all lengths contract in the same ratio." Or, to take another example, suppose someone said, "All humans are mortal." And suppose we find a human who is two hundred years old. Would the defender of the above assertion admit it was falsified? Suppose we actually found a Struldburg like Gulliver describes in his voyage to Laputa. (The Struldburgs never die. Some are centuries old. They grow like ordinary people, but whereas most people who live to be ninety or one hundred die, the Struldburgs continue to live, though they suffer the deformities of extreme age.) Suppose the defender still maintained that the Struldburgs are bound to die sometime. At this point we would begin to see that *his claim* is such that it is not falsifiable. The reason for this is most likely that the defender is defining "human" partially in terms of mortality. This being the case, it would be logically impossible to falsify his statement. If the statement or statements in an explicans were like these two examples, that is, not falsifiable, then, if we follow Popper's criterion, they are to be regarded as pseudoscientific explanations.

Let us now consider some examples of scientific explanations which, according to Popper, satisfy, and some which fail to satisfy this demarcation criterion. In the following quotation Popper considers three explanations— one of Freud's, one of Adler's, and one of Einstein's. The first two are pseudoexplanations because they fail to satisfy (4), whereas the third is a genuine explanation since it fulfills (4).[11]

> ... every conceivable case could be interpreted in the light of Adler's theory, or equally of Freud's. I may illustrate this by two very different examples of human behavior: that of a man who pushes a child into the water with the intention of drowning it; and that of a man who sacrifices his life in an attempt to save the child. Each of these two cases can be explained with equal ease in Freudian and in Adlerian terms. According to Freud the first man suffered from repression (say, of some component of his Oedipus complex), while the second man had achieved sublimation. According to Adler the first man suffered from feelings of inferiority (producing perhaps the need to prove

[11] Ibid., pp. 35–36. Used by permission.

to himself that he dared to commit some crime), and so did the second man (whose need was to prove to himself that he dared to rescue the child). I could not think of any human behavior which could not be interpreted in terms of either theory. It was precisely this fact—that they always fitted, that they were always confirmed—which in the eyes of their admirers constituted the strongest argument in favour of these theories. It began to dawn on me that this apparent strength was in fact their weakness.

With Einstein's theory the situation was strikingly different. Take one typical instance—Einstein's prediction, just then confirmed by the findings of Eddington's expedition. Einstein's gravitational theory had led to the result that light must be attracted by heavy bodies (such as the sun), precisely as material bodies were attracted. As a consequence it could be calculated that light from a distant fixed star whose apparent position was close to the sun would reach the earth from such a direction that the star would seem to be slightly shifted away from the sun; or, in other words, that stars close to the sun would look as if they had moved a little away from the sun, and from one another. This is a thing which cannot normally be observed since such stars are rendered invisible in daytime by the sun's overwhelming brightness; but during an eclipse it is possible to take photographs of them. If the same constellation is photographed at night one can measure the distances on the two photographs, and check the predicted effect.

According to Popper, Freud's and Adler's explanations for human actions are such that they are not falsifiable. No conceivable action could be imagined which would not be compatible with these explanations. On the other hand, from Einstein's gravitational theory a consequence follows which is such that observation could show either that it is true or that it is false. In a word, conceivable observable data could be incompatible with Einstein's theory.

The falsifiability criterion, like criteria (1), (2), and (3), does set off some recognized pseudoscientific explanations from some clear-cut genuine scientific explanations. But it is thought by some that this criterion of demarcation is both too restrictive (under it some genuine explanations would be excluded) and too broad (some pseudoexplanations would be included). We will now consider these two objections.

First Objection. Popper clearly makes the distinction between theoretical explanations and empirical explanations. Thus when he says that theoretical explanations are falsifiable he means that observable consequences can be deduced from the explanations, as in Newton's gravitational theory, which *can* either conflict or accord with observation. He does not maintain that the statements of the theory can directly conflict, and hence be falsified, or not conflict with observation. But does the falsification of such consequences imply the falsity of the theoretical explanation? This issue, it will be recalled, was discussed in Chapter 12. It was argued there that theories can be dealt death blows through the falsification of such consequences, but this does not entail the falsity of the theory. And the only way open to supposedly falsify a theoretical explanation is to deduce some consequence which conflicts with observation, since the explanation cannot directly conflict with observation. Thus unless in "falsifiability" Popper means to include "capable of being dealt a death blow," his criterion would exclude theoretical explanations from the class of genuine scientific explanations.

Second Objection. Even supposing that theoretical explanations are falsifiable, it does not follow that if an explanation is a pseudoexplanation, then it is not made up of falsifiable statements. And if falsifiability is to be a satisfactory criterion of demarcation, it must be true that obvious pseudo-explanations must not contain falsifiable explicans. But there are explanations which no one would call genuine scientific explanations and which have explicans which are made up of falsifiable statements. For example, the homeostasis example is falsifiable. Another example of a falsifiable pseudo-explanation would be this:

> Why does opium produce sleep?
> Explanation: Because it has dormitive power.

We assume that here "dormitive power" is not regarded as a defining criterion for "opium." Each of these explanations is clearly circular.

Conditions for a Genuine (Nonpseudo) Scientific Explanation

The conditions we will examine in this section result from noting in what way a group of commonly recognized genuine scientific explanations differ from a group of commonly recognized pseudoexplanations. It might well be that we could come across explanations which could not be classed definitely in either group. Thus our suggested demarcation criterion (the following two conditions) should be understood as a criterion which generally distinguishes genuine from pseudoscientific explanations. Here, then, are the two conditions which must generally be met in order for an explanation not to be a pseudoexplanation:

1. The statements of the explicans do not follow from the explicandum.

This is a *logical* condition for adequacy. An explanation which fails to meet this logical condition would be a form of what is called a circular argument. No circular explanation would be ranked as a genuine scientific explanation; and formally, no statement S_1 which is logically equivalent to S_2 can be regarded as a genuine scientific explanation of S_2. This condition would thus rule out the homeostatis and the opium explanations as genuine explanations.

2. The statements in the explicans must be testable either directly or indirectly.

An explanation is directly testable when it is possible in principle to see by observation whether the things related to the terms in the statements of the explanation are in fact related in the way stated. Empirical explanations can in principle be directly tested. From time to time, due to technical or physical difficulties, such explanations must be indirectly tested. All empirical hypotheses are clearly falsifiable. If the things referred to are observed to be related in the way stated, the statement is true; if not, then the statement is false. The second condition (2) as it applies to empirical explanations would be the same as Popper's falsifiability criterion.

An explanation is indirectly testable when it is possible to deduce, with the help of other assumptions, consequences which can in principle be directly tested. All theoretical hypotheses are open to indirect but not direct testing. Sometimes such testing results in a death blow to a theory with the consequence that the theory is given up. As pointed out, if "falsifiable" is understood to include "capable of being dealt a death blow," then this second condition would be the same as Popper's falsifiability criterion.

Three examples of statements which cannot be tested were just considered. If the way Popper regards Freud's and Adler's explanations for actions of the two men is correct, then their explanations for the two acts would be examples of untestable explanations and thus would fail to fulfill condition (2). All the explanations so far considered—the Galenic theory, Torricelli's "sea of air" explanation, Huygens' wave theory, Galileo's explanations, Blackett's explanation, and so forth—are clear-cut cases of testable explanations. And since they all fulfill the first condition (1) they are all examples of genuine scientific explanations.

From time to time an explanation is so formulated that consequences follow from the theory which are capable of conflicting with observation. But when these consequences are found, through experiment, to conflict with observation, the theory is sometimes so modified that it can no longer be tested. For example during the nineteenth century it was thought by most authorities that light waves travel through what was called "ether" in the way in which sound travels through air and in the way in which a wave travels through water. Luminiferous ether was thought of as a motionless substance filling all space. If light waves (indicated by the dotted lines) were sent out from the center of a sphere traveling through space in this manner:

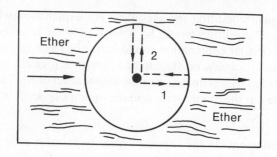

and reflected from the inner surface of the sphere as indicated, then the ether theory, as it was regarded at one time, implies that the waves would not return to the center simultaneously. The ether theory predicted that the first light wave would take longer than the second to make the trip because of the adverse effect of "bucking" the flow of ether. The situation was thought to be analogous to the adverse effect of a river current on the speed of a boat going upstream then back downstream, compared to going across the current and then back. The famous Michelson–Morley experiment in 1887 showed that light waves in such a situation will return simultaneously. There were several modifications that could be made of the ether theory that would make it compatible with the Michelson–Morley experiment. For example, it could be argued that the bodies carry their ether with them—that is, drag it along with them—or that bodies contract as they travel through the ether thus shortening the distance the first ray had to travel. Michelson suggested the first modification, and the second possible modification is known as the Lorentz–Fitzgerald Contraction Hypothesis. Michelson's suggestion was upset by Lodge's experiment in 1893 with massive discs. This experiment showed that objects do not drag the ether with them. The Contraction Hypothesis is retained today, but for reasons other than to explain the velocity of light through ether. However, the effects of this modification and others was that ether was regarded as not having any effects on the electrical, optical, or mechanical properties of matter. In a word, no experiment, however ingenious or varied, should show any trace of or detect in any way the ether's effects on anything. Thus, because the theory was reformulated to explain why the ether had no detectable effects, no experiment could possibly conflict with a consequence of the reformulated ether theory.[12]

Satisfactory and Unsatisfactory Explanations

If an explanation fulfills the two conditions introduced below, then, generally, it is a satisfactory explanation. [Actually (3) overlaps (4).] Generally, if an explanation fails to fulfill one of these conditions, then it is an unsatisfactory explanation—*assuming* it meets conditions (1) and (2) (discussed in the last section). For if it fails to meet (1) and (2), then it is not an unsatisfactory explanation but a pseudoexplanation.

3. The explicans must be supported by evidence other than the evidence upon which the acceptance of the explicandum is based.

---

[12] This was Lorentz's idea. One could (and most physicists later did) regard Lorentz's ingenious calculations as showing that there was no such thing as ether—or, at least, that the concept was not needed in physics.

This condition avoids what are generally called *ad hoc* explanations. Michelson's suggestion that the sphere carries its own ether and the Lorentz–Fitzgerald hypothesis were both *ad hoc* hypotheses at the time they were introduced. They were introduced to make the ether theory compatible with the results of the Michelson–Morley experiment. The only "evidence" for them was that they explained how the ether theory was compatible with the experimental data. An explanation that is *merely ad hoc* and is not supported by data other than that which it purports to explain is obviously unsatisfactory. However, a hypothesis introduced in this way can be either rejected or established by further investigations. For example, the Lorentz–Fitzgerald hypothesis has been retained within Einstein's relativity theory. Many hypotheses at the time of formulation are *ad hoc* in the sense that all that justifies the assertion of the hypothesis at the time of formulation is merely the fact that it explains the given set of phenomena which prompted it. An explanation ceases to be *ad hoc* when it fulfills (4), below, or when evidence other than that which it is devised to explain is provided for it.

4. The explicans must be true or corroborated.

In the preceding chapters we came across a number of explanations which failed to meet (4)—for example, the caloric theory of heat, the Galenic theory of the blood system, the corpuscular theory of light, and the Ptolemaic theory of the solar system. Notice that all of these theories satisfy condition (2). If they had not, then they could not have been shown to be false or not to hold. Thus all of these theories were genuine explanations, but since they were shown to be false or not to hold, they were unsatisfactory genuine explanations.

Examples of Pseudo- and Unsatisfactory Scientific Explanations

The four conditions described in the preceding sections will become clearer as we examine three additional examples of explanations which violate them.

Example 1: Why does the existence of strongly knit social bonds between members of a community help to sustain human beings during periods of personal stress? (explicandum) Explicans: Such societies have a great deal of social cohesion.

Assuming that "social cohesion" and "strongly knit social bonds between members of a community" are approximate synonyms, this explanation violates the first condition (1), for the explicans can be seen to follow from the explicandum.

Example 2:[13] In the case of normal development of an embryo, a definite part develops into an eye, another part into a foot, and so forth. Hans Driesch, a famous biologist, thought he had shown by experiment that if such parts are removed, the mature organism will not necessarily lack an eye or foot, since the formation of these organs will be taken over by other parts of the embryo. If, for example, the upper part of a certain organism (tabularia) is cut off, a new part grows from the surface of the amputation. If, however, the organism is divided in another way, then the very same surface which in the first case produced a head may now sprout a tail. Thus, Driesch concluded, one and the same part of a certain organism contains different "developmental potentialities" out of which may develop different parts according to what is needed for the development of a complete organism. What explains this "developmental potential" of organisms? Driesch says that it is determined by some factor which is nonspatial. He called it *entelechy*. All organic processes are in fact distinguished from inorganic processes by the presence of these entelechies. The entelechy, according to Driesch, is "a teleologically directing factor of nature. . . . There is nothing like it in the inorganic world. . . . Entelechy is not an energy, not a force, not an intensity, not a constant, but—entelechy. . . . Entelechy relates to space, thus belongs to nature; but entelechy is not *in* space—it acts not in space but into space."[14] It is, Driesch, says, "indivisible" and "nonlocalized."

There is some question whether the cutting experiments with the tabularia supported his conclusions about them. But this is not our interest. Rather, we want to know whether his explicans is a genuine explanation. It turns out that it is not, for it fails to fulfill the second condition (2). The notion of entelechy is so formulated as to remove the *possibility* of any kind of testing—direct testing, indirect testing, corroboration, and so on.

Example 3: In 1950 Immanuel Velikovsky published a book which became a best-seller, entitled *Worlds in Collision*. The theory found in the book is, in brief, that a giant comet once erupted from the planet Jupiter, passed close to the Earth on two occasions, the first about 1500 B.C., and then became the planet Venus. The comet's first encounter caused the Earth either to stop spinning or to slow down. There was a short retreat and a second passing which caused thunder, earthquakes, and so forth. Several years later a precipitate of carbohydrates formed in the comet's tail fell to the Earth. The second encounter occurred 52 years later and had similar effects on the Earth. The theory is held up as explaining what caused the Red Sea to divide (the slowing of the Earth's spin), the conditions which prevailed for Moses on Mount Sinai, the manna from heaven which kept the Israelites alive for

---

[13] Taken from Moritz Schlick's "Philosophy of Organic Life," *Readings in the Philosophy of Science*, edited by Herbert Feigl and May Brodbeck (Appleton-Century-Crofts, 1953).

[14] Hans Driesch, *History and Theory of Vitalism*, trans. C. K. Ogden (New York: Macmillan, 1914).

four years (the precipitate from the comet's tail), Joshua's making the sun stand still (the second encounter), and Joshua's toppling the walls with the trumpets (earthquake produced by the Earth's cooling).

Velikovsky's explanation for the Old Testament stories fulfills the first two conditions (1) and (2). It is thus a genuine, as opposed to a pseudoscientific explanation. However, it is an unsatisfactory explanation because it fails to fulfill conditions (3) and (4). It is essentially an *ad hoc* explanation. The supposed evidence for the theory consists almost entirely of the stories which the theory explains.[15] And the explicans conflict with facts—for example, no marks which would have resulted from such upheavals have been found on the Earth.

Summary

Generally, genuine explanations in science are distinguished from pseudoexplanations if and only if (1) the statements of the explicans do not follow from the explicandum, and (2) the statements of the explicans are testable either directly or indirectly. Generally, satisfactory scientific explanations are distinguished from unsatisfactory ones if and only if (3) the explicans is supported by evidence based on data other than the observational data upon which the acceptance of the explicandum is based, and (4) the explicans is true or corroborated.

EXERCISES 13.2

Using the four characteristics (1, 2, 3, and 4) discussed in this chapter, classify the following as genuine or pseudoexplanations and classify the genuine explanations as satisfactory or unsatisfactory explanations. Justify your choice.

1. "Most of the scientists I know," says Boston University Theologian Edwin Booth, "believe in the immanent principle of life in the organic universe. If they are religious, they call it God. If they are not religious, they have awe and reverence for this principle. But it isn't refined, nor is it personal. It is greater than personal—it is absolutely essential to the principle of life itself."   (*Time*, June 29, 1962)

2. According to Marxism, revolution is inevitable. One reason for this is the operation of "The Law of the Transformation of Quantity into

---

[15] V. Bargmann (Princeton Physics Dept.) and L. Motz (Columbia, Astronomy) in a letter in *Science*, Vol. 38, December 1962, urged reconsideration of Velikovsky's conclusion, on new observation, though they disagreed with his theory.

Quality." All things change by imperceptible steps until there arrives a point, which Hegel calls the "node," beyond which a thing cannot vary while remaining the same. That this law exists can be seen when water turns to steam at 100°C and into ice at 0°C. This change occurs abruptly so that water is at one moment water and at the next moment steam or ice.

3. How do artists come to their material? Freud in his "The Relation of the Poet to Daydreaming" (in *Collected Papers*) writes that some cue in the environment arouses unfulfilled wishes. Rather than just repress these wishes as some of us do, only to have them fulfilled in dreams or in daydreams, the artist also fulfills the wish in artistic work. All people have these wishes: erotic wishes, wishes for power, honor, riches, and fame. Those who can fulfill them in real life are happy people. Those who cannot, because they lack the various means to fulfill them, are unhappy people. The artist, who has more intense wishes than other people to begin with, cannot fulfill these wishes in real life, but instead fulfills them in dreaming, daydreaming, and in his work. He is, of course, unhappy, but the explanation for how he comes to his material is in his being unhappy.

4. Tonight I want to tell you a little about astrology, and in particular to explain its foundations. It has sometimes been claimed by unscientific astrologers that stars and planets compel our every action. As a scientific astrologer my first task is to correct that impression. The stars do not compel, they impel. There is a distinction here which I am sure you are all subtle enough to grasp without my pausing to explain it. I shall therefore go on now to talk about how we know they impel, and how they impel.

   Strangely enough, the main support for the truth of astrology came upon the scene only recently, several thousands of years after men began to practice our most ancient of sciences. Modern physics teaches us that the stars are huge bodies, some of them thousands of times the size and mass of our own sun. Now these great bodies are constantly giving off vibrations. Ask any astronomer and he will tell you, for example, that the stars are the source of cosmic rays whose power in terms of electron-volts is fantastically high. Nor is there reason to think that cosmic rays are the only kinds of vibrations stars emit, or even the strongest kind. Well, astrologers have known for centuries how great is the force of stellar vibrations. The rediscovery of such forces in modern times occasions no surprise on our part.

   Now what about these vibrations? Did it every occur to you how sensitive an instrument the human body is? You must have realized long ago that nothing is more intricate and responsive than the mind and nervous system of a creature who is capable of being affected powerfully by a new idea or by the words of someone long dead. Go to a physiologist or a psychologist and ask him about the machinery of the brain if you doubt me.

Next, put these two facts together: first, the incalculable forces involved in the vibrations given off by stars, and second, the exceedingly frail and responsive machinery of the human mind. How can any man in his right mind deny the likelihood that so delicate an instrument should respond to so gigantic an influence? Doesn't the seismograph at Fordham register earthquakes in the Sea of Japan? Of course, yet the seismograph is not nearly so sensitive as the mind, nor are the greatest quakes comparable in force to the vibrations given off by a star.

It stands to reason, therefore, that the colossal vibrations of the stars and planets we are born under must set their stamp somehow on each human being. The truth of astrology is this: over the centuries these character-shaping influences have gradually been measured, so that today astrology belongs among the exact sciences. Every newborn child's personality, plastic at birth, is given its character and permanent cast by the peculiar configuration of heavenly bodies at the time of the child's birth. The truth has the further merit of explaining why no two persons are exactly alike. Even with so-called identical twins, the moment of birth is not the same, and with the passing of a few moments the star-picture can change significantly. We know, then, that astrology is an exact science, because if an accurate horoscope is given but fails to agree with the facts of a person's life, it can only mean that the person has made an error in reporting the time or place of his birth!

People who dislike astrology will sometimes say, out of malice, that the stars' distances are sufficient to make the effects of their vibrations negligible. This is easily refuted. First, the space between the earth and stars is nearly a vacuum, empty enough to let vibrations pass almost undiminished in vigor. Second, the Chicago Exposition in 1935 was opened by a ray of light from the star Arcturus hitting a photoelectric cell. If a star as remote at Arcturus can open a fair in Illinois, it is very careless to argue that the stars are too far away to affect our lives.

(JOHN A. OESTERLE, *Logic*)[16]

5. Some psychologists claim that ESP (extra-sensory perception—telepathy, clairvoyance, and the like) has been demonstrated by means of tests with ESP cards. One person turns up cards with five symbols—a square, circle, cross, star and wavy lines. The subject, who cannot see the cards, is asked to tell what card is up. Many subjects have scores which are higher than the laws of chance allow. PK, an abbreviation of "psychokinesis," has also been demonstrated. This is the ability of the mind to control matter, as found in mediumistic levitations, faith

---

[16] Reprinted from John A. Oesterle, *Logic: The Art of Defining and Reasoning*, 2nd ed. © 1963. Prentice-Hall, Inc., Englewood Cliffs, N.J. Used by permission of Prentice-Hall, Inc. and Professor Harry Nielsen, who devised this example.

healing, haunted house phenomena, etc. By having subjects concentrate on certain faces of dice, it has been found that these faces show up more than the laws of chance allow. ESP and PK are free of space and time restrictions. They both, for example, work just as well when the subject is separated by great distances from the cards or dice. This independence from time and space make these phenomena such that they cannot be explained by any *physical* theory. We must employ *mental* notions as distinct from the physical world. The subjects must be believers in psychic phenomena to have the ESP and PK. This is because a disbeliever will upset the delicate operation of the subject's psi-ability. (Adapted from MARTIN GARDNER, *Fads and Fallacies in the Name of Science*)

6. Housewives consistently report that one of the most pleasurable tasks of the home is making a cake. Psychologists were put to work exploring this phenomenon for merchandising clues. James Vicary made a study of cake symbolism and came up with the conclusion that "baking a cake traditionally is acting out the birth of a child" so that when a woman bakes a cake for her family she is symbolically presenting the family with a new baby, an idea she likes very much. Mr. Vicary cited the many jokes and old wives' tales about cake making as evidence: the quip that brides whose cakes fall obviously can't produce a baby yet; the married jest about "leaving a cake in the oven"; the myth that a cake is likely to fall if the woman baking it is menstruating. A psychological consulting firm in Chicago also made a study of cake symbolism and found that "women experience making a cake as making a gift of themselves to their family," which suggests much the same thing.

The food mixes—particularly the cake mixes—soon found themselves deeply involved in this problem of feminine creativity and encountered much more resistance than the makers, being logical people, ever dreamed possible. The makers found themselves trying to cope with negative and guilt feelings on the part of women who felt that use of ready mixes was a sign of poor housekeeping and threatened to deprive them of a traditional source of praise.

(VANCE PACKARD, *The Hidden Persuaders*)

7. According to Count Alfred Korzybski, the General Semanticist, people are "unsane" when their mental maps of reality are slightly out of correspondence with the real world. If the inner world is too much askew, they become "insane." A principal cause of all this is the Aristotelian mental orientation, which distorts reality. It assumes, for example, that an object is either a chair or not a chair, when clearly there are all kinds of objects which may or may not be called chairs depending on how you define "chair." But a precise definition is impossible. "Chair" is simply a word we apply to a group of things more or less alike, but which fade off in all directions, along continuums, into other objects which are not called chairs. . . .

The non-Aristotelian mental attitude is, in essence, a recognition of the above elementary fact. There is no such thing as pure "chairishness." There are only chair 1, chair 2, chair 3, et cetera! This assigning of numbers is a process Korzybski called "indexing." In similar fashion, the same chair changes constantly in time. Because of weathering, use, and so forth, it is not the same chair from one moment to the next. We recognize this by the process of "dating." We speak of chair 1952, chair 1953, et cetera! The Count was convinced that the unsane, and many insane, could be helped back to sanity by teaching them to think in these and similar non-Aristotelian ways. For example, a neurotic may hate all mothers. The reason may be that a childhood situation caused him to hate his own mother. Not having broken free of Aristotelian habits, he thinks all mothers are alike because they are all called by the same word. But the word, as Korzybski was fond of repeating, is not the thing. When a man learns to index mothers—that is, call them mother 1, mother 2, mother 3, et cetera—he then perceives that other mothers are not identical with his own mother. In addition, even *his* mother is not the same mother she was when he was a child. Instead there are mother 1910, mother 1911, mother 1912, et cetera. Understanding all this, the neurotic's hatred for mothers is supposed to diminish greatly.

(MARTIN GARDNER, *Fads and Fallacies in the Name of Science*)

8. Dowsing is the art of finding underground water or other substances by means of a divining rod, which is usually a forked stick. The method works with a good dowser. Sometimes a good dowser has difficulty, but this is because of such factors as fatigue, lack of concentration, poor physical condition, worry, too much friction on soles of shoes, all sorts of atmospheric conditions, the presence of electric lines in the area, humidity of soil, tree roots, and so forth. Although an effort can be made to take them all into account, they are so numerous that in practice to take them all into account would be virtually impossible. This is the major reason that controlled experiment has failed to show that dowsing works. Also it should be kept in mind that the digging often diverts the water which is located by dowsing.

9. Some people think the earth is rotating at a speed of 1,000 miles an hour. But this is clearly impossible. For one thing, if it were moving like this and I threw a rock straight up into the air, then during the seconds that the rock took for its descent, the earth would have moved over a mile, so the rock would hit a mile away. But the rock lands very near the point from which I threw it. Also, if a bird on a tree were to let go, it would be rushed away if the earth is moving anything like 1,000 miles per hour. Just think of those paper cups that we let go when the car is

doing a mere sixty! Or suppose the bird sees a worm and lets go of the tree. The earth, in the meantime, goes whirling by at this enormous rate, and obviously, no matter how hard the bird flaps its wings, it can never achieve sufficient speed to reach the worm. But this is ridiculous! Birds catch worms constantly!

10. It is no longer possible to doubt seriously the existence of intelligent life on other planets. True, before the invention of the airplane and radar tracking devices, the thousands of reported sightings of UFO's or "unidentified flying objects" were not enough to constitute convincing evidence. They served only to provoke wonder. But in our own century things have happened which change the picture entirely. In the first place we have on record the sworn testimony of many World War II and Korean pilots, as well as commercial airline pilots, to the effect that their planes were paced for minutes at a time, in bright daylight, by ships of a construction never attempted on earth. Gen. James Doolittle, leader of the first raid on the Japanese mainland, has given testimony of such an occurrence. When human pilots attempted to swing closer for a better look, the strange craft sped away at fantastic speeds, estimated at over 2000 mph.

Beyond such testimony as the above, we know that radar stations have tracked not only giant single ships, such as the one which Captain Mantell, an Air Force officer stationed near Washington D.C., tried to investigate at the cost of his life, but also, in hundreds of instances, whole squadrons of smaller ships flying in tight formations. Radar experts have testified that the speed, sharp turns, and close formation of these fleets rule out any possibility of finding an explanation in weather phenomena. The blips on the radar screens were unmistakably those of solid objects, some of great size, and these experts, remember, speak from a background of military experience in which there was no room allowed for loose interpretations or confusions of one kind of object with another.

It is plain from the mass of such testimony that the UFO's are not patches of vapor, nor are their radar blips anything like what might be produced by experiments with light reflections in the atmosphere. Their speeds exceed anything achieved on earth, their changes of direction and high rates of acceleration bespeak a degree of engineering knowledge not to be found on earth even at the drawing-board stage.

The core of my argument is this: when we have exhausted all terrestrial possibilities that might explain these objects, our only alternative is the extraterrestrial hypothesis. And it is fairly easy to exhaust the terrestrial possibilities. The speeds, accelerations, and structural features of these UFO's are simply beyond what our civilization has shown evidence that it is able to produce. Further, the number of such craft indicates an engineering program of dimensions impossible to conceal on earth, even in a territory as vast as the U.S.S.R. Besides, it is obvious that the Russians could not be responsible, for their pioneer work in sputniks is of an order far inferior to the performance of UFO's. If any more is needed to absolve the Russians, we may recall that UFO's have been sighted for many years, whereas the U.S.S.R. has only in the last decade made its great industrial strides.

The simple impossibility, then, of explaining UFO's by reference to what man on earth is capable of, forces us to this hypothesis: there is, quartered somewhere far out in space, a civilization technologically in advance of our own. It is managed by intelligent beings. These beings have shown a sustained interest in what goes on on earth. Their mastery of space and speed keeps them safe from any attempts of ours to study them closely. But that they exist, there cannot be any doubt.[17]

11.   . . . there is another experiment one can do at home, this time using an adult as a subject rather than a child. Buy two presents for your wife, again choosing things that you are reasonably sure she will find about equally attractive. Find some plausible excuse for having both of them in your possession, show them to your wife and ask her to tell you how attractive each one is to her. After you have obtained a good measure of attractiveness, tell her that she can have one of them, whichever she chooses. The other you will return to the store. After she has made her choice, ask her once more to evaluate the attractiveness of each of them. If you compare the evaluations of attractiveness before and after the choice, you will probably find that the chosen present has increased in attractiveness and the rejected one decreased.

Such behavior can be explained by a new theory concerning "cognitive dissonance." This theory centers around the idea that if a person knows various things that are not psychologically consistent with one another, he will, in a variety of ways, try to make them more consistent. Two items of information that psychologically do not fit together are said to be in a dissonant relation to each other. The items of information may be about behavior, feelings, opinions, things in the environment and so on. The word "cognitive" simply emphasizes that the theory deals with relations among items of information.

(LEON FESTINGER, "Cognitive Dissonance")

ANSWERS

6.   Very likely true and the evidence for it is the increasingly large sales of cake mixes when the mixes were altered so that the housewife was

---

[17] This example was created by Prof. Harry Nielsen, and we use it here with his permission.

required, or allowed, to add eggs and milk. However, it is also true that the cakes from mixes (and especially the first ones) were not as good as the homemade cakes.

7. The belief in dowsing shows the extent of human credulity. There are unlimited reasons why a dowser will fail to find water, and no sensible reason why he should succeed, except for the widespread groundwater in certain parts of the country. That is, there is no connection, causal or otherwise, between the rod and the water.

14

Probability

In any inductive argument the conclusion is not regarded as following by necessity from the premises; rather, the conclusion is regarded as acceptable relative to the premises because the evidence cited in the premises renders the conclusion *probable*. It seems thus that the logic of probability is relevant to any discussion of inductive arguments, and it appears inevitable that any *system* of inductive logic, if such a system is possible, will have to have as one of its important parts what is called the calculus of probability. In this chapter this calculus, which consists of rules governing the calculation of probabilities under certain stringent conditions, is introduced.

Four Problems in Probability Theory

In any discussion of the topic of probability as it comes up in logic, four problems enter: First, what is the meaning of probability sentences? A probability sentence is a sentence which indicates a probability for some event. Examples of typical probability sentences would be the following:

The probability that a head will turn up on a toss of a coin is $\frac{1}{2}$.
The probability of rolling a 5 on one toss of a die is 1 out of 6.
The probability of death in their thirty-ninth year among American males is .012.
The probability that the train will be on time is 0.4.
If there is any probability that God exists, you should believe that He does.
The quantum theory is probably true.

The second problem that enters any discussion of probability in logic is how does one obtain initial numerical values of probability? For example, how does one determine that the probability of drawing a spade from a standard deck of bridge cards is $\frac{1}{4}$? Or that the probability that a given birth will be a male birth is 0.5, or thereabouts?

The third problem is how does one calculate with initially given probabilities to obtain other probabilities? Suppose the probability of a female student taking a certain course is 0.2. Once a female is in the course, however, the probability that she will read the text is 0.6. What is the probability that a female student will enter the course *and* read the text?

The final problem which comes up is how do we apply probabilities in the determination of the acceptability of a conclusion in an inductive argument? At present little can be said in response to this problem in addition to the obvious, namely: accept that hypothesis which has a high probability relative to the evidence cited in the premise; or accept that hypothesis which has the maximum probability of all those considered.

Though little can be said in response to the last problem, much has been written about the meaning of probability statements (the first problem), though there is no general agreement about it. We begin with proposed solutions to this problem and then turn to the second and third problems, which, with certain restrictions, have been answered with mathematical precision.

Problem 1: The Meaning of Probability

There are several different views concerning the meaning of probability statements. Perhaps the word "probability" has only one meaning, and no account has identified it precisely. This is almost inconceivable. More likely, the word is ambiguous, in some complicated way, and we mean different things by the word in different contexts, in which case more than one view could be partially true. Let us consider the three prominent views of the meaning of "probability."

Physical Interpretation. According to the physical interpretation of probability sentences, probability sentences are about features of things. Consider the following probability statement:

1. The probability of throwing a 6 on one throw of a die is $\frac{1}{6}$.

On this view (1) is construed as the statement: a die has the disposition of turning up a 6 about one sixth of the time in the long run; or the relative frequency (in the long run) of tossing a 6 with a fair die is $\frac{1}{6}$. That a die has such properties is determined by observation. So prior to observation we have no reason at all to assign a probability to any event. Probability sentences on this view are like the following: "The temperature of the room is 70° F"; "The weight of the stone is 14 pounds"; "The length of the bridge is 105 feet." They are statements justified by observation.

Logical Interpretation. On this view probability statements such as (1) above are logical truths if they are true and logical falsehoods if they are false (see Chapter 10). So (1) is a logical truth, since it is true, and the following, for example, is a logical falsehood, since it is a false probability statement: "The probability of throwing a 6 with a die is $\frac{1}{2}$." Why this view, the logical interpretation of probability statements, is plausible will be seen shortly.

Psychological Interpretation. Probability statements, following the psychological interpretation, are about the degree of belief rational persons have. They indicate or express psychological attitudes towards the occurrence of certain events. They are about belief-states. For example, to utter (1) is to say that a rational person would be willing to offer 6 to 1 odds that a 6 will come up.

There are, of course, reasons for advancing these different views, some of which will appear as we progress. The chief reason, however, for the logical interpretation of probability statements is that, for example, the die can be regarded as an *ideal* die with perfectly distributed weight and exact edges. So regarded, when one says that the probability of throwing a 6 on one throw of a die is $\frac{1}{6}$, one is implicitly assuming in making the utterance that there are exactly six possible states for the die—a 1 showing up, a 2 showing up, and so on—and that each has an absolutely equal chance of occurring. If one makes this assumption with respect to (1), then it is not at all implausible to construe (1) as a logical truth if true. However, the die can also be regarded as it actually is, not as an ideal die. So regarded, the physical interpretation of (1) seems in order. In uttering (1) in this context we are saying something about an ordinary, nonideally construed die, and our basis for saying (1) is what we know about the behavior of dice from the past.

Problem 2: Ways to Determine Initial Probabilities

There are different ways used to measure the initial probability of an event. Three of these ways which are especially important are the classical way, the relative frequency way, and the personal odds way. Probability sentences determined in the first way lend support to the logical interpretation of probability, whereas probability sentences determined by the second way support the physical interpretation, and those determined in the third way seem to support the psychological interpretation. Since each way is sometimes used to determine a probability, it is likely that indeed the word "probability" is ambiguous. Let us now consider the three ways to measure the initial probability of an event.

The Classical Way. If an event can occur in any one of *n* equally possible ways, and if *m* of these ways are considered favorable, then according to the classical way of determining probability, often called the *classical theory*, the probability of event *A* occurring, *P(A)*, *A* being a favorable event, is given by this formula:

$$P(A): \text{Probability of event } A = \frac{m: \text{number of favorable events whose probability is to be measured}}{n: \text{number of equally possible events of certain kind}}$$

or, briefly:

$$P(A) = \frac{m}{n}$$

To illustrate: One has a standard fifty-two-card deck of bridge cards. What is the probability that a spade will turn up if a card is drawn from the deck? In this problem *P(A)* is the probability that a spade turns up from a standard deck of bridge cards. There are, let us suppose, fifty-two equally possible events relevant to *P(A)*. Hence the *n* here, the denominator of the fraction, is 52. There are thirteen possible favorable cases since there are thirteen spades in the deck. Thus *P(A)* equals $\frac{13}{52}$, that is $\frac{1}{4}$, or 0.25. Note that the probability of an event can range between two limits: 1.0 and 0. If an event *A* is certain to occur, then $P(A) = 1$, whereas if it is certain not to occur, $P(A) = 0$. To take another illustration, suppose a single die is tossed, what is the probability that an even number will turn up? In this problem, *P(A)* is the probability that an even number will turn up from a toss of a die. In this problem, *n*, let us suppose, is 6, and the number of possible favorable cases, the number of possible even numbers out of the six possible is 3. Thus the probability of an even number turning up on the toss of a die is $\frac{3}{6}$, or $\frac{1}{2}$, or 0.50.

As the preceding cases illustrate, for the classic theory to be applied we begin with a measure of *m* and *n* and we suppose that equally possible events make up the class *m* and the class *n*. But how does one determine when each of a set of events is equally possible? This is the great difficulty facing the classical theory. One answer is that in applying the theory we assume the so-called *principle of indifference*, according to which any set of events is to be considered equally possible in the absence of any reason for considering the events not to be equally possible. One can challenge the principle of indifference by pointing out that just because we do not know one event is not equally possible does not mean that it is. (*Ad ignoratiam* fallacy?) It should be noted that, in contrast, neither of the next two methods of determining initial probability makes use of the principle of indifference, and this is a point in their favor, since it would be preferable to avoid *all* controversial assumptions in a theory.

Relative Frequency Way. According to this method of determining probability, probabilities are relative frequencies. The way to arrive at probabilities is not to compute numbers of equally likely alternatives, but to count instances of the occurrences of favorable events. For example, to calculate the probability of tossing a 3 with a given die, one tosses the die, and counts the times that 3 turns up. After a number of trials note the favorable instances as contrasted with actual number of tosses to obtain relative frequency of 3 turning up. This ratio will be the probability of 3 turning up. Thus according to the relative frequency theory:

$$P(A) = \frac{m \text{ (actual occurrence of favorable events)}}{n \text{ (actual number of events)}}$$

To illustrate: Suppose we wish to calculate the probability of death of an American male of the white-collar class during his thirty-ninth year. We look at records. Suppose we find that out of a representative sample of 2,400 white-collar males, twenty-four die in their thirty-ninth year. In this case $P(A)$ is the probability that an AMWC dies during his thirty-ninth year. On the basis of the statistics, n is 2,400 and m is 24. Thus $P(A)$ is $\frac{24}{2400}$, or $\frac{1}{100}$, or 0.01. Probability sentences emerging out of this context seem amenable to the physical interpretation. For instance, to say, "The probability that a given birth will be male is 0.51," on the basis of the frequency method seems to amount to saying, "The relative frequency of male births to the total number of births equals 0.51."

Personal Odds Way. According to the personal odds theory there are two steps in obtaining an initial numerical probability for an event. First determine the highest odds a rational and knowledgeable person would be willing to offer in a bet on the event in question. Second, if the odds in favor of the event are m to n, then the probability of the event is

$$P(A) = \frac{m}{m+n}$$

For example, Jimmy the Greek gives 5 to 4 odds that Arizona State will beat Notre Dame this year. What is the probability that Arizona will win if we calculate the probability using the personal odds theory? Answer: Assuming Jimmy is a rational person and knowledgeable, the probability that Arizona State will win is

$$\frac{5}{5+4} = \frac{5}{9} = 0.55$$

The probability that Notre Dame will win is thus 0.45, $1 - 0.55$. Probability statements which have such an origin can easily be construed as being about belief states. For example, to say that it is more probable that Arizona State will win than that Notre Dame will win is to say that those (presumably) in the know are willing to offer odds that Arizona State will win.

EXERCISES 14.1

A. Using the classic theory, answer the following:

1. Suppose an ideal die is tossed. What is the probability that
   a. a 6 turns up.
   b. a number less than 6 turns up.
   c. an odd number turns up.
   d. a number greater than 2 but less than 6 turns up.

2. There are nine Volkswagens and seven Toyotas in Joe's Import used car lot. Suppose he sells one car. What is the probability that
   a. It is a Volkswagen.
   b. It is a Toyota.

B. Using the frequency theory answer the following:

1. Joe of Joe's Import sold eighty-nine Volkswagens this year. He sold twenty of them with radial tires. What is the probability of his selling a Volkswagen with radial tires next year?

2. Suppose a survey of some university juniors and seniors is taken and that it is reasonable to suppose that this sample is a representative sample. The results of the survey are as follows:

	Support R.O.T.C.	Do not support R.O.T.C.
Juniors	60	10
Seniors	20	40

What is the probability that
   a. A student supports R.O.T.C.
   b. A junior supports R.O.T.C.
   c. A senior supports R.O.T.C.
   d. Nonsupporting upper classmen will be seniors.
   e. They will be juniors.

C. 1. Jimmy the Greek gives 4 to 1 odds that the Cowboys will beat the Dophins this year.
   a. What is the probability that the Cowboys will win?
   b. What is the probability that the Dolphins will win?

2. A certain distinguished stock analyst gives the following odds for appreciation of the following stocks in the coming year:

ATT	5:4
Kodak	1:6
Boise Cascade	3:2
Motorola	2:2

What is the probability that each of these stocks will appreciate in the coming year?

The Calculus of Probability

So far we have considered the questions as to how initial probabilities might be calculated. We now consider the question as to how, given certain probabilties, other probabilities can be calculated from them. The probability calculus has been developed to answer this question and it is part of all more general theories of probability. In this section an informal account of the basic principles of the probability theory is given.

Some pairs of events are such that the occurrence of one of them has an effect on the occurrence of the other. For example, drawing an ace from a deck of cards (without putting it back into the deck) has an effect on the chances of getting an ace on the next draw. But other pairs of events are such that the occurrence of one has no effect on the other. For example, drawing an ace from a deck of cards has no effect on the chances of getting an ace on the next draw if the ace has been put back into the deck before the second draw. If two events are such that the occurrence of one has no effect on the occurrence of the second, they are said to be *independent events.*

In addition, some pairs of events are such that it is logically possible for both of them to occur. For example, it is logically possible for a die to land face 1 up on its first throw and also land face 1 up on its second throw. But other pairs of events are such that it is not logically possible for both to occur. For example, it is not logically possible for face 1 and face 2 to land up on a single throw of a die. If two events are such that it is not logically possible for both to occur, they are said to be *mutually exclusive events.*

Let P continue to be an abbreviation for the expression "the probability that" and A and B be variables that range over names of events. The first basic rule of the probability calculus can be stated as follows:

Special Multiplication Principle. If A and B are independent events:

$$P(A \text{ and } B) = P(A) \times P(B)$$

How this principle can be applied is illustrated in this problem: The probability of getting a 1 on a given throw of a die (A) is $\frac{1}{6}$ and the probability of getting a 1 on some other throw of the die (B) is also $\frac{1}{6}$. Since A and B are independent of each other, the probability of getting a 1 on both throws of the die is equal to the probability of getting a 1 on the first throw times the probability of getting a 1 on the second throw. The special multiplication principle can be applied in this case. Thus the probability of getting 1's on both throws equals $\frac{1}{6}$ times $\frac{1}{6}$, or $\frac{1}{36}$. To take another example: Urn 1 contains three white and five red balls. Urn 2 contains four white and three red balls. One ball is drawn from each urn. What is the probability that they are both red? Let $P(A)$ be the probability of drawing a red ball from urn 1, which is $\frac{5}{8}$. Let $P(B)$ be the probability of drawing a red ball from urn 2, which is $\frac{3}{7}$. Since A and B are independent events the special multiplication principle can be applied. Thus the $P(A$ and $B)$, the probability that they are both red is $\frac{5}{8} \times \frac{3}{7} = \frac{15}{56} = 0.27$.

General Multiplication Principle. If A and B are dependent events, then the multiplication principle is

$$P(A \text{ and } B) = P(A) \times P(B \text{ given } A)$$

Its application to the problem of the probability of drawing two spades in a row without replacement is as follows:

   $P(A)$ (the probability that one spade will be drawn) is $\frac{1}{4}$
   $P(B$ given $A)$ (the probability of drawing a spade given that a spade has been drawn and not replaced) is $\frac{12}{51}$.

Thus applying the general multiplication principle:

$$P(A \text{ and } B) = \frac{1}{4} \times \frac{12}{51} = 0.094.$$

If A and B are two mutually exclusive events, the $P(A$ or $B)$ can be calculated using the special addition principle.

Special Addition Principle. If A and B are two mutually exclusive events:

$$P(A \text{ or } B) = P(A) + P(B)$$

What is the probability of drawing an ace or a picture card from an ordinary deck of fifty-two cards? To solve this problem we must use the special addition principle, since event A and event B are two mutually exclusive events they cannot both occur at the same time. The solution is as follows:

   $P(A)$ (the probability of drawing an ace) $= \frac{4}{52}$
   $P(B)$ (the probability of drawing a picture card) $= \frac{12}{52}$
   Thus $P(A$ or $B)$ is $\frac{4}{52} + \frac{12}{52} = \frac{16}{52} = \frac{4}{13} = 0.309$

Sometimes events are not mutually exclusive. For example, if a single die is tossed, what is the probability that either an odd number or a number greater than 3 will appear? Here A and B are not mutually exclusive events. To solve this problem we need to make use of the general addition principle.

General Addition Principle.

$$P(A \text{ or } B) = P(A) + P(B) - P(A \text{ and } B)$$

To solve this last problem we set it out as follows:

$P(A)$ (the probability that the die is an odd number) $= \frac{3}{6}$
$P(B)$ (the probability that the die is a number greater than 3) $= \frac{3}{6}$
$P(A \text{ and } B)$ (the probability that the die number is odd and greater than 3) = (by the general multiplication principle) $\frac{1}{3} \times \frac{1}{2} = \frac{1}{6}$.
$P(A \text{ or } B) = (\frac{3}{6} + \frac{3}{6}) - \frac{1}{6} = \frac{5}{6} = 0.83$.

In addition, it is customary to assume in the calculus of probability that the probability of an event A and the nonoccurrence of A (its complement $\bar{A}$) occurring is 0, whereas the probability of either A or its complement occurring is 1. That is,

5. $P(A \text{ and } \bar{A}) = 0$
6. $P(A \text{ or } \bar{A}) = 1$

From this is follows that

7. $P(\bar{A}) = 1 - P(A)$

An application of (7) would be this: If the probability that Smith is a reform Democrat is put at 0.4, what is the probability that Smith is not such a Democrat? Let

$P(A)$ (the probability that Smith is a reform Democrat) = 0.4
$P(\bar{A})$ (the probability that Smith is not a reform Democrat) $= 1 - 0.4 = 0.6$ [following (7)]

It is easy to see how formula (7) follows from (5) and (6). Since A and $\bar{A}$ are mutually exclusive events by rule 3

$$P(A \text{ or } \bar{A}) = P(A) + P(\bar{A})$$

so from (6) it follows that

$$P(A) + P(\bar{A}) = 1$$

If $P(A)$ is subtracted from both sides we obtain (7).

In the following problems use either the classical, frequency, or personal odds theory in obtaining initial probabilities. Use one or more of the rules from the calculus of probability to arrive at the final answer.

1. Urn 1 contains seven white and fifteen red balls. Urn 2 contains twelve white and three red balls. One ball is drawn from each urn. What is the probability that they are both red?

2. What is the probability of drawing two aces in a row from a deck of bridge cards with replacement? With no replacement?

3. There is a probability of 0.2 that the children will go swimming today and 0.5 that they will stay home and watch T.V. What is the probability that they will either go swimming or stay home and watch T.V.?

4. Half of the metaphysicians in the world write poetry and a fourth of them play chess. What is the probability that a metaphysician either writes poetry or plays chess?

5. Two students are taking the final exam in introductory logic, along with others, of course. Student x has a 50 percent chance of passing while the odds of student y passing are 7 to 9. What is the probability that
   a. Both students will pass the test.
   b. Both students will fail the test.
   c. Either student will pass the test.
   d. Either x will fail or y will fail.

ANSWERS

4. $P(A)$ (the probability of metaphysicians writing poetry) $= 0.50$. $P(B)$ (the probability of metaphysicians playing chess) $= 0.25$. Assuming they are independent events: $P(A \text{ and } B) = 0.125$. Assuming they are not mutually exclusive events: $P(A \text{ or } B) = (0.50 + 0.25) - 0.125 = 0.625$.

5. $P(A)$ (the probability that x will pass) $= \frac{1}{2} = 0.50$; $P(\bar{A}) = 0.50$; $P(B)$ (the probability that y will pass) $= \frac{7}{16} = 0.437$; $P(\bar{B}) = 0.563$.
   a. $P(A \text{ and } B) = \frac{1}{2} \times \frac{7}{16} = \frac{7}{32} = 0.219$
   b. $P(\bar{A} \text{ and } \bar{B}) = 0.50 \times .563 = 0.281$
   c. $P(A \text{ or } B) = (0.50 + 0.437) - 0.219 = 0.718$
   d. $P(\bar{A} \text{ or } \bar{B}) = 1 - \frac{7}{32} = 0.781$

NAME INDEX

A

Adler, A., 421–422, 424
Agnew, Spiro, 98
Alexander, Shana, 137
Alinsky, Saul, 93
Anselm, 83
Aquinas, Thomas, 83
Arago, J., 378
Aristotle, 241, 351
Arizona Republic, 17, 24, 66, 87, 103
Arrow, Kenneth, 24
Ascoli, Max, 158
Austin, J. L., 141n.
Avogadro, 368

B

Babson, Roger, 60
Bacon, Francis, 45
Bagdikian, Ben, 403
Baker, Russell, 40
Ball, George, 97
Bargmann, V., 428
Batten, Louis J., 409
Baxter, Richard, 407
Becher, J. J., 382
Bell, Griffin, 158
Bellamy, Edward, 53

Ben-Veniste, Richard, 82
Bernays, Paul, 327
Bernback, William, 93
Blackett, P. M. S., 404, 424
Booth, Edwin, 428
Boring, Edwin G., 383
Brandeis, Louis, 143
Brewster, David, 366
Brodback, Mary, 427
Brodeur, Paul, 10
Broder, David, 48f
Brown, Bill, 81
Brown, Edmund G. "Pat," 48, 81
Brown, Jerry, 37, 48f, 109
Brutus, 107
Bryant, Anita, 100
Buchanan, Partrick, 56
Burger, Warren, 90
Burke, Edmund, 6
Bush, Prescott, 85
Byrd, Robert C., 6, 80

C

Carroll, Lewis, 135, 141, 268–270
Carter, Jimmy, 7, 24, 26, 58f, 67, 85f, 109, 158
Castro, Fidel, 76

Cavendish, Henry, 382
Cavert, Samuel McCrea, 55
Chase, Stuart, 36
Cleese, John, 90
Cohen, Bernard, 398
Cohen, Jerry, 6, 42f
Conant, James, 366
Console, A. Dale, 156
Cope, Edward D., 413–414
Copernicus, 399–400
Crile, George, Jr., 7

D

Darwin, Charles, 358n.
Davis, Kingsley, 416
Diggs, Charles, 102
Dole, Robert, 89
Donnelly, Frank A., 43
Donovan, Robert J., 56
Dreisch, Hans, 427
Drew, Elizabeth, 37, 86
Dubos, René, 381, 394–395, 414
Duhem, P., 374n.

E

Eddington, A. S., 422
Eijkmann, Christian, 391–392
Einstein, Albert, 363, 421–422, 426
Eiseley, Loren C., 414
Ellsberg, Daniel, 27, 154
Empedocles, 101
Engels, Frederich, 80
Erasistratus, 351
Erlichman, John, 82
Euthyphro, 135

F

Fabricius, 353
Feigl, Herbert, 427n.
Festinger, Leon, 434
Feyerabend, P. K., 359n.
Fialka, John, 68

Fibiger, Johannes, 364–365
Fitzgerald, G. F., 425–426
Flanders, Senator, 85
Flood, Daniel, 17
Ford, Gerald, 26, 55, 80, 89
Foucault, J., 377–378
Frampton, George, Jr., 82
Freud, Sigmund, 58, 412–413, 421–422, 424, 429
Friendly, Fred W., 57
Fulbright, William, 157

G

Galbraith, John Kenneth, 28, 410–411
Galen, 352, 424
Galileo, 350, 365–366, 398f, 424
Gallup, George, 108
Gardner, Martin, 60, 431–432
Gemar, Joanne, 388n.
Glaser, Hugo, 392
Goldwater, Barry, 147, 159
Goodfield, June, 89
Gray, L. Patrick, III, 158
Griffith, Thomas, 98
Grunbaum, A., 374n.

H

Haldeman, Robert, 82
Hall, A. R., 353n.
Hall, Alexander, 44
Hammond, E. Cuyler, 393
Hanna, Richard, 17
Harris, Louis, 108
Harvey, William, 351–354, 359
Hayakawa, S. I., 19
Hegel, G. W. F., 429
Herberg, Will, 53
Herbers, John, 69
Herophilus, 351
Herschensohn, Bruce, 34, 91
Hilgard, Ernest, 416
Hobbes, Thomas, 66
Hoffman, Abbie, 88

Holmes, Sherlock, 90
Hull, Clark L., 415
Hume, David, 108
Hunt, E. Howard, 154
Hutton, James, 380f
Huygens, C., 378–379, 424

I

Ingen-Housz, Jan, 395

J

Jackson, Henry, 87f
Jacobs, W. P., 371
James, William, 143f, 159
Javits, Jacob K., 69
Jaworski, Leon, 56
Jefferson, Thomas, 80
Jesus Christ, 7, 57, 107
Jevons, W. S., 75
Joffe, Bernard, 365
Johnson, Charles K., 87
Johnson, Edwin, 85
Johnson, Lyndon, 58, 81, 101
Johnson, Ronald J., 24
Jones, Harry A., 149
Jordan, Barbara, 62f
Joshua, 428
Joyce, James, 142
Julius Caesar, 107

K

Kaufman, Lloyd, 383–384
Kearns, Doris, 101
Kennedy, John F., 79, 82
Kennedy, Robert, 58
King Lear, 98
Kock, Edward, 109
Korzybski, Alfred, 431–432
Kripke, Saul, 123

L

LaFollette, R. M., 84
Laird, Melvin, 157
Lander, Bernard, 413
Landon, Alfred, 64f
LaPrade, J. Wallace, 158
Laurenti, Luigi, 388f
Lavoisier, Antoine, 367, 382
Lekachman, Robert, 26
Lenin, 80
Lewis, C. I., 135
Lincoln, Abraham, 56
Lippman, Walter, 159
Literary Digest, 65
Lodge, O. J., 425
Lorentz, H. A., 425–426
Lukasiewicz, Jan, 340

M

McCarthy, Eugene, 27
McCarthy, Joe, 57, 84f
McGovern, George, 40, 56, 88
McKie, Douglas, 382
McNamara, Robert, 404
Mair, Alex, 136
Mair, George, 109
Mandel, Leon, 33, 137
Mantell, Captain, 433
Marsak, Robt. E., 417
Marston, David, 109
Marx, Groucho, 286
Marx, Karl, 80, 83, 103
Mason, S. F., 380n.
Means, Gardiner, 411
Meany, George, 89
Meno, 106
Michelson, A. A., 425–426
Mill, John Stuart, 23, 51, 373, 384f
Milton, John, 110
Mintz, Morton, 6, 42f
Mitchell, E. D., 58
Mondale, Walter, F., 89f
Moore, Wilbert E., 416

Morley, E. W., 425–426
Moses, 427
Motz, L., 428
Murchison, R. I., 381
Myerson, Bess, 79

N

Naftulin, Donald H., 43
Nagel, Ernest, 351n.
Napolitan, Joe, 40
Newton, Isaac, 354–356, 358–359, 362, 377–379, 398, 400f
Nielsen, Harry, 430n., 434n.
Nietzsche, Friedrich, 32
Nixon, Richard, 27, 35, 40, 56, 63f, 68, 80f, 82, 88, 89, 91, 98, 102, 106, 154, 157, 158
Nobel, A., 101
Nossiter, Bernard, 411

O

Oedipus, 50
Oesterle, John A., 430
Ogden, C. K., 427
Ognibene, Peter J., 88
Olmstead, Roy, 142f
Opfer, David, 157
Orwell, George, 49, 111, 134, 153

P

Packard, Vance, 431
Page, Melvin, 60
Pascal, B., 350, 361–362, 387
Pasteur, Louis, 366, 381, 394–395
Perk, Ralph, 55
Peters, Charles, 7
Pittman, Stuart, 58
Plato, 39, 134, 135
Popper, Karl, 358n., 360, 362, 420f
Post, Emil, 337
Priestley, J. B., 395
Proxmire, William, 156
Ptolemy, 399–400

R

Rappoport, Anatol, 412
Rather, Dan, 56, 99
Rayleigh, J. W. S., 373
Reagan, Ronald, 55, 63, 67f, 81
Redi, Francesco, 366
Reid, Thomas, 95
Rock, Irvin, 383–384
Roosevelt, Franklin D., 64f, 99, 102
Rossignol, 394
Rovere, Richard, 57, 84f
Rubin, Jerry, 88
Rumford, Count, 356–359, 361, 374, 376
Rush, Benjamin, 80
Russell, Bertrand, 92, 101f, 160, 324, 327

S

Schlick, Morris, 427n.
Schorr, Daniel, 78
Sedgwick, Adam, 381
Servetus, 353
Shakespeare, William, 83, 98, 107
Shylock, 83
Skyrms, Brian, 347
Socrates, 38, 106, 135
Sophocles, 50
Spitz, René, 395–396
Stahl, G. E., 382
Stalin, Josef, 80
Stebbing, L. S., 385n., 386n.
Stevens, Theodore D., 138
Stone, I. F., 158
Stratton, William, 148
Swift, Jonathan, 84
Symington, Stuart, 404

T

Theobald, Robert, 47, 91
Thompson, Robert, 42
Toricelli, 349–351, 354, 358–359, 361, 363–364, 424

Toynbee, Arnold, 93
Truman, Harry, 55f, 57, 82, 323

U

Ulysses, 142

V

Velikovsky, Immanuel, 427–428
Venn, John, 243
Vesalius, 352
Vicary, James, 431
Von Frisch, Karl, 371
Von Mayer, Julius R., 410

W

Wallace, George, 158, 160
Wallace, Henry A., 88
Walton, Harold, 414
Ware, John E. Jr., 43
Watkins, Senator, 85
Wattenburg, Ben, 88
Weber, Max, 406f

Welch, Robert, 41f
Wells, William, 393–394
Werner, Abraham, 379f
Whately, Richard, 45
Whitehead, A. N., 324, 327
Whitehead, Clay, 56, 157
Williams, Edward B., 84f
Williams, Samuel, 367
Witcover, Jules, 67, 68, 90
Wittgenstein, Ludwig, 118, 159
Woolsey, John M., 142
Wootten, James, 86, 160
Workman, W. D., 83
Wylie, Frank, 33–34

Y

Yeats, W. B., 50
Young, Andrew, 97
Yukawa, Hideki, 416–417

Z

Ziegler, Ron, 137
Zwicker, General, 85

SUBJECT INDEX

A

A sentence, 242
Absolute consistency, 334
Accent fallacy, 75–78
Accident fallacy, 72
Accidental correlation fallacy, 61
Ad baculum fallacy, 39
Addition (Add), 216
Ad hoc explanations, 426
Ad hominem fallacy, 31–36
  abusive, 31
  circumstantial, 31
Ad ignorantiam fallacy, 43–46
Ad populum fallacy, 36–41
Ad misericordiam fallacy, 38
Ad verecundiam fallacy, 41–43
Algebra, Boolean, 274–277
Ambiguity
  contextual, 131
  of an expression, 73
  fallacies of, 30, 72–78
  lexical, 131
  syntactical, 72–75
Amphibolous sentence, 73
Analogies
  argumentative, 94–95
  evaluating analogical arguments, 96–97

  fallacy of weak analogy, 96
Analytic sentence, 322
And (·), 177–179
Antecedent, 105, 180
Argument diagrams, 18–23
Argument indicator words, 4
Argument patterns, 168
  validity of, 169
  validity of sentential, 196
  validity of syllositic, 250
  validity of predicate, 291–295
Arguments, 3, 165, 345
  ad hoc, 60
  analogical, 94–95
  circular, 45
  conclusion of, 3
  correctness or incorrectness of, 12–16
  deductive, 10–11, 165
  demonstrative, 236
  predicate, 173, 278
  premises of, 3
  reductio ad absurdum (RAA), 232–234
  sentential, 173
  soundness, 18
  valid, 12
Association (Assoc), 222
Assumed premise, 228

Attitude disputes, 145
Axiom system for sentential logic, 323–326
Axiomatic methods, 323–324
Axioms, 324

B

Biconditional (≡), 184
Biased statistics fallacy, 63–65
Black-and-white fallacy, 105
Boolean algebra, 274–277
Borderline cases, 129

C

Calculus of probability, 422–444
Categorical sentences, 242
  and classes, 258
  disguised, 246–247
  distribution of terms of, 250
  major and minor terms of, 249
  particular affirmative (*I*), 242
  particular negative (*O*), 242
  universal affirmative (*A*), 242
  universal negative (*E*), 242
  and Venn diagrams, 243–245
Causal theory of reference, 123
Charity, principle of, 8
Circular argument, 45
Class
  complement, 258
  intersection, 259
  union, 275
Classical theory of probability, 439
Commutation (Comm), 222
Complement of a term, 251
Complete systems in logic
  axiom system for sentential logic (PM), 327, 337–340
  natural deduction system for sentential logic, 217
  predicate logic, 301
  traditional syllogistic logic, 261

Complex question, 50
Composition fallacy, 74–75
Compound sentence, 175
  truth functional, 176
Conclusion, 3
  intermediate, 19
Conditional (⊃), 180–183
Conditional proof rule (RCP), 228–230
  validity of, 234
Conjunct, 184
Conjunction (Conj), 169, 216
Conjunctive normal form (CNF), 337
Connotation, 112
Consequent, 105, 180
Consistency of PM, 326–327, 333–334
Consistent set of sentences, 237
Constant
  individual, 289
  logical, 173, 320
Constructive dilemma (CD), 216
Contextual ambiguity, 131
  vagueness, 131
Contradiction, 46, 232, 264
Contradictories, 264
Contrapositive, 265
Contrapositive (Contra), 222
Contraries, 264
Contrary-to-fact conditionals, 182
Converse, 265
Converse fallacy of accident, 72
Corroboration, 360
Counterexamples, 13, 117, 170–172
Criteria
  for an expression, 115
  for genuine scientific explanations, 418–424
  for satisfactory scientific explanations, 418–424
Crucial experiments, 373–379
  and death blows, 376–378
  and empirical hypotheses, 359
  and fact of the cross, 378–379
  and theoretical hypotheses, 359

D

Death blow to a theory, 376–378
Deductive arguments, 10–11, 165
  in science, 363
Deductive explanations, 397–402
Deductive logic, 346
Definitional dispute, 140
Definitional transformation, 325
Definitions
  by enumerations, 113
  exact, 116
  and intension of a word, 112
  intensional, 112
  nominal, 128
  ostensive, 113
  persuasive, 155
  real, 128
Demarcation, problem of, 417–425
Demonstrative argument, 236
DeMorgan's Theorem (DeM), 222
Denotation, 112
Derived rule in PM, 331
Descriptive theory of reference, 112
Dilemmas, 103–105
  and black-and-white fallacy, 105
  complex, 104
  constructive, 104
  criticizing, 104
  destructive, 104
  simple, 104
Disagreement in attitudes, 145
Discharged assumed premise, 228, 232
Disjunct, 184
Disjunction (∨), 179–180
Disjunctive syllogism (DS), 169, 216
Distribution (Dist), 222
Division fallacy, 74–75
Domains, 287
Double negation (DN), 169, 222

E

E sentence, 242
Elementary disjunction, 337

Emotive words, 151–156
Empathetic explanations, 406–408
Empty set, 259
Empty term, 112, 242, 259
Entelechy, 427
Enthymemes, 8, 269–270
Equivalence (Equiv), 222
Equivocation fallacy, 69–72
Euphemism, 152
Exact definition, 116
Exclusive sense of "or", 179
Extension, 112
Existential generalization (EG), 304, 310
Existential import, 243
Existential instantiation (EI), 306, 310
Existential quantifier, 280
Explicandum, 397
Explicans, 397
Exportation (Exp), 222
Extending a word, 141
Extension, 112
Extensional vagueness, 131

F

Fact of the cross, 378–379
Factual dispute, 139
Fallacies
  of ambiguity, 30
  of accent, 76
  of accident, 72
  accidental correlation, 61
  ad baculum, 39
  ad hominem, 31
  ad ignorantiam, 43
  ad misericordiam, 38
  ad populum, 36
  ad verecundiam, 41
  black-and-white, 105
  of affirming the consequent, 202
  of ambiguity, 69–78
  and amphibolous sentences, 73
  of biased statistics, 63
  circular argument, 45

Fallacies (*cont.*)
  complex question, 50
  composition, 74
  converse, of accident, 72
  of denying the antecedent, 202
  of false dilemma, 104
  division, 74
  equivocation, 69
  false cause, 59
  formal, 29, 201, 272
  genetic, 50
  hasty generalization, 63
  of illicit major term, 257
  of illicit minor term, 257
  of inconsistency, 47
  of insufficient evidence, 30
  of invalid dilemma, 203
  of invalid hypothetical syllogism, 203
  material, 30
  petitio principii, 45
  post hoc, 59
  of quoting out of context, 76
  of relevance, 30
  of small sample, 63
  special pleading, 61
  straw man, 52
  of syntactical ambiguity, 73
  tu quoque, 35–36
  of undistributed middle term, 257
  of weak analogy, 96
Fallacious arguments, 29
False cause fallacy, 59–61
False dilemma fallacy, 103–106
Falsifiability, 420–423
Family resemblance, 119
Figure of a syllogism, 249
Formation rules in PM, 324
Formal fallacy, 29, 201, 257, 272
  formal sentential fallacies, 201–203
  formal syllogistic fallacies, 257
Functional explanations, 405–402

G

Galileo's law of motion, 401

General addition principle, 444
General sentence, 280
  truth-functional expansion of, 289
  instance of, 302
General term, 242, 168
Genetic fallacy, 50–51
Generalization on the basis of a sample,
  14–16, 63, 361–363

H

Hasty generalization fallacy, 63
Historical explanations, 403–405
Hypotheses
  corroboration of, 360
  direct testing of, 354, 423–425
  discovery and justification of, 362
  empirical (or experimental), 359,
    373–374
  and "free creation of mind," 363
  William Harvey's hypothesis, 351–
    354
  indirect testing of, 354, 423–425
  and inductivism, 362
  Lorenz-Fitzgerald contraction hypo-
    thesis, 425
  Newton's corpuscular hypothesis,
    354–356
  Rumford's hypothesis, 356–358
  theoretical, 359, 374–375
  theoretical entities in, 359
  Torricelli's hypothesis, 349–351
  Velikovsky's hypothesis, 427–428
  see also Theories *and* Scientific
    explanations
Hypothetical syllogism (HS), 169, 216

I

I sentence, 242
If and only if (≡), 184
If, then (⊃), 180–183
Immediate inferences in syllogistic logic,
  263–266

Implication (Imp), 222
Implicit premise, 8, 269–270
Inclusive sense of "or", 179
Inconsistency, fallacy of, 46–49
Inconsistent triad test, 258–261
Independence
    of axioms of PM, 327, 335–336
    of rules in natural deduction system
        for sentential logic, 217
Individual variable, 279
    constant, 279–289
Induction and deduction compared, 10–
    11, 361–364
    by enumeration, 362
    and sampling, 14–16, 63–65, 345
    see also Mill's methods
Inductive arguments, 11, 345
    correctness of, 14–16, 346
Inductive logic, 11, 345–348
Inductivism, 362
Informal fallacies, see Fallacies
Intension, 112
Intensional vagueness, 131
Intermediate conclusion, 19
Interpretations
    of an argument pattern, 169
    of a sentential argument pattern, 197
    of a monadic predicate argument
        pattern, 291–292, 320
Invalid dilemma, 203
Invalid hypothetical syllogism, 203
Invalidity, 12–13, 166; see also Coun-
    terexamples
"is" of predication, 71
"is" of identity, 71

L

Laws of nature
    empirical, 360
    theoretical, 360–361
Lexical ambiguity, 131
Logic, 3
Logical equivalence in sentential logic,
    191

Logical falsehood, 322
Logical form, 13, 167–169
Logical term, 173, 322
Logical truth, 320–322

M

Main connective, 185, 193
Major premise, 249
Major term, 249
Material fallacies, 30
    of insufficient evidence, 59–65
Meaning
    new theory of, 127
    of a word, 112
    of a name, 121–125
    traditional theory of, 127
Metalogic, 333
Michelson-Morley experiment, 425
Middle term, 249
Mill's methods, 384–391
    method of agreement, 385
    method of agreement and difference,
        386
    method of concomitant variations,
        386–387
    method of difference, 385–386
    method of residue, 386
    using Mill's methods, 387–391
Minor premise, 249
Minor term, 249
Modus ponens (MP), 169, 216
Modus tollens (MT), 169, 216
Monadic predicate argument pattern,
    295
Monadic predicate, 280
Mood of a syllogism, 249
Mutually exclusive events, 442

N

n-place predicate, 280
Names, *see* Singular terms
    proper, 121–125

Natural deduction system for predicate logic
  completeness of, 301
  rules for, 302–313
  soundness of, 301
Natural deduction system for sentential logic
  completeness of, 217
  proof in, 215
  rules for 216, 222, 228, 232
  soundness of, 217
Necessary condition, 184
Negation completeness, 337
Negation consistency of PM, 326, 332–334
New theory of meaning, 127
Newton's laws of motion, 401
Nominal kinds, 127
Nominal definition, 126–128
Nonscientific explanations, 425–428
Not (~), 176–177

O

O sentence, 242
Observation and scientific explanations, 419–420
Obverse, 265
One-place predicate, 280
Open sentence, 279
Or (∨), 179–180
  exclusive use, 179
  inclusive use, 179
Ostensive definition, 113

P

PM, 324
  axioms of, 326
  completeness of, 327, 337–340
  consistency of, 326–327, 333–334
  derived rules, 331–332
  formation rules of, 324
  independence of, 327, 335–336
  proof in, 326
  properties of, 326–327
  rules of inference in, 326
  theorems of, 326, 328–332
  vocabulary for, 324
Paradigm example, 115
Particular affirmative (*I*), 242
Particular negative (*O*), 242
Personal odds theory of probability, 440
Persuasive definition, 155
Petitio principii fallacy, 45–46
Post hoc fallacy, 60
Predicate argument, 173, 278
Predicate constant, 279
Predicate logic, 173, 278; *see also* Natural deduction system for predicate logic
Predicate variable, 291
Predicates
  monadic, 280
  n-place, 280–281
  relational, 312
Premise, 3
Primitive, undefined expression, 324–325
Principia Mathematica system, *see* PM
Principle of charity, 8
Principle of indifference, 439
Probabilistic explanations, 402–403
Probabilistic (or statistical) generality, 402
Probability
  logical interpretation, 438
  physical interpretation, 437
  psychological interpretation, 438
  theories of measuring, 438–441
Proof
  in natural deduction system for sentential logic, 215
  in PM, 326
Proper name, 121–125
Pseudo-dispute, 140

Q

Quantifier, 173, 280
  negation rules, 283, 311

Quantifier (*cont.*)
   rules in predicate logic, 310–313
   existential, 280
   universal, 280
Quoting out of context fallacy, 76–78

R

Real definition, 126–128
Reductio ad absurdum
   rule (RAA), 232–234
   test for monadic predicate logic, 296
   truth table test, 205
   validity of RAA, 229–230
Reference
   causal theory of, 123
   descriptive theory of, 122
   semantic, 124
   speaker's, 124
Reinforced syllogisms, 250
Relational predicate logic, 311–313
Relational predicate, 280–281, 312
Relative frequency view of probability,
   440
Replacement rules in sentential logic,
   220–224
Rule of conditional proof (RCP), 228
   validity of, 229–230
Rules
   derived, 217, 233
   of inference in sentential logic, 214–
   234
   of inference in predicate logic, 301–
   310
   replacement rules in sentential logic,
   220–224
   for statement connectives, 186
   syllogistic, 256

S

Sampling, 14–16, 63–65, 347
Science
   and deduction, 363
   ideal of, 349

and induction, 361–362
   practical aim of, 348
   theoretical aim of, 349
   and types of explanations, 397–408
Scientific explanations
   corroboration of, 360
   deductive, 397–402
   direct and indirect testing of, 423–
   425
   empathetic, 406–408
   and falsifiability, 420
   functional, 405–406
   genuine and pseudo scientific, 423
   historical, 403–405
   laws in, 360–361
   and observation, 419–420
   patterns of, 397–408
   probabilistic, 402–403
   reasons and, 402
   satisfactory and unsatisfactory, 418–
   425
   see also Hypotheses
Scope
   of a connective, 184–186, 193
   of a quantifier, 308
Semantic completeness of PM, 327,
   337–340
Semantic feature, 115
Semantic reference, 124
(Truth functional) sentence connectives,
   175–184
   " · " and English "and," 177–179
   " ≡ " and English "if and only if," 184
   " ⊃ " and English "if, then," 180–183
   " ~ " and English "not," 176–177
   " ∨ " and English "or," 179–180
   truth functionality of, 176
   scope of, 184–186
   and truth tables, 190–191
Sentential
   arguments, 173
   argument patterns, 173, 189
   connectives, 173
   logic, 173
Simple statement, 175

Simplification (Simp), 169, 216
Single formula, 337
Singular sentence, 242
  in traditional syllogistic logic, 247
  in predicate logic, 279
Singular terms, 247, 279
Small sample fallacy, 63–65
Sound argument, 18
Sound systems in logic
  axiom system for sentential logic (PM), 327
  predicate logic, 301
  natural deduction system for sentential logic, 217
  syllogistic logic, 217
Sorites, 268
Speaker's reference, 124
Special addition principle, 443
Special multiplication principle, 442
Special pleading fallacy, 61–63
Square of opposition, 264
Strategies in constructing proofs
  in sentential logic, 233–234
  in predicate logic, 305
Straw man fallacy, 52–54
Subalternation, 264
Subcontraries, 265
Substitution rule (in PM), 326
Sufficient condition, 184
Syllogistic
  argument, 248
  logic, 241
  chains, 268
  rules for validity, 257
Syllogism, 248
  mood, 249
  figure, 249
  validity of, 250
Symbolizing
  categorical sentences, 246–247
  general sentences, 283–284
  sentence connectives, 208–210
Syntactical ambiguity, 72–75

Syntactical ambiguity fallacy, 72–74
Synthetic sentence, 322

T

Tautology (Taut), 222
Tautologies, 276, 319
Terms
  empty, 112, 242, 259
  general, 168, 242
  logical, 173
  major, 249
  middle, 249
  minor, 249
  natural kind, 126
  singular, 279
Theorems
  in axiom system, 324
  in logic, 321
  in PM, 326
Theories
  abandonment of, see Crucial experiments
  caloric theory, 356
  causal theory of reference, 123
  classical theory of probability, 439
  Copernicus' theory, 399
  descriptive theory of reference, 122
  Einstein's gravitational theory, 422
  empirical and theoretical, see Hypotheses
  ether theory, 424
  Galenic theory, 352
  Huygens' wave theory, 378
  Kinetic theory, 358
  Newton's corpuscular theory, 354–356, 377
  new theory of meaning, 127
  personal odds theory, 440
  Ptolemaic theory, 398
  relative frequency theory, 440
  traditional theory of meaning, 127
Traditional theory of meaning, 127

Truth functional
    expansion of general sentences, 289
    compounds, 176
    implication, 214
    sentence connectives, 175–184
Truth tables, 190
    and logical equivalence, 191
    for the sentence connectives, 190–191
    short-cut method, 205–207
    in testing argument patterns, 196–198
    in testing arguments, 199
Truths of logic, 320–322
Tu quoque fallacy, 35–36

U

Universal affirmative (*A*), 242
Universal generalization (UG), 308, 310
Universal instantiation (UI), 302, 310
Universal negative (*E*), 242
Universal quantifier, 280
Universal set, 275

V

Vagueness, 129–133
    contextual, 131
    extensional, 131
    intensional, 131

Validity
    of argument patterns, 169
    of arguments, 12, 165
    of Boolean equations, 276–277
    of deductive arguments, 12, 165
    of monadic predicate argument
        patterns, 291–295
    of predicate rules, 302
    of sentential arguments, 196–200,
        319
    of sentential argument patterns, 196
    of syllogisms, 250
    truth table methods of establishing,
        196–198
    of truth functional rules of inference,
        214, 229–230, 234
Variable, 167
Venn diagrams
    for categorical sentences, 243–245
    test, 253–256
Verbal definition, 113–114
Verstehen, 407

W

Well-formed formula (wff), 324
Word extension dispute, 141